MICROSOFT AZURE VIRTUAL DESKTOP SPECIALTY

CONFIGURING AND OPERATING MICROSOFT AZURE VIRTUAL DESKTOP

- ✓ MASTER THE EXAM (AZ-140)
- ✓ 10 PRACTICE TESTS
- ✓ 500 RIGOROUS EXAM QUESTIONS
- ✓ 490+ EXAM FOCUSED TIPS
- ✓ 495+ CAUTION ALERTS
- ✓ SOLID FOUNDATIONS
- ✓ GAIN WEALTH OF INSIGHTS
- ✓ EXPERT EXPLANATIONS AND
- ✓ ONE ULTIMATE GOAL

2025 UPGRADED EDITION | PASS ON YOUR FIRST TRY

ANAND M
AMEENA PUBLICATIONS

Copyright © 2025 ANAND M
All rights reserved.
ISBN: 9798325388002

DEDICATION

To the Visionaries in My Professional Odyssey

This book is dedicated to the mentors and leaders who guided me through triumph and adversity in my professional universe. Your guidance has illuminated the path to success and taught me to seize opportunities and surmount obstacles. Thank you for imparting the advice to those who taught me the value of strategic thinking and the significance of innovation to transform obstacles into stepping stones. Your visionary leadership has inspired my creativity and motivated me to forge new paths.

Thank you for sharing the best and worst of your experiences with me, kind and severe employers. As I present this book to the world, I am aware that you have been my inspiration. All of your roles as mentors, advisors, and even occasional adversaries have helped me become a better professional and storyteller.

This dedication is a tribute to your impact on my journey, a narrative woven with threads of gratitude, introspection, and profound gratitude for the lessons you've inscribed into my story.

With deep gratitude and enduring respect,
Anand M

FROM TECH TO LIFE SKILLS – MY EBOOKS COLLECTION

Dive into my rich collection of eBooks, curated meticulously across diverse and essential domains.

  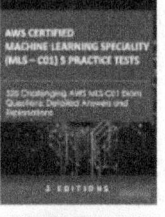 

Pro Tips and Tricks Series: Empower yourself with life-enhancing skills and professional essentials with our well-crafted guides.

Hot IT Certifications and Tech Series: Stay ahead in the tech game. Whether you're eyeing certifications in AWS, PMP, or prompt engineering, harnessing the power of ChatGPT with tools like Excel, PowerPoint, Word, and more!, we've got you covered!

Essential Life Skills: Embark on a journey within. From yoga to holistic well-being, Master the art of culinary, baking, and more delve deep and rediscover yourself.

Stay Updated & Engaged
For an entire world of my knowledge, tips, and treasures, follow me on Amazon
https://www.amazon.com/author/anandm

Your Feedback Matters!
Your support, feedback, and ratings are the wind beneath my wings. It drives me to curate content that brings immense value to every aspect of life. Please take a moment to share your thoughts and rate the books. Together, let's keep the flame of knowledge burning bright!

Best Regards,

ANAND M

INTRODUCTION

Welcome to **MICROSOFT AZURE VIRTUAL DESKTOP SPECIALTY: CONFIGURING AND OPERATING MICROSOFT AZURE VIRTUAL DESKTOP**. This book is your ultimate companion to mastering the Microsoft AZ-140 certification exam. Designed with precision and depth, it provides everything you need to excel: **10 practice tests, 500 rigorous exam questions, 490+ exam-focused tips, and 495+ caution alerts**—all crafted to build your confidence and expertise in Azure Virtual Desktop.

Achieving the **Microsoft Azure Virtual Desktop Specialty certification** signifies a deep mastery of configuring and operating Azure Virtual Desktop environments. It highlights your ability to design, implement, and manage virtual desktop infrastructures that promote agility and efficiency in business operations. This book is an essential tool for anyone aiming to excel in the field of virtual desktop technologies, guiding you through the complexities of Azure Virtual Desktop, and ensuring your preparation goes beyond merely passing the exam to gaining a deep insight into practical virtual desktop applications.

In the ever-evolving landscape of cloud computing and virtualization, the **Microsoft Azure Virtual Desktop Specialty** certification stands as a testament to your expertise and capabilities in leveraging the power of Azure to provide scalable and secure virtual desktop experiences. This credential is highly regarded in the industry, unlocking numerous career opportunities and enabling professional growth.

As you delve into this book, here are the key details about the Microsoft Azure Virtual Desktop exam:

- ✓ **Level:** Specialty
- ✓ **Length:** The exam is 180 minutes long, providing ample time to showcase your virtual desktop management skills.
- ✓ **Cost:** The exam fee is detailed on the official Microsoft website.
- ✓ **Format:** The exam features various question types, assessing both your practical abilities and theoretical knowledge in configuring and operating Microsoft Azure Virtual Desktop.
- ✓ **Delivery Method:** The exam is available at authorized testing centers or as an online proctored exam, offering flexibility and convenience.

Each question in this book comes with expert explanations, clarifying complex scenarios and providing valuable insights into virtual desktop management. Our goal is to guide you through the landscape of Microsoft Azure Virtual Desktop, ensuring a well-rounded and comprehensive preparation.

Embark on this enriching journey with **"MICROSOFT AZURE VIRTUAL DESKTOP SPECIALTY: MASTER THE EXAM (AZ-140)"**. Arm yourself with the knowledge, insights, and strategies essential for success in achieving your Microsoft Azure Virtual Desktop Specialty certification. Let this book be your guide, illuminating your path to excellence in the world of Azure Virtual Desktop.

ADVANTAGES OF CERTIFICATION

As you embark on the journey to earn the **Microsoft Azure Virtual Desktop Specialty certification**, it's crucial to understand the myriad of benefits that this prestigious credential offers. This certification is more than a demonstration of your expertise in virtual desktop infrastructure; it's a gateway to numerous professional advantages:

Elevated Professional Recognition: In the rapidly evolving field of cloud computing and virtualization, Microsoft Azure Virtual Desktop holds a significant position. Earning the Azure Virtual Desktop Specialty certification distinguishes you as an expert in deploying and managing virtual desktops within the Microsoft ecosystem. It validates your skills in creating scalable and secure virtual desktop environments, thereby enhancing your professional credibility in the tech community.

Career Advancement Opportunities: This certification is a powerful endorsement of your virtual desktop capabilities. It serves as a stepping stone for career growth, often leading to more senior roles and better opportunities in the spheres of cloud services, virtualization, and IT infrastructure management.

Financial Rewards: Achieving specialized certifications like this one is frequently linked to an increase in salary potential. Professionals with the Azure Virtual Desktop Specialty certification are often rewarded with higher pay, reflecting the value of their expertise and the investment made in their professional development.

Competitive Edge in the Job Market: In the competitive domain of IT and cloud services, holding the Azure Virtual Desktop Specialty certification sets you apart. It aligns you with specialized roles that match your expertise and career goals, making you a sought-after candidate for prestigious positions within organizations seeking to optimize their IT operations through virtualization.

Comprehensive Understanding and Hands-On Expertise: This certification goes beyond theoretical knowledge, placing a strong emphasis on practical, hands-on experience with Microsoft Azure Virtual Desktop's tools and services. As a certified Azure Virtual Desktop Specialist, you demonstrate not just knowledge, but also proficiency in implementing, managing, and securing virtual desktops that support remote workforces and offer scalable solutions.

In conclusion, the **Microsoft Azure Virtual Desktop Specialty certification** is not just a mere accolade; it's a significant milestone in your career path. It equips you with the skills, knowledge, and connections needed to confidently navigate the complex and dynamic landscape of cloud computing and virtual desktop technologies.

EXAM OBJECTIVE

Welcome to the Microsoft Azure Virtual Desktop Specialty question bank, your essential resource for mastering the AZ-140 certification exam. Below is a comprehensive breakdown of the exam domains and their respective weightings:

Exam Section & Weightage

Domain	Weightage
Plan and implement an Azure Virtual Desktop infrastructure	40–45%
Plan and implement identity and security	15–20%
Plan and implement user environments and apps	20–25%
Monitor and maintain an Azure Virtual Desktop infrastructure	10–15%

Domain 1: Plan and implement an Azure Virtual Desktop infrastructure (40–45%)
This domain focuses on designing and deploying a robust Azure Virtual Desktop infrastructure. Topics include creating host pools, managing virtual machines, configuring session hosts, and implementing high availability. Mastering this section ensures you can design scalable, secure, and efficient desktop solutions tailored to business needs.

Domain 2: Plan and implement identity and security (15–20%)
In this domain, you'll delve into configuring Azure Active Directory, managing user access, and implementing security controls. You'll learn to secure identities, enforce compliance policies, and protect Azure Virtual Desktop environments from threats. Proficiency here is critical for safeguarding virtual desktop infrastructures in the cloud.

Domain 3: Plan and implement user environments and apps (20–25%)
This section emphasizes configuring and managing user experiences. Topics include installing and managing applications, customizing user profiles, and implementing FSLogix for seamless user data access. Understanding these concepts is essential for creating personalized and efficient virtual desktop environments that enhance productivity.

Domain 4: Monitor and maintain an Azure Virtual Desktop infrastructure (10–15%)
This domain covers monitoring performance, troubleshooting issues, and optimizing Azure Virtual Desktop environments. You'll learn to use tools like Azure Monitor and Log Analytics to ensure system health and efficiency. Developing these skills ensures you can maintain stable and high-performing desktop solutions.

This Exam Objectives section serves as your roadmap for the AZ-140 certification journey, guiding you through each domain's focus and importance in mastering Microsoft Azure Virtual Desktop. Let this guide be your pathway to certification success, helping you build expertise in configuring and operating Azure Virtual Desktop environments.

QUESTION BANK AND EXAM OBJECTIVE MAP

This question bank is meticulously aligned with the Microsoft Azure Virtual Desktop Specialty (AZ-140) exam syllabus, offering comprehensive coverage of all essential concepts related to planning, configuring, and managing Azure Virtual Desktop environments. Each question is thoughtfully designed to mirror real-world scenarios and challenges, highlighting the practical application of Azure Virtual Desktop concepts and functionalities.

The questions in this book are crafted to build a clear and focused understanding of Azure Virtual Desktop principles. They enable you to quickly grasp critical topics, pinpoint areas that need improvement, and apply your knowledge effectively in real-world situations. By engaging with these questions, you'll enhance your ability to design virtual desktop solutions, implement identity and security, configure user environments, and monitor system performance efficiently.

Each question is further supported by targeted exam tips and strategic caution alerts. These insights are designed to sharpen your exam preparation by emphasizing key concepts, highlighting important considerations, and identifying common pitfalls. This ensures you are thoroughly equipped to approach the exam with confidence and precision.

The following table maps each question to the corresponding knowledge areas in the exam syllabus, ensuring that your preparation is both comprehensive and strategically aligned for success.

DOMAIN 1 - PLAN AND IMPLEMENT AN AZURE VIRTUAL DESKTOP INFRASTRUCTURE (40-45%)

Note: P indicates Practice Test and Q indicates Question

S.No	KNOWLEDGE AREA	MAPPED QUESTIONS
1	Assess Network Capacity and Speed Requirements	P1Q1,P2Q1,P3Q1,P4Q1,P5Q1
2	Azure Virtual Network Connectivity Planning	P6Q1,P7Q1,P8Q1,P9Q1,P10Q1
3	Internet and On-premises Network Connectivity Management	P1Q2,P2Q2,P3Q2,P4Q2,P5Q2
4	Implement RDP Shortpath and QoS Policies	P6Q2,P7Q2,P8Q2,P9Q2,P10Q2
5	Implement Azure Private Link with AVD	P1Q3,P2Q3,P3Q3,P4Q3,P5Q3
6	Name Resolution Management for AVD	P6Q3,P7Q3,P8Q3,P9Q3,P10Q3
7	Monitor and Troubleshoot Network Connectivity	P1Q4,P2Q4,P3Q4,P4Q4,P5Q4
8	Plan Storage for AVD User Data	P6Q4,P7Q4,P8Q4,P9Q4,P10Q4
9	Implement Storage for FSLogix Components	P1Q5,P2Q5,P3Q5,P4Q5,P5Q5
10	Implement Storage Accounts and File Shares	P6Q5,P7Q5,P8Q5,P9Q5,P10Q5
11	Implement Azure NetApp Files	P1Q6,P2Q6,P3Q6,P4Q6,P5Q6
12	Recommend Resource Groups, Subscriptions, and Management Groups	P6Q6,P7Q6,P8Q6,P9Q6,P10Q6
13	Recommend an Operating System for AVD Implementation	P1Q7,P2Q7,P3Q7,P4Q7,P5Q7
14	Licensing Model Recommendations for AVD	P6Q7,P7Q7,P8Q7,P9Q7,P10Q7

S.No	KNOWLEDGE AREA	MAPPED QUESTIONS
15	Plan Host Pools Architecture	P1Q8,P2Q8,P3Q8,P4Q8,P5Q8
16	Calculate Performance Requirements Configuration	P6Q8,P7Q8,P8Q8,P9Q8,P10Q8
17	VM Capacity Requirements Configuration	P1Q9,P2Q9,P3Q9,P4Q9,P5Q9
18	Create Host Pools and Session Hosts Using Azure Portal	P6Q9,P7Q9,P8Q9,P9Q9,P10Q9
19	Automate Host and Host Pool Creation	P1Q10,P2Q10,P3Q10,P4Q10,P5Q10
20	Configure Host Pool and Session Host Settings	P6Q10,P7Q10,P8Q10,P9Q10,P10Q10
21	Apply a Windows Client or Windows Server License to a Session Host	P1Q11,P2Q11,P3Q11,P4Q11,P5Q11
22	Create a Golden Image Manually	P6Q11,P7Q11,P8Q11,P9Q11,P10Q11
23	Use Azure Virtual Machine Image Builder for Golden Images	P1Q12,P2Q12,P3Q12,P4Q12,P5Q12
24	Modify a Session Host Image	P6Q12,P7Q12,P8Q12,P9Q12,P10Q12
25	Lifecycle Management for Images	P1Q13,P2Q13,P3Q13,P4Q13,P5Q13
26	Apply OS and Application Updates to an Image	P6Q13,P7Q13,P8Q13,P9Q13,P10Q13
27	Use a Golden Image to Create a Session Host	P1Q14,P2Q14,P3Q14,P4Q14,P5Q14
28	Implement Image Storage	P6Q14,P7Q14,P8Q14,P9Q14,P10Q14
29	Manage Azure Compute Gallery	P1Q15,P2Q15,P3Q15,P4Q15,P5Q15
30	Advanced Networking for AVD	P6Q15,P7Q15,P8Q15,P9Q15,P10Q15
31	Security Practices for Azure Virtual Desktop	P1Q16,P2Q16,P3Q16,P4Q16,P5Q16
32	Compliance Management in AVD	P6Q16,P7Q16,P8Q16,P9Q16,P10Q16
33	Performance Tuning for Azure Virtual Desktop	P1Q17,P2Q17,P3Q17,P4Q17,P5Q17
34	Cost Optimization Strategies for AVD	P6Q17,P7Q17,P8Q17,P9Q17,P10Q17
35	Integration of AVD with Microsoft 365	P1Q18,P2Q18,P3Q18,P4Q18,P5Q18
36	Scalability Solutions for Azure Virtual Desktop	P6Q18,P7Q18,P8Q18,P9Q18,P10Q18
37	User Experience Optimization in AVD	P1Q19,P2Q19,P3Q19,P4Q19,P5Q19
38	Disaster Recovery Planning for AVD	P6Q19,P7Q19,P8Q19,P9Q19,P10Q19
39	Automation of Azure Virtual Desktop Management	P1Q20,P2Q20,P3Q20,P4Q20,P5Q20
40	Monitoring and Reporting in Azure Virtual Desktop	P6Q20,P7Q20,P8Q20,P9Q20,P10Q20

DOMAIN 2 - PLAN AND IMPLEMENT IDENTITY AND SECURITY (15-20%)

Note: P indicates Practice Test and Q indicates Question

S.No	KNOWLEDGE AREA	MAPPED QUESTIONS
41	Choose an Identity Management and Authentication Method	P1Q21,P2Q21,P3Q21,P4Q21,P5Q21
42	Azure Virtual Desktop Requirements for AD DS	P6Q21,P7Q21,P8Q21,P9Q21,P10Q21
43	Microsoft Entra Domain Services and Microsoft Entra ID	P1Q22,P2Q22,P3Q22,P4Q22,P5Q22
44	Implement Azure Roles and RBAC for Azure Virtual Desktop	P6Q22,P7Q22,P8Q22,P9Q22,P10Q22
45	Implement Conditional Access Policies for AVD Connections	P1Q23,P2Q23,P3Q23,P4Q23,P5Q23
46	Implement Multifactor Authentication in Azure Virtual Desktop	P6Q23,P7Q23,P8Q23,P9Q23,P10Q23
47	Manage Roles, Groups, and Rights Assignments on AVD Session Hosts	P1Q24,P2Q24,P3Q24,P4Q24,P5Q24

S.No	KNOWLEDGE AREA	MAPPED QUESTIONS
48	Security Management Using Microsoft Defender for Cloud	P6Q24,P7Q24,P8Q24,P9Q24,P10Q24
49	Configure Microsoft Defender Antivirus for Session Hosts	P1Q25,P2Q25,P3Q25,P4Q25,P5Q25
50	Network Security for Azure Virtual Desktop Connections	P6Q25,P7Q25,P8Q25,P9Q25,P10Q25
51	Configure Azure Bastion or JIT for Administrative Access	P1Q26,P2Q26,P3Q26,P4Q26,P5Q26
52	Implement Windows Threat Protection Features	P6Q26,P7Q26,P8Q26,P9Q26,P10Q26
53	Confidential VM and Trusted Launch in AVD Host Pool Provisioning	P1Q27,P2Q27,P3Q27,P4Q27,P5Q27
54	Identity Integration Planning	P6Q27,P7Q27,P8Q27,P9Q27,P10Q27
55	RBAC and Azure Role Management	P1Q28,P2Q28,P3Q28,P4Q28,P5Q28
56	Conditional Access Implementation for AVD	P6Q28,P7Q28,P8Q28,P9Q28,P10Q28
57	Multifactor Authentication Setup and Management	P1Q29,P2Q29,P3Q29,P4Q29,P5Q29
58	Managing Security Configurations for Session Hosts	P6Q29,P7Q29,P8Q29,P9Q29,P10Q29
59	Network Security Enhancements for AVD Connections	P1Q30,P2Q30,P3Q30,P4Q30,P5Q30
60	Administrative Security Practices for Azure Virtual Desktop	P6Q30,P7Q30,P8Q30,P9Q30,P10Q30

DOMAIN 3 - PLAN AND IMPLEMENT USER ENVIRONMENTS AND APPS (20-25%)

Note: P indicates Practice Test and Q indicates Question

S.No	KNOWLEDGE AREA	MAPPED QUESTIONS
61	Recommend FSLogix Configuration	P1Q31,P2Q31,P3Q31,P4Q31,P5Q31
62	Install and Configure FSLogix	P6Q31,P7Q31,P8Q31,P9Q31,P10Q31
63	Configure Profile Containers	P1Q32,P2Q32,P3Q32,P4Q32,P5Q32
64	Configure Office Containers	P6Q32,P7Q32,P8Q32,P9Q32,P10Q32
65	Configure Cloud Cache	P1Q33,P2Q33,P3Q33,P4Q33,P5Q33
66	Choose an Azure Virtual Desktop Client and Deployment Method	P6Q33,P7Q33,P8Q33,P9Q33,P10Q33
67	Deploy and Troubleshoot Azure Virtual Desktop Clients	P1Q34,P2Q34,P3Q34,P4Q34,P5Q34
68	Configure Device Redirection	P6Q34,P7Q34,P8Q34,P9Q34,P10Q34
69	Configure Multimedia Redirection	P1Q35,P2Q35,P3Q35,P4Q35,P5Q35
70	Configure Printing and Universal Print	P6Q35,P7Q35,P8Q35,P9Q35,P10Q35
71	Configure User Settings through Group Policy and Microsoft Intune Policies	P1Q36,P2Q36,P3Q36,P4Q36,P5Q36
72	Configure RDP Properties on a Host Pool	P6Q36,P7Q36,P8Q36,P9Q36,P10Q36
73	Configure Session Timeout Properties	P1Q37,P2Q37,P3Q37,P4Q37,P5Q37
74	Implement Start Virtual Machine on Connect	P6Q37,P7Q37,P8Q37,P9Q37,P10Q37
75	Assign and Unassign Personal Desktops	P1Q38,P2Q38,P3Q38,P4Q38,P5Q38
76	Choose a Method for Deploying Apps to Azure Virtual Desktop	P6Q38,P7Q38,P8Q38,P9Q38,P10Q38
77	Configure Dynamic Application Delivery Using MSIX App Attach	P1Q39,P2Q39,P3Q39,P4Q39,P5Q39
78	Publish an Application as a RemoteApp	P6Q39,P7Q39,P8Q39,P9Q39,P10Q39
79	Implement FSLogix Application Masking	P1Q40,P2Q40,P3Q40,P4Q40,P5Q40
80	Implement and Manage OneDrive, Including Multisession Environments	P6Q40,P7Q40,P8Q40,P9Q40,P10Q40

81	Implement and Manage Microsoft Teams, Including the Remote Desktop WebRTC Redirector Service	P1Q41,P2Q41,P3Q41,P4Q41,P5Q41
82	Implement and Manage Microsoft 365 Apps on Azure Virtual Desktop Session Hosts	P6Q41,P7Q41,P8Q41,P9Q41,P10Q41
83	Implement and Manage Browsers for Azure Virtual Desktop Sessions	P1Q42,P2Q42,P3Q42,P4Q42,P5Q42
84	Create and Configure an Application Group	P6Q42,P7Q42,P8Q42,P9Q42,P10Q42

DOMAIN 4 - MONITOR AND MAINTAIN AVD INFRASTRUCTURE (10-15%)

Note: P indicates Practice Test and Q indicates Question

S.No	KNOWLEDGE AREA	MAPPED QUESTIONS
85	Monitor AVD Host Pools	P1Q43,P2Q43,P3Q43,P4Q43,P5Q43
86	Manage AVD Session Health	P6Q43,P7Q43,P8Q43,P9Q43,P10Q43
87	Utilize Azure Monitor for AVD	P1Q44,P2Q44,P3Q44,P4Q44,P5Q44
88	Implement Diagnostic Settings	P6Q44,P7Q44,P8Q44,P9Q44,P10Q44
89	Manage User Profiles and Data	P1Q45,P2Q45,P3Q45,P4Q45,P5Q45
90	Update Management for Session Hosts	P6Q45,P7Q45,P8Q45,P9Q45,P10Q45
91	Scale and Optimize AVD Resources	P1Q46,P2Q46,P3Q46,P4Q46,P5Q46
92	Network Performance and Connectivity Monitoring	P6Q46,P7Q46,P8Q46,P9Q46,P10Q46
93	Security Compliance and Auditing	P1Q47,P2Q47,P3Q47,P4Q47,P5Q47
94	Cost Management and Optimization	P6Q47,P7Q47,P8Q47,P9Q47,P10Q47
95	Automated Remediation Techniques	P1Q48,P2Q48,P3Q48,P4Q48,P5Q48
96	Disaster Recovery Planning and Implementation	P6Q48,P7Q48,P8Q48,P9Q48,P10Q48
97	Licensing and Compliance Management	P1Q49,P2Q49,P3Q49,P4Q49,P5Q49
98	User Experience and Feedback Analysis	P6Q49,P7Q49,P8Q49,P9Q49,P10Q49
99	Application Performance Monitoring	P1Q50,P2Q50,P3Q50,P4Q50,P5Q50
100	Log Management and Analysis	P6Q50,P7Q50,P8Q50,P9Q50,P10Q50

CONTENTS

PRACTICE TEST 1 - QUESTIONS ONLY 1

PRACTICE TEST 1 - ANSWERS ONLY 14

PRACTICE TEST 2 - QUESTIONS ONLY 33

PRACTICE TEST 2 - ANSWERS ONLY 46

PRACTICE TEST 3 - QUESTIONS ONLY 65

PRACTICE TEST 3 - ANSWERS ONLY 78

PRACTICE TEST 4 - QUESTIONS ONLY 98

PRACTICE TEST 4 - ANSWERS ONLY 111

PRACTICE TEST 5 - QUESTIONS ONLY 130

PRACTICE TEST 5 - ANSWERS ONLY 143

PRACTICE TEST 6 - QUESTIONS ONLY 163

PRACTICE TEST 6 - ANSWERS ONLY 176

PRACTICE TEST 7 - QUESTIONS ONLY 196

PRACTICE TEST 7 - ANSWERS ONLY 209

PRACTICE TEST 8 - QUESTIONS ONLY 229

PRACTICE TEST 8 - ANSWERS ONLY 242

PRACTICE TEST 9 - QUESTIONS ONLY 262

PRACTICE TEST 9 - ANSWERS ONLY 275

PRACTICE TEST 10 - QUESTIONS ONLY 295

PRACTICE TEST 10 - ANSWERS ONLY 308

ABOUT THE AUTHOR 328

PRACTICE TEST 1 - QUESTIONS ONLY

QUESTION 1

You are overseeing the deployment of AVD for a global consulting firm with employees across multiple regions. You need to simulate the anticipated network load to:
• Ensure bandwidth sufficiency for high-resolution video conferencing.
• Identify potential performance bottlenecks.
• Optimize network configurations for different regional offices.
What PowerShell script would best simulate network traffic and help analyze bandwidth needs for this scenario?

A) Use the Test-NetConnection cmdlet
B) Utilize the Start-PacketTrace cmdlet
C) Invoke the Simulate-AVDLoad script with parameters for video payload
D) Apply the Measure-Command cmdlet on network processes
E) Execute the New-AVDNetworkProfile with default settings

QUESTION 2

You are configuring internet connectivity for an AVD implementation that must support secure, high-performance access for users worldwide. Key considerations include:
• Implementing MFA for enhanced security.
• Optimizing VPN settings for reliable performance.
• Using Azure Bastion for secure, seamless access.
Which PowerShell command would you use to configure MFA settings for Azure AD, integral to securing AVD internet connectivity?

```
A) Set-AzureADStrongAuthenticationRequirement
B) New-AzADApplication
C) Enable-AzADDirectoryRole
D) Set-AzApplicationGatewayAuthentication
E) Install-AzADServicePrincipal
```

QUESTION 3

- You are tasked with optimizing user experience in an Azure Virtual Desktop (AVD) environment.
- You need to ensure efficient monitoring of user connections for troubleshooting purposes.
- Your goal is to identify the appropriate Log Analytics table for this task.

Which table should you query to obtain detailed information about user connections, including client IP addresses and session host details?

```
A) WVDCheckpoints
B) WVDConnections
C) WVDUserSessions
D) WVDSessionHostManagement
E) WVDServiceHealth
```

QUESTION 4

Your organization has deployed Azure Virtual Desktop (AVD) for remote access to applications and desktops. As the IT administrator, you need to monitor the network performance of the AVD infrastructure to ensure optimal user experiences. Which tools and methods would you utilize for monitoring AVD network performance? Select THREE.

A) Azure Monitor for monitoring network latency and bandwidth usage

B) Network Performance Monitor (NPM) for real-time network monitoring and diagnostics
C) Azure Network Watcher for analyzing network traffic and diagnosing connectivity issues
D) Performance Monitor (PerfMon) for tracking network throughput and packet loss
E) PowerShell scripts for querying network performance counters and generating reports

QUESTION 5

You are tasked with creating a host pool in Azure Virtual Desktop and need to automate the process using an ARM template. The following script has been provided. Identify any issues or optimizations that could be made.

```json
{
 "type": "Microsoft.DesktopVirtualization/hostpools",
 "apiVersion": "2021-09-03-preview",
 "name": "[parameters('hostPoolName')]",
 "location": "[parameters('location')]",
 "properties": {
 "hostPoolType": "Pooled",
 "loadBalancerType": "BreadthFirst",
 "maxSessionLimit": 10,
 "customRdpProperty": "audiomode:i:0",
 }
}
```

A) Incorrect apiVersion
B) Incorrect hostPoolType
C) MaxSessionLimit too low
D) Syntax error in JSON
E) All are correct

QUESTION 6

You need to implement a cost-effective solution for managing session hosts in an Azure Virtual Desktop (AVD) environment to optimize resource usage. The solution must meet the following requirements:
- Automatically scale session hosts based on user demand.
- Ensure that session hosts are only active during business hours.
- Minimize administrative overhead.
Which Azure service or feature should you use?

A) Azure Automation Runbooks
B) Azure DevOps pipelines
C) Azure Functions
D) Azure Monitor Autoscale
E) Azure Policy

QUESTION 7

Your organization is planning to implement Azure Virtual Desktop (AVD) and is evaluating different operating system options. As the Azure architect, you need to consider the criteria for choosing the most suitable OS for AVD implementation. Which criteria should you consider? Select THREE.

A) Application compatibility and support for virtualization technologies
B) Security features and compliance with organizational standards
C) Performance metrics, including resource utilization and responsiveness

D) Licensing costs and subscription requirements
E) Integration capabilities with Microsoft 365 and other productivity tools

QUESTION 8

Your organization is in the process of designing host pools for Azure Virtual Desktop (AVD) and needs to adhere to specific design principles. As the Azure architect, you are responsible for outlining these principles. What should you emphasize? Select THREE.

A) Scalability and Elasticity
B) Fault Tolerance and High Availability
C) Resource Utilization and Optimization
D) Network Segmentation and Isolation
E) Cost Efficiency and Optimization

QUESTION 9

You are tasked with implementing autoscale for host pools in an Azure Virtual Desktop (AVD) environment to optimize resource usage. Consider the following requirements:
- Ensure that session hosts are available during peak usage hours.
- Minimize manual intervention and administrative overhead.
- Scale resources dynamically based on user demand.
Which of the following options meets these requirements for autoscaling? Select TWO.

A) Each host pool must contain at least one session host.
B) Specify the minimum and maximum number of session hosts for each host pool.
C) Deploy host pools in Azure regions that support autoscale.
D) Enable autoscale at the subscription level.
E) Deploy a custom script to each session host to facilitate autoscaling.

QUESTION 10

As an Azure administrator, you are tasked with setting up a new storage account optimized for AVD environments. You must use the Azure CLI to create the account. Identify the correct command to use.
bash
```
az storage account create --name MyStorageAccount --resource-group MyResourceGroup --location eastus --sku Standard_LRS --kind StorageV2
```

A) Command is correct
B) Incorrect location parameter
C) Incorrect SKU for AVD
D) Kind parameter is not suitable for AVD
E) Resource group does not exist

QUESTION 11

Your organization is planning to deploy Azure Virtual Desktop (AVD) with Windows Server operating systems for session hosts. As the Azure administrator, you need to understand the licensing requirements and apply licenses to the session hosts. What are the critical steps in this process? Select THREE.

A) Verify License Availability and Eligibility
B) Retrieve License Key from Microsoft Volume Licensing Center
C) Access Azure Portal and Navigate to AVD Service
D) Select Session Hosts and Choose License Assignment Method

E) Confirm License Application and Validate Activation Status

QUESTION 12

You are responsible for designing a disaster recovery strategy for an Azure Virtual Desktop (AVD) infrastructure. Consider the following requirements:
- Ensure host pools can be restored to a secondary Azure region in the event of a primary region outage.
- Minimize downtime by replicating host pools to the secondary region.

Which of the following solutions should you include in the strategy?

A) Azure Backup
B) Azure Migrate
C) Azure Resource Manager (ARM)
D) Azure Site Recovery
E) Azure Blob Storage

QUESTION 13

Your organization is seeking strategies for effective lifecycle management of Azure Virtual Desktop (AVD) images to ensure smooth operations and minimize disruptions. As the Azure specialist, you need to evaluate different approaches for image lifecycle management. Which of the following strategies are commonly used for effective lifecycle management of AVD images? Select THREE.

A) Rolling Updates
B) Immutable Infrastructure
C) Blue-Green Deployment
D) Scheduled Maintenance Windows
E) Image Versioning and Tagging

QUESTION 14

Your organization is planning to create session hosts from golden images in Azure Virtual Desktop (AVD) to streamline deployment processes and ensure consistency across virtual desktop environments. As the Azure specialist, you need to outline the steps involved in creating session hosts from a golden image. What are the steps to create a session host from a golden image in AVD? Select THREE.

A) Prepare a Generalized Virtual Machine Image
B) Provision a New Virtual Machine from the Golden Image
C) Customize Session Host Settings in AVD Management Portal
D) Assign App Groups and Users to the Session Host
E) Validate User Access and Application Availability

QUESTION 15

As the Azure admin, you need to set up a Compute Gallery to optimize the management of VM images for AVD deployments. Which PowerShell command correctly creates a new Compute Gallery?
`New-AzGallery -ResourceGroupName "RG1" -Location "East US" -Name "AVDGallery"`

A) Correct command
B) Incorrect ResourceGroupName
C) Location should be "West US"
D) Gallery name is inappropriate
E) Command is missing required parameters

QUESTION 16

Your organization is planning to implement comprehensive security measures for Azure Virtual Desktop (AVD) deployments to ensure the protection of sensitive data and resources. As the Azure specialist, you need to recommend a set of security practices aligned with industry standards. What are the recommended comprehensive security measures for AVD deployments? Select THREE.

A) Enable Network Segmentation and Isolation
B) Implement Role-Based Access Control (RBAC) for User Permissions
C) Utilize Endpoint Protection Solutions for Device Security
D) Enable Data Encryption for Data-at-Rest and Data-in-Transit
E) Implement Continuous Monitoring and Threat Detection Solutions

QUESTION 17

Your organization is deploying Azure Virtual Desktop (AVD) to provide remote access to a wide range of applications for its employees. However, there are concerns about the performance of AVD, particularly during peak usage times. As the Azure specialist, you need to optimize AVD performance to ensure smooth operation. Which techniques can you employ to optimize AVD performance? Select THREE.

A) Implementing FSLogix Profile Containers for User Profile Management
B) Configuring Azure Load Balancer for Traffic Distribution
C) Enabling Azure Monitor for Performance Monitoring and Analysis
D) Utilizing Azure Resource Manager (ARM) Templates for Infrastructure Deployment
E) Deploying Azure Application Gateway for Application Delivery

QUESTION 18

As an Azure Virtual Desktop (AVD) administrator, you're tasked with ensuring seamless updates for session hosts. Considering the infrastructure with a host pool containing 25 session hosts, you need to update the Azure Virtual Desktop agent efficiently. What should be your approach given the following criteria and challenges:
- Minimize downtime during updates
- Ensure all session hosts are updated to the latest agent version
- Simplify the update process for administrative efficiency?

A) Configure a scaling plan.
B) Configure diagnostic settings.
C) Enable drain mode.
D) Enable Scheduled Agent Updates.
E) Deploy a new host pool.

QUESTION 19

Your organization is planning to scale its Azure Virtual Desktop (AVD) infrastructure to accommodate peak usage times efficiently. Critical factors include leveraging Azure's scalability features, optimizing costs, and ensuring uninterrupted service. How would you approach scaling the AVD infrastructure while balancing performance and cost considerations? Select TWO.

A) Utilize VM Scale Sets
B) Implement Azure Bastion for secure RDP access
C) Optimize VM configurations for peak performance

QUESTION 20

As an Azure administrator, you are tasked with automating the deployment of AVD instances to streamline operations.

You decide to use ARM templates for deployment consistency. You must ensure the deployment scales automatically based on user load and integrates seamlessly with existing identity management solutions. Consider security protocols to avoid exposing sensitive data. What ARM template adjustment is necessary to meet these requirements?

```json
{
 "type": "Microsoft.Network/networkInterfaces",
 "properties": {
 "enableAcceleratedNetworking": true
 }
}
```

A) Add identity management integration
B) Enable diagnostics settings
C) Configure auto-scale settings
D) Secure sensitive data with parameters
E) Template is correct as is

QUESTION 21

You are configuring Azure Virtual Desktop to integrate with an on-premises Active Directory domain. You need to implement a Group Policy setting to optimize network connectivity. Which Group Policy setting should you configure for this purpose?

A) Enable RDP Shortpath for managed networks
B) Allow remote connections to this computer
C) Configure Windows Firewall for RDP access
D) Enable Remote Desktop Protocol (RDP)
E) Implement Network Level Authentication (NLA)

QUESTION 22

Your organization is considering the implementation of Microsoft Entra Domain Services (MEDS) for Azure Virtual Desktop (AVD) environments and seeks to understand the overview and benefits of this service. The focus is on evaluating how MEDS can enhance identity and access management in AVD deployments. Which benefits are associated with Microsoft Entra Domain Services (MEDS) for AVD environments? Select THREE.

A) Seamless integration with Azure AD for centralized identity management
B) Compatibility with existing on-premises Active Directory environments
C) Simplified deployment and management of domain controllers in Azure
D) Enhanced security through automatic patching and threat detection
E) Scalability to support growing AVD deployments with ease

QUESTION 23

Your organization is planning to implement Conditional Access policies for Azure Virtual Desktop (AVD) connections to enhance security. The focus is on creating and implementing these policies effectively to ensure secure access to AVD resources. What steps are involved in creating and implementing Conditional Access policies for AVD connections? Select CORRECT answers that apply.

A) Define access controls based on user identity and device state
B) Configure conditional access rules in Azure AD
C) Specify conditions for accessing AVD resources, such as location or device compliance
D) Assign Conditional Access policies to AVD user groups or roles
E) Monitor policy effectiveness and adjust settings as needed

QUESTION 24

Your organization plans to deploy Azure Virtual Desktop in a multi-geo scenario to enhance performance. The deployment must leverage existing Azure infrastructure and comply with data residency requirements. Which of the following steps should you prioritize? Select THREE.

A) Configure a multi-session environment.
B) Deploy regional host pools.
C) Implement Azure Site Recovery.
D) Enable geo-redundant storage.
E) Integrate with Azure Traffic Manager.

QUESTION 25

You are configuring Microsoft Defender Antivirus on Azure Virtual Desktop session hosts to ensure robust security. The setup must automatically update antivirus definitions and report detection incidents. What PowerShell command enables Defender's real-time protection and scheduled scans on AVD session hosts?

A) `Set-MpPreference -DisableRealtimeMonitoring $false`
B) `Set-MpPreference -DisableRealtimeMonitoring $true`
C) `Update-MpSignature`
D) `Enable-MpRealtimeProtection`
E) `Set-MpPreference -ScanScheduleDay Everyday`

QUESTION 26

Your organization is planning to enhance the security of Azure Virtual Desktop (AVD) management by implementing Azure Bastion. The focus is on understanding the steps required to set up Azure Bastion for secure AVD management. What are the steps involved in setting up Azure Bastion for secure AVD management? Select THREE.

A) Provision Azure Bastion in the same virtual network (VNET) as AVD session hosts
B) Configure network security groups (NSGs) to allow inbound traffic on ports required by Azure Bastion
C) Associate Azure Bastion with the AVD workspace for seamless RDP/SSH access to session hosts
D) Assign appropriate RBAC roles to administrators for access to Azure Bastion
E) Enable Azure Bastion diagnostics logging for monitoring and troubleshooting

QUESTION 27

Your organization needs to enhance the security of its Azure Virtual Desktop (AVD) environment to address the following requirements: advanced threat protection, secure remote access, and integration with existing security infrastructure. Which solutions should you implement? Select THREE.

A) Deploy Azure Firewall.
B) Implement Microsoft Defender for Endpoint.
C) Use Azure VPN Gateway for secure remote access.
D) Configure Azure Active Directory Conditional Access.
E) Integrate with third-party SIEM tools.

QUESTION 28

Your organization is in the process of designing an effective RBAC model for Azure Virtual Desktop (AVD) environments to ensure secure and efficient access management. The focus is on understanding the key considerations for designing the RBAC model. What are the key considerations for designing an effective RBAC model for AVD environments? Select THREE.

A) Define granular roles based on job functions and responsibilities

B) Implement role hierarchies to simplify role assignment and management
C) Use Azure AD groups to streamline role assignment and membership management
D) Regularly review and update role assignments based on changing requirements
E) Utilize built-in Azure AD roles for standardized access control policies

QUESTION 29

Your organization is planning to set up Multi-Factor Authentication (MFA) for Azure Virtual Desktop (AVD) to enhance security. The focus is on providing a comprehensive guide to setting up MFA. What are the steps involved in setting up MFA for Azure Virtual Desktop? Select THREE.

A) Enable MFA for Azure AD users in the Azure portal
B) Configure Conditional Access policies to enforce MFA for AVD access
C) Implement Azure AD Security Defaults for automatic MFA enforcement
D) Integrate MFA with on-premises Active Directory using Azure AD Connect
E) Educate users on MFA setup and usage best practices

QUESTION 30

You are tasked with setting up secure network communication for AVD using PowerShell. You need to ensure that the Network Security Group (NSG) only allows RDP access from a specific IP range and that it is configured to prioritize this rule over others. Additionally, the configuration must adhere to compliance requirements for restricted access. Review the PowerShell script below for setting up the NSG and select the appropriate configuration.

```
New-AzNetworkSecurityGroup -Name "AVDNSG" -ResourceGroupName "AVDResources"
New-AzNetworkSecurityRuleConfig -Name "AllowRDP" -Access Allow -Protocol Tcp -Direction
Inbound -Priority 100 -SourceAddressPrefix "203.0.113.0/24" -SourcePortRange "*" -
DestinationAddressPrefix "*" -DestinationPortRange 3389 -NetworkSecurityGroup "AVDNSG"
```

A) Correct configuration
B) SourceAddressPrefix should be broader
C) DestinationPortRange should include more ports
D) NSG name does not follow naming conventions
E) Priority should be lower to take precedence

QUESTION 31

Your organization is planning to deploy FSLogix to enhance user profile management for Azure Virtual Desktop (AVD) environments. The focus is on criteria for recommending specific FSLogix settings. What criteria should be considered when recommending specific FSLogix settings for AVD environments? Select THREE.

A) User environment complexity and customization requirements
B) Performance impact on session host resources and storage utilization
C) Compatibility with third-party applications and plugins
D) Network latency and bandwidth constraints for profile storage
E) Support for multi-session host configurations and load balancing

QUESTION 32

As an Azure Virtual Desktop administrator tasked with optimizing user experience, you need to enhance the performance of Profile Containers to ensure efficient desktop environments. In this scenario, consider the following:
 - The solution should accommodate a growing number of users without compromising performance.
 - Optimal performance should be achieved while minimizing resource consumption.

- Enhancements should lead to a seamless and responsive desktop experience for end-users.
What techniques can optimize Profile Containers performance? Select THREE.

A) Implement folder redirection.
B) Utilize FSLogix Cloud Cache.
C) Configure Profile Containers to store only essential user settings.
D) Implement data deduplication within Profile Containers.
E) Enable Profile Containers compression.

QUESTION 33

In a finance company, you need to secure AVD session hosts to comply with regulations, ensure encrypted connections, and facilitate secure administrative access. What configurations should be implemented? Select THREE.

A) Deploy Azure Bastion for secure RDP and SSH access.
B) Configure network security groups (NSGs) to restrict traffic.
C) Enable Azure Defender for virtual machines.
D) Use Azure Policy to enforce security standards.
E) Implement Just-In-Time (JIT) VM access.

QUESTION 34

Your organization is planning to deploy Azure Virtual Desktop (AVD) clients to provide remote access to corporate resources. Consider the following scenario:
- The organization has users spread across multiple geographical locations, each with varying network conditions.
- Some users require high-definition multimedia applications, while others need lightweight access to office productivity tools.
- IT administrators aim to optimize client deployment strategies to ensure optimal performance and user experience across diverse scenarios.

Which deployment strategies should you consider for the given scenario? Select THREE.

A) Deploy AVD clients using MSIX App Attach for dynamic application provisioning.
B) Utilize Azure Bastion for secure RDP access to AVD instances without exposing them to the public internet.
C) Implement GPU-accelerated virtual machines (VMs) for users requiring high-definition multimedia applications.
D) Optimize network Quality of Service (QoS) settings to prioritize AVD traffic based on application requirements.
E) Leverage Azure AD Conditional Access policies to enforce multi-factor authentication (MFA) for user access to AVD sessions.

QUESTION 35

You are tasked with setting up multimedia redirection to enhance the performance of Azure Virtual Desktop environments for a design team using heavy video content. Ensure the redirection settings optimize the usage of GPU resources and are compatible with the team's applications. Review the PowerShell script below for configuring multimedia redirection:

```
Set-RDSessionCollectionConfiguration -CollectionName "DesignTeam" -CustomRdpProperty
"redirectclipboard:i:1;audiocapturemode:i:1;videoplaybackmode:i:1"
```

A) Script is correctly configured for optimal performance
B) Videoplaybackmode should be disabled
C) Audiocapturemode is incorrectly configured
D) GPU usage is not optimized
E) Redirectclipboard should be disabled

QUESTION 36

A government agency uses Azure Virtual Desktop for classified data handling. The security requirements are: no direct internet access, SSL encryption for all connections, and administrative access via Azure portal only. Which configurations should you implement? Select THREE.

A) Configure Azure Bastion for secure access.
B) Deploy Azure Firewall with strict rules.
C) Use Azure Private Link for private connectivity.
D) Implement Azure Application Proxy.
E) Enable Just-in-Time (JIT) VM access.

QUESTION 37

You are configuring session timeout properties for Azure Virtual Desktop (AVD) to optimize user experience and security. The finance department requires longer session durations due to the nature of their work. Which approach would best meet their needs while ensuring security compliance?

A) Adjusting session timeouts based on Azure AD group membership
B) Implementing Multi-Factor Authentication (MFA) for all finance users
C) Enforcing complex password policies for finance department users
D) Integrating FSLogix for persistent user profiles
E) Configuring Just-In-Time (JIT) access for administrative tasks

QUESTION 38

In your role as an Azure Virtual Desktop (AVD) administrator, you need to ensure efficient utilization of resources and cost-effectiveness. Considering the potential focus area of "Implement Start Virtual Machine on Connect," which benefit aligns with configuring this feature?

A) Reducing VM idle time and associated costs by powering on VMs only when users connect
B) Increasing VM availability and responsiveness by pre-starting VMs before user connection
C) Enhancing user experience by minimizing login delays and wait times for VM availability
D) Improving security by isolating user sessions and data on dedicated VMs
E) Streamlining management by automatically scaling VM capacity based on user demand

QUESTION 39

A healthcare organization requires a secure AVD setup that allows only designated staff to access patient records, ensures compliance with health data regulations, and maintains operational continuity. What configurations are essential? Select THREE.

A) Deploy Azure Bastion for secure access.
B) Configure Azure AD with Conditional Access policies.
C) Implement Azure Site Recovery across multiple regions.
D) Create a dedicated subnet named AzureBastionSubnet.
E) Enable disk encryption with Azure Disk Encryption.

QUESTION 40

You are tasked with configuring FSLogix Application Masking on AVD to limit access to specific applications for certain user groups. Use the PowerShell script below to achieve this:

```
$AppGroup = "HR_Tools"
$MaskingRule = "App1.exe"
New-FSLogixAppMaskingRule -Name $AppGroup -FilePath $MaskingRule -AssignedUser AD\HRDept
```

Choose the correct adjustment to ensure the rule is applied correctly.

A) Use Set-FSLogixAppMaskingRule instead of New-FSLogixAppMaskingRule to apply the rule.
B) Change $MaskingRule = "App1.exe" to $MaskingRule = "C:\Program Files\App1\App1.exe" for a full path specification.
C) Change -AssignedUser AD\HRDept to -AssignedUser "AD\HRDept" to correct syntax errors in the user assignment.
D) Add -Enabled $true at the end of the command to ensure the rule is active.
E) No changes are needed; the script is correct as it is.

QUESTION 41

You are configuring Microsoft Teams optimization for AVD using PowerShell. Your goal is to implement the WebRTC redirector service to enhance video and audio performance. Which of the following PowerShell scripts correctly configures the required settings?
Set-AVDTeamsConfig -EnableWebRTC $true -OptimizeMedia $true

A) Script is correct as is.
B) Add -UseRDPTransport $false to disable RDP transport and ensure WebRTC is used.
C) Replace -EnableWebRTC $true with -WebRTCRedirector $true.
D) Change -OptimizeMedia $true to -MediaOptimization $true.
E) Add -SessionHost $vmName to specify the AVD session host explicitly.

QUESTION 42

You are setting up FSLogix profile containers in an Azure Virtual Desktop environment to improve user profile management. Which registry settings must be configured to optimize the performance of profile loading? Select THREE.

A) HKLM\SOFTWARE\FSLogix\Profiles\Type
B) HKLM\SOFTWARE\FSLogix\Profiles\Enabled
C) HKLM\SOFTWARE\Policies\FSLogix\ODFC\Size
D) HKLM\SOFTWARE\FSLogix\Profiles\VHDLocations
E) HKLM\SYSTEM\CurrentControlSet\Services\frxccd\Start

QUESTION 43

You are responsible for monitoring the performance metrics of Azure Virtual Desktop (AVD) host pools to ensure optimal user experience. The AVD environment serves users across multiple regions, and you need to identify potential performance bottlenecks. Which tool allows you to effectively monitor these metrics and identify performance issues in real-time?

A) Utilize Azure Monitor to collect and analyze performance data
B) Run PowerShell script to extract host pool metrics
C) Configure Azure Log Analytics to track host pool performance
D) Enable Diagnostic Settings in Azure Portal for host pool monitoring
E) Utilize Network Performance Monitor for host pool analysis

QUESTION 44

You are tasked with configuring Azure Monitor for detailed analytics of Azure Virtual Desktop (AVD) deployments in your organization. To ensure effective monitoring and analysis, you must consider:
1. The granularity of metrics required for comprehensive analysis, including user session performance and resource utilization.
2. The impact of monitoring on AVD performance and cost, balancing the need for detailed analytics with resource consumption.
3. The integration of Azure Monitor logs with existing monitoring tools and workflows for centralized management.

What is the most appropriate initial step to enable detailed monitoring and analysis of AVD deployments using Azure Monitor?

A) Enable Azure Monitor logs for AVD
B) Configure Azure Monitor Alerts for AVD
C) Integrate Azure Monitor with Azure Log Analytics
D) Deploy Azure Monitor Workbooks for AVD
E) Enable Azure Monitor Application Insights for AVD

QUESTION 45

You are configuring Azure Backup to protect user profiles stored with FSLogix. Write a PowerShell script to automate the backup of the FSLogix profile containers stored in an Azure File Share named 'ProfileStorage' within the 'AVDResourceGroup'.
PowerShell
New-AzRecoveryServicesBackupProtectionPolicy -Name "DailyBackup" -WorkloadType "AzureFiles" -BackupFrequency "Daily"

A) Correct as is.
B) Add -ResourceGroupName "AVDResourceGroup" -FileShareName "ProfileStorage" -PolicyName "DailyBackup" to the script.
C) Replace New-AzRecoveryServicesBackupProtectionPolicy with Set-AzRecoveryServicesBackupPolicy.
D) Include -SchedulePolicy Default in the script.
E) Change -BackupFrequency "Daily" to -BackupScheduleType Daily.

QUESTION 46

As an Azure Virtual Desktop (AVD) administrator, you are tasked with implementing dynamic scaling techniques to efficiently manage resources based on fluctuating user demands. The company experiences peak usage during certain times of the day, leading to performance issues. Additionally, cost optimization is a key concern for the organization. Which method allows for dynamic scaling of AVD resources, ensuring optimal performance and cost-effectiveness?

A) Auto-scaling with Azure Logic Apps
B) Manual scaling using PowerShell scripts
C) Scheduled scaling with Azure Automation
D) Adaptive scaling with Azure Monitor
E) Static scaling with Azure Resource Manager templates

QUESTION 47

As an Azure Virtual Desktop (AVD) administrator, you are tasked with implementing security policies to enforce compliance and mitigate risks in AVD environments. Which security policy should be prioritized to enhance security posture?

A) Role-Based Access Control (RBAC)
B) Multi-Factor Authentication (MFA)
C) Just-In-Time (JIT) access
D) Network Security Groups (NSGs)
E) Azure Security Center policies

QUESTION 48

For a media company deploying AVD to handle high-resolution video editing, what FSLogix settings are essential to manage large file sizes, ensure high performance, and maintain data security? Select THREE.

A) HKLM\SOFTWARE\FSLogix\Profiles\VHDLocations
B) HKLM\SOFTWARE\FSLogix\Profiles\CloudCache
C) HKLM\SOFTWARE\FSLogix\Profiles\DynamicVHDAllocation
D) HKLM\SOFTWARE\FSLogix\Profiles\Encrypt
E) HKLM\SOFTWARE\FSLogix\Profiles\LocalCacheSize

QUESTION 49

A company is designing disaster recovery strategies for its Azure Virtual Desktop (AVD) environment to ensure business continuity. Which considerations should be prioritized when designing disaster recovery strategies for AVD? Select THREE.

A) Implementing cross-region replication for AVD resources
B) Configuring Azure Site Recovery for automated failover and recovery
C) Utilizing Azure Backup for data protection and retention
D) Implementing RBAC policies for access control during disaster recovery
E) Leveraging Azure Bastion for secure RDP/SSH access to AVD resources

QUESTION 50

A company is experiencing performance issues with applications deployed on Azure Virtual Desktop (AVD). They need to monitor and optimize application performance to ensure a smooth user experience. Which tools and strategies should they consider for this task? Select THREE.

A) Azure Application Insights for tracking application performance metrics
B) Microsoft Endpoint Analytics for analyzing user experience metrics
C) Azure Monitor for monitoring resource utilization and performance
D) Implementing FSLogix for optimizing application load times
E) Utilizing Azure Log Analytics for tracking application errors and exceptions

PRACTICE TEST 1 - ANSWERS ONLY

QUESTION 1

Answer - C) Invoke the Simulate-AVDLoad script with parameters for video payload
Option A - Incorrect. Test-NetConnection is used for basic network diagnostics, not for simulating AVD loads.
Option B - Incorrect. There is no Start-PacketTrace cmdlet in PowerShell for AVD context.
Option C - Correct. This custom script (hypothetical) would simulate AVD load, specifically with video-intensive processes.
Option D - Incorrect. Measure-Command measures the time a script block takes to run, not network capacity.
Option E - Incorrect. New-AVDNetworkProfile does not exist; used for illustration only.

EXAM FOCUS	*You need to simulate network traffic using tools tailored for AVD. The custom Simulate-AVDLoad script provides realistic video payloads. Avoid generic diagnostics like Test-NetConnection. Focus on tools designed for video conferencing and regional analysis. Eliminate commands unrelated to AVD context or payload simulation.*
CAUTION ALERT	*Stay alert to fictitious cmdlets like Start-PacketTrace or invalid tools like New-AVDNetworkProfile. Always ensure commands are suitable for realistic AVD scenarios and support payload-specific analysis. Verify that scripts align with organizational requirements.*

QUESTION 2

Answer - A) Set-AzureADStrongAuthenticationRequirement
Option A - Correct. Directly relates to configuring MFA for Azure AD.
Option B - Incorrect. For creating new Azure AD applications, not MFA.
Option C - Incorrect. Enables directory roles, not related to MFA.
Option D - Incorrect. Configures authentication for application gateways.
Option E - Incorrect. Installs service principals for Azure applications.

EXAM FOCUS	*To configure MFA for Azure AD, always use Set-AzureADStrongAuthenticationRequirement. Eliminate choices like New-AzADApplication or Enable-AzADDirectoryRole, which are for unrelated Azure AD tasks. Ensure MFA integrates seamlessly with AVD for high-security environments. Utilize role-specific MFA configurations for optimal outcomes.*
CAUTION ALERT	*Avoid confusing MFA-specific commands with application setup or directory role tasks. Stay clear of redundant configurations that do not enhance security for AVD. Ensure MFA aligns with the overall identity management strategy and user access policies.*

QUESTION 3

Answer - [B]

Option B - WVDConnections: This table contains detailed information about user connections, including client IP addresses and session host details, making it the correct choice.
Option A - WVDCheckpoints: This table typically contains checkpoint data related to session activities, not detailed user connection information.
Option C - WVDUserSessions: Although it sounds relevant, this table usually stores information about user session activities rather than connection details.
Option D - WVDSessionHostManagement: This table focuses more on the management of session hosts rather than user connections.
Option E - WVDServiceHealth: This table provides information about the health of the Azure Virtual Desktop service, not specific user connection details.

EXAM FOCUS	*Use the WVDConnections table for detailed insights into user sessions. This table tracks connection endpoints, session host details, and IP addresses. Avoid choices like WVDUserSessions or WVDSessionHostManagement, which don't focus on connection-specific details. Prioritize user session monitoring over broader system health metrics.*
CAUTION ALERT	*Don't confuse connection data (WVDConnections) with session or health data tables. Stay alert to choosing tables that only partially address your monitoring needs. Ensure the table you query aligns with your troubleshooting objectives and session connectivity requirements.*

QUESTION 4

Answer - A) Azure Monitor for monitoring network latency and bandwidth usage; B) Network Performance Monitor (NPM) for real-time network monitoring and diagnostics; C) Azure Network Watcher for analyzing network traffic and diagnosing connectivity issues

Option A - Correct. Azure Monitor provides insights into network latency and bandwidth usage, allowing for proactive monitoring of AVD network performance. Option B - Correct. Network Performance Monitor offers real-time monitoring and diagnostics, helping identify and resolve network issues in AVD environments.

Option C - Correct. Azure Network Watcher enables analysis of network traffic and diagnosis of connectivity issues, facilitating troubleshooting in AVD setups. Option D - Incorrect. While Performance Monitor can track network metrics, it may not offer the same level of visibility and analysis as dedicated Azure monitoring tools. Option E - Incorrect. While PowerShell scripts can be useful for automation, they may not provide comprehensive network performance monitoring capabilities compared to specialized tools like Azure Monitor and Network Performance Monitor.

EXAM FOCUS	*For AVD network performance, leverage Azure Monitor, Network Performance Monitor (NPM), and Azure Network Watcher. These tools provide latency, traffic diagnostics, and bandwidth insights. Avoid overreliance on basic tools like PerfMon or PowerShell for detailed monitoring tasks. Always prioritize comprehensive, real-time solutions.*
CAUTION ALERT	*Avoid using Performance Monitor for AVD environments; it lacks the granularity of Azure tools. Stay clear of assuming PowerShell alone can address all diagnostic needs. Use tools designed specifically for Azure networks and AVD performance requirements.*

QUESTION 5

Answer - D) Syntax error in JSON

Option A - Correct: The apiVersion is outdated and should be updated to a more recent version.
Option B - Incorrect: The hostPoolType 'Pooled' is valid for this scenario.
Option C - Incorrect: The maxSessionLimit is set appropriately for a pooled environment.
Option D - Correct: There is a syntax error in JSON due to an extra comma after "audiomode:i:0".
Option E - Incorrect: Not all options are correct.

EXAM FOCUS	*Double-check JSON syntax in ARM templates. The extra comma after "audiomode:i:0" causes errors. Keep the apiVersion updated to prevent compatibility issues. Ensure that parameters match current Azure specifications to streamline deployment. Eliminate assumptions about correct configuration without syntax validation.*
CAUTION ALERT	*Stay alert to minor syntax errors, like misplaced commas, which can disrupt deployments. Avoid using outdated apiVersion values as they can cause compatibility issues. Always validate JSON templates with Azure's schema before deploying host pools.*

QUESTION 6

Answer - [D]

Option D - Azure Monitor Autoscale: This option allows you to automatically scale resources, such as session hosts, based on predefined metrics or schedules, meeting the specified requirements and minimizing administrative overhead. Option A - Azure Automation Runbooks: While Runbooks can automate tasks, Azure Monitor Autoscale is more suitable for dynamically scaling resources based on demand.

Option B - Azure DevOps pipelines: DevOps pipelines are used for continuous integration and continuous deployment (CI/CD), not for managing resource scaling. Option C - Azure Functions: Functions are event-driven serverless compute, which is not specifically designed for scaling AVD session hosts based on demand. Option E - Azure Policy: Policies are used for enforcing rules and standards across resources but are not designed for managing resource scaling based on demand.

EXAM FOCUS	*Use Azure Monitor Autoscale to manage resources dynamically. It meets all requirements for scaling session hosts based on usage patterns and time schedules. Eliminate options like Azure Automation Runbooks, which lack demand-based scaling. Prioritize services designed for resource optimization in AVD environments.*
CAUTION ALERT	*Avoid relying on services like Azure Functions for autoscale; they are event-driven and not tailored for resource management. Stay cautious about using generic automation solutions instead of dedicated scaling services optimized for Azure Virtual Desktop.*

QUESTION 7

Answer - A) Application compatibility and support for virtualization technologies; B) Security features and compliance with organizational standards; C) Performance metrics, including resource utilization and responsiveness

Option A - Correct. Application compatibility and support for virtualization technologies are crucial for ensuring that all necessary applications can run efficiently within the AVD environment. Option B - Correct. Security features and compliance with organizational standards help maintain data integrity and protect against potential vulnerabilities within the AVD deployment.

Option C - Correct. Performance metrics such as resource utilization and responsiveness directly impact user experience and overall productivity in AVD implementations. Option D - Incorrect. While licensing costs are important, they are not the only criteria for choosing an OS for AVD, especially considering other factors like application compatibility and security. Option E - Incorrect. While integration with Microsoft 365 and other productivity tools is valuable, it is not the primary criterion for selecting an OS for AVD.

EXAM FOCUS	*Focus on OS selection criteria like application compatibility, virtualization support, security features, and performance. Avoid distractions like licensing costs or integration tools unless they directly impact AVD operations. Prioritize core functionalities to ensure smooth user experience and compliance.*
CAUTION ALERT	*Avoid over-prioritizing licensing or integration features when selecting an OS for AVD. Stay alert to core requirements like performance, compatibility, and compliance standards, which are more critical for the successful deployment of Azure Virtual Desktop environments.*

QUESTION 8

Answer - A) Scalability and Elasticity; B) Fault Tolerance and High Availability; C) Resource Utilization and Optimization

Option A - Correct. Scalability and elasticity are essential design principles for host pools in AVD, ensuring that deployments can adapt to changing user demands and workload requirements. Option B - Correct. Fault tolerance and high availability help maintain service continuity and minimize downtime in AVD environments, enhancing user experience and productivity.

Option C - Correct. Resource utilization and optimization ensure efficient use of computing resources within host pools, maximizing performance and cost-effectiveness. Option D - Incorrect. While network segmentation and isolation are important for security, they are not directly related to design principles for host pools in AVD deployments. Option E - Incorrect. While cost efficiency and optimization are crucial considerations, they are encompassed within the broader design principles of scalability, fault tolerance, and resource utilization.

EXAM FOCUS	*Emphasize design principles like scalability, fault tolerance, and resource optimization for host pools. Avoid unrelated considerations like network segmentation or cost alone. Always align your design to workload demands and user requirements while ensuring high availability and efficient resource utilization.*
CAUTION ALERT	*Don't mistake network or cost-specific strategies for core host pool design principles. Stay cautious about overemphasizing secondary considerations that don't directly address performance, fault tolerance, or resource efficiency in AVD host pool design.*

QUESTION 9

Answer - [B, C]

Option B - Specify the minimum and maximum number of session hosts for each host pool: This allows for dynamic scaling based on demand while ensuring session hosts are available during peak usage hours.
Option C - Deploy host pools in Azure regions that support autoscale: This ensures that autoscaling functionality can be utilized effectively to meet resource demands.

Option A - Each host pool must contain at least one session host: While generally true, it is not a specific requirement for enabling autoscale. Option D - Enable autoscale at the subscription level: Autoscale is enabled at the host pool level, not the subscription level. Option E - Deploying custom scripts to each session host is not necessary for autoscaling in AVD environments and adds unnecessary complexity.

EXAM FOCUS	*Use autoscale with specified minimum and maximum session hosts to manage resource allocation dynamically. Deploy host pools in regions that support autoscale features. Eliminate custom scripting or enabling autoscale at the subscription level, as these approaches don't align with AVD scaling strategies.*
CAUTION ALERT	*Avoid implementing custom scripts for autoscaling, as Azure provides built-in capabilities. Stay alert to region limitations for autoscale support; not all Azure regions fully support this feature. Verify your region and configuration compatibility beforehand.*

QUESTION 10

Answer - A) Command is correct

Option A - Correct: The command is correctly set up for creating a storage account in Azure.
Option B - Incorrect: The location 'eastus' is valid.
Option C - Incorrect: 'Standard_LRS' is a suitable SKU for general purposes in AVD.
Option D - Incorrect: 'StorageV2' is the correct kind for this setup.
Option E - Incorrect: Existence of the resource group cannot be determined from the command itself.

EXAM FOCUS	*Ensure the Azure CLI command for creating storage accounts is accurate by using parameters like Standard_LRS and StorageV2. Confirm that the resource group exists to prevent errors. Avoid changing valid parameters like location or kind unless your requirements differ significantly from the default setup.*
CAUTION ALERT	*Don't overlook verifying resource group existence before running the command. Stay clear of arbitrary changes to CLI parameters unless dictated by deployment requirements. Ensure all specified values are compatible with Azure Virtual Desktop storage needs.*

QUESTION 11

Answer - A) Verify License Availability and Eligibility; C) Access Azure Portal and Navigate to AVD Service; D) Select

Session Hosts and Choose License Assignment Method

Option A - Correct. Before applying licenses, it's essential to ensure that sufficient licenses are available and that the organization meets eligibility criteria based on licensing agreements. Option C - Correct. Accessing the Azure portal and navigating to the AVD service allows administrators to manage session hosts and apply licenses within the AVD deployment.

Option D - Correct. Selecting session hosts and choosing the appropriate license assignment method (e.g., user-based or device-based) is a critical step in the licensing process to ensure compliance and proper resource allocation. Option B - Incorrect. While retrieving the license key is necessary for some licensing scenarios, AVD leverages subscription-based licensing models, and license keys are not directly obtained from the Microsoft Volume Licensing Center. Option E - Incorrect. While confirming license application and validating activation status are important, they are typically automatic processes after selecting the license assignment method and applying licenses within the Azure portal.

EXAM FOCUS	*Always verify licensing requirements. Ensure session hosts are assigned proper licenses (user-based or device-based) through the Azure portal. Eliminate choices involving manual retrieval of license keys; AVD uses subscription-based models. Prioritize navigating to the AVD service for licensing tasks.*
CAUTION ALERT	*Avoid assuming manual license key retrieval is necessary; AVD handles licensing differently. Stay alert to mixing Windows Server and client OS licensing processes. Ensure compliance with licensing agreements to avoid errors in production.*

QUESTION 12

Answer - [D]

Option D - Azure Site Recovery: Azure Site Recovery provides disaster recovery as a service and supports replication and failover of Azure Virtual Desktop host pools to a secondary region, meeting the requirements for disaster recovery.
Option A - Azure Backup is primarily used for data backup and does not provide the capability to failover host pools to a secondary region.

Option B - Azure Migrate is used for workload migration, not disaster recovery for AVD host pools.
Option C - Azure Resource Manager (ARM) is a management service and does not provide disaster recovery capabilities for AVD host pools. Option E - Azure Blob Storage is a storage service and is not directly related to disaster recovery for AVD host pools.

EXAM FOCUS	*Always include Azure Site Recovery for disaster recovery strategies involving host pool failovers to secondary regions. Eliminate Azure Migrate and Blob Storage as these focus on migration and storage. ARM and Azure Backup are also unsuitable for real-time failover needs.*
CAUTION ALERT	*Avoid confusing backup and migration services with disaster recovery. Stay clear of relying on Azure Backup alone, as it cannot replicate host pools or handle failover. Focus on services explicitly designed for DR like Azure Site Recovery.*

QUESTION 13

Answer - B) Immutable Infrastructure; C) Blue-Green Deployment; E) Image Versioning and Tagging

Option A - Incorrect. Rolling updates are typically associated with software deployments and are not specific to image lifecycle management in AVD.

Option B - Correct. Immutable infrastructure involves deploying new instances rather than modifying existing ones, providing consistency and reliability in image lifecycle management. Option C - Correct. Blue-Green Deployment involves maintaining two identical environments (blue and green) and switching between them during updates, minimizing downtime and risk in image lifecycle management. Option D - Incorrect. While scheduling maintenance windows is important for overall system maintenance, it is not a strategy specific to image lifecycle management.

Option E - Correct. Image versioning and tagging help track changes and versions, facilitating rollback and compliance in image lifecycle management.

EXAM FOCUS	*Use immutable infrastructure, blue-green deployments, and image versioning/tagging for effective lifecycle management. Eliminate rolling updates, which are software-specific, and maintenance windows, which apply to broader systems, not images. Prioritize consistency and rollback capabilities.*
CAUTION ALERT	*Avoid associating rolling updates with image management—they focus on application deployment. Stay alert to overlooking tagging/versioning; they simplify rollbacks and compliance audits. Ensure strategies maintain operational reliability during updates.*

QUESTION 14

Answer - A) Prepare a Generalized Virtual Machine Image; B) Provision a New Virtual Machine from the Golden Image; D) Assign App Groups and Users to the Session Host

Option A - Correct. Before creating session hosts, it's essential to prepare a generalized virtual machine image that serves as the golden image template. Option B - Correct. After preparing the golden image, provision new virtual machines from this image to create session hosts in AVD. Option C - Incorrect. Customizing session host settings typically occurs after provisioning the virtual machine and configuring AVD properties, not during the initial creation from the golden image. Option D - Correct. Once session hosts are created, app groups and users need to be assigned to them to grant access to applications and desktops.

Option E - Incorrect. While validating user access and application availability is essential, it typically occurs after the session hosts are created and configured.

EXAM FOCUS	*Prepare a generalized VM image, provision VMs from it, and assign app groups/users for consistent session host deployment. Eliminate steps like session customization or post-validation that occur later in the workflow. Focus on efficient provisioning and assigning access to minimize errors.*
CAUTION ALERT	*Don't confuse initial provisioning steps with post-deployment configurations like application assignment or access validation. Stay clear of skipping generalization—it ensures compatibility across session hosts. Always validate the image before deployment.*

QUESTION 15

Answer - A) Correct command

Option A - Correct: This command properly sets up a new Compute Gallery.
Option B - Incorrect: 'ResourceGroupName' is valid assuming 'RG1' exists.
Option C - Incorrect: 'East US' is a valid location, but depending on data sovereignty needs, 'West US' could be considered.
Option D - Incorrect: 'AVDGallery' is an appropriate name for a gallery dedicated to Azure Virtual Desktop.
Option E - Incorrect: The command includes all required parameters to create a gallery.

EXAM FOCUS	*Always verify New-AzGallery command includes valid resource group, location, and name parameters. Eliminate choices about gallery names or incorrect locations unless requirements dictate otherwise. Ensure Compute Gallery names are meaningful for easier management.*
CAUTION ALERT	*Avoid skipping validation of the resource group's existence. Stay alert to potential typos in gallery names or incorrect regions that could fail compliance checks. Always use logical naming conventions aligned with organizational standards.*

QUESTION 16

Answer - A) Enable Network Segmentation and Isolation; B) Implement Role-Based Access Control (RBAC) for User

Permissions; D) Enable Data Encryption for Data-at-Rest and Data-in-Transit

Option A - Correct. Network segmentation and isolation help prevent lateral movement of threats within the network, enhancing security for AVD deployments. Option B - Correct. RBAC ensures that users have appropriate permissions, reducing the risk of unauthorized access to AVD resources. Option C - Incorrect. While endpoint protection solutions are important, they may not be directly related to AVD security practices.

Option D - Correct. Data encryption for data-at-rest and data-in-transit ensures that sensitive information remains protected from unauthorized access or interception in AVD deployments. Option E - Incorrect. While continuous monitoring and threat detection are valuable, they may not be specific security measures for AVD deployments.

EXAM FOCUS	*Implement network segmentation, RBAC, and data encryption to secure AVD deployments. Avoid focusing on endpoint protection or continuous monitoring—they are important but not specific to AVD security. Prioritize measures that reduce exposure and meet compliance standards.*
CAUTION ALERT	*Stay clear of conflating endpoint-specific solutions with broader AVD security practices. Don't ignore encryption for both data-in-transit and at-rest. Ensure RBAC aligns with the principle of least privilege for minimizing unauthorized access risks.*

QUESTION 17

Answer - A) Implementing FSLogix Profile Containers for User Profile Management; B) Configuring Azure Load Balancer for Traffic Distribution; C) Enabling Azure Monitor for Performance Monitoring and Analysis

Option A - Correct. Implementing FSLogix Profile Containers helps optimize AVD performance by efficiently managing user profiles and reducing logon times. Option B - Correct. Configuring Azure Load Balancer allows for traffic distribution across AVD resources, optimizing performance and ensuring scalability during peak usage times.

Option C - Correct. Enabling Azure Monitor enables performance monitoring and analysis, allowing for proactive identification and resolution of performance issues in AVD deployments. Option D - Incorrect. While ARM templates are useful for infrastructure deployment, they may not directly impact AVD performance optimization. Option E - Incorrect. Deploying Azure Application Gateway focuses on application delivery and may not specifically address performance optimization for AVD deployments.

EXAM FOCUS	*Use FSLogix profile containers, Azure Load Balancer, and Azure Monitor for performance optimization. Eliminate unrelated solutions like ARM templates or Azure Application Gateway. Focus on tools that directly address AVD logon times, traffic distribution, and proactive issue resolution.*
CAUTION ALERT	*Avoid using ARM templates for optimization—they're better suited for deployment. Stay clear of general traffic delivery solutions like Application Gateway unless they specifically address AVD challenges. Ensure optimizations are tailored to workload requirements.*

QUESTION 18

Answer - [D]

Option D - Enable Scheduled Agent Updates: This option ensures that Azure Virtual Desktop agents across all session hosts are automatically updated according to a predefined schedule, minimizing downtime and administrative effort. Option A - Configuring a scaling plan is unrelated to updating Azure Virtual Desktop agents and is used for scaling session hosts based on demand. Option B - Configuring diagnostic settings is useful for monitoring and troubleshooting but does not involve updating Azure Virtual Desktop agents.

Option C - Enabling drain mode is used for gracefully removing session hosts from service but does not involve updating Azure Virtual Desktop agents. Option E - Deploying a new host pool is unnecessary for updating Azure Virtual Desktop agents and would require additional configuration and migration steps.

EXAM	*Enable Scheduled Agent Updates to automate agent updates across session hosts. Eliminate options like*

FOCUS	deploying new pools or configuring diagnostic settings, which do not address updating. Drain mode is useful for removing hosts temporarily but isn't needed for scheduled updates.
CAUTION ALERT	Avoid assuming that updating agents requires new host pools—it adds unnecessary complexity. Stay alert to missing schedules, as manual updates are time-consuming and error-prone. Ensure scheduled updates are enabled across all host pools.

QUESTION 19

Answer - A) Utilize VM Scale Sets; C) Optimize VM configurations for peak performance

Option A - Correct. VM Scale Sets enable automatic scaling of AVD session hosts based on demand, optimizing resource utilization and reducing costs during off-peak times. Option B - Incorrect. Azure Bastion provides secure RDP access to virtual machines but does not directly address scalability considerations in AVD deployments. Option C - Correct. Optimizing VM configurations ensures efficient resource allocation, enhancing AVD performance without unnecessary costs.

EXAM FOCUS	Utilize VM Scale Sets for dynamic scaling and optimize VM configurations for performance. Eliminate options like Azure Bastion, which is unrelated to scaling, or manual approaches that add administrative overhead. Prioritize automatic scaling to balance cost and resource efficiency.
CAUTION ALERT	Avoid relying solely on manual configurations or security solutions like Bastion for scaling tasks. Stay clear of overprovisioning resources during off-peak hours—leverage autoscaling to dynamically adjust based on actual demand.

QUESTION 20

Answer - D) Secure sensitive data with parameters

Option A - Incorrect: Identity management integration is essential but not directly configurable via this network interface template. Option B - Incorrect: Diagnostics settings are important for monitoring but not requested in the scenario. Option C - Incorrect: Auto-scaling settings are vital for handling user load but should be defined in a compute or application insights resource, not a network interface.

Option D - Correct: Using secure parameters to manage sensitive data, such as API keys or connection strings, ensures that security protocols are adhered to and that data exposure is minimized. Option E - Incorrect: The scenario requires specific enhancements to meet the outlined requirements, which the current template does not fully address.

EXAM FOCUS	Secure sensitive data using parameters in ARM templates. Eliminate incorrect solutions like enabling diagnostics or adding identity settings unrelated to network configurations. Prioritize templates that align with auto-scaling and identity management needs without exposing sensitive information.
CAUTION ALERT	Don't ignore securing sensitive data—leaving parameters unprotected increases risk. Stay alert to adding unnecessary diagnostics or identity settings to network templates. Focus on solutions that meet scaling, security, and operational requirements effectively.

QUESTION 21

Answer - A

Option A - Enabling RDP Shortpath for managed networks optimizes network connectivity for Azure Virtual Desktop, particularly for managed networks. This setting improves performance by reducing latency and enhancing user experience. Option B - Allowing remote connections to the computer is a general setting for enabling RDP access but does not specifically optimize network connectivity for Azure Virtual Desktop.

Option C - Configuring Windows Firewall for RDP access focuses on security configurations rather than network optimization.

Option D - Enabling Remote Desktop Protocol (RDP) is a basic setting for enabling RDP access but does not address network optimization for Azure Virtual Desktop. Option E - Implementing Network Level Authentication (NLA) enhances security by requiring authentication before establishing an RDP connection, but it does not specifically optimize network connectivity.

EXAM FOCUS	*You should enable RDP Shortpath for managed networks to optimize AVD connectivity. This reduces latency by leveraging a direct UDP-based transport. Always verify that your network infrastructure supports this setting.*
CAUTION ALERT	*Avoid assuming general RDP or firewall settings are sufficient for optimization. Stay clear of overlooking the specific requirement for managed networks to enable RDP Shortpath effectively.*

QUESTION 22

Answer - A) Seamless integration with Azure AD for centralized identity management; B) Compatibility with existing on-premises Active Directory environments; E) Scalability to support growing AVD deployments with ease

Option A - Correct. MEDS seamlessly integrates with Azure AD, providing centralized identity management for AVD environments. Option B - Correct. MEDS is compatible with existing on-premises Active Directory environments, facilitating hybrid identity scenarios. Option E - Correct. MEDS offers scalability to support growing AVD deployments, ensuring performance and availability.

Option C - Incorrect. While MEDS simplifies deployment and management, it is not specifically related to domain controller management in Azure. Option D - Incorrect. While MEDS enhances security, automatic patching and threat detection are not specific benefits associated with this service.

EXAM FOCUS	*Make sure to leverage Microsoft Entra Domain Services for seamless integration with Azure AD and hybrid identity. Its scalability ensures you can adapt to growing AVD demands while maintaining centralized identity management.*
CAUTION ALERT	*Avoid confusing MEDS benefits with full domain controller management. Stay alert to scenarios where MEDS might not replace certain on-premises AD dependencies, as it is a managed service with specific capabilities.*

QUESTION 23

Answer - A) Define access controls based on user identity and device state; B) Configure conditional access rules in Azure AD; C) Specify conditions for accessing AVD resources, such as location or device compliance; D) Assign Conditional Access policies to AVD user groups or roles

Option A - Correct. Defining access controls based on user identity and device state allows for granular control over access to AVD resources. Option B - Correct. Configuring conditional access rules in Azure AD enables the enforcement of access policies based on specific conditions. Option C - Correct. Specifying conditions for accessing AVD resources, such as location or device compliance, helps ensure secure access.

Option D - Correct. Assigning Conditional Access policies to AVD user groups or roles ensures that the policies are applied to the appropriate users. Option E - Incorrect. While monitoring policy effectiveness is important, it is not specifically a step involved in creating and implementing Conditional Access policies.

EXAM FOCUS	*You need to define Conditional Access policies based on user and device conditions. Always assign policies to specific AVD user groups and roles to control access effectively. Regularly review configurations for compliance.*
CAUTION ALERT	*Avoid applying Conditional Access policies broadly without specific criteria. Stay clear of assuming monitoring policy effectiveness is part of the initial creation process—it is a follow-up activity.*

QUESTION 24

Answer - B, D, E

A) Incorrect - Configuring a multi-session environment is not directly related to data residency or performance issues across multiple geographies. B) Correct - Deploying regional host pools will help in adhering to data residency laws and improve access times for users in different geographical areas. C) Incorrect - Azure Site Recovery is primarily for disaster recovery, not for initial deployment to manage data residency or performance.

D) Correct - Enabling geo-redundant storage ensures that data is replicated in multiple regions, aiding compliance with data residency requirements. E) Correct - Integrating Azure Traffic Manager can optimize traffic and improve user experience across different regions.

EXAM FOCUS	*Prioritize deploying regional host pools and geo-redundant storage for performance and compliance. Integrating Azure Traffic Manager can optimize user experience by intelligently directing traffic to the nearest resources.*
CAUTION ALERT	*Avoid assuming Azure Site Recovery or multi-session configurations are directly related to multi-geo setups. Stay clear of missing data residency laws when configuring regional deployments.*

QUESTION 25

Answer - A) Set-MpPreference -DisableRealtimeMonitoring $false

Option A - Correct: Enables real-time monitoring which is crucial for immediate threat detection.
Option B - Incorrect: Disables real-time monitoring, reducing protection.
Option C - Incorrect: Updates definitions but doesn't configure protection settings.
Option D - Incorrect: Command does not exist.
Option E - Incorrect: Sets scan schedule but does not enable real-time protection.

EXAM FOCUS	*Always enable real-time monitoring with Set-MpPreference -DisableRealtimeMonitoring $false to maintain robust security on AVD session hosts. Automate definition updates to ensure up-to-date threat protection.*
CAUTION ALERT	*Avoid disabling real-time monitoring or relying solely on manual updates for antivirus definitions. Stay cautious about commands that may not specifically enable real-time protection features.*

QUESTION 26

Answer - A) Provision Azure Bastion in the same virtual network (VNET) as AVD session hosts; B) Configure network security groups (NSGs) to allow inbound traffic on ports required by Azure Bastion; C) Associate Azure Bastion with the AVD workspace for seamless RDP/SSH access to session hosts

Option A - Correct. Provisioning Azure Bastion in the same VNET as AVD session hosts ensures proximity and optimized network performance. Option B - Correct. Configuring NSGs to allow inbound traffic on ports required by Azure Bastion enables secure communication. Option C - Correct. Associating Azure Bastion with the AVD workspace facilitates seamless RDP/SSH access to session hosts through the Azure portal. Option D - Incorrect. While assigning RBAC roles is important, it is not specifically mentioned in the context of setting up Azure Bastion for secure AVD management as described in the question. Option E - Incorrect. While enabling diagnostics logging is valuable for monitoring and troubleshooting, it is not directly related to setting up Azure Bastion for secure AVD management as described in the question.

EXAM FOCUS	*Provision Azure Bastion in the same VNET as AVD session hosts for secure and optimized access. Configure NSGs appropriately and associate Bastion with the AVD workspace for seamless RDP/SSH management.*
CAUTION	*Avoid overlooking NSG configurations when setting up Azure Bastion. Stay clear of deploying Bastion in a*

| ALERT | separate VNET, as this can lead to performance and connectivity issues. |

QUESTION 27

Answer - B, C, D

A) Incorrect - While Azure Firewall provides network protection, it does not specifically address advanced threat protection for endpoints. B) Correct - Microsoft Defender for Endpoint offers advanced threat protection capabilities that are critical for securing AVD environments.

C) Correct - Azure VPN Gateway provides a secure method for remote access, protecting against unauthorized access.

D) Correct - Azure Active Directory Conditional Access allows integration with existing security infrastructure to enforce security policies based on conditions.

E) Incorrect - Third-party SIEM tools integration is useful for monitoring but does not directly address the specified requirements.

EXAM FOCUS	*Implement Defender for Endpoint for advanced threat protection, Azure VPN Gateway for secure remote access, and Conditional Access for enforcing identity-based security policies in AVD. Regularly review integrated solutions.*
CAUTION ALERT	*Avoid relying solely on network-level protections like Azure Firewall for endpoint security. Stay alert to gaps in Conditional Access configurations that might leave resources exposed.*

QUESTION 28

Answer - A) Define granular roles based on job functions and responsibilities; C) Use Azure AD groups to streamline role assignment and membership management; D) Regularly review and update role assignments based on changing requirements

Option A - Correct. Defining granular roles based on job functions and responsibilities ensures that users have appropriate access permissions tailored to their specific tasks, enhancing security and efficiency. Option B - Incorrect. While role hierarchies can simplify role assignment and management in some cases, they are not always necessary or appropriate for all RBAC models. Option C - Correct. Using Azure AD groups helps streamline role assignment and membership management by allowing administrators to assign roles to groups rather than individual users, reducing administrative overhead.

Option D - Correct. Regularly reviewing and updating role assignments based on changing requirements ensures that access permissions remain aligned with organizational needs and security policies. Option E - Incorrect. While utilizing built-in Azure AD roles can provide standardized access control policies, they may not always meet the specific needs of an organization, necessitating the creation of custom roles.

EXAM FOCUS	*Define granular roles in your RBAC model and use Azure AD groups to simplify assignment. Regularly update roles to reflect changes in organizational needs while minimizing over-permissioning.*
CAUTION ALERT	*Avoid relying only on built-in roles, as they may not meet all requirements. Stay cautious about creating overly complex hierarchies that can complicate role management and increase administrative overhead.*

QUESTION 29

Answer - A) Enable MFA for Azure AD users in the Azure portal; B) Configure Conditional Access policies to enforce MFA for AVD access; E) Educate users on MFA setup and usage best practices

Option A - Correct. Enabling MFA for Azure AD users in the Azure portal is the first step in setting up MFA for AVD access, ensuring that users are prompted to set up MFA. Option B - Correct. Configuring Conditional Access policies to enforce MFA for AVD access provides granular control over when and how MFA is required.

Option C - Incorrect. While Azure AD Security Defaults can enforce MFA, it may not provide the flexibility required for AVD-specific access scenarios. Option D - Incorrect. While integrating MFA with on-premises Active Directory using Azure AD Connect is important for hybrid environments, it is not directly related to setting up MFA for AVD access. Option E - Correct. Educating users on MFA setup and usage best practices ensures smooth adoption and compliance with MFA requirements.

EXAM FOCUS	*Enable MFA for Azure AD users and enforce it through Conditional Access policies. Educate users on best practices to ensure smooth adoption and compliance. Review access scenarios to ensure MFA aligns with organizational security goals.*
CAUTION ALERT	*Avoid relying on Azure AD Security Defaults for nuanced AVD access scenarios. Stay alert to incomplete Conditional Access configurations that fail to enforce MFA across all intended resources.*

QUESTION 30

Answer - A) Correct configuration

Option A - Correct: The script correctly sets up an NSG to allow RDP access from a specific IP range on the standard port, following best practices for secure remote access. Option B - Incorrect: A broader IP range would reduce the security effectiveness of the rule.

Option C - Incorrect: Limiting the destination port range to 3389 (RDP) enhances security by restricting access to the necessary service only. Option D - Incorrect: The NSG name "AVDNSG" is appropriately descriptive for Azure Virtual Desktop. Option E - Incorrect: Priority 100 is typically adequate to ensure the rule is evaluated properly without interfering with other potential rules.

EXAM FOCUS	*Use specific IP ranges and strict destination ports like 3389 for RDP in NSG rules to enhance security. Ensure priority settings like 100 make the rule effective while adhering to compliance requirements for restricted access.*
CAUTION ALERT	*Avoid broad IP ranges that increase exposure risk. Stay cautious about assigning a lower priority for critical rules, as it can lead to unintended consequences with conflicting configurations.*

QUESTION 31

Answer - A) User environment complexity and customization requirements; B) Performance impact on session host resources and storage utilization; D) Network latency and bandwidth constraints for profile storage

Option A - Correct. User environment complexity and customization requirements influence the choice of FSLogix settings to ensure optimal user experience and profile management. Option B - Correct. Considering the performance impact on session host resources and storage utilization helps maintain system performance and scalability.

Option C - Incorrect. While compatibility with third-party applications is important, it may not directly influence the selection of FSLogix settings. Option D - Correct. Evaluating network latency and bandwidth constraints ensures efficient profile storage and retrieval across distributed AVD environments. Option E - Incorrect. While support for multi-session host configurations is important, it may not be directly related to selecting specific FSLogix settings.

EXAM FOCUS	*You should consider user customization needs, session host performance, and network constraints when configuring FSLogix. Always validate how settings align with organizational workflows and data transfer requirements. Tailor configurations to balance system scalability and user experience effectively.*
CAUTION ALERT	*Avoid assuming all FSLogix configurations are universally optimal. Stay alert to misconfigurations that could lead to high resource usage, especially in environments with limited network bandwidth or heavy session host loads.*

QUESTION 32

Answer - A) Implement folder redirection, B) Utilize FSLogix Cloud Cache, C) Configure Profile Containers to store only essential user settings.

A) Implement folder redirection - Redirecting folders such as Documents, Downloads, and Desktop to network shares reduces the size of Profile Containers and enhances performance. B) Utilize FSLogix Cloud Cache - FSLogix Cloud Cache caches user profiles and reduces load times by storing profile data locally.

C) Configure Profile Containers to store only essential user settings - Storing only essential user settings in Profile Containers reduces their size and improves performance. D) Implement data deduplication within Profile Containers - Data deduplication may not be effective within Profile Containers and can increase processing overhead. E) Enable Profile Containers compression - Enabling compression may increase CPU usage and affect performance without significant storage savings.

EXAM FOCUS	*Make sure to implement folder redirection for critical data, enable FSLogix Cloud Cache for better profile load times, and configure containers to store only essential settings. These methods improve performance, scalability, and resource allocation for growing AVD deployments.*
CAUTION ALERT	*Don't enable compression or deduplication without assessing their impact. These can lead to higher CPU overhead and may negate performance benefits, especially in environments with intensive workloads or numerous concurrent users.*

QUESTION 33

Answer - A, B, E

A) Correct - Azure Bastion provides secure RDP and SSH access through Azure's infrastructure, preventing exposure over the internet. B) Correct - NSGs help restrict traffic to the VMs, ensuring that only authorized traffic reaches the session hosts.

C) Incorrect - Azure Defender is essential for threat protection but does not directly address secure administrative access or encrypted connections. D) Incorrect - While Azure Policy enforces standards, it is not specific to secure administrative access or encrypted connection requirements. E) Correct - JIT VM access minimizes the attack surface by allowing access to VMs only at required times, enhancing security for administrative tasks.

EXAM FOCUS	*You need to secure AVD hosts using Azure Bastion for private access, NSGs for traffic restriction, and JIT access to reduce attack surface. These measures ensure compliance, encrypted sessions, and minimal exposure to public networks.*
CAUTION ALERT	*Avoid relying solely on Azure Defender for administrative security. Stay clear of overly broad NSG rules, which can introduce vulnerabilities. Always validate firewall rules against regulatory and organizational security standards.*

QUESTION 34

Answer - A) Deploy AVD clients using MSIX App Attach for dynamic application provisioning, C) Implement GPU-accelerated virtual machines (VMs) for users requiring high-definition multimedia applications, D) Optimize network Quality of Service (QoS) settings to prioritize AVD traffic based on application requirements.

A) Deploy AVD clients using MSIX App Attach for dynamic application provisioning - MSIX App Attach simplifies application management by dynamically attaching packaged applications to user sessions, enhancing flexibility and resource utilization. C) Implement GPU-accelerated virtual machines (VMs) for users requiring high-definition multimedia applications - GPU-accelerated VMs enhance performance for graphics-intensive applications, ensuring smooth multimedia experiences for users. D) Optimize network Quality of Service (QoS) settings to prioritize AVD traffic based on application requirements - QoS optimization ensures consistent performance by prioritizing AVD traffic over the network, especially for latency-sensitive applications.

B) Utilize Azure Bastion for secure RDP access to AVD instances without exposing them to the public internet - While Azure Bastion enhances access security, it may not directly relate to deployment strategies for optimizing performance and user experience. E) Leverage Azure AD Conditional Access policies to enforce multi-factor authentication (MFA) for user access to AVD sessions - While Conditional Access policies enhance security, they may not directly address deployment strategies for optimizing performance and user experience.

EXAM FOCUS	*Always consider using MSIX App Attach for dynamic app provisioning, GPU-accelerated VMs for multimedia-heavy tasks, and QoS to prioritize AVD traffic. These strategies ensure optimal resource allocation and enhanced user experience across geographies.*
CAUTION ALERT	*Don't assume Azure Bastion or Conditional Access policies directly optimize client performance. Stay cautious about neglecting network adjustments, as QoS settings are crucial for latency-sensitive applications in remote locations.*

QUESTION 35

Answer - A) Script is correctly configured for optimal performance

Option A - Correct: The script properly configures multimedia redirection for video and audio, optimizing user experience for video-intensive applications. Option B - Incorrect: Disabling videoplaybackmode would negate the benefits of multimedia redirection for video content. Option C - Incorrect: Audiocapturemode is set correctly to capture audio which is necessary for complete multimedia redirection.

Option D - Incorrect: The script assumes GPU optimization elsewhere; this setting is about enabling redirection. Option E - Incorrect: Clipboard redirection is unrelated to multimedia performance and generally useful.

EXAM FOCUS	*You should configure multimedia redirection settings like videoplaybackmode and audiocapturemode to optimize performance. Always validate compatibility with GPU resources and ensure the settings align with application requirements for video-heavy environments.*
CAUTION ALERT	*Avoid disabling key redirection features such as videoplaybackmode, as this undermines multimedia performance. Stay alert to GPU resource misconfigurations, which could lead to degraded experiences in high-definition video workflows.*

QUESTION 36

Answer - A, B, C

A) Correct - Azure Bastion allows secure SSL access and eliminates the need for public IPs, meeting the no direct internet access requirement. B) Correct - Azure Firewall can enforce rules that prevent direct internet access while allowing secure, monitored connections. C) Correct - Azure Private Link ensures that the connection remains on the Microsoft network, not exposing data to the public internet.

D) Incorrect - Azure Application Proxy is typically used for secure remote access to internal applications, not for VM management. E) Incorrect - JIT VM access is for managing when VMs can be accessed, not how they are accessed or the encryption of those connections.

EXAM FOCUS	*Use Azure Bastion, Private Link, and Firewall for secure AVD configurations. These prevent public exposure, enable private connectivity, and enforce SSL encryption. Always test configurations against compliance standards for sensitive data handling.*
CAUTION ALERT	*Avoid assuming Application Proxy or JIT access fully meets stringent security needs. Stay cautious about improperly configured firewall rules that could inadvertently allow unwanted traffic or compromise network isolation requirements.*

QUESTION 37

Answer - A) Adjusting session timeouts based on Azure AD group membership

Adjusting session timeouts based on Azure AD group membership allows for tailored configurations to meet departmental needs while maintaining security compliance. Option B - Incorrect. While MFA enhances security, it is not directly related to session timeout configurations for specific departments. Option C - Incorrect. Password policies are important but do not address session duration requirements.

Option D - Incorrect. FSLogix provides profile management but does not control session timeouts. Option E - Incorrect. JIT access is unrelated to session duration configurations.

EXAM FOCUS	*Adjust session timeouts using Azure AD groups to meet departmental needs while maintaining security compliance. Tailored configurations ensure critical teams like finance can work uninterrupted while adhering to organization-wide access policies and regulations.*
CAUTION ALERT	*Don't enforce uniform session timeouts without considering varying departmental workflows. Stay cautious about extending durations excessively, as this may compromise security, especially in compliance-focused environments.*

QUESTION 38

Answer - A) Reducing VM idle time and associated costs by powering on VMs only when users connect

Configuring Start VM on Connect reduces idle time and costs by powering on VMs only when users connect, ensuring efficient resource utilization and cost-effectiveness. Option B - Incorrect. Pre-starting VMs may increase resource usage without guaranteeing user connections.

Option C - Incorrect. While it may enhance user experience, this is not the primary benefit of configuring Start VM on Connect. Option D - Incorrect. Security benefits are not directly related to this feature. Option E - Incorrect. While automatic scaling may improve management, it is not specific to Start VM on Connect.

EXAM FOCUS	*Implement Start VM on Connect to power on VMs only when needed. This reduces idle time, optimizes resource utilization, and ensures cost savings. Always monitor usage patterns to refine configurations for peak and off-peak operations.*
CAUTION ALERT	*Avoid pre-starting VMs unnecessarily, as this wastes resources and costs. Stay alert to configurations that leave VMs running outside business hours, negating potential savings from optimized AVD deployments.*

QUESTION 39

Answer - A, B, D

A) Correct - Azure Bastion provides secure and private access to virtual machines, crucial for healthcare environments handling sensitive data. B) Correct - Azure AD Conditional Access ensures that only authorized personnel can access certain resources, crucial for compliance and security. C) Incorrect - While important for continuity, Azure Site Recovery is not specific to the secure access of session hosts.

D) Correct - A dedicated subnet named AzureBastionSubnet is required to deploy Azure Bastion, ensuring the infrastructure is correctly set up for secure access. E) Incorrect - While disk encryption is important, it is not part of the specific requirements for accessing VMs securely or managing access.

EXAM FOCUS	*Use Azure Bastion for private VM access, Conditional Access for role-based security, and AzureBastionSubnet for proper infrastructure setup. These ensure compliance, secure sessions, and minimal data exposure in healthcare AVD environments.*
CAUTION ALERT	*Avoid assuming disk encryption alone ensures compliance or security. Stay cautious about neglecting Conditional Access policies, as these are critical for role-based access control and protecting sensitive healthcare data.*

QUESTION 40

Answer - C

Option A - Incorrect. New-FSLogixAppMaskingRule is used for creating new rules, not Set-FSLogixAppMaskingRule which is for modifying existing ones. Option B - Incorrect. While using a full path is good practice, it is not necessary for the rule to work if the executable name is unique. Option C - Correct. The user assignment string should be enclosed in quotes to prevent syntax errors.

Option D - Incorrect. The -Enabled $true is not necessary as rules are enabled by default upon creation. Option E - Incorrect. There is a syntax error with the user assignment that needs correction.

EXAM FOCUS	*Always enclose user assignments like -AssignedUser in quotes to avoid syntax errors. Verify configurations carefully when using FSLogix Application Masking to limit app access and ensure settings align with user group requirements.*
CAUTION ALERT	*Avoid neglecting syntax validation in PowerShell commands, as minor errors can disrupt rule creation. Stay alert to assigning incorrect paths or user groups, as this can lead to misapplied masking rules or failed deployments.*

QUESTION 41

Answer - D

Option A - Incorrect. While enabling WebRTC is correct, the parameter for optimizing media is not accurate. Option B - Incorrect. Adding -UseRDPTransport $false is unnecessary as enabling WebRTC already implies not using RDP for media transport.

Option C - Incorrect. The parameter -EnableWebRTC $true is correct. Option D - Correct. The correct parameter for media optimization in PowerShell is -MediaOptimization $true. Option E - Incorrect. Specifying the session host is not required in this command as it applies globally to the AVD environment.

EXAM FOCUS	*You need to use -MediaOptimization $true for media optimization when configuring Teams for AVD. Make sure WebRTC redirector service is enabled for improved audio and video. Validate PowerShell parameters carefully, ensuring commands apply across all session hosts effectively.*
CAUTION ALERT	*Avoid misconfiguring PowerShell parameters. Stay alert to deprecated options like -UseRDPTransport $false, which may conflict with WebRTC optimization. Ensure syntax correctness to avoid operational issues during Teams optimization.*

QUESTION 42

Answer - B, D

A) Incorrect - The 'Type' setting is not directly involved in performance but specifies the type of container used. B) Correct - Enabling FSLogix Profiles is essential for the feature to function and directly affects performance by ensuring profiles are handled efficiently. C) Incorrect - 'Size' under ODFC is not a recognized setting for optimizing performance in FSLogix. D) Correct - Specifying 'VHDLocations' is crucial for defining where user profile disks are stored, impacting load times and performance. E) Incorrect - The 'Start' setting under 'frxccd' service is not relevant to FSLogix profile performance but relates to the service startup type.

EXAM FOCUS	*Always configure HKLM\SOFTWARE\FSLogix\Profiles\Enabled to activate FSLogix and VHDLocations for optimized storage. Ensure profile paths are valid and accessible. These settings directly impact user profile load times, scalability, and AVD session efficiency.*
CAUTION ALERT	*Avoid leaving Enabled or VHDLocations unset, as this can cause profiles to fail loading. Stay alert to incorrect registry paths, which may disrupt FSLogix's functionality and negatively impact session performance.*

QUESTION 43

Answer - C) Configure Azure Log Analytics to track host pool performance

Option A - Incorrect. While Azure Monitor provides overall monitoring, Azure Log Analytics offers more granular insights into AVD host pool performance, allowing for real-time tracking and analysis. Option B - Incorrect. While PowerShell can automate tasks, it may not provide real-time monitoring of host pool performance and lacks the depth of Azure Log Analytics. Option C - Correct. Azure Log Analytics allows for tracking and analysis of specific metrics for AVD host pools in real-time, providing insights into potential performance bottlenecks. Option D - Incorrect. Diagnostic Settings in Azure Portal may provide basic monitoring but may not offer the detailed insights provided by Azure Log Analytics. Option E - Incorrect. Network Performance Monitor focuses on network traffic, not specific performance metrics related to AVD host pools.

EXAM FOCUS	*Use Azure Log Analytics for in-depth and real-time AVD host pool performance monitoring. Configure relevant queries and dashboards for actionable insights into resource utilization and bottlenecks. Integration with Azure Monitor enhances centralized management.*
CAUTION ALERT	*Don't rely solely on Diagnostic Settings or PowerShell for comprehensive performance tracking. Stay cautious about overlooking specific metrics like CPU or memory trends that directly influence user session experience in AVD.*

QUESTION 44

Answer - A) Enable Azure Monitor logs for AVD

Option A - Enabling Azure Monitor logs for AVD allows the collection of detailed telemetry data, including performance metrics and operational logs, essential for comprehensive monitoring and analysis. Option B - Configuring Azure Monitor Alerts for AVD focuses on alerting, not initial monitoring setup.

Option C - Integrating Azure Monitor with Azure Log Analytics is part of the monitoring setup but doesn't directly enable detailed monitoring of AVD deployments. Option D - Deploying Azure Monitor Workbooks for AVD is more for visualizing data, not for initial monitoring setup. Option E - Enabling Azure Monitor Application Insights for AVD focuses on application-level monitoring, not infrastructure monitoring.

EXAM FOCUS	*Enable Azure Monitor logs for AVD to collect detailed metrics like session performance, resource consumption, and user trends. Integrating these logs with existing tools ensures centralized monitoring and actionable analysis for proactive troubleshooting.*
CAUTION ALERT	*Don't skip enabling telemetry collection when configuring Azure Monitor logs. Stay cautious about collecting excessive metrics, which can increase costs and degrade system performance. Focus on data that directly supports actionable insights.*

QUESTION 45

Answer - B

Option A - Incorrect. The script creates a policy but doesn't apply it to the file share.
Option B - Correct. Extending the script to specify the resource group, file share name, and policy ensures that the Azure File Share storing the FSLogix profiles is correctly targeted for daily backups.
Option C - Incorrect. Set-AzRecoveryServicesBackupPolicy modifies an existing policy, not create a new one.
Option D - Incorrect. -SchedulePolicy is not a valid parameter for this cmdlet.
Option E - Incorrect. -BackupFrequency "Daily" is already correctly specified for creating a daily backup policy.

EXAM FOCUS	*Always specify -ResourceGroupName, -FileShareName, and -PolicyName to ensure FSLogix profiles are correctly targeted for backups. Use the daily frequency option to maintain consistency and reduce*

	administrative overhead in data protection efforts.
CAUTION ALERT	*Avoid creating a backup policy without applying it to specific resources. Stay alert to skipping parameters like FileShareName, which may lead to incomplete configurations and leave critical profiles unprotected.*

QUESTION 46

Answer - D) Adaptive scaling with Azure Monitor

Option D - Adaptive scaling with Azure Monitor dynamically adjusts AVD resources based on real-time performance metrics, ensuring optimal resource allocation and cost-effectiveness. It automatically scales resources up or down based on user demand and predefined rules, addressing both performance and cost concerns.

Option A - Auto-scaling with Azure Logic Apps may lack the real-time performance monitoring required for dynamic scaling. Option B - Manual scaling using PowerShell scripts may not be efficient for addressing peak usage and cost optimization simultaneously. Option C - Scheduled scaling with Azure Automation may not respond effectively to sudden changes in user demands, potentially leading to performance issues during peak times. Option E - Static scaling with Azure Resource Manager templates does not provide the flexibility needed for dynamic resource allocation to address fluctuating usage patterns.

EXAM FOCUS	*Use Azure Monitor adaptive scaling for dynamic adjustments based on real-time metrics. This ensures cost-effective resource allocation during peak and off-peak hours. Define scaling rules in advance to handle fluctuating user demands efficiently.*
CAUTION ALERT	*Don't depend on static scaling or manual intervention during peak loads. Stay cautious about incomplete scaling rules, as they can lead to resource overutilization or downtime, impacting user experience and operational efficiency.*

QUESTION 47

Answer - E) Azure Security Center policies

Option E - Azure Security Center policies enable administrators to define and enforce security configurations, including compliance standards, threat detection rules, and vulnerability assessments, ensuring adherence to industry regulations and best practices in AVD environments.

Option A - Role-Based Access Control (RBAC) provides granular access control but may not directly address compliance requirements or threat detection. Option B - Multi-Factor Authentication (MFA) enhances authentication security but may not specifically focus on security policy enforcement. Option C - Just-In-Time (JIT) access limits administrative access duration but may not directly enforce security policies for user roles. Option D - Network Security Groups (NSGs) control network traffic but may not cover comprehensive security policy enforcement as Azure Security Center does.

EXAM FOCUS	*Prioritize Azure Security Center policies for comprehensive threat detection and compliance enforcement. Use these policies to define configurations for vulnerability management, data protection, and regulatory alignment within your AVD environment.*
CAUTION ALERT	*Avoid assuming RBAC or MFA alone fulfills compliance needs. Stay cautious about overlooking policies specific to security posture management, which are essential for identifying misconfigurations and vulnerabilities proactively.*

QUESTION 48

Answer - A, C, D

A) Correct - 'VHDLocations' helps optimize where large files are stored, impacting file access speed and system performance. B) Incorrect - While 'CloudCache' is crucial for redundancy, it does not directly manage large file sizes or performance. C) Correct - 'DynamicVHDAllocation' is essential for efficiently managing disk space when dealing with large video files, preventing waste and enhancing performance.

D) Correct - 'Encrypt' ensures that all stored data, especially sensitive high-resolution videos, is secure from unauthorized access. E) Incorrect - 'LocalCacheSize' affects local storage but is secondary to VHD management and encryption in terms of performance and security priorities for video editing.

EXAM FOCUS	*Configure VHDLocations for optimal storage, DynamicVHDAllocation to manage disk space efficiently, and Encrypt to secure sensitive data. These FSLogix settings are crucial for high-performance environments handling large files like video content.*
CAUTION ALERT	*Avoid neglecting disk encryption or dynamic allocation, as these are critical for performance and data security. Stay cautious about redundant cloud storage configurations that may increase costs without benefiting performance.*

QUESTION 49

Answer - A) Implementing cross-region replication for AVD resources
B) Configuring Azure Site Recovery for automated failover and recovery
C) Utilizing Azure Backup for data protection and retention

A) Implementing cross-region replication for AVD resources - Cross-region replication ensures data redundancy and availability in case of region-wide failures. B) Configuring Azure Site Recovery for automated failover and recovery - Azure Site Recovery automates the failover process and ensures rapid recovery of AVD resources. C) Utilizing Azure Backup for data protection and retention - Azure Backup provides reliable backup and recovery solutions for AVD data and configurations. D, E) While RBAC policies and Azure Bastion are important for access control and secure access, they are not directly related to designing disaster recovery strategies for AVD.

EXAM FOCUS	*Implement cross-region replication and Azure Site Recovery for robust disaster recovery. Combine with Azure Backup for reliable data protection. These ensure high availability, data redundancy, and operational continuity for AVD environments.*
CAUTION ALERT	*Don't assume RBAC or Bastion configurations replace disaster recovery strategies. Stay cautious about overlooking cross-region replication, as localized failures can cause significant disruptions without adequate redundancy measures.*

QUESTION 50

Answer - A) Azure Application Insights for tracking application performance metrics
C) Azure Monitor for monitoring resource utilization and performance
E) Utilizing Azure Log Analytics for tracking application errors and exceptions

A) Azure Application Insights for tracking application performance metrics - Azure Application Insights provides detailed insights into application performance metrics, helping identify bottlenecks and optimize performance. C) Azure Monitor for monitoring resource utilization and performance - Azure Monitor enables monitoring of resource utilization and performance, allowing proactive identification and resolution of performance issues. E) Utilizing Azure Log Analytics for tracking application errors and exceptions - Azure Log Analytics helps track application errors and exceptions, enabling rapid troubleshooting and resolution of issues. B, D) While Microsoft Endpoint Analytics and FSLogix are valuable for analyzing user experience and optimizing application load times, they are not specifically focused on monitoring and optimizing application performance in AVD.

EXAM FOCUS	*Use Azure Application Insights for app performance tracking, Azure Monitor for system metrics, and Azure Log Analytics for error diagnostics. Together, they provide a comprehensive view for monitoring and optimizing application performance in AVD environments.*
CAUTION ALERT	*Avoid overlooking application-level monitoring tools like Application Insights. Stay cautious about assuming infrastructure monitoring alone identifies app-specific issues, as these may require granular diagnostics for resolution.*

PRACTICE TEST 2 - QUESTIONS ONLY

QUESTION 1

As part of the AVD implementation team for a software development company, you are concerned about the impact of network latency on the developers' productivity and real-time collaboration tools. Your goals are to:
- Evaluate network latency between your virtual network and Azure services.
- Determine the real-time collaboration tools' performance.
- Provide recommendations for network improvements.

Which Azure CLI command would you use to evaluate network latency effectively in this scenario?

```
A) az network vnet check-gateway
B) az network vnet test-latency
C) az network watcher test-ip-flow
D) az network watcher show-next-hop
E) az network watcher test-connection
```

QUESTION 2

As an Azure administrator, you're tasked with integrating an on-premises network with AVD using ExpressRoute to ensure compliance with industry regulations requiring secure and private connectivity. Your focus areas are:
- Configuring ExpressRoute circuits for dedicated connectivity.
- Ensuring end-to-end encryption.
- Leveraging Azure RBAC for access control.

What Azure CLI command would you use to create an ExpressRoute circuit?

```
A) az network express-route create
B) az network vpn-gateway create
C) az network vnet subnet create
D) az network vnet peering add
E) az network express-route list-circuit
```

QUESTION 3

- Your responsibility is to ensure the performance optimization of Azure Virtual Desktop (AVD) session hosts.
- You are required to monitor critical performance metrics to identify any potential bottlenecks.
- Your task involves selecting the appropriate Log Analytics table to retrieve performance data.

Which table in Log Analytics should you consult to monitor the health and performance of the session hosts, including CPU and memory usage?

```
A) WVDConnections
B) WVDPerformanceCounters
C) WVDHostRegistrations
D) WVDAgentHealth
E) WVDServiceHealth
```

QUESTION 4

Your organization's Azure Virtual Desktop (AVD) users are experiencing intermittent connectivity issues when accessing resources hosted on the AVD infrastructure. As the IT support specialist, you are tasked with troubleshooting these common network connectivity issues to ensure uninterrupted service delivery. Which steps would you take to troubleshoot these issues effectively? Select THREE.

A) Check DNS resolution for AVD resources using nslookup

B) Review Azure Network Security Group (NSG) rules for port blocking issues
C) Analyze Azure Virtual Network Gateway logs for VPN connectivity problems
D) Monitor Azure ExpressRoute circuit status and bandwidth utilization
E) Verify Azure Virtual Desktop session host availability and resource utilization

QUESTION 5

As an Azure administrator, you're configuring a session host using PowerShell to optimize its performance for graphics-intensive applications. Which PowerShell cmdlet correctly sets up a GPU-enabled VM?

`New-AzVM -ResourceGroupName "ResourceGroup1" -Name "VM1" -Size "Standard_NV6" -Image "Win10"`

A) Command uses an incorrect VM size
B) Command lacks network configuration
C) Image specification is incorrect
D) Correct command for GPU setup
E) Command needs additional storage options

QUESTION 6

Your organization is seeking to reduce costs in its Azure Virtual Desktop (AVD) environment by implementing an efficient solution for managing session host usage. The solution must meet the following requirements:
- Automatically start session hosts at 7:00 AM and shut them down at 7:00 PM.
- Be effective every day of the week.
- Minimize manual intervention.

Which Azure service should you leverage to achieve this?

A) Azure Monitor
B) Azure Logic Apps
C) Azure Policy
D) Azure Automation with Azure Functions
E) Azure Virtual Machine Scale Sets

QUESTION 7

Your organization is debating between Windows 10 Multi-Session and Windows Server as the operating system for Azure Virtual Desktop (AVD) deployments. As the Azure specialist, you need to compare the two options to help make an informed decision. How do these options differ? Select THREE.

A) Windows 10 Multi-Session provides a desktop-like experience with better application compatibility for end-users
B) Windows Server offers enhanced scalability and resource utilization for multi-user environments
C) Windows 10 Multi-Session includes built-in security features such as Windows Defender Antivirus and Windows Defender Firewall
D) Windows Server supports Remote Desktop Services (RDS) roles and features for centralized desktop and application delivery
E) Windows 10 Multi-Session requires less frequent patching and updates compared to Windows Server

QUESTION 8

Your organization is implementing host pools in Azure Virtual Desktop (AVD) and requires effective scaling and load balancing strategies to ensure optimal performance and resource allocation. As the Azure specialist, you are tasked with selecting the most suitable approaches. Which strategies should you consider? Select TWO.

A) Auto Scaling and Dynamic Provisioning

B) Capacity Planning and Reserved Instances
C) Geo-Redundancy and Disaster Recovery
D) Weighted Round-Robin and Session Affinity
E) Vertical Scaling and Resource Overcommitment

QUESTION 9

You need to configure autoscale for host pools in an Azure Virtual Desktop (AVD) environment to optimize resource usage. Consider the following factors:
- Scalability based on demand to accommodate varying user loads.
- Efficient utilization of session hosts during peak and off-peak hours.
- Minimization of administrative effort for managing resource scaling.
Which Azure service should you leverage to achieve these objectives?

A) Azure Automation
B) Azure Monitor
C) Azure Resource Manager templates
D) Azure Logic Apps
E) Azure Virtual Machine Scale Sets

QUESTION 10

You need to configure file shares in Azure for a high-traffic AVD environment. Your task includes setting up the share with appropriate access and scalability settings. Review this PowerShell snippet for potential issues.
`New-AzRmStorageShare -StorageAccountName "AVDStorage" -Name "AVDFiles" -Quota 512 -EnabledProtocol "SMB"`

A) Quota too low for high-traffic
B) Incorrect protocol for AVD
C) Command syntax is incorrect
D) Storage account name is inappropriate
E) Command is correctly configured

QUESTION 11

Your organization is experiencing issues with applying Windows Client licenses to session hosts in Azure Virtual Desktop (AVD). As the Azure specialist, you are tasked with troubleshooting the problem. What common issues might you encounter during the license application process? Select THREE.

A) Invalid License Key or Activation Code
B) Incorrect License Type for Session Host OS
C) Network Connectivity Issues Preventing License Activation
D) Incompatibility Between License and AVD Subscription
E) Insufficient User or Device CALs for License Assignment

QUESTION 12

You are configuring a disaster recovery strategy for an Azure Virtual Desktop (AVD) environment with multi-region deployment. Consider the following requirements:
- Enable failover of AVD host pools to a secondary region in case of a regional outage.
- Ensure minimal data loss and downtime during failover operations.
Which combination of Azure services should you leverage to meet these requirements? Select TWO.

A) Azure Backup

B) Azure Traffic Manager
C) Azure Site Recovery
D) Azure Load Balancer
E) Azure Blob Storage

QUESTION 13

Your organization needs to track and update Azure Virtual Desktop (AVD) images efficiently to ensure the latest software versions and security patches are applied. As the Azure specialist, you need to identify suitable tools and techniques for tracking and updating images. Which of the following tools and techniques are commonly used for tracking and updating AVD images? Select TWO.

A) Azure Monitor Logs
B) Azure Security Center
C) Azure Automation Update Management
D) Git Version Control System
E) Azure DevOps Pipelines

QUESTION 14

Your organization is evaluating the benefits of using golden images in Azure Virtual Desktop (AVD) deployments to optimize management and consistency. As the Azure specialist, you need to identify the advantages of utilizing golden images in AVD environments. What are the benefits of using golden images in AVD deployments? Select THREE.

A) Streamlined Deployment Processes
B) Consistency Across Virtual Desktop Environments
C) Simplified Patch Management and Updates
D) Enhanced Security with Preconfigured Settings
E) Reduced Storage Costs due to Shared Image Repository

QUESTION 15

You are tasked with integrating the Compute Gallery with your AVD setup to streamline image management. What Azure CLI command should you use to add an image definition to your gallery?

```bash
az sig image-definition create --resource-group MyResourceGroup --gallery-name MyGallery --gallery-image-definition MyImage --publisher "MyOrg" --offer "AVDOffer" --sku "2021" --os-type Windows
```

A) Command is correct
B) Incorrect gallery-image-definition parameter
C) Publisher should be "Microsoft"
D) SKU should be "Standard_DS1_v2"
E) os-type should be Linux

QUESTION 16

Azure Security Center plays a crucial role in managing security for Azure Virtual Desktop (AVD) environments by providing insights, recommendations, and threat protection capabilities. As the Azure specialist, you need to explain the role of Azure Security Center in managing AVD security effectively. What is the role of Azure Security Center in managing AVD security? Select THREE.

A) Continuous Monitoring and Security Assessments
B) Integration with Azure AD for Identity Protection

C) Threat Detection and Incident Response Automation
D) Secure Configuration Management for AVD Resources
E) Vulnerability Management and Patch Management for AVD Deployments

QUESTION 17

Your organization is planning to deploy Azure Virtual Desktop (AVD) for its workforce, and you need to ensure optimal resource allocation to maintain performance across all user sessions. However, you're faced with the challenge of balancing resource allocation effectively. What strategies can you implement to balance resource allocation for optimal performance in AVD deployments? Select THREE.

A) Implementing Dynamic Scaling of Virtual Machines based on User Demand
B) Configuring Azure Policy for Resource Quotas and Allocation Policies
C) Utilizing Azure Load Balancer for Traffic Distribution and Load Management
D) Enabling Autoscaling Policies for AVD Host Pools
E) Allocating Dedicated GPUs for Graphics-Intensive Applications

QUESTION 18

You're managing an Azure Virtual Desktop (AVD) environment and facing performance issues due to outdated Azure Virtual Desktop agents in one of the host pools. Considering this challenge, what action should you take to address the issue effectively?
- Ensure all session hosts in the affected pool have the latest agent version
- Minimize disruption to user sessions
- Streamline the update process for administrative efficiency

A) Configure a scaling plan.
B) Enable diagnostic logging.
C) Deploy Azure Policy.
D) Enable drain mode.
E) Update the Azure Virtual Desktop agent manually.

QUESTION 19

Your organization is integrating Azure Virtual Desktop (AVD) with Microsoft 365 to enhance productivity and collaboration. Critical considerations include seamless identity and access management, application compatibility, and data security. How would you ensure a smooth integration while addressing these key aspects effectively? Select TWO.

A) Configure Azure AD for seamless identity management
B) Utilize FSLogix for user profile management
C) Implement Azure Information Protection for data security

QUESTION 20

You are integrating automation with existing IT workflows using PowerShell scripts to manage AVD settings. The script should configure network settings, apply security patches, and report on the status of these operations to ensure compliance with organizational policies. Which PowerShell command should you include to update AVD session hosts with the latest security patches automatically?

```
Update-AzAVDSessionHost -ResourceGroupName "RG1" -HostPoolName "HP1" -Name "SessionHost01" -Restart
```

A) Command is correct
B) Add logging of operation status
C) Include error handling mechanisms

D) Script needs to force a restart
E) Add a parameter to check for updates only

QUESTION 21

You need to ensure that Azure Virtual Desktop users can securely access resources on-premises via Remote Desktop Gateway (RD Gateway). Which port should you configure for RD Gateway in the firewall rules?

A) 80
B) 443
C) 3389
D) 8080
E) 8443

QUESTION 22

Your organization is planning to configure Microsoft Entra ID for user authentication in Azure Virtual Desktop (AVD) environments and needs guidance on the necessary configuration steps. The focus is on understanding the process of configuring Entra ID to enable secure and seamless user access to AVD resources. What are the essential configuration steps for implementing Microsoft Entra ID in AVD environments? Select THREE.

A) Provisioning Entra ID accounts for AVD users
B) Configuring Azure AD Connect for user synchronization
C) Enabling Azure AD authentication for AVD session hosts
D) Integrating Entra ID with Azure Bastion for secure RDP access
E) Configuring AVD session host permissions for Entra ID authentication

QUESTION 23

Your organization is considering implementing Conditional Access policies for Azure Virtual Desktop (AVD) to address various use cases while balancing security with user experience. The focus is on understanding the different scenarios where Conditional Access can be applied effectively. In which scenarios can Conditional Access be effectively used in Azure Virtual Desktop (AVD) environments? Select CORRECT answers that apply.

A) Enforcing multi-factor authentication (MFA) for AVD connections
B) Restricting access based on user location or IP address
C) Implementing device compliance checks for accessing AVD resources
D) Granting access to AVD based on user role or group membership
E) Blocking access to AVD for devices with outdated software or security patches

QUESTION 24

You are configuring an Azure Virtual Desktop environment that needs to support a large number of remote users during peak hours without compromising on performance. What configurations should be considered? Select THREE.

A) Implement scaling automation.
B) Increase the size of the VMs.
C) Deploy a single large host pool.
D) Use persistent desktops.
E) Implement FSLogix profile containers.

QUESTION 25

As part of compliance, you need to customize Microsoft Defender Antivirus settings on AVD session hosts to exclude specific directories from scanning, which are used for non-persistent data. How do you configure this setting using

PowerShell?

A) `Add-MpPreference -ExclusionPath "C:\Temp"`
B) `Set-MpPreference -ExclusionPath "C:\Temp"`
C) `Add-MpPreference -ExclusionProcess "C:\Temp"`
D) `Remove-MpPreference -ExclusionPath "C:\Temp"`
E) `Get-MpPreference -ExclusionPath`

QUESTION 26

Your organization is evaluating options for administrative access to Azure Virtual Desktop (AVD) session hosts and considering implementing Just-In-Time (JIT) access. The focus is on understanding the advantages of JIT access over traditional methods. What are the advantages of Just-In-Time (JIT) access over traditional methods for administrative access to AVD session hosts? Select THREE.

A) Reduced attack surface by limiting access to session hosts only when needed
B) Enhanced security posture with temporary access granted based on predefined conditions and approval workflows
C) Improved compliance with regulatory requirements by enforcing least privileged access principles
D) Mitigation of insider threats by minimizing the window of opportunity for unauthorized access
E) Simplified access management through centralized control and audit trails for administrative activities

QUESTION 27

To comply with industry regulations, your AVD deployment must ensure data integrity, prevent data breaches, and allow for security audits. What actions should you prioritize? Select THREE.

A) Encrypt all data at rest and in transit.
B) Regularly update session hosts.
C) Implement role-based access controls (RBAC).
D) Utilize Azure Security Center for continuous monitoring.
E) Enable Microsoft Defender for Cloud.

QUESTION 28

Your organization is considering custom role creation and management in Azure for fine-grained access control in Azure Virtual Desktop (AVD) environments. The focus is on understanding the process of custom role creation and management. What are the steps involved in custom role creation and management in Azure? Select THREE.

A) Identify the permissions required for the custom role
B) Define role assignments to assign the custom role to users or groups
C) Use Azure Policy to enforce compliance with custom role permissions
D) Test the custom role in a non-production environment before deployment
E) Monitor and audit usage of the custom role for security and compliance

QUESTION 29

Your organization has implemented Multi-Factor Authentication (MFA) for Azure Virtual Desktop (AVD) to enhance security. However, some users are experiencing difficulties with the MFA setup process, leading to support requests. The focus is on user education and support for MFA. How can you effectively support users in setting up MFA for Azure Virtual Desktop? Select THREE.

A) Provide step-by-step guides and video tutorials for MFA setup
B) Offer live webinars or virtual training sessions on MFA setup and usage best practices
C) Establish a dedicated helpdesk or support team to assist users with MFA setup
D) Send regular email communications with tips and reminders for MFA setup and usage

E) Integrate MFA setup prompts and instructions directly into the AVD user interface

QUESTION 30

Implement an Azure CLI command to configure a network security group (NSG) that effectively blocks all inbound traffic except for HTTPS and SSH to your AVD environment. This setup should adhere to organizational security policies that require minimizing open ports and maintaining high levels of traffic security. Analyze the Azure CLI script below for potential adjustments needed to align with best practices for securing AVD access.
bash
az network nsg rule create --nsg-name "AVDNSG" --name "AllowHTTPS" --priority 100 --direction Inbound --access Allow --protocol Tcp --destination-port-ranges 443 22

A) Correct as is
B) Separate rules for HTTPS and SSH required
C) Set higher priority for the rule
D) Specify source IP ranges
E) Change access to Deny except for specified ports

QUESTION 31

Your organization is concerned about the potential impact of FSLogix configurations on system performance in Azure Virtual Desktop (AVD) environments. The focus is on the impact of FSLogix configurations on system performance. What factors contribute to the impact of FSLogix configurations on system performance in AVD environments? Select THREE.

A) Profile container size and disk I/O operations during user logon and logoff
B) Frequency of profile disk merges and optimizations performed by FSLogix
C) Concurrent user logon and logoff activities affecting profile access and loading times
D) Utilization of network bandwidth for profile synchronization and replication
E) Compatibility of FSLogix with virtual machine sizes and disk types

QUESTION 32

As an Azure Virtual Desktop administrator responsible for maintaining data security, you need to ensure proper segregation of user data within Profile Containers. Consider the following factors:
- Sensitive data must be segregated to prevent unauthorized access.
- Segregation should align with industry regulations and compliance standards.
- Segregation methods should not compromise administrative tasks or user experience.
How can data segregation be achieved in Profile Containers? Select THREE.

A) Segregate user data based on departmental roles.
B) Utilize separate Profile Containers for different user groups.
C) Implement access controls to restrict data access within Profile Containers.
D) Leverage Azure AD dynamic groups for data segregation.
E) Encrypt Profile Containers to ensure data isolation.

QUESTION 33

To optimize AVD for a tech company's global workforce, you must ensure low latency, high availability, and compliance with international data protection laws. What actions are crucial? Select THREE.

A) Distribute host pools across multiple Azure regions.
B) Implement Azure Front Door for global load balancing.
C) Use Azure Site Recovery for business continuity.
D) Enable geo-redundant storage (GRS).

E) Configure data residency with Azure Policy.

QUESTION 34

You encounter performance issues with Azure Virtual Desktop (AVD) clients, leading to user complaints about slow responsiveness and application lag. Consider the following scenario:
- Users access AVD sessions from diverse devices and locations, experiencing inconsistent performance across different scenarios.
- Some users report connectivity issues and session disruptions, while others notice significant delays in application loading times.
- IT administrators aim to identify common troubleshooting techniques to address performance issues and improve user experience effectively.

What common troubleshooting techniques should you apply for the given scenario? Select THREE.

A) Analyze FSLogix Profile Containers for disk space utilization and profile loading times.
B) Monitor Azure Monitor logs for insights into client connectivity issues and session failures.
C) Check network latency between clients and AVD resources using Azure Network Watcher tools.
D) Evaluate AVD session host performance metrics, including CPU, memory, and disk usage.
E) Review Azure AD authentication logs for errors related to user sign-in and access permissions.

QUESTION 35

As an Azure administrator, ensure multimedia redirection does not compromise the security of the virtual desktop environment. Evaluate the JSON configuration below used to implement codec settings for secure multimedia redirection:

```json
{
  "Codec": "H.264",
  "Encryption": true,
  "Quality": "High"
}
```

A) Configuration is secure and efficient
B) Encryption should be set to false
C) H.264 is not recommended for secure environments
D) Quality setting should be lowered to save bandwidth
E) JSON format is incorrect

QUESTION 36

In a financial institution's AVD setup, the business requirements are to ensure transaction security, regulatory compliance for data protection, and resilience against data loss. What configurations should you prioritize? Select THREE.

A) Enable Azure Site Recovery across regions.
B) Configure network security groups (NSGs) for strict traffic control.
C) Implement Azure Information Protection.
D) Use Azure Policy to enforce compliance standards.
E) Deploy Azure Key Vault to manage encryption keys.

QUESTION 37

You are tasked with monitoring and managing session timeouts for Azure Virtual Desktop (AVD) users in a large enterprise environment. Which Azure service would be most suitable for tracking user session activity and enforcing session duration policies based on specific criteria?

A) Azure Monitor
B) Azure Security Center
C) Azure Active Directory Identity Protection
D) Azure Log Analytics
E) Azure Resource Graph

QUESTION 38

When implementing Start VM on Connect in Azure Virtual Desktop (AVD), understanding the impact on resource utilization is essential. Consider the following scenario: Your organization experiences peak user activity during specific times of the day, requiring additional VM capacity. How does configuring Start VM on Connect impact resource provisioning and allocation in this scenario?

A) Allocating resources dynamically based on user demand to ensure optimal performance
B) Pre-allocating resources to accommodate peak user activity periods and prevent performance degradation
C) Scaling VM capacity automatically to maintain a consistent user experience across sessions
D) Releasing resources promptly after user sessions to minimize idle VMs and associated costs
E) Utilizing advanced resource scheduling algorithms to prioritize critical workloads and optimize resource allocation

QUESTION 39

For a financial institution using AVD, ensuring high security for transaction processing, strict access controls, and auditability are key. What configurations should be prioritized? Select THREE.

A) Implement Azure Bastion for all VM access.
B) Use Azure Policy to enforce governance and compliance.
C) Enable logging and monitoring with Azure Monitor.
D) Create an NSG with inbound and outbound rules tailored to business needs.
E) Set up a new application group for transaction processing teams.

QUESTION 40

A security engineer needs to update FSLogix application masking rules to reflect recent organizational changes. Which of the following PowerShell commands correctly updates the existing rule to mask a new application for all users except the IT department?

```
$RuleName = "GeneralApps"
$NewApp = "Calculator.exe"
Update-FSLogixAppMaskingRule -Name $RuleName -AddFilePath $NewApp -ExcludeUser "AD\ITDept"
```

A) Correct as is.
B) Replace Update-FSLogixAppMaskingRule with Set-FSLogixAppMaskingRule.
C) Change -AddFilePath to -FilePath and remove -ExcludeUser.
D) Add -Enabled $true to ensure the rule is active after the update.
E) Replace "AD\ITDept" with AD\ITDept without quotes.

QUESTION 41

As an Azure administrator, you are tasked with ensuring that Microsoft Teams can effectively handle simultaneous connections in a multisession AVD environment without compromising security. Which ARM template configuration best secures the Teams deployment while maintaining performance?

```
{ "type": "Microsoft.AVD/sessions", "properties": { "teamsOptimization": { "enabled": true, "security": "high" } } }
```

A) Configuration is correct.
B) Add "encryption": "enabled" to enhance data protection.
C) Change "security": "high" to "securityLevel": "standard" for optimal performance.
D) Include "multisession": "enabled" to explicitly enable support for multiple sessions.
E) Replace "teamsOptimization": { "enabled": true } with "teamsFeatures": { "WebRTC": "enabled", "optimize": "true" }.

QUESTION 42

An organization is implementing FSLogix on Azure Virtual Desktop for high-availability user environments. Which registry modifications should you consider to ensure profile availability and redundancy? Select THREE.

A) HKLM\SOFTWARE\FSLogix\Profiles\CloudCacheLocations
B) HKLM\SOFTWARE\FSLogix\Profiles\DeleteLocalProfileWhenVHDShouldApply
C) HKLM\SOFTWARE\Policies\FSLogix\ODFC\Enabled
D) HKLM\SOFTWARE\FSLogix\Profiles\CloudCacheConnectionString
E) HKLM\SOFTWARE\FSLogix\Profiles\DiskType

QUESTION 43

As an Azure server administrator, you need to proactively address potential performance issues in AVD host pools by setting performance thresholds and alerts. The AVD environment caters to a large user base, and timely detection of performance anomalies is critical. Which Azure service allows you to configure these thresholds and alerts effectively to ensure continuous monitoring?

A) Azure Security Center
B) Azure Monitor Alerts
C) Azure Log Analytics Alerts
D) Azure Policy
E) Azure Resource Health

QUESTION 44

As part of optimizing Azure Virtual Desktop (AVD) performance, you need to customize log queries for analyzing specific AVD metrics. To achieve this effectively, you should consider:
1. The specific performance indicators relevant to AVD deployments, such as session latency and connection failures.
2. The complexity and syntax of the query language required for querying AVD telemetry data.
3. The scalability and performance impact of custom log queries on Azure Monitor Logs and associated costs.
Which query language provides the most suitable syntax and capabilities for analyzing AVD telemetry data within Azure Monitor Logs?

A) Kusto Query Language (KQL)
B) SQL Query Language
C) PowerShell
D) Python
E) ARM Templates

QUESTION 45

As part of data compliance, you need to ensure all AVD user data is encrypted both at rest and in transit. Which Azure CLI command should be used to enforce encryption for Azure Files where user data is stored?

```
az storage account update --name "storageaccount" --resource-group "AVDResourceGroup" --
https-only true --default-action Allow
```

A) Correct as is.
B) Change --https-only true to --https-only allowed.
C) Add --require-encryption true to enforce encryption.
D) Replace --default-action Allow with --allow-encrypted-only true.
E) Modify the command to include both --https-only true and --encryption-services blob file.

QUESTION 46

Analyzing usage patterns is essential for optimizing resource allocation in Azure Virtual Desktop (AVD) environments. As an AVD administrator, you need to identify usage trends and bottlenecks to improve performance and user experience. Which tool provides insights into user activity and resource utilization, enabling administrators to identify optimization opportunities?

A) Azure Resource Graph
B) Azure Log Analytics
C) Azure Cost Management + Billing
D) Azure Advisor
E) Azure Monitor

QUESTION 47

In an Azure Virtual Desktop (AVD) deployment, ensuring compliance with industry standards and regulations is crucial for data protection and risk management. Which tool should be used for auditing and compliance reporting in AVD environments?

A) Azure Policy
B) Azure Sentinel
C) Azure Log Analytics
D) Azure Security Center
E) Azure Monitor

QUESTION 48

You are planning an Azure Virtual Desktop deployment for a financial services firm that requires regulatory compliance, high availability, and support for remote access. Which Windows operating systems should be deployed on session hosts to meet these requirements? Select THREE.

A) Windows 10 Enterprise multi-session
B) Windows Server 2019
C) Windows 11 Enterprise
D) Windows Server 2022
E) Windows 10 Pro

QUESTION 49

An organization seeks to automate disaster recovery processes in its Azure Virtual Desktop (AVD) environment to minimize downtime and ensure quick recovery. Which automation techniques should the organization consider for effective disaster recovery in AVD? Select TWO.

A) Implementing Azure Policy initiatives for continuous compliance monitoring
B) Configuring Azure Automation runbooks for automated troubleshooting
C) Leveraging PowerShell scripts for real-time monitoring and remediation

D) Integrating Azure Monitor alerts with Logic Apps for automated responses
E) Utilizing Azure DevOps pipelines for automated deployment of AVD updates and patches

QUESTION 50

An organization is looking for tools to effectively manage application performance in its Azure Virtual Desktop (AVD) environment. Which options should they consider for application performance management? Select TWO.

A) Azure Monitor for tracking performance metrics and user activity
B) Microsoft Endpoint Manager for optimizing application delivery and performance
C) Utilizing Azure Application Insights for monitoring application performance and user interactions
D) Implementing Azure Log Analytics for analyzing application usage and performance trends
E) Microsoft 365 Usage Analytics for tracking application adoption and user engagement

PRACTICE TEST 2 - ANSWERS ONLY

QUESTION 1

Answer - E) az network watcher test-connection

Option A - Incorrect. This command checks gateway configurations.
Option B - Incorrect. This command does not exist in Azure CLI.
Option C - Incorrect. Tests IP packet flow, not latency.
Option D - Incorrect. This shows the route a packet takes, not latency.
Option E - Correct. This command tests connectivity and measures latency.

EXAM FOCUS	*Always use az network watcher test-connection to measure latency and troubleshoot network connectivity. Make sure Network Watcher is enabled in your subscription. Focus on evaluating real-time collaboration tools' network dependency to optimize configurations.*
CAUTION ALERT	*Avoid commands like az network vnet test-latency, which do not exist. Stay alert to misinterpreting results or overlooking dependencies like DNS and NSGs that could influence connectivity metrics.*

QUESTION 2

Answer - A) az network express-route create

Option A - Correct. Specifically creates an ExpressRoute circuit.
Option B - Incorrect. For VPN gateways, not ExpressRoute circuits.
Option C - Incorrect. Creates a subnet within a VNet, unrelated to ExpressRoute.
Option D - Incorrect. Adds peering, not creating ExpressRoute circuits.
Option E - Incorrect. Lists existing circuits, doesn't create new ones.

EXAM FOCUS	*Use az network express-route create for dedicated private connectivity. Ensure encryption is enabled for compliance. Leverage Azure RBAC to assign least-privilege roles for secure access control. Validate bandwidth and provider options during setup.*
CAUTION ALERT	*Avoid confusing ExpressRoute with VPN gateways (az network vpn-gateway create), as these are separate solutions. Stay cautious about overprovisioning bandwidth, which may inflate costs unnecessarily without measurable benefits.*

QUESTION 3

Answer - [B]

Option B - WVDPerformanceCounters: This table contains performance metrics for session hosts, such as CPU and memory usage, making it the correct choice.
Option A - WVDConnections: This table focuses on user connections rather than host performance.
Option C - WVDHostRegistrations: This table deals with host registration details, not performance metrics.
Option D - WVDAgentHealth: This is not a standard table for performance monitoring in Azure Virtual Desktop.
Option E - WVDServiceHealth: This provides overall service health information, not host-specific performance metrics.

EXAM FOCUS	*Use the WVDPerformanceCounters table in Azure Log Analytics to monitor key metrics like CPU, memory usage, and disk I/O. This provides granular insights into host performance and helps proactively address bottlenecks before they impact user experience.*
CAUTION ALERT	*Avoid relying on tables like WVDConnections for performance monitoring; they are connection-specific. Stay alert to incomplete data ingestion in Log Analytics due to misconfigured data collection rules in your environment.*

QUESTION 4

Answer - A) Check DNS resolution for AVD resources using nslookup; B) Review Azure Network Security Group (NSG) rules for port blocking issues; E) Verify Azure Virtual Desktop session host availability and resource utilization

Option A - Correct. Checking DNS resolution helps identify issues with resolving AVD resources, which can impact connectivity for users. Option B - Correct. Reviewing NSG rules ensures that port blocking issues are not causing connectivity problems for AVD users. Option C - Incorrect. Analyzing Virtual Network Gateway logs may be relevant for VPN connectivity issues but may not directly address common network connectivity issues in AVD deployments.

Option D - Incorrect. Monitoring ExpressRoute circuit status is important for hybrid network setups but may not be directly related to troubleshooting connectivity issues within AVD environments. Option E - Correct. Verifying session host availability and resource utilization is essential for identifying potential bottlenecks or resource constraints affecting AVD connectivity.

EXAM FOCUS	*Always start troubleshooting AVD connectivity issues with DNS resolution (nslookup) and NSG rule review. Verifying session host availability provides direct insights into potential resource bottlenecks impacting connectivity for users.*
CAUTION ALERT	*Don't waste time analyzing ExpressRoute or VPN issues unless hybrid connectivity is confirmed as the root cause. Stay cautious about overlooking session host metrics, which often pinpoint performance-related connectivity problems.*

QUESTION 5

Answer - D) Correct command for GPU setup

Option A - Incorrect: "Standard_NV6" is a valid size for GPU-enabled VMs.
Option B - Incorrect: Network configuration is not mandatory in the initial setup command.
Option C - Incorrect: "Win10" is a valid image for this setup.
Option D - Correct: This is the correct command to set up a GPU-enabled VM.
Option E - Incorrect: Additional storage options are not required for the basic setup of a GPU-enabled VM.

EXAM FOCUS	*Use New-AzVM with the Standard_NV6 size for GPU-enabled workloads. Ensure the VM is configured with the correct GPU driver and compatible software. Validate that GPU-enabled VMs match the workload demands, particularly for graphics-intensive applications.*
CAUTION ALERT	*Avoid incorrect sizing for GPU VMs. Using non-GPU sizes will degrade graphics application performance. Stay clear of configurations lacking proper storage, as GPU workloads typically require high IOPS and storage capacity for efficiency.*

QUESTION 6

Answer - [E]

Option E - Azure Virtual Machine Scale Sets: This option allows you to automatically scale up or down the number of session hosts based on a schedule, meeting the specified requirements and minimizing manual intervention.
Option A - Azure Monitor: While Monitor provides monitoring capabilities, it does not directly handle the automatic starting and stopping of session hosts based on a schedule.

Option B - Azure Logic Apps: Logic Apps are used for automating workflows, but they are not specifically designed for managing the lifecycle of session hosts. Option C - Azure Policy: Policies are used for enforcing rules and standards across resources but are not designed for managing the lifecycle of session hosts. Option D - Azure Automation with Azure Functions: While Azure Automation can perform scheduled tasks, using Virtual Machine Scale Sets is more suitable for this scenario as it is specifically designed for scaling resources based on a schedule.

EXAM	*Leverage Azure Virtual Machine Scale Sets to schedule and automate host lifecycle management. Define*

FOCUS	clear scaling schedules to align with business hours. Use predictive autoscaling for seamless operations during fluctuating user demands, minimizing cost.
CAUTION ALERT	Avoid relying on manual PowerShell scripts for daily scaling tasks; they lack automation benefits. Stay cautious about overusing Azure Automation when a dedicated scaling solution like VM Scale Sets offers better optimization features.

QUESTION 7

Answer - A) Windows 10 Multi-Session provides a desktop-like experience with better application compatibility for end-users; B) Windows Server offers enhanced scalability and resource utilization for multi-user environments; D) Windows Server supports Remote Desktop Services (RDS) roles and features for centralized desktop and application delivery

Option A - Correct. Windows 10 Multi-Session provides a familiar desktop experience for end-users and offers better application compatibility, making it suitable for organizations transitioning from traditional desktop environments. Option B - Correct. Windows Server is designed for multi-user environments and offers enhanced scalability and resource utilization capabilities, making it suitable for larger deployments with higher user densities. Option C - Incorrect. While Windows 10 Multi-Session includes security features, they are not unique to this OS option and are also available in Windows Server.

Option D - Correct. Windows Server supports RDS roles and features, enabling centralized desktop and application delivery, which is crucial for AVD deployments. Option E - Incorrect. Windows 10 Multi-Session and Windows Server both require regular patching and updates, and the frequency may vary based on deployment configurations and organizational policies.

EXAM FOCUS	Windows 10 Multi-Session suits end-user workloads needing app compatibility. Use Windows Server for environments requiring RDS roles or scalability. Evaluate app compatibility and user density to choose the OS that aligns best with your organization's needs.
CAUTION ALERT	Avoid assuming Windows 10 Multi-Session is identical to Windows Server in scaling or app compatibility. Stay alert to licensing implications for each OS type, as they vary significantly between server and multi-session configurations.

QUESTION 8

Answer - A) Auto Scaling and Dynamic Provisioning; D) Weighted Round-Robin and Session Affinity

Option A - Correct. Auto scaling and dynamic provisioning adjust resources based on workload demand, ensuring efficient scaling of host pools in AVD deployments.

Option D - Correct. Weighted round-robin and session affinity are load balancing techniques that distribute incoming connections evenly across session hosts, optimizing resource utilization and user experience. Option B - Incorrect. While capacity planning and reserved instances are relevant for resource management, they are not specific strategies for scaling and load balancing host pools in AVD. Option C - Incorrect. Geo-redundancy and disaster recovery focus on ensuring service availability and data protection but do not directly address scaling and load balancing concerns. Option E - Incorrect. Vertical scaling and resource overcommitment refer to resource allocation methods but do not specifically address scaling and load balancing strategies for host pools in AVD.

EXAM FOCUS	Combine auto scaling and dynamic provisioning with weighted round-robin load balancing for optimal AVD performance. Configure session affinity for consistent user experience when reconnecting to session hosts, improving resource utilization.
CAUTION ALERT	Avoid overcommitting resources with vertical scaling, which could degrade performance. Stay cautious about disregarding user connection patterns when configuring load balancing rules, as it directly affects host pool efficiency.

QUESTION 9

Answer - [E]

Option E - Azure Virtual Machine Scale Sets: Scale sets allow for dynamic scaling of session hosts based on demand, enabling efficient utilization of resources and minimizing administrative effort.

Option A - Azure Automation: While useful for automation tasks, it is not specifically tailored for autoscaling AVD session hosts. Option B - Azure Monitor: Provides monitoring and analytics capabilities but does not directly facilitate autoscaling of AVD session hosts. Option C - Azure Resource Manager templates: Used for deploying and managing Azure resources, but not specifically designed for autoscaling AVD session hosts. Option D - Azure Logic Apps: Used for creating workflows and automation tasks, but not tailored for autoscaling AVD session hosts.

EXAM FOCUS	*Use Azure Virtual Machine Scale Sets for efficient resource scaling based on real-time user demand. Define minimum and maximum host thresholds to manage costs effectively during peak and off-peak hours. Integrate scaling metrics with Azure Monitor for alerts.*
CAUTION ALERT	*Avoid relying solely on static templates for scaling; they lack dynamic capabilities. Stay cautious about missing predefined thresholds, which may lead to under-provisioning or excessive resource usage during peak user demands.*

QUESTION 10

Answer - E) Command is correctly configured

Option A - Incorrect: A 512 GB quota is generally sufficient for initial setup but may need adjustment based on actual usage.
Option B - Incorrect: 'SMB' is the correct protocol for file shares used with AVD.
Option C - Incorrect: The command syntax is correct.
Option D - Incorrect: 'AVDStorage' is a valid storage account name.
Option E - Correct: The command is configured appropriately for setting up file shares.

EXAM FOCUS	*SMB protocol and a quota of 512 GB work well for initial file share setup in high-traffic AVD environments. Validate quotas periodically to match storage demands. Ensure the storage account has redundancy (e.g., LRS or ZRS) for reliability and scalability.*
CAUTION ALERT	*Avoid using unsupported protocols like NFS for AVD-specific use cases. Stay cautious about underestimating quota requirements, especially for environments with high user concurrency or data-intensive workloads, leading to performance bottlenecks.*

QUESTION 11

Answer - A) Invalid License Key or Activation Code; B) Incorrect License Type for Session Host OS; C) Network Connectivity Issues Preventing License Activation

Option A - Correct. Invalid license keys or activation codes can prevent successful license application and activation on session hosts within the AVD deployment. Option B - Correct. Using the incorrect license type for the session host operating system (e.g., Windows Client license applied to a Windows Server OS) can result in licensing errors and compliance issues. Option C - Correct. Network connectivity issues, such as firewall restrictions or DNS configuration problems, may prevent session hosts from communicating with the licensing servers for activation. Option D - Incorrect. Incompatibility between the license and AVD subscription is less common and typically addressed during the initial setup rather than during the license application process. Option E - Incorrect. Insufficient user or device CALs (Client Access Licenses) may impact user access but are not directly related to license application issues on session hosts.

EXAM FOCUS	*You need to focus on technical issues that hinder license activation: invalid keys (Option A), wrong license types for the OS (Option B), and network issues blocking activation servers (Option C). Eliminate Option E, as AVD doesn't use CALs, and Option D is less likely during application.*

CAUTION ALERT	*Avoid confusing AVD licensing with traditional CAL requirements; AVD relies on per-user licenses from eligible subscriptions. Stay alert to network configurations that may block licensing traffic, causing activation failures on session hosts.*

QUESTION 12

Answer - [B, C]

Option B - Azure Traffic Manager: Azure Traffic Manager enables DNS-based traffic routing to the closest available endpoint, facilitating failover to a secondary region in case of a regional outage. Option C - Azure Site Recovery: Azure Site Recovery supports replication and failover of AVD host pools to a secondary region, ensuring minimal data loss and downtime during failover operations.

Option A - Azure Backup is not designed for failover and does not provide real-time replication or failover capabilities for AVD host pools. Option D - Azure Load Balancer is a network load balancer and does not provide failover capabilities at the application level for AVD host pools. Option E - Azure Blob Storage is a storage service and is not directly related to failover and disaster recovery for AVD host pools.

EXAM FOCUS	*You should use Azure Site Recovery (Option C) for replicating host pools to a secondary region, ensuring minimal data loss. Azure Traffic Manager (Option B) enables failover by routing users to the active region. Eliminate Azure Backup (Option A) as it doesn't support real-time replication.*
CAUTION ALERT	*Avoid assuming Azure Backup provides failover capabilities; it is meant for data backup and recovery, not live replication. Stay cautious about options like Azure Load Balancer, which doesn't offer cross-region failover for AVD host pools.*

QUESTION 13

Answer - C) Azure Automation Update Management; E) Azure DevOps Pipelines

Option A - Incorrect. Azure Monitor Logs are primarily used for monitoring and analyzing data, not for tracking and updating AVD images.

Option B - Incorrect. Azure Security Center focuses on security posture management and threat protection rather than image tracking and updating. Option C - Correct. Azure Automation Update Management provides automated patching and update capabilities for AVD images, ensuring they are up-to-date with the latest software versions and security patches. Option D - Incorrect. Git Version Control System is used for source code management and version control, not specifically for tracking and updating AVD images. Option E - Correct. Azure DevOps Pipelines allow for continuous integration and deployment, enabling efficient tracking and updating of AVD images through automation.

EXAM FOCUS	*Implement Azure Automation Update Management (Option C) for automated patching of AVD images. Use Azure DevOps Pipelines (Option E) to track image versions and automate deployments. Eliminate Azure Monitor Logs and Security Center as they focus on monitoring, not updating images. Disregard Git, which is for code versioning.*
CAUTION ALERT	*Don't confuse code versioning tools like Git with image management. Stay alert to the primary functions of Azure services; Monitoring tools don't facilitate image updates. Ensure you select solutions designed for image tracking and updating tasks.*

QUESTION 14

Answer - A) Streamlined Deployment Processes; B) Consistency Across Virtual Desktop Environments; C) Simplified Patch Management and Updates

Option A - Correct. Using golden images streamlines the deployment of session hosts by providing a pre-configured template, reducing setup time and effort. Option B - Correct. Golden images ensure consistency across virtual desktop environments by providing a standardized base configuration for session hosts. Option C - Correct. Golden images simplify patch management and updates by allowing administrators to apply changes to a single image, which can then be propagated to all session hosts. Option D - Incorrect. While golden images may enhance security by including preconfigured settings, this is not their primary benefit. Option E - Incorrect. While shared image repositories may reduce storage costs, it is not directly related to the benefits of using golden images in AVD deployments.

EXAM FOCUS	*You should recognize that golden images streamline deployments (Option A), ensure consistency (Option B), and simplify updates (Option C). Eliminate Option D as enhanced security is a secondary benefit. Disregard Option E; while storage savings are possible, they're not a primary advantage of golden images in AVD.*
CAUTION ALERT	*Avoid overestimating the impact of golden images on security or storage costs without proper configuration. Stay cautious about assuming that all benefits apply equally; focus on the primary advantages relevant to deployment and management efficiency.*

QUESTION 15

Answer - A) Command is correct

Option A - Correct: The command correctly adds an image definition to a Compute Gallery.
Option B - Incorrect: The 'gallery-image-definition' parameter is correctly used.
Option C - Incorrect: The publisher name "MyOrg" is valid if that is the organization's identifier.
Option D - Incorrect: 'SKU' in this context refers to the image SKU, not the VM size.
Option E - Incorrect: 'os-type Windows' is correct for AVD deployments, assuming the image is Windows-based.

EXAM FOCUS	*Verify that the Azure CLI command is correct (Option A). Ensure parameters like publisher, offer, SKU, and OS type match your organizational standards. Eliminate Options B, C, D, and E by checking each parameter's correctness against documentation, confirming that none require changes in this context.*
CAUTION ALERT	*Don't confuse SKU with VM sizes; in image definitions, SKU refers to the image version. Stay alert to incorrect parameter names or values, which can cause deployment failures. Always double-check command syntax and parameters for accuracy.*

QUESTION 16

Answer - A) Continuous Monitoring and Security Assessments; C) Threat Detection and Incident Response Automation; D) Secure Configuration Management for AVD Resources

Option A - Correct. Azure Security Center provides continuous monitoring and security assessments to identify and remediate security risks in AVD deployments. Option B - Incorrect. While integration with Azure AD is important, it may not be a specific role of Azure Security Center for managing AVD security. Option C - Correct. Azure Security Center offers threat detection and incident response automation capabilities to detect and respond to security threats in AVD environments. Option D - Correct. Secure configuration management ensures that AVD resources are configured according to security best practices, reducing the attack surface and mitigating security risks. Option E - Incorrect. While vulnerability management and patch management are essential, they may not be specific roles of Azure Security Center for managing AVD security.

EXAM FOCUS	*You should leverage Azure Security Center for continuous monitoring (Option A), threat detection (Option C), and secure configuration management (Option D). Eliminate Option B, as identity protection is more aligned with Azure AD. Disregard Option E; vulnerability management isn't a primary role here.*
CAUTION ALERT	*Avoid assuming Azure Security Center handles identity integration with Azure AD. Stay cautious about overestimating its role in vulnerability and patch management; while it provides recommendations, it doesn't directly manage these aspects.*

QUESTION 17

Answer - A) Implementing Dynamic Scaling of Virtual Machines based on User Demand; C) Utilizing Azure Load Balancer for Traffic Distribution and Load Management; D) Enabling Autoscaling Policies for AVD Host Pools

Option A - Correct. Implementing dynamic scaling of virtual machines based on user demand allows for efficient resource allocation and ensures optimal performance in AVD deployments. Option B - Incorrect. While Azure Policy can help with resource governance, it may not specifically address dynamic resource allocation for AVD performance optimization. Option C - Correct. Utilizing Azure Load Balancer enables traffic distribution and load management, ensuring balanced resource utilization and optimal performance in AVD deployments.

Option D - Correct. Enabling autoscaling policies for AVD host pools allows for automatic adjustment of resources based on workload demand, maintaining optimal performance for users. Option E - Incorrect. While allocating dedicated GPUs may improve performance for graphics-intensive applications, it may not address the broader challenge of balancing resource allocation for optimal performance across all user sessions in AVD deployments.

EXAM FOCUS	*Implement dynamic VM scaling based on user demand (Option A), use Azure Load Balancer for efficient traffic distribution (Option C), and enable autoscaling for host pools (Option D). Eliminate Azure Policy (Option B) as it governs resources but doesn't optimize performance. Disregard dedicated GPUs (Option E) for general performance balancing.*
CAUTION ALERT	*Don't confuse resource governance (Azure Policy) with performance optimization strategies. Stay alert to the specific needs of your environment; dedicated GPUs are beneficial for graphics-intensive workloads but not for overall resource balancing.*

QUESTION 18

Answer - [E]

Option E - Update the Azure Virtual Desktop agent manually: This action ensures that all session hosts in the affected pool are promptly updated to the latest agent version, addressing the performance issues effectively while minimizing disruption to user sessions.

Option A - Configuring a scaling plan is unrelated to updating Azure Virtual Desktop agents and is used for dynamically adjusting the number of session hosts based on demand. Option B - Enabling diagnostic logging helps in monitoring and troubleshooting but does not involve updating Azure Virtual Desktop agents. Option C - Deploying Azure Policy is not directly related to updating Azure Virtual Desktop agents and is used for enforcing organizational standards and compliance. Option D - Enabling drain mode is used for gracefully removing session hosts from service but does not involve updating Azure Virtual Desktop agents.

EXAM FOCUS	*You need to manually update the AVD agent (Option E) to address performance issues promptly. Eliminate Options A-D, as they don't directly resolve outdated agent problems. Remember, updating agents minimizes disruptions and improves performance without affecting user sessions significantly.*
CAUTION ALERT	*Avoid assuming that enabling drain mode or deploying policies will update the agents. Stay cautious about delaying updates; outdated agents can lead to performance degradation. Focus on direct actions that address the core issue effectively.*

QUESTION 19

Answer - A) Configure Azure AD for seamless identity management; B) Utilize FSLogix for user profile management

Option A - Correct. Configuring Azure AD enables seamless identity management across AVD and Microsoft 365, enhancing user experience and security. Option B - Correct. FSLogix ensures consistent user experiences by managing user profiles efficiently, improving application compatibility in AVD environments. Option C - Incorrect. Azure Information Protection focuses on data security but does not directly contribute to seamless integration between AVD and Microsoft 365.

EXAM FOCUS	Configure Azure AD for seamless identity management (Option A) and use FSLogix for efficient profile management (Option B). Eliminate Option C; while Azure Information Protection enhances data security, it doesn't directly impact integration or application compatibility. Focus on solutions that address identity and profile challenges.
CAUTION ALERT	Don't assume data protection tools facilitate integration or compatibility. Stay alert to the distinct roles of each service; ensure that identity and profile management solutions align with integration objectives between AVD and Microsoft 365.

QUESTION 20

Answer - A) Command is correct

Option A - Correct: The command correctly updates the AVD session hosts and includes a restart, which is typically required to apply security patches.

Option B - Incorrect: While logging is critical for compliance, it must be set up as part of a broader operational or monitoring solution, not within this command. Option C - Incorrect: Error handling is crucial for automation scripts but would be implemented through additional scripting logic around this command, not within the command itself. Option D - Incorrect: The command already includes a restart, which is necessary for applying patches. Option E - Incorrect: Checking for updates only without applying them does not fulfill the requirement to apply security patches as specified.

EXAM FOCUS	Recognize that the PowerShell command is correct (Option A) for automating updates and reboots. Eliminate Options B-E by noting that logging and error handling are script-level concerns, not parameters of this command. The restart parameter suffices; forcing a restart isn't necessary unless specific conditions require it.
CAUTION ALERT	Avoid neglecting broader script practices like logging and error handling; while not parameters in the command, they are essential for compliance. Stay cautious about unnecessary parameters that don't contribute to the required operation in context.

QUESTION 21

Answer - B

Option B - Port 443 is used for secure HTTPS communication, including traffic through RD Gateway for Azure Virtual Desktop. Configuring firewall rules to allow port 443 ensures secure access to on-premises resources via RD Gateway.
Option C - Port 3389 is the default port for RDP connections but is not specifically used for RD Gateway communication.
Option D - Port 8080 is often used for alternative web services but is not standard for RD Gateway connections.
Option E - Port 8443 is sometimes used for secure web services but is not the default port for RD Gateway connections.
Option A - Port 80 is typically used for unencrypted HTTP traffic and is not suitable for secure RD Gateway connections.

EXAM FOCUS	Always configure port 443 for RD Gateway in AVD, as it ensures secure HTTPS communication. Eliminate port 3389, which is only for direct RDP. Remember, port 80 is for HTTP, unsuitable for secure traffic. Understand each port's protocol before making configurations.
CAUTION ALERT	Don't confuse RD Gateway's use of port 443 with direct RDP connections on 3389. Avoid leaving port 3389 open, as it increases the attack surface. Never use unencrypted HTTP (port 80) for secure AVD communications to protect user data.

QUESTION 22

Answer - A) Provisioning Entra ID accounts for AVD users; C) Enabling Azure AD authentication for AVD session hosts; E) Configuring AVD session host permissions for Entra ID authentication

Option A - Correct. Provisioning Entra ID accounts ensures that AVD users have the necessary credentials for authentication.

Option C - Correct. Enabling Azure AD authentication for AVD session hosts allows users to authenticate using Entra ID credentials. Option E - Correct. Configuring AVD session host permissions for Entra ID authentication ensures that users can access resources using Entra ID credentials. Option B - Incorrect. While Azure AD Connect is important for user synchronization, it is not specifically related to Entra ID configuration for AVD environments. Option D - Incorrect. Azure Bastion provides secure RDP access but is not directly related to Entra ID configuration for AVD.

EXAM FOCUS	*Provision Entra ID accounts, enable Azure AD authentication for session hosts, and set proper permissions. Eliminate Azure AD Connect, which focuses on synchronization, not direct AVD configuration. Understand authentication vs. identity synchronization concepts clearly.*
CAUTION ALERT	*Avoid assuming Azure AD Connect is mandatory; it's for hybrid identity setups. Stay cautious about skipping session host permissions—it's critical for allowing Entra ID to authenticate users. Incorrect configurations lead to failed access.*

QUESTION 23

Answer - A) Enforcing multi-factor authentication (MFA) for AVD connections; B) Restricting access based on user location or IP address; C) Implementing device compliance checks for accessing AVD resources; D) Granting access to AVD based on user role or group membership

Option A - Correct. Enforcing multi-factor authentication (MFA) for AVD connections adds an extra layer of security to verify user identities.

Option B - Correct. Restricting access based on user location or IP address helps prevent unauthorized access to AVD resources. Option C - Correct. Implementing device compliance checks ensures that only compliant devices can access AVD resources, enhancing security. Option D - Correct. Granting access to AVD based on user role or group membership allows for fine-grained access control tailored to organizational needs. Option E - Incorrect. While blocking access to AVD for devices with outdated software or security patches is a valid use case, it is not specifically mentioned in the question.

EXAM FOCUS	*Conditional Access policies enhance AVD by enforcing MFA, restricting by location/IP, and ensuring compliant devices. Eliminate vague scenarios like "blocking outdated devices" unless explicitly configured. Focus on specific, enforceable conditions for better exam clarity.*
CAUTION ALERT	*Don't confuse Conditional Access policies with device management tools like Intune. Policies need precise rules for location, device compliance, or MFA—broad assumptions about blocking outdated devices or roles won't address exam scenarios effectively.*

QUESTION 24

Answer - A, B, E

A) Correct - Implementing scaling automation allows for dynamically adjusting resources based on user load, which is crucial during peak hours. B) Correct - Increasing the size of the VMs can provide additional resources necessary to handle increased load during peak times. C) Incorrect - A single large host pool can create bottlenecks and management difficulties; multiple smaller pools are generally more efficient. D) Incorrect - Persistent desktops are not necessarily beneficial for performance during peak loads but are more about user experience and data retention. E) Correct - Using FSLogix profile containers optimizes user profile management and enhances performance, particularly in large deployments.

EXAM FOCUS	*Use scaling automation, FSLogix for profile management, and larger VMs for peak loads. Eliminate single large host pools, which create bottlenecks. FSLogix minimizes login delays. Understand when to scale resources dynamically to maintain performance under heavy usage.*
CAUTION ALERT	*Avoid persistent desktops—they're resource-heavy and not suitable for handling peak loads dynamically. Stay clear of oversizing individual VMs unless justified by workload. Mismanaged pools or scaling configurations lead to inefficiencies.*

QUESTION 25

Answer - A) Add-MpPreference -ExclusionPath "C:\Temp"

Option A - Correct: Adds an exclusion path to the Defender settings, preventing scanning of specified directories.
Option B - Incorrect: Incorrect usage of Set command for exclusions.
Option C - Incorrect: Adds a process exclusion, not a path.
Option D - Incorrect: Removes an exclusion, opposite of requirement.
Option E - Incorrect: Retrieves current settings without making changes.

EXAM FOCUS	*Use Add-MpPreference for Defender exclusions. Remember, Set-MpPreference adjusts settings but doesn't add exclusions. Validate paths carefully to avoid critical directory exclusions. Always distinguish between process and path exclusions for accurate configurations.*
CAUTION ALERT	*Avoid using Remove-MpPreference—it deletes exclusions. Don't confuse process exclusions (applied to executables) with path exclusions (applied to directories). Misconfigurations can weaken security by excluding sensitive directories unintentionally.*

QUESTION 26

Answer - A) Reduced attack surface by limiting access to session hosts only when needed; B) Enhanced security posture with temporary access granted based on predefined conditions and approval workflows; D) Mitigation of insider threats by minimizing the window of opportunity for unauthorized access

Option A - Correct. JIT access reduces the attack surface by granting access to AVD session hosts only when needed, minimizing exposure to potential security threats. Option B - Correct. JIT access enhances security posture by providing temporary access based on predefined conditions and approval workflows, reducing the risk of unauthorized access. Option D - Correct. JIT access mitigates insider threats by minimizing the window of opportunity for unauthorized access to AVD session hosts, enhancing overall security.

Option C - Incorrect. While improving compliance with regulatory requirements is important, it is not specifically mentioned in the context of advantages of JIT access over traditional methods for administrative access to AVD session hosts as described in the question. Option E - Incorrect. While centralized control and audit trails are beneficial, they are not directly related to the advantages of JIT access over traditional methods for administrative access to AVD session hosts as described in the question.

EXAM FOCUS	*JIT access enhances security by granting temporary, conditional access to session hosts, reducing attack surfaces. Eliminate choices focused solely on compliance or centralized control—JIT is about limiting unauthorized access. It complements, not replaces, RBAC policies.*
CAUTION ALERT	*Avoid assuming JIT access applies to all administrative activities without proper configuration. Stay alert to misconfigurations that leave hosts unnecessarily exposed. JIT must be paired with RBAC to enforce least-privilege principles effectively.*

QUESTION 27

Answer - A, C, D

A) Correct - Encrypting data at rest and in transit is fundamental to ensuring data integrity and preventing breaches.
B) Incorrect - Regular updates are important for security but do not directly address compliance needs for audits.
C) Correct - Implementing RBAC is essential for managing access controls and is a compliance requirement in many industries. D) Correct - Utilizing Azure Security Center helps in continuous security monitoring and is crucial for compliance with security audits. E) Incorrect - While Microsoft Defender for Cloud provides broad security management and threat protection, it is not specifically required to meet these three requirements.

EXAM FOCUS	*Prioritize encrypting data at rest/in-transit, enabling RBAC, and leveraging Azure Security Center for continuous monitoring. Eliminate less impactful measures like basic updates or generalized threat*

CAUTION ALERT	*protection unless explicitly required. Focus on compliance and audit-readiness.* *Don't assume general threat protection like Microsoft Defender for Cloud fully meets compliance needs. Encryption and RBAC are critical for audits. Ensure every measure directly supports data integrity, auditability, and regulatory standards.*

QUESTION 28

Answer - A) Identify the permissions required for the custom role; B) Define role assignments to assign the custom role to users or groups; D) Test the custom role in a non-production environment before deployment

Option A - Correct. Identifying the permissions required for the custom role is the first step in custom role creation, ensuring that the role includes the necessary access permissions for users or groups. Option B - Correct. Defining role assignments to assign the custom role to users or groups ensures that the role is effectively applied to the appropriate entities, enabling fine-grained access control.

Option C - Incorrect. While Azure Policy can enforce compliance with permissions, it is not directly involved in custom role creation and management. Option D - Correct. Testing the custom role in a non-production environment before deployment helps identify any potential issues or conflicts with existing roles or permissions, ensuring a smooth deployment process. Option E - Incorrect. While monitoring and auditing usage of the custom role are important for security and compliance, they are not directly related to the process of custom role creation and management.

EXAM FOCUS	*Define permissions, assign roles, and test in non-production environments. Eliminate Azure Policy—it enforces standards but doesn't create roles. Always test custom roles to avoid conflicts. Focus on precision when aligning roles with organizational requirements.*
CAUTION ALERT	*Avoid skipping the testing phase—it leads to deployment failures. Don't assume that Azure Policy or monitoring replaces role management. Misaligned permissions can overexpose or under-restrict access, leading to operational or security issues.*

QUESTION 29

Answer - A) Provide step-by-step guides and video tutorials for MFA setup; B) Offer live webinars or virtual training sessions on MFA setup and usage best practices; C) Establish a dedicated helpdesk or support team to assist users with MFA setup

Option A - Correct. Providing step-by-step guides and video tutorials for MFA setup offers users clear instructions for completing the process independently. Option B - Correct. Offering live webinars or virtual training sessions on MFA setup and usage best practices allows for interactive learning and troubleshooting. Option C - Correct. Establishing a dedicated helpdesk or support team ensures that users can receive personalized assistance and troubleshooting for MFA setup.

Option D - Incorrect. While sending regular email communications can be helpful, it may not provide immediate support or address specific user questions and concerns. Option E - Incorrect. While integrating MFA setup prompts into the AVD user interface can streamline the process, it may not provide sufficient guidance for users who require assistance.

EXAM FOCUS	*Provide detailed MFA setup guides, webinars, and helpdesk support. Integrate step-by-step tutorials to address varied user skills. Eliminate passive measures like generic emails, which don't provide real-time troubleshooting for setup complexities.*
CAUTION ALERT	*Don't rely on email campaigns—they're insufficient for resolving user challenges. Avoid assuming all users can follow setup intuitively. Interactive sessions and clear instructions tailored to different technical levels ensure smoother adoption.*

QUESTION 30

Answer - A) Correct as is

Option A - Correct: The rule correctly allows only HTTPS and SSH traffic, blocking all other inbound traffic.
Option B - Incorrect: A single rule can cover multiple ports if the same action applies.
Option C - Incorrect: Priority 100 is typically sufficient for custom rules unless overridden by other rules.
Option D - Incorrect: Specifying source IP ranges is not required in the scenario.
Option E - Incorrect: The current access setting is appropriate to allow the specified traffic.

EXAM FOCUS	*The provided rule correctly allows HTTPS and SSH while blocking all other traffic. Focus on simplicity—avoid adding unnecessary IP ranges unless explicitly required. Validate rule priorities to avoid conflicts with existing security configurations.*
CAUTION ALERT	*Don't assume rules with lower priority (higher numbers) will override this setup. Always verify existing rules for overlaps. Avoid overcomplicating configurations with unnecessary conditions—it can inadvertently open unintended access.*

QUESTION 31

Answer - A) Profile container size and disk I/O operations during user logon and logoff; B) Frequency of profile disk merges and optimizations performed by FSLogix; C) Concurrent user logon and logoff activities affecting profile access and loading times

Option A - Correct. Profile container size and disk I/O operations during user logon and logoff significantly impact system performance and responsiveness. Option B - Correct. The frequency of profile disk merges and optimizations performed by FSLogix affects overall system performance and storage utilization. Option C - Correct. Concurrent user logon and logoff activities can lead to profile access conflicts and increase loading times, impacting user experience. Option D - Incorrect. While network bandwidth usage is relevant for profile synchronization, it may not directly impact system performance in all scenarios.

Option E - Incorrect. While FSLogix compatibility with virtual machine sizes and disk types is important, it may not directly correlate with system performance impacts.

EXAM FOCUS	*You need to monitor profile container size and disk I/O as they directly impact performance. Analyze the frequency of FSLogix profile merges, which affect storage and performance. Concurrent logons can strain the system; plan resources accordingly for peak load.*
CAUTION ALERT	*Don't overlook network bandwidth or VM compatibility—these factors indirectly affect performance but aren't primary contributors to FSLogix-specific impacts. Mismanagement of disk I/O or logons may lead to extended profile load times.*

QUESTION 32

Answer - A) Segregate user data based on departmental roles, B) Utilize separate Profile Containers for different user groups, C) Implement access controls to restrict data access within Profile Containers.

A) Segregate user data based on departmental roles - Segregating data based on departmental roles ensures that users only have access to relevant information. B) Utilize separate Profile Containers for different user groups - Each user group can have its Profile Container, ensuring data isolation and access control. C) Implement access controls to restrict data access within Profile Containers - Access controls ensure that only authorized users can access specific data within Profile Containers.

D) Leverage Azure AD dynamic groups for data segregation - While dynamic groups can help with user management, they are not directly related to data segregation within Profile Containers. E) Encrypt Profile Containers to ensure data isolation - Encryption secures data within Profile Containers but does not directly address segregation based on user roles or groups.

EXAM FOCUS	Always segregate Profile Containers by user group or department to ensure secure and compliant access. Implement access controls for granular security and align segregation with regulations. Eliminate methods that only provide encryption but not role-based data control.
CAUTION ALERT	Avoid relying solely on encryption for segregation; encryption secures data but doesn't separate access by roles. Misconfiguration in access controls or dynamic groups may lead to unauthorized access, violating compliance standards.

QUESTION 33

Answer - A, B, E

A) Correct - Distributing host pools across regions reduces latency by serving users from the nearest location and enhances availability. B) Correct - Azure Front Door facilitates global load balancing, improving application responsiveness and user experience across geographies. C) Incorrect - Site Recovery is crucial for disaster recovery but does not directly impact latency or compliance with data laws.

D) Incorrect - GRS is vital for data durability but does not address latency or legal compliance directly.
E) Correct - Configuring data residency settings in Azure Policy ensures compliance with international data protection laws, crucial for global operations.

EXAM FOCUS	Distribute host pools geographically to reduce latency for users. Use Azure Front Door for global load balancing and Azure Policy for enforcing data residency to maintain compliance. Eliminate redundant disaster recovery setups unrelated to latency optimization.
CAUTION ALERT	Avoid assuming Azure Site Recovery directly affects latency; it's for disaster recovery. Geo-redundant storage is crucial for durability but does not directly solve latency or compliance requirements—ensure tools match objectives.

QUESTION 34

Answer - A) Analyze FSLogix Profile Containers for disk space utilization and profile loading times, C) Check network latency between clients and AVD resources using Azure Network Watcher tools, D) Evaluate AVD session host performance metrics, including CPU, memory, and disk usage.

A) Analyze FSLogix Profile Containers for disk space utilization and profile loading times - FSLogix Profile Containers may impact performance if disk space is insufficient or profile loading times are excessive, requiring optimization. C) Check network latency between clients and AVD resources using Azure Network Watcher tools - Network latency affects client-server communication, and identifying latency issues helps optimize network performance for AVD sessions.

D) Evaluate AVD session host performance metrics, including CPU, memory, and disk usage - Monitoring session host performance metrics identifies resource bottlenecks affecting AVD client performance, enabling targeted optimization efforts. B) Monitor Azure Monitor logs for insights into client connectivity issues and session failures - While Azure Monitor logs provide valuable insights, they may not directly address performance issues impacting AVD clients. E) Review Azure AD authentication logs for errors related to user sign-in and access permissions - While authentication logs provide security insights, they may not directly assist in troubleshooting performance issues with AVD clients.

EXAM FOCUS	Investigate FSLogix profile usage and session host performance metrics for bottlenecks. Network latency issues must be diagnosed using Azure Network Watcher. Eliminate actions unrelated to user performance, such as Azure AD log reviews, unless access issues are reported.
CAUTION ALERT	Avoid assuming all lag is from network issues. Mismanaged FSLogix profiles or overburdened session hosts are common culprits. Don't dismiss connectivity diagnostics, as they often uncover overlooked latency factors.

QUESTION 35

Answer - A) Configuration is secure and efficient

Option A - Correct: H.264 with encryption and high quality is suitable for secure, high-performance multimedia redirection. Option B - Incorrect: Encryption is crucial for securing data streams in a virtual desktop environment. Option C - Incorrect: H.264 is widely used and appropriate if encrypted. Option D - Incorrect: Quality is a balance of performance and resource use, and 'High' is acceptable if bandwidth permits. Option E - Incorrect: The JSON is correctly formatted and configured for the purpose.

EXAM FOCUS	*Use codecs like H.264 with encryption for secure multimedia redirection, balancing high quality and performance. Avoid lowering quality unnecessarily unless bandwidth is critical. Ensure configurations align with multimedia and security policies to optimize user experience.*
CAUTION ALERT	*Don't disable encryption—doing so compromises security in a virtual desktop environment. Avoid codecs that are not standard or supported in enterprise environments. Misaligned configurations may cause streaming issues or bandwidth overload.*

QUESTION 36

Answer - B, D, E

A) Incorrect - Azure Site Recovery is crucial for business continuity but does not directly address transaction security or compliance. B) Correct - NSGs will control traffic flow to and from VMs, enhancing security for transactions. C) Incorrect - Azure Information Protection is more about data classification and protection, not specifically compliance or transaction security in an AVD context.

D) Correct - Azure Policy helps enforce regulatory compliance standards, essential in financial institutions. E) Correct - Azure Key Vault manages encryption keys securely, ensuring data protection and supporting compliance with regulations.

EXAM FOCUS	*Use NSGs to control traffic, ensuring secure transaction environments. Apply Azure Policy to enforce compliance. Leverage Key Vault for secure encryption key management to safeguard sensitive financial data. Eliminate non-critical configurations like Azure Information Protection.*
CAUTION ALERT	*Don't assume Azure Site Recovery alone guarantees compliance or transaction security—it's for recovery. Avoid misconfiguring NSGs, which may leave critical ports open, exposing your environment to threats. Focus on explicit security needs.*

QUESTION 37

Answer - A) Azure Monitor

Azure Monitor provides specialized monitoring capabilities for AVD sessions, allowing for tracking of user activity and enforcement of session duration policies based on specific criteria. Option B - Incorrect. While Azure Security Center provides security insights, it does not focus on session monitoring or management. Option C - Incorrect. Identity Protection is primarily for detecting identity-based risks, not session management. Option D - Incorrect. While Log Analytics collects and analyzes data, Azure Monitor offers more specialized monitoring capabilities for AVD sessions. Option E - Incorrect. Azure Resource Graph provides a programmatic interface to query Azure resources but does not directly address session management.

EXAM FOCUS	*Azure Monitor is essential for tracking session activity and enforcing timeout policies. Leverage it for analyzing performance trends and applying duration limits. Eliminate tools like Log Analytics, which provide raw data without session-specific tracking capabilities.*
CAUTION ALERT	*Avoid overcomplicating session tracking with tools like Identity Protection—it's for identity risks, not timeouts. Ensure Azure Monitor rules are precise to avoid unintentional session terminations or gaps in timeout enforcement.*

QUESTION 38

Answer - B) Pre-allocating resources to accommodate peak user activity periods and prevent performance degradation

Configuring Start VM on Connect pre-allocates resources, ensuring sufficient capacity during peak user activity periods and preventing performance degradation due to resource constraints.
Option A - Incorrect. Dynamic allocation may not guarantee resource availability during peak periods.
Option C - Incorrect. While automatic scaling may help, it is not specific to pre-allocation.
Option D - Incorrect. Releasing resources promptly is unrelated to pre-allocation.
Option E - Incorrect. Resource scheduling algorithms may optimize but do not specifically address pre-allocation.

EXAM FOCUS	*Start VM on Connect ensures VM resources are pre-allocated for peak activity periods, avoiding delays during user logins. It's best for environments with predictable peak times. Avoid solutions requiring real-time scaling during spikes, as they can result in performance lags.*
CAUTION ALERT	*Don't assume dynamic allocation is enough—pre-allocation ensures readiness during peak times. Misconfigured scaling policies can lead to under-provisioning or unnecessary costs if resources remain idle outside business hours.*

QUESTION 39

Answer - A, B, C

A) Correct - Azure Bastion secures access to VMs by providing a more secure and manageable environment for accessing session hosts. B) Correct - Azure Policy helps enforce security policies and compliance with financial regulations. C) Correct - Azure Monitor for logging and monitoring ensures that all actions are auditable, which is critical for financial institutions.

D) Incorrect - NSGs are crucial for network security but were not specified as a primary requirement in this scenario.
E) Incorrect - Creating a new application group is helpful for management but does not directly impact security or compliance.

EXAM FOCUS	*Use Azure Bastion for secure VM access, Azure Policy for compliance enforcement, and Azure Monitor for auditing. Eliminate redundant setups like additional application groups unless explicitly required. Ensure configurations align with transaction and security demands.*
CAUTION ALERT	*Avoid solely relying on NSGs for transaction security—layered tools like Bastion and Monitor are critical. Don't skip detailed audit logging; financial institutions need it for regulatory and operational transparency.*

QUESTION 40

Answer - A

Option A - Correct. The command correctly uses Update-FSLogixAppMaskingRule to update the rule, appropriately adds a new application, and correctly excludes a user group.

Option B - Incorrect. Set-FSLogixAppMaskingRule is used for modifying existing properties, not adding new paths or exclusions. Option C - Incorrect. -AddFilePath is necessary to add new applications without removing existing ones, and -ExcludeUser is correctly used. Option D - Incorrect. The -Enabled $true is unnecessary as the rule remains active unless explicitly disabled. Option E - Incorrect. User groups should be enclosed in quotes to prevent syntax errors.

EXAM FOCUS	*The Update-FSLogixAppMaskingRule command correctly updates masking rules. Use -ExcludeUser to selectively exempt departments like IT. Validate syntax and ensure masking rules do not disrupt operations or unintended applications. Check rules' active status post-update.*
CAUTION ALERT	*Don't replace Update with Set; it modifies properties but doesn't add new rules. Avoid excluding entire directories when only specific users or applications need masking. Mismanaged exclusions may lead to*

| | *compromised masking effectiveness.* |

QUESTION 41

Answer - B

Option A - Incorrect. While the configuration enhances security, it lacks explicit encryption for data protection.

Option B - Correct. Adding "encryption": "enabled" ensures that all data transmitted during Teams sessions is protected. Option C - Incorrect. The security level should not be reduced as it compromises the secure deployment of Teams. Option D - Incorrect. The multisession attribute is not required here as Teams automatically supports AVD multisessions. Option E - Incorrect. The proposed syntax is not valid for ARM templates focusing on Teams optimization configurations.

EXAM FOCUS	*Ensure Teams optimization includes encryption settings for compliance and security. Adding "encryption": "enabled" protects transmitted data. Avoid redundant attributes like multisession, as Teams already supports AVD multisession configurations. Test configurations for efficiency.*
CAUTION ALERT	*Don't compromise security by lowering security values. Avoid incorrect syntax or non-ARM compatible options like "teamsFeatures": { "WebRTC": "enabled" }. Misconfigured settings can degrade performance or weaken encryption.*

QUESTION 42

Answer - A, C, D

A) Correct - 'CloudCacheLocations' allows for specifying multiple storage locations, providing redundancy and high availability. B) Incorrect - 'DeleteLocalProfileWhenVHDShouldApply' is relevant for local profile cleanup, not for availability or redundancy. C) Correct - Enabling ODFC (Office Data File Container) can help manage office data separately, enhancing profile availability.

D) Correct - 'CloudCacheConnectionString' is essential for configuring connections to cloud storage, crucial for profile data redundancy and availability. E) Incorrect - 'DiskType' relates to the type of disk used but does not directly impact high-availability settings for profiles.

EXAM FOCUS	*Always configure CloudCacheLocations and CloudCacheConnectionString to enable redundancy in FSLogix setups. Ensure ODFC is enabled for managing Office data efficiently. Prioritize configurations that directly enhance high availability of profiles.*
CAUTION ALERT	*Don't rely on irrelevant keys like DiskType for high availability—it controls hardware specifics, not redundancy. Misuse of settings like DeleteLocalProfile can inadvertently cause data loss in high-availability environments.*

QUESTION 43

Answer - B) Azure Monitor Alerts

Option A - Incorrect. Azure Security Center focuses on security posture and may not provide the necessary tools for configuring performance thresholds and alerts for AVD host pools.

Option B - Correct. Azure Monitor Alerts enables the configuration of performance thresholds and alerts based on predefined conditions, allowing for proactive monitoring and timely detection of performance anomalies. Option C - Incorrect. While Azure Log Analytics Alerts may provide insights, Azure Monitor Alerts offers more comprehensive tools specifically tailored for setting performance thresholds and alerts.

Option D - Incorrect. Azure Policy is used for governance and compliance and may not be suitable for configuring performance thresholds and alerts. Option E - Incorrect. Azure Resource Health provides insights into the health of

Azure resources but does not offer the specific tools needed for configuring performance thresholds and alerts.

EXAM FOCUS	*Use Azure Monitor Alerts for setting precise thresholds and receiving notifications for performance anomalies. Customize alert rules for critical metrics like CPU, memory, and session load to proactively manage AVD host pool performance.*
CAUTION ALERT	*Avoid using Azure Security Center for performance thresholds; it focuses on security. Misconfiguring alerts or thresholds can lead to missed critical events or excessive, non-actionable notifications, disrupting system monitoring.*

QUESTION 44

Answer - A) Kusto Query Language (KQL)

Option A - Kusto Query Language (KQL) is the query language used within Azure Monitor Logs for retrieving and analyzing log and metric data, including AVD telemetry, providing powerful querying capabilities.
Option B - SQL Query Language is not used for querying Azure Monitor Logs.
Option C - PowerShell and Python are scripting languages and not query languages for Azure Monitor Logs.
Option D - ARM Templates are used for infrastructure deployment, not for querying telemetry data.

EXAM FOCUS	*Leverage Kusto Query Language (KQL) for custom log analysis in Azure Monitor Logs. Optimize queries for performance by focusing on essential metrics like latency and session failures. Use query optimization techniques to reduce cost and improve scalability.*
CAUTION ALERT	*Don't attempt to use PowerShell, SQL, or ARM Templates for telemetry queries—they're not suitable for Azure Monitor Logs. Inefficient KQL queries can escalate costs and impact Azure Monitor's performance during heavy usage periods.*

QUESTION 45

Answer - E

Option A - Incorrect. The command only enforces HTTPS but does not ensure encryption of stored data.
Option B - Incorrect. --https-only allowed is not a valid parameter value.
Option C - Incorrect. --require-encryption true is not a valid Azure CLI parameter for this purpose.
Option D - Incorrect. --allow-encrypted-only true does not exist; it should focus on enabling encryption services specifically.
Option E - Correct. Specifying --https-only true ensures data is encrypted in transit, and --encryption-services blob file configures encryption at rest for both blobs and files, meeting compliance requirements for AVD user data.

EXAM FOCUS	*Enforce encryption for data compliance by combining --https-only true and --encryption-services blob file in the Azure CLI command. Ensure encryption at both rest and transit to meet regulatory standards and protect user data.*
CAUTION ALERT	*Avoid assuming HTTPS alone ensures compliance; encryption for stored data must be explicitly configured. Misusing non-existent parameters like --require-encryption true or --allow-encrypted-only can lead to deployment errors.*

QUESTION 46

Answer - B) Azure Log Analytics

Option B - Azure Log Analytics provides detailed insights into user activity and resource utilization in AVD environments, allowing administrators to analyze usage patterns and identify optimization opportunities. It offers logs and metrics for performance monitoring and troubleshooting, addressing the need for improving performance and user experience.

Option A - Azure Resource Graph focuses on querying Azure resources and may not provide granular usage data required for optimization. Option C - Azure Cost Management + Billing focuses on cost analysis and optimization but may not provide detailed usage insights for AVD environments. Option D - Azure Advisor offers recommendations for improving Azure resource utilization but may not provide the detailed usage analytics needed for AVD optimization.

Option E - Azure Monitor focuses on monitoring and alerting but may not provide the detailed usage insights required for resource optimization in AVD environments.

EXAM FOCUS	*Use Azure Log Analytics to analyze detailed AVD usage patterns, including user activity and resource utilization. Customize dashboards to track trends and bottlenecks for optimizing resource allocation and improving user experience.*
CAUTION ALERT	*Don't rely solely on Azure Cost Management—it tracks financials, not detailed user behavior. Misconfigured Log Analytics queries can omit key insights, leading to missed optimization opportunities in AVD resource management.*

QUESTION 47

Answer - D) Azure Security Center

Option D - Azure Security Center provides auditing and compliance reporting capabilities, including continuous monitoring, regulatory compliance assessments, and security recommendations, enabling administrators to maintain compliance with industry standards and regulations in AVD environments.

Option A - Azure Policy focuses on governance and compliance but may not offer detailed auditing and reporting features required for AVD environments. Option B - Azure Sentinel offers security information and event management (SIEM) but may not specialize in compliance reporting for AVD environments. Option C - Azure Log Analytics allows querying log data but may require additional configuration for compliance reporting in AVD environments. Option E - Azure Monitor focuses on monitoring Azure services but may not provide dedicated compliance reporting features.

EXAM FOCUS	*Leverage Azure Security Center for comprehensive compliance reporting in AVD. It provides regulatory compliance assessments, recommendations, and auditing capabilities. Use built-in standards templates to streamline compliance workflows.*
CAUTION ALERT	*Avoid assuming Azure Policy alone covers compliance—it enforces governance, not audits. Misunderstanding compliance tool functionalities may lead to gaps in reporting or incomplete risk assessments in regulatory environments.*

QUESTION 48

Answer - A, B, D

A) Correct - Windows 10 Enterprise multi-session supports multiple simultaneous user sessions and meets regulatory compliance for financial institutions.
B) Correct - Windows Server 2019 supports Remote Desktop Services for high availability and is commonly used in environments requiring stable, long-term support. C) Incorrect - Windows 11 Enterprise does support the latest security features but is not specifically required for regulatory compliance in financial services.

D) Correct - Windows Server 2022 offers the latest security and performance improvements suitable for critical applications in financial services. E) Incorrect - Windows 10 Pro does not support multi-session capabilities required for high availability in enterprise environments.

EXAM FOCUS	*Deploy Windows 10 Enterprise multi-session for scalability and compliance. Use Windows Server 2019 or 2022 for stability and enterprise-level features. Eliminate options like Windows 10 Pro, which lack multi-session support for AVD.*
CAUTION ALERT	*Avoid deploying non-multi-session OS like Windows 10 Pro for AVD host pools. While Windows 11 offers modern features, it may not align with regulatory compliance or established financial standards compared to Server OS options.*

QUESTION 49

Answer - B) Configuring Azure Automation runbooks for automated troubleshooting
D) Integrating Azure Monitor alerts with Logic Apps for automated responses

B) Configuring Azure Automation runbooks for automated troubleshooting - Automation runbooks can execute predefined tasks to troubleshoot and resolve AVD issues, minimizing downtime. D) Integrating Azure Monitor alerts with Logic Apps for automated responses - Logic Apps can execute workflows in response to Azure Monitor alerts, facilitating automated disaster recovery processes.

A, C, E) While Azure Policy initiatives, PowerShell scripts, and Azure DevOps pipelines are useful for automation, they are not specifically tailored for disaster recovery in AVD.

EXAM FOCUS	*Use Azure Automation runbooks for troubleshooting and Logic Apps integrated with Monitor alerts for automated recovery workflows. Automating disaster recovery minimizes downtime and ensures timely responses to incidents.*
CAUTION ALERT	*Don't assume PowerShell scripts alone provide complete automation—they require integration for real-time execution. Misaligned workflows or absent recovery logic in Logic Apps may delay disaster responses, undermining automation objectives.*

QUESTION 50

Answer - C) Utilizing Azure Application Insights for monitoring application performance and user interactions
D) Implementing Azure Log Analytics for analyzing application usage and performance trends

C) Utilizing Azure Application Insights for monitoring application performance and user interactions - Azure Application Insights is ideal for monitoring application performance and user interactions, providing valuable insights into performance metrics and user behavior. D) Implementing Azure Log Analytics for analyzing application usage and performance trends - Azure Log Analytics enables organizations to analyze application usage and performance trends, facilitating optimization and troubleshooting.

A, B, E) While Azure Monitor, Microsoft Endpoint Manager, and Microsoft 365 Usage Analytics have their respective benefits, they are not specifically tailored for application performance management in AVD.

EXAM FOCUS	*Employ Azure Application Insights for real-time application performance tracking and Azure Log Analytics for trend analysis. These tools complement each other in managing application performance and diagnosing issues effectively.*
CAUTION ALERT	*Avoid relying solely on Azure Monitor—it lacks specialized application insights. Misuse of analytics tools without correlating metrics may lead to incomplete diagnostics, hampering application performance improvements in AVD environments.*

PRACTICE TEST 3 - QUESTIONS ONLY

QUESTION 1

Your task is to ensure that a newly planned AVD deployment for a healthcare provider is network-ready, particularly for handling sensitive patient data. You need to:
- Assess the network's capacity to handle AVD-specific traffic.
- Ensure compliance with data security regulations.
- Optimize the network setup for peak times.

Which tool or technique would you use to assess network readiness specifically for AVD in this scenario?

A) Network Performance Monitor
B) Azure Speed Test
C) AVD Planning Toolkit
D) Azure Advisor
E) FSLogix Agent Diagnostics

QUESTION 2

You are enhancing AVD setup to include robust monitoring and optimization of network traffic, particularly focusing on:
- Implementing QoS to prioritize AVD traffic.
- Using Azure Monitor to track performance metrics.
- Applying Azure Network Watcher for real-time network diagnostics.

Which ARM template would be most appropriate for deploying Network Watcher to monitor AVD traffic?

```
A) {"type": "Microsoft.Network/networkWatcher", "properties": {}}
B) {"type": "Microsoft.Network/virtualNetwork", "properties": {}}
C) {"type": "Microsoft.Network/trafficManager", "properties": {}}
D) {"type": "Microsoft.Compute/virtualMachines", "properties": {}}
E) {"type": "Microsoft.Storage/storageAccounts", "properties": {}}
```

QUESTION 3

- As an Azure Virtual Desktop (AVD) administrator, you are troubleshooting authentication issues impacting user access.
- You need to access detailed logs related to user authentication attempts to identify and resolve the issue.
- Your task involves selecting the appropriate Log Analytics table for this purpose.

Which table should you query to access detailed logs related to user authentication attempts?

```
A) WVDConnections
B) WVDAuditLogs
C) WVDServiceMetadata
D) WVDAgentHealth
E) WVDSecurityEvents
```

QUESTION 4

Your organization's Azure Virtual Desktop (AVD) deployment is experiencing network connectivity issues, impacting user productivity. The IT team needs to diagnose and resolve these issues promptly to restore service availability. How would you leverage Azure Network Watcher in diagnosing network problems within the AVD infrastructure? Select TWO.

A) Use Connection Monitor to test connectivity between AVD session hosts and client devices
B) Analyze Network Security Group (NSG) flow logs to identify blocked traffic and rule violations
C) Run IP flow verify to validate traffic flow and detect packet drops or routing issues

D) Utilize VPN diagnostics to troubleshoot connectivity problems for remote users
E) Monitor ExpressRoute circuits for bandwidth utilization and performance metrics

QUESTION 5

In setting up Azure Virtual Desktop, you need to ensure that RDP connections are secured using Multi-Factor Authentication. The following Azure CLI script is proposed. Identify the correct implementation.

```bash
az vm extension set --publisher Microsoft.Azure.ActiveDirectory --name AADLoginForWindows --resource-group MyResourceGroup --vm-name MyVM
```

A) Correct implementation
B) Wrong extension name
C) Wrong publisher
D) Missing MFA setup
E) Incorrect resource group name

QUESTION 6

You are tasked with implementing a cost optimization strategy for managing session hosts in an Azure Virtual Desktop (AVD) environment. The solution must meet the following requirements:
- Dynamically scale session hosts based on user demand to optimize resource usage.
- Ensure that session hosts are available during business hours only.
- Minimize manual intervention.
Which Azure service or feature should you use?

A) Azure Monitor Autoscale
B) Azure Resource Manager templates
C) Azure Functions
D) Azure Automation with Azure Runbooks
E) Azure Policy

QUESTION 7

Your organization is concerned about the impact of the chosen operating system on performance and scalability in Azure Virtual Desktop (AVD) deployments. As the Azure architect, you need to explain how the OS choice influences these aspects. What considerations should you highlight? Select THREE.

A) Windows 10 Multi-Session offers better performance for graphics-intensive applications and multimedia content
B) Windows Server is optimized for resource efficiency and can support a larger number of concurrent users with lower hardware requirements
C) Both OS options may require optimization and tuning to achieve optimal performance and scalability in AVD deployments
D) Windows 10 Multi-Session is more suitable for small to medium-sized deployments, while Windows Server is preferred for large-scale enterprise environments
E) The choice between OS options may impact the allocation of virtual machine resources, including CPU, memory, and storage

QUESTION 8

Your organization prioritizes security in the design of Azure Virtual Desktop (AVD) host pools and requires thorough considerations in the architecture. As the Azure architect, you need to highlight key security considerations. What should you emphasize? Select THREE.

A) Role-Based Access Control (RBAC) and Least Privilege
B) Network Isolation and Micro-Segmentation
C) Data Encryption and Data Loss Prevention (DLP)
D) Identity and Access Management (IAM)
E) Threat Detection and Intrusion Prevention

QUESTION 9

You are planning to implement autoscale for host pools in an Azure Virtual Desktop (AVD) environment to optimize resource utilization. Consider the following criteria:
- Scale resources dynamically based on user demand to ensure optimal performance.
- Ensure that session hosts are available during business hours and scaled down during off-peak hours.
- Minimize manual intervention for managing resource scaling.
Which of the following actions can you perform with autoscale to meet these criteria? Select TWO.

A) Automatically shut down session hosts during off-peak hours.
B) Automatically add session hosts based on CPU usage.
C) Automatically adjust virtual machine sizes based on network bandwidth.
D) Automatically archive inactive user profiles.
E) Automatically allocate additional storage to session hosts.

QUESTION 10

Implementing secure access to Azure file shares is critical. Assume you are configuring access using RBAC and Azure AD credentials. What adjustments should be made to this ARM template snippet?

```json
{
 "type": "Microsoft.Storage/storageAccounts/fileServices/shares",
 "apiVersion": "2019-06-01",
 "properties": {
 "enabledProtocols": "SMB",
 "rootSquashType": "NoRootSquash"
 }
}
```

A) Update API version
B) Change enabledProtocols to NFS
C) Add an RBAC role assignment
D) Remove rootSquashType for SMB
E) No changes needed

QUESTION 11

Your organization is considering deploying Windows 10 Enterprise multi-session (E3 or E5) licenses for session hosts in Azure Virtual Desktop (AVD). As the Azure architect, you need to understand the impact of licensing on session host functionality. What are key considerations in this regard? Select THREE.

A) Access to Advanced Security Features and Compliance Tools
B) Enhanced User Experience with Virtual Desktop Infrastructure (VDI)
C) Support for Resource-Intensive Applications and Workloads
D) Integration with Microsoft Defender for Endpoint and Endpoint Manager
E) Compatibility with MSIX App Attach and Profile Containers

QUESTION 12

You are tasked with implementing a disaster recovery strategy for an Azure Virtual Desktop (AVD) environment to ensure business continuity. Consider the following factors:
- Ability to failover AVD host pools to a secondary Azure region.
- Minimize downtime and ensure seamless user experience during failover.
Which Azure service should you use to meet these requirements?

A) Azure Storage replication
B) Azure Site Recovery
C) Azure Backup
D) Azure Traffic Manager
E) Azure Front Door

QUESTION 13

Your organization is striving to balance performance and security considerations in the lifecycle management of Azure Virtual Desktop (AVD) images. As the Azure specialist, you need to assess strategies that achieve this balance effectively. Which of the following strategies can help achieve a balance between performance and security in AVD image lifecycle management? Select TWO.

A) Implementing Network Segmentation for Image Repositories
B) Leveraging Cached Images for Faster Deployment
C) Encrypting Image Data at Rest and in Transit
D) Using Lightweight Base Images for Rapid Provisioning
E) Enforcing Role-Based Access Control (RBAC) for Image Modification

QUESTION 14

Your organization requires customizations to be applied to session hosts at the time of creation in Azure Virtual Desktop (AVD) to meet specific user requirements and application needs. As the Azure specialist, you need to identify options for customizing session hosts during creation. Which options are available for customizing session hosts at the time of creation in AVD? Select THREE.

A) Installing Additional Applications
B) Configuring User Profiles and Permissions
C) Enabling FSLogix Profile Containers
D) Joining the Session Host to Active Directory Domain
E) Applying Group Policy Settings for Desktop Environment

QUESTION 15

Your organization requires strict version management of images used in AVD. How can you ensure each image version is preserved and managed correctly using Azure CLI?

```bash
az sig image-version create --resource-group MyResourceGroup --gallery-name MyGallery --gallery-image-definition MyImage --gallery-image-version "1.0.0" --target-regions "East US" --managed-image "/subscriptions/subID/resourceGroups/MyResourceGroup/providers/Microsoft.Compute/images/MyManagedImage"
```

A) Correct setup
B) Version syntax is incorrect
C) Target-regions should include multiple locations

D) Managed image path is wrong
E) Command needs additional flags

QUESTION 16

Implementing Multi-Factor Authentication (MFA) and conditional access policies are essential security practices for Azure Virtual Desktop (AVD) deployments to ensure secure user access. As the Azure specialist, you need to outline the steps for implementing MFA and conditional access effectively. What are the key steps for implementing MFA and conditional access for AVD deployments? Select THREE.

A) Configure Azure AD Conditional Access Policies
B) Enable MFA for User Sign-In to AVD Resources
C) Define Access Controls Based on User Roles and Locations
D) Integrate Azure Security Center with Conditional Access Policies
E) Utilize Azure Bastion for Secure Remote Access to AVD Resources

QUESTION 17

As an Azure specialist, you're responsible for monitoring and tuning the performance of Azure Virtual Desktop (AVD) deployments to ensure smooth operation and user satisfaction. Which tools can you use for performance monitoring and tuning in AVD environments? Select THREE.

A) Azure Monitor for Metrics Collection and Performance Analysis
B) Azure Policy for Resource Governance and Optimization
C) Azure Security Center for Threat Detection and Response
D) Azure Log Analytics for Log Collection and Analysis
E) Azure Application Insights for Application Performance Monitoring

QUESTION 18

You're responsible for ensuring that all session hosts in an Azure Virtual Desktop (AVD) host pool have the latest security patches and updates applied. Considering the criticality of this task, what actions should you take to meet the requirements effectively?
- Automate the application of security patches and updates
- Ensure minimal administrative effort
- Enable centralized management of update deployment Select TWO.

A) Configure a scaling plan.
B) Implement diagnostic logging.
C) Enable drain mode.
D) Configure Azure Update Management.
E) Manually update each session host.

QUESTION 19

Your organization aims to optimize the user experience in Azure Virtual Desktop (AVD) deployments by customizing user environments for maximum productivity. Critical factors include personalized application access, profile management, and data synchronization. How would you prioritize these factors to enhance user satisfaction and productivity effectively? Select TWO.

A) Implement MSIX App Attach for dynamic application provisioning
B) Configure FSLogix for profile management and data synchronization
C) Utilize Azure Bastion for secure remote access

QUESTION 20

To enhance AVD management efficiency, you are automating user environment setups using JSON configurations in Azure CLI. The automation must support dynamic application attachment based on user roles, enforce a strict logout policy, and provide detailed logging for audit purposes. How should you modify the JSON configuration to include a logout policy?

```json
{
 "userType": "dynamic",
 "applications": ["Office", "Teams"],
 "logging": "detailed"
}
```

A) Add logout policy settings
B) Integrate role-based application management
C) Ensure logging covers security audits
D) JSON is configured correctly
E) Modify userType to static

QUESTION 21

You are tasked with configuring firewall rules to allow traffic for Remote Desktop Protocol (RDP) connections in an Azure Virtual Desktop environment. Which port should you specify in the firewall rules for RDP traffic?

A) 80
B) 443
C) 3389
D) 8080
E) 8443

QUESTION 22

Your organization is interested in leveraging Microsoft Entra services to enhance security in Azure Virtual Desktop (AVD) environments and wants to understand the security enhancements provided by these services. The focus is on evaluating how Entra services contribute to strengthening security posture and protecting AVD deployments from threats. Which security enhancements are provided by Microsoft Entra services for AVD environments? Select THREE.

A) Integration with Azure Sentinel for advanced threat detection and response
B) Implementation of role-based access control (RBAC) for granular access management
C) Enforcement of multi-factor authentication (MFA) for user sign-in
D) Automatic encryption of data at rest and in transit within AVD environments
E) Integration with Microsoft Defender for Cloud for endpoint protection and vulnerability management

QUESTION 23

Your organization aims to balance security requirements with user experience when implementing Conditional Access policies for Azure Virtual Desktop (AVD). The focus is on ensuring that security measures do not overly impact user productivity. How can Conditional Access policies be configured to balance security with user experience in AVD environments? Select THREE.

A) Implement Conditional Access policies with granular controls based on risk assessments
B) Define policies that allow for adaptive authentication based on user behavior and context
C) Utilize risk-based access policies to dynamically adjust security measures based on threat levels

D) Implement Conditional Access policies with predefined access controls to minimize user disruptions
E) Leverage session controls to allow users to access AVD resources from any device securely

QUESTION 24

As an Azure security engineer, you are tasked with securing Azure Virtual Desktop deployments against potential breaches. What are the most effective measures to take? Select THREE.

A) Configure conditional access policies.
B) Enable multi-factor authentication.
C) Use Azure Security Center.
D) Restrict user access based on geolocation.
E) All session hosts should be domain-joined.

QUESTION 25

To optimize the performance of AVD environments, you are tasked with adjusting the Defender Antivirus settings to limit CPU usage during scans. Which PowerShell command correctly sets the maximum CPU usage for Defender scans?

```
A) Set-MpPreference -ScanAvgCPULoadFactor 20
B) Set-MpPreference -ScanMaxCPULoadFactor 50
C) Set-MpPreference -ScanMaxCPULoadFactor 20
D) Set-MpPreference -REMScanAvgCPULoadFactor 20
E) Configure-MpCPULoad -ScanMaxCPULoad 20
```

QUESTION 26

Your organization is implementing Just-In-Time (JIT) access for administrative access to Azure Virtual Desktop (AVD) session hosts to enhance security. The focus is on configuring JIT settings for optimal security. What settings should be configured for optimal security when implementing Just-In-Time (JIT) access for administrative access to AVD session hosts? Select THREE.

A) Define a maximum session duration for JIT access to AVD session hosts
B) Implement multi-factor authentication (MFA) for all JIT access requests
C) Configure access approval workflows with designated approvers for JIT access requests
D) Enable logging and auditing of all JIT access activities for compliance and security monitoring
E) Restrict JIT access to specific IP ranges or trusted networks to prevent unauthorized access

QUESTION 27

Your AVD environment is targeted by a sophisticated cyber attack. To enhance your defensive strategy, you must improve real-time threat detection, ensure endpoint security, and maintain system resilience. Which configurations would be most effective? Select THREE.

A) Integrate with Azure Sentinel.
B) Implement Microsoft Defender for Identity.
C) Configure geo-redundancy for AVD.
D) Enable Azure Monitor.
E) Deploy Endpoint Detection and Response (EDR) solutions.

QUESTION 28

Your organization is tasked with assigning roles based on the least privilege principle in Azure Virtual Desktop (AVD) environments to minimize the risk of unauthorized access. The focus is on understanding the concept of least privilege and its application in role assignment. How does the concept of least privilege apply to role assignment in AVD environments? Select TWO.

A) Assign roles with only the permissions necessary to perform specific tasks
B) Limit administrative access to critical resources and functions
C) Regularly review and update role assignments based on changing requirements
D) Implement role hierarchies to enforce strict access control policies
E) Utilize built-in Azure AD roles for standardized access control policies

QUESTION 29

Your organization has implemented Multi-Factor Authentication (MFA) for Azure Virtual Desktop (AVD) to enhance security. However, there are concerns about balancing security requirements with user convenience and usability. The focus is on balancing security and usability in MFA setups. How can you balance security and usability when implementing MFA for Azure Virtual Desktop? Select THREE.

A) Implement MFA only for high-risk activities or privileged users
B) Offer alternative authentication methods, such as biometric or token-based authentication
C) Adjust MFA settings based on user feedback and usage patterns to minimize disruption
D) Provide temporary bypass options for MFA during critical business operations or emergencies
E) Enforce MFA only during specific time windows or from certain locations

QUESTION 30

Your role involves implementing advanced machine learning-based network monitoring to detect anomalies in AVD traffic. This integration should enhance security by analyzing network flow data to identify unusual patterns and potential threats. Determine if the Azure service configured in the script below effectively utilizes machine learning for traffic analysis and suggest necessary modifications to optimize anomaly detection.

```bash
az network watcher flow-log configure --enabled true --nsg "AVDNSG" --storage-account "AVDStorage" --workspace "AVDWorkspace"
```

A) Correct configuration
B) Enable Traffic Analytics
C) Use a different storage account
D) Integrate with Azure Sentinel
E) Change workspace to a more secure one

QUESTION 31

Your organization is planning a large-scale deployment of FSLogix for Azure Virtual Desktop (AVD) environments and needs to consider scalability considerations. The focus is on scalability considerations for FSLogix deployments. What scalability considerations should be evaluated when deploying FSLogix for large-scale AVD environments? Select THREE.

A) Scalability of storage infrastructure to accommodate growing profile container sizes
B) Ability to distribute profile management tasks across multiple file servers or storage locations
C) Impact of user profile growth and increased logon/logoff activities on FSLogix performance
D) Support for load balancing and high availability configurations for FSLogix components
E) Integration with Azure Monitor for performance monitoring and capacity planning

QUESTION 32

As an Azure Virtual Desktop administrator tasked with optimizing storage for user profiles, you need to explore integration options with cloud storage solutions. Consider the following aspects:
 - The solution should scale seamlessly to accommodate growing user profiles.

- Data should be backed up and accessible from multiple locations for redundancy.
- Integration should offer cost-effective storage solutions without compromising performance.

How can Profile Containers be integrated with cloud storage solutions? Select THREE.

A) Integrate Profile Containers with Azure Blob Storage.
B) Utilize OneDrive for Business as a storage solution for Profile Containers.
C) Leverage Azure File Sync to synchronize Profile Containers across multiple locations.
D) Implement Azure Backup for Profile Containers.
E) Utilize Azure NetApp Files for Profile Container storage.

QUESTION 33

Your AVD setup needs enhanced monitoring, proactive threat detection, and compliance with healthcare regulations. Which configurations should you prioritize? Select THREE.

A) Integrate with Azure Monitor and Azure Log Analytics.
B) Enable Azure Security Center Standard tier.
C) Implement network segmentation using Azure Firewall.
D) Apply Azure Policy health compliance standards.
E) Use Azure Sentinel for SIEM.

QUESTION 34

Your organization plans to monitor Azure Virtual Desktop (AVD) client deployments to ensure optimal performance and user experience. Consider the following scenario:
- The organization operates in a highly regulated industry with strict compliance requirements for data protection and privacy.
- Users access AVD sessions from both corporate-owned and personal devices, requiring comprehensive monitoring of client activities.
- IT administrators aim to implement monitoring tools and techniques that provide visibility into client performance, connectivity, and security events.

Which monitoring tools and techniques should you implement for the given scenario? Select THREE.

A) Utilize Azure Monitor for real-time monitoring of AVD session host performance and resource utilization.
B) Implement Azure Log Analytics to collect and analyze logs from AVD clients and session hosts for troubleshooting and performance optimization.
C) Configure Azure Security Center to detect and remediate security threats targeting AVD clients and associated resources.
D) Leverage Azure Application Insights to track user interactions and application performance within AVD sessions for usability analysis.
E) Use Azure Network Watcher to monitor network traffic between clients and AVD resources and identify connectivity issues.

QUESTION 35

Implement a balanced configuration for multimedia redirection that considers both resource usage and user experience. You need to adjust settings dynamically based on network conditions. Which Azure CLI command or configuration approach would best manage these requirements?
Consider this pseudocode for dynamic adjustment:

```
pseudo
if networkSpeed > 100Mbps
 enableHighQualityMode()
else
 enableStandardMode()
```

A) Implement as a real-time scripted solution
B) Adjust manually as needed
C) Use Azure Automation to apply settings
D) This approach is not supported by Azure
E) Only static settings are possible

QUESTION 36

A healthcare provider needs to use Azure Virtual Desktop to ensure high availability, HIPAA compliance, and secure patient data access. What should be configured? Select THREE.

A) Deploy Azure Bastion for secure RDP access.
B) Use Azure ExpressRoute for dedicated network connectivity.
C) Configure Azure Health Data Services.
D) Enable Multi-Factor Authentication for data access.
E) Implement Azure Private Link to secure data exchanges.

QUESTION 37

You are troubleshooting session timeout issues reported by Azure Virtual Desktop (AVD) users who experience frequent disconnections during peak hours. Which tool or feature should you utilize to analyze network latency and identify potential bottlenecks affecting session stability?

A) Azure Network Watcher
B) Azure Virtual Network
C) Azure Application Gateway
D) Azure Load Balancer
E) Azure Traffic Manager

QUESTION 38

Security considerations are paramount when implementing Start VM on Connect in Azure Virtual Desktop (AVD) environments. Consider the following scenario: Your organization deals with sensitive data and strict compliance requirements. What security measure is crucial to mitigate risks associated with starting VMs upon user connection?

A) Implementing Network Security Groups (NSGs) to control traffic flow and restrict unauthorized access
B) Enforcing Just-In-Time (JIT) access policies to limit VM access to specific times and users
C) Configuring Role-Based Access Control (RBAC) to restrict administrative privileges and access to VM resources
D) Utilizing Azure Bastion to provide secure RDP access to VMs without exposing public IPs
E) Enabling Azure Security Center to detect and respond to threats across AVD resources and user sessions

QUESTION 39

An international law firm needs its AVD setup to ensure data confidentiality, enable secure remote access for global partners, and meet international compliance standards. What should you configure? Select THREE.

A) Configure Azure Bastion with AzureBastionSubnet.
B) Implement Azure VPN Gateway for secure remote connections.
C) Use Azure Information Protection for data classification and loss prevention.
D) Enable Multi-Factor Authentication across all user accounts.
E) Set up Conditional Access policies based on user location and device compliance.

QUESTION 40

In an effort to streamline application visibility on AVD sessions for non-administrative staff, you are deploying an FSLogix rule using the following script. Identify the error:

```
$RuleName = "NonAdminApps"
$AppPath = "Notepad.exe"
New-FSLogixAppMaskingRule -Name $RuleName -FilePath $AppPath -ExcludeGroup "NonAdmins"
```

A) The script is correct.
B) Replace New-FSLogixAppMaskingRule with Set-FSLogixAppMaskingRule.
C) Change -ExcludeGroup to -AssignedGroup as non-admins should not see the app.
D) Modify $AppPath = "Notepad.exe" to $AppPath = "C:\Windows\Notepad.exe" to specify the full path.
E) The rule should include -Enabled $true to be effective.

QUESTION 41

Troubleshooting Teams connectivity issues in AVD often requires analyzing network configurations. What PowerShell command should you use to check the network performance metrics specific to Teams sessions?
`Get-AVDNetworkStats -Filter "TeamsSessions"`

A) Command is correct as is.
B) Replace -Filter "TeamsSessions" with -SessionType "Teams".
C) Add -Detailed $true for comprehensive metrics.
D) Use Get-TeamsAVDStats instead of Get-AVDNetworkStats.
E) Remove -Filter and use the command without parameters for a general overview.

QUESTION 42

In an AVD setup requiring enhanced security measures for FSLogix profile containers, which registry changes are necessary to secure and manage user data effectively? Select THREE.

A) HKLM\SOFTWARE\FSLogix\Profiles\Encrypt
B) HKLM\SOFTWARE\Policies\FSLogix\ODFC\EncryptProfile
C) HKLM\SOFTWARE\FSLogix\Profiles\ProfileType
D) HKLM\SOFTWARE\FSLogix\Apps\Hide
E) HKLM\SOFTWARE\FSLogix\Profiles\PreventLoginWithFailure

QUESTION 43

You have been tasked with maintaining optimal performance of Azure Virtual Desktop (AVD) host pools to ensure a seamless user experience. The AVD environment serves users across different geographical locations, and reducing latency is crucial. Which best practice should you prioritize to optimize performance and minimize latency for users accessing AVD resources?

A) Regularly update FSLogix profiles for users
B) Implement Quality of Service (QoS) policies for network traffic
C) Monitor GPU utilization and adjust resources accordingly
D) Deploy AVD session hosts in proximity to user locations
E) Increase VM sizes for better performance

QUESTION 44

You need to proactively manage Azure Virtual Desktop (AVD) deployments by setting up alerts for critical events and performance thresholds. In designing the alerting strategy, consider:

1. The threshold values for alerts, balancing sensitivity with the avoidance of false positives.
2. The frequency and notification channels for alert notifications, ensuring timely responses to critical events.
3. The correlation of alerts with broader infrastructure health and performance metrics for holistic monitoring.

What is the most suitable mechanism for proactively managing AVD deployments through alerting?

A) Azure Monitor Logs
B) Azure Policy
C) Azure Automation
D) Azure Monitor Alerts
E) Azure Security Center

QUESTION 45

A software training center needs Azure Virtual Desktop for instructional labs that require support for multiple programming environments, rapid provisioning, and snapshot capabilities. They have VM1 with Windows 10 Pro, VM2 with Windows 11 Enterprise, VM3 with Windows Server 2019, and VM4 with Windows Server 2022. Which VMs should be configured?

A) VM2 and VM4
B) VM1, VM2, and VM3
C) VM3 and VM4
D) VM1, VM3, and VM4
E) VM2 and VM3

QUESTION 46

Cost management is a crucial aspect of scaling Azure Virtual Desktop (AVD) resources efficiently. As an AVD administrator, you need to implement strategies to optimize costs while ensuring adequate resource availability. Which strategy helps optimize costs by automatically adjusting resource allocation based on predefined criteria?

A) Manual scaling with Azure Logic Apps
B) Reserved capacity for AVD resources
C) Budget alerts in Azure Cost Management + Billing
D) Scheduled scaling with Azure Automation
E) Dynamic scaling with Azure Monitor

QUESTION 47

Managing user access and security roles is essential for maintaining security and compliance in Azure Virtual Desktop (AVD) environments. Which method should be used to enforce least privilege access control for AVD resources?

A) Role-Based Access Control (RBAC)
B) Conditional Access policies
C) Group-based licensing
D) Azure AD Privileged Identity Management (PIM)
E) Azure AD Identity Protection policies

QUESTION 48

An educational institution needs to deploy Azure Virtual Desktop to facilitate remote learning with considerations for cost-efficiency, easy maintenance, and broad device support. Which operating systems should you choose for the session hosts? Select THREE.

A) Windows 11 N
B) Windows Server 2012 R2

C) Windows 10 Enterprise multi-session
D) Windows Server 2022
E) Windows 8.1 Enterprise

QUESTION 49

A company is planning to test and validate its disaster recovery procedures for the Azure Virtual Desktop (AVD) environment. What steps should the company take to ensure thorough testing and validation of its recovery procedures? Select TWO.

A) Simulating failover scenarios in a non-production AVD environment
B) Conducting regular performance testing to assess failover impact on AVD performance
C) Documenting recovery procedures and conducting tabletop exercises
D) Leveraging Azure Monitor for real-time monitoring during failover testing
E) Implementing Azure Sentinel for automated threat detection during recovery testing

QUESTION 50

A company is facing application-specific issues in its Azure Virtual Desktop (AVD) environment, impacting user productivity. What strategies should they employ to effectively resolve these issues? Select THREE.

A) Utilizing Azure Advisor for identifying performance optimization opportunities
B) Implementing Microsoft Defender Antivirus for protecting against application vulnerabilities
C) Leveraging Azure Policy for enforcing application-specific configurations and security policies
D) Conducting application compatibility testing and remediation using MSIX App Attach
E) Azure Resource Manager (ARM) for deploying application updates and patches

PRACTICE TEST 3 - ANSWERS ONLY

QUESTION 1

Answer - C) AVD Planning Toolkit

Option A - Incorrect. Monitors performance but not specifically for AVD readiness.
Option B - Incorrect. Tests general internet speed, not specific to AVD.
Option C - Correct. Specifically designed tool for AVD network readiness assessment.
Option D - Incorrect. Provides broad Azure optimization recommendations.
Option E - Incorrect. FSLogix is for managing user profiles, not network testing.

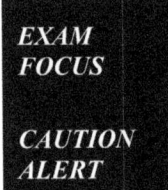

You should leverage the AVD Planning Toolkit for a detailed assessment of network readiness. It's specifically designed for AVD deployments, ensuring compliance and performance optimization. Avoid generic tools that don't account for AVD-specific traffic nuances.

Don't rely solely on tools like Azure Speed Test or FSLogix diagnostics—they don't address AVD-specific network readiness. Ensure all configurations meet regulatory requirements for handling sensitive patient data in healthcare environments.

QUESTION 2

Answer - A) {"type": "Microsoft.Network/networkWatcher", "properties": {}}

Option A - Correct. Specifically for deploying Network Watcher.
Option B - Incorrect. Deploys a virtual network, not for monitoring.
Option C - Incorrect. Manages traffic distribution, not network monitoring.
Option D - Incorrect. Deploys VMs, not related to network diagnostics.
Option E - Incorrect. Creates storage accounts, unrelated to network monitoring.

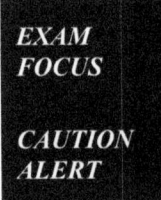

Use the Microsoft.Network/networkWatcher ARM template to deploy Network Watcher for AVD monitoring. This ensures visibility into traffic flow and enables diagnostics. Always prioritize tools tailored for network performance monitoring.

Avoid misusing templates like Microsoft.Compute/virtualMachines—these are unrelated to network diagnostics. Misconfigured templates may result in incomplete monitoring, leaving AVD traffic issues unresolved and causing performance degradation.

QUESTION 3

Answer - [B]

Option B - WVDAuditLogs: This table contains detailed logs related to user authentication attempts, making it essential for troubleshooting authentication issues. Option A - WVDConnections: This table provides information about user connections but not detailed authentication logs.

Option C - WVDServiceMetadata: This contains metadata about the Azure Virtual Desktop service rather than authentication logs. Option D - WVDAgentHealth: This deals with agent health status, not authentication.
Option E - WVDSecurityEvents: While it may contain security-related events, it typically does not focus specifically on authentication logs.

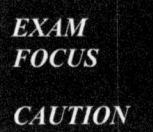

Always query the WVDAuditLogs table for detailed authentication logs in AVD. This is the go-to resource for troubleshooting user access issues. Eliminate tables like WVDConnections that focus on connection metrics instead of authentication.

Don't confuse WVDAgentHealth or WVDSecurityEvents with detailed authentication logs. These tables

| ALERT | serve different purposes and won't provide actionable insights for resolving authentication-related problems in AVD environments. |

QUESTION 4

Answer - A) Use Connection Monitor to test connectivity between AVD session hosts and client devices; C) Run IP flow verify to validate traffic flow and detect packet drops or routing issues

Option A - Correct. Using Connection Monitor helps test connectivity between AVD session hosts and client devices, aiding in diagnosing network connectivity issues. Option B - Incorrect. While NSG flow logs provide insights into network traffic, they may not directly diagnose connectivity problems within AVD deployments.

Option C - Correct. Running IP flow verify validates traffic flow and detects packet drops or routing issues, assisting in diagnosing network problems in AVD setups. Option D - Incorrect. VPN diagnostics are relevant for VPN connectivity issues but may not address network problems specific to AVD infrastructures. Option E - Incorrect. Monitoring ExpressRoute circuits focuses on bandwidth utilization and performance metrics, which may not directly help diagnose network connectivity issues within AVD deployments.

| EXAM FOCUS | Use Connection Monitor to test AVD host-client connectivity and IP Flow Verify to validate traffic flow. These tools pinpoint routing issues and blocked traffic. Always test across multiple paths to ensure comprehensive diagnostics. |
| CAUTION ALERT | Don't over-rely on NSG flow logs; they don't directly test connectivity between clients and AVD hosts. Misinterpreting VPN diagnostics as AVD-specific troubleshooting can lead to delayed resolution of network issues. |

QUESTION 5

Answer - D) Missing MFA setup

Option A - Incorrect: This command does not setup MFA.
Option B - Incorrect: The extension name is correct for enabling Azure AD login.
Option C - Incorrect: The publisher is correct for this type of extension.
Option D - Correct: This script does not include MFA setup, which is necessary for securing RDP connections.
Option E - Incorrect: The resource group name can vary and is correct as long as it exists.

| EXAM FOCUS | Ensure RDP connections are secured with Multi-Factor Authentication (MFA). Add MFA setup explicitly to the script as it's not included by default. Always verify resource group and extension compatibility with AVD requirements. |
| CAUTION ALERT | Don't assume Azure AD login alone secures RDP connections. Misconfigured MFA or missing setup steps can leave connections vulnerable. Avoid overlooking specific commands needed to integrate MFA with AVD environments. |

QUESTION 6

Answer - [A]

Option A - Azure Monitor Autoscale: This option allows you to automatically scale resources, such as session hosts, based on predefined metrics or schedules, meeting the specified requirements and minimizing manual intervention.
Option B - Azure Resource Manager templates: While templates enable you to deploy and manage Azure resources, they are not specifically designed for dynamically scaling resources based on demand.

Option C - Azure Functions: Functions are event-driven serverless compute, which is not specifically designed for scaling AVD session hosts based on demand. Option D - Azure Automation with Azure Runbooks: While Azure Automation can perform scheduled tasks, using Azure Monitor Autoscale is more suitable for dynamically scaling resources based on demand.

Option E - Azure Policy: Policies are used for enforcing rules and standards across resources but are not designed for managing resource scaling based on demand.

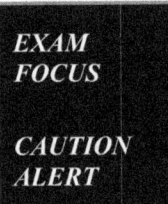

Use Azure Monitor Autoscale for dynamic scaling of session hosts. It meets business hour availability and minimizes manual intervention by automating scale operations based on predefined metrics. Schedule actions for cost efficiency.

Don't use tools like Azure Policy or Resource Manager templates for scaling—they lack automation capabilities tailored to dynamic resource scaling. Misconfigurations can result in resource wastage or under-provisioned host pools.

QUESTION 7

Answer - B) Windows Server is optimized for resource efficiency and can support a larger number of concurrent users with lower hardware requirements; C) Both OS options may require optimization and tuning to achieve optimal performance and scalability in AVD deployments; E) The choice between OS options may impact the allocation of virtual machine resources, including CPU, memory, and storage

Option B - Correct. Windows Server is optimized for resource efficiency and can handle a larger number of concurrent users with lower hardware requirements, making it more scalable for AVD deployments. Option C - Correct. Both OS options may require optimization and tuning to achieve optimal performance and scalability based on specific workload requirements and deployment configurations.

Option A - Incorrect. While Windows 10 Multi-Session may offer better performance for certain applications, it is not universally superior to Windows Server in all scenarios. Option D - Incorrect. Both Windows 10 Multi-Session and Windows Server can be suitable for deployments of various sizes, depending on factors such as user density, application requirements, and organizational preferences. Option E - Correct. The choice between OS options can impact resource allocation, including CPU, memory, and storage, which are critical for ensuring adequate performance and scalability in AVD deployments.

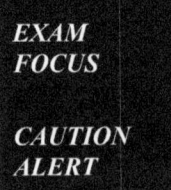

Windows Server is ideal for large-scale deployments due to its efficiency. Both OS options require tuning for optimal performance. Ensure CPU, memory, and storage are allocated appropriately to meet user and application demands.

Don't assume Windows 10 Multi-Session always outperforms Server OS. Avoid neglecting the resource implications of the chosen OS, as poor optimization can lead to bottlenecks and reduced scalability in AVD environments.

QUESTION 8

Answer - A) Role-Based Access Control (RBAC) and Least Privilege; B) Network Isolation and Micro-Segmentation; C) Data Encryption and Data Loss Prevention (DLP)

Option A - Correct. Role-Based Access Control (RBAC) and least privilege principles ensure that users have appropriate permissions within host pools, reducing the risk of unauthorized access and data breaches. Option B - Correct. Network isolation and micro-segmentation enhance security by restricting communication between session hosts and other network resources, limiting the attack surface and potential lateral movement of threats. Option C - Correct. Data encryption and data loss prevention (DLP) measures protect sensitive information within host pools, safeguarding against data breaches and unauthorized disclosure.

Option D - Incorrect. While identity and access management (IAM) are critical for security, they are broader considerations that encompass RBAC and least privilege, making option A more specific. Option E - Incorrect. Threat detection and intrusion prevention are important security measures but are not directly related to host pool design considerations in AVD deployments.

EXAM FOCUS	Implement RBAC with least privilege, network isolation, and data encryption to secure AVD host pools. These measures reduce unauthorized access, minimize attack surfaces, and protect sensitive data in compliance with regulations.
CAUTION ALERT	Don't overlook network isolation—it's critical for preventing lateral movement of threats. Avoid relying solely on IAM as it doesn't address host-level security intricacies like encryption or network segmentation in AVD setups.

QUESTION 9

Answer - [A, B]

Option A - Automatically shut down session hosts during off-peak hours: This ensures resources are scaled down during periods of low demand, meeting the requirement to minimize manual intervention and optimize resource utilization.
Option B - Automatically add session hosts based on CPU usage: Scaling based on CPU usage helps accommodate varying user loads and ensures optimal performance.

Option C - Automatically adjusting virtual machine sizes based on network bandwidth is not a typical use case for autoscaling in AVD environments and does not directly address the stated criteria.
Option D - Automatically archiving inactive user profiles is a management task unrelated to autoscaling session hosts.
Option E - Automatically allocating additional storage to session hosts is not a function typically performed by autoscale and does not address the specified criteria.

EXAM FOCUS	Configure autoscaling to shut down session hosts during off-peak hours and add hosts based on CPU usage. These actions dynamically balance costs and performance. Monitor metrics regularly to fine-tune scaling settings for optimal results.
CAUTION ALERT	Don't use autoscaling for non-resource tasks like archiving profiles or adjusting VM sizes based on bandwidth—it's not designed for these purposes. Misuse of scaling policies can disrupt availability during peak demand.

QUESTION 10

Answer - D) Remove rootSquashType for SMB

Option A - Correct: Updating the API version can ensure compatibility with the latest features.
Option B - Incorrect: 'SMB' is correct for Azure file shares in an AVD context.
Option C - Correct: Adding an RBAC role assignment is necessary for securing access with Azure AD.
Option D - Correct: 'rootSquashType' is not applicable for SMB protocol and should be removed.
Option F - Incorrect: Changes are needed to optimize security settings.

EXAM FOCUS	Remove rootSquashType when using the SMB protocol and add RBAC role assignments for securing Azure file shares. Update the API version to align with the latest Azure capabilities and ensure compatibility with AVD file-sharing requirements.
CAUTION ALERT	Don't configure SMB with irrelevant attributes like rootSquashType. Misconfigured ARM templates can lead to insecure access or non-functional file shares, compromising AVD performance and compliance standards.

QUESTION 11

Answer - A) Access to Advanced Security Features and Compliance Tools; C) Support for Resource-Intensive Applications and Workloads; D) Integration with Microsoft Defender for Endpoint and Endpoint Manager

Option A - Correct. Windows 10 Enterprise multi-session licenses (E3 or E5) provide access to advanced security features, such as Windows Defender Advanced Threat Protection (ATP) and Microsoft Information Protection, enhancing security and compliance within the AVD environment.

Option C - Correct. These licenses support resource-intensive applications and workloads, leveraging features like GPU acceleration and high-performance computing capabilities for optimal performance. Option D - Correct. Integration with Microsoft Defender for Endpoint and Microsoft Endpoint Manager allows administrators to enforce security policies, manage devices, and protect against threats across session hosts within the AVD deployment.

Option B - Incorrect. While Windows 10 Enterprise multi-session licenses enhance user experience with VDI, this aspect is not the primary focus when considering the impact of licensing on session host functionality. Option E - Incorrect. Compatibility with MSIX App Attach and profile containers is important for application management and user experience but is not directly tied to the licensing model of Windows 10 Enterprise multi-session.

EXAM FOCUS	*Always choose licensing options that offer advanced security features (e.g., Defender ATP) for compliance needs. Ensure licenses support resource-intensive workloads and integrate with Endpoint Manager for streamlined security management across session hosts.*
CAUTION ALERT	*Don't confuse application compatibility (e.g., MSIX App Attach) with license-specific features. Avoid overlooking the performance benefits of Windows 10 multi-session licenses in demanding environments.*

QUESTION 12

Answer - [B]

Option B - Azure Site Recovery: Azure Site Recovery provides disaster recovery as a service and supports replication and failover of AVD host pools to a secondary region, minimizing downtime and ensuring seamless user experience during failover.

Option A - Azure Storage replication replicates data between storage accounts but does not provide application-level failover capabilities for AVD host pools. Option C - Azure Backup is primarily used for data backup and recovery, not for failover and disaster recovery of AVD host pools. Option D - Azure Traffic Manager provides DNS-based traffic routing but does not directly support failover and disaster recovery for AVD host pools. Option E - Azure Front Door is a content delivery network (CDN) service and is not designed for failover and disaster recovery of AVD host pools.

EXAM FOCUS	*You should use Azure Site Recovery for failover of AVD host pools. It provides application-level replication and ensures minimal downtime, meeting business continuity needs effectively. Plan for regular disaster recovery drills to validate configurations.*
CAUTION ALERT	*Avoid relying on tools like Azure Backup or Traffic Manager for AVD disaster recovery—they don't offer application-level failover. Misconfigured failover settings may lead to extended downtime and user dissatisfaction.*

QUESTION 13

Answer - C) Encrypting Image Data at Rest and in Transit; D) Using Lightweight Base Images for Rapid Provisioning

Option A - Incorrect. While network segmentation enhances security, it does not directly impact the performance of AVD image lifecycle management. Option B - Incorrect. Leveraging cached images may improve deployment speed but does not inherently address the balance between performance and security in AVD image lifecycle management.

Option C - Correct. Encrypting image data at rest and in transit enhances security without significantly compromising performance, thus achieving a balance between the two aspects. Option D - Correct. Using lightweight base images reduces deployment time and resource usage while maintaining security, contributing to the balance between performance and security in AVD image lifecycle management.

Option E - Incorrect. Role-Based Access Control (RBAC) is essential for controlling access but is not directly related to achieving a balance between performance and security in AVD image lifecycle management.

EXAM FOCUS	Ensure AVD images are encrypted at rest and in transit for robust security. Using lightweight base images helps speed up deployment while maintaining compliance. Always balance speed and security to achieve optimal lifecycle management outcomes.
CAUTION ALERT	Don't skip encryption steps for image security—it's critical for compliance. Avoid using cached images without verifying compatibility and security standards, as they may compromise the balance between performance and security.

QUESTION 14

Answer - A) Installing Additional Applications; B) Configuring User Profiles and Permissions; C) Enabling FSLogix Profile Containers

Option A - Correct. During session host creation, administrators can install additional applications to meet user requirements and workload demands. Option B - Correct. Configuring user profiles and permissions ensures that users have appropriate access and settings on the session host.

Option C - Correct. Enabling FSLogix Profile Containers provides a solution for managing user profiles in non-persistent AVD environments, enhancing user experience and customization. Option D - Incorrect. Joining the session host to Active Directory typically occurs as a separate step after the initial creation process. Option E - Incorrect. Applying group policy settings for the desktop environment is a configuration task that may occur post-creation and is not specific to the creation process itself.

EXAM FOCUS	Customize session hosts during creation by installing necessary applications and enabling FSLogix for profile management. This ensures user requirements are met from the start, enhancing deployment efficiency and user satisfaction.
CAUTION ALERT	Don't assume group policy settings or Active Directory joins occur during initial session host creation—these steps often happen post-deployment. Avoid mismanaging profile configurations, as it impacts user experience significantly.

QUESTION 15

Answer - A) Correct setup

Option A - Correct: This command sets up a new image version correctly in the specified Compute Gallery.
Option B - Incorrect: The version syntax "1.0.0" is correctly formatted for Azure image versioning.
Option C - Incorrect: Including multiple locations is best practice, but not mandatory if the region meets the organization's requirements.
Option D - Incorrect: The managed image path is correctly formatted.
Option E - Incorrect: The command includes the necessary flags for creating an image version, additional flags are optional depending on further specifications.

EXAM FOCUS	Always preserve image versioning with the correct Azure CLI syntax for image lifecycle management. Use the Compute Gallery for structured image deployment across regions, ensuring consistency and availability. Include all mandatory parameters.
CAUTION ALERT	Don't neglect region redundancy in image configurations—it ensures resilience during outages. Avoid incomplete commands, as missing parameters like target regions can disrupt versioning and deployment workflows.

QUESTION 16

Answer - A) Configure Azure AD Conditional Access Policies; B) Enable MFA for User Sign-In to AVD Resources; C) Define Access Controls Based on User Roles and Locations

Option A - Correct. Configuring Azure AD Conditional Access Policies allows administrators to enforce access controls based on conditions such as device health or user location in AVD deployments. Option B - Correct. Enabling MFA for user sign-in adds an extra layer of security by requiring users to verify their identity using a second authentication factor in AVD environments.

Option C - Correct. Defining access controls based on user roles and locations ensures that only authorized users can access AVD resources, reducing the risk of unauthorized access. Option D - Incorrect. While integrating with Azure Security Center is valuable, it may not be a specific step for implementing MFA and conditional access for AVD deployments. Option E - Incorrect. While Azure Bastion provides secure remote access, it may not be directly related to implementing MFA and conditional access for AVD deployments.

EXAM FOCUS	*Configure Conditional Access policies and enable MFA for user authentication. Define role- and location-based access controls to enhance security while maintaining flexibility. Regularly review access policies for compliance and adaptability.*
CAUTION ALERT	*Don't rely on Azure Bastion or Security Center for MFA and Conditional Access setups—they serve different purposes. Overlooking policy reviews can lead to outdated or insecure configurations in AVD environments.*

QUESTION 17

Answer - A) Azure Monitor for Metrics Collection and Performance Analysis; D) Azure Log Analytics for Log Collection and Analysis; E) Azure Application Insights for Application Performance Monitoring

Option A - Correct. Azure Monitor allows for metrics collection and performance analysis, providing insights into the health and performance of AVD deployments. Option B - Incorrect. While Azure Policy is useful for resource governance, it may not be specifically designed for performance monitoring and tuning in AVD environments.

Option C - Incorrect. Azure Security Center focuses on threat detection and response, which is important for security but may not directly address performance monitoring and tuning. Option D - Correct. Azure Log Analytics enables log collection and analysis, allowing for deep insights into AVD performance and identifying areas for optimization. Option E - Correct. Azure Application Insights provides application performance monitoring capabilities, helping identify performance bottlenecks and optimizing application performance in AVD deployments.

EXAM FOCUS	*Use Azure Monitor for real-time metrics, Log Analytics for detailed insights, and Application Insights for application performance tuning. Together, they provide a comprehensive monitoring solution for optimizing AVD deployments.*
CAUTION ALERT	*Don't rely solely on Azure Policy or Security Center—they don't provide in-depth performance analytics. Misinterpreting general security recommendations as performance solutions may lead to inefficiencies in managing AVD environments.*

QUESTION 18

Answer - [D, E]

Option D - Configure Azure Update Management: This option automates the application of security patches and updates to all session hosts in the host pool, ensuring compliance with security requirements while minimizing administrative effort. Option E - Manually update each session host: Alternatively, manual updating ensures that security patches and updates are applied promptly, providing greater control over the update process.

Option A - Configuring a scaling plan is unrelated to applying security patches and updates and is used for dynamically adjusting the number of session hosts based on demand. Option B - Implementing diagnostic logging is used for monitoring and troubleshooting but does not involve applying security patches and updates. Option C - Enabling drain mode is used for gracefully removing session hosts from service but does not involve applying security patches and updates.

EXAM FOCUS	Automate updates with Azure Update Management to ensure all session hosts remain secure and compliant. Centralized management reduces manual effort and minimizes downtime. Enable reporting to verify successful patch applications.
CAUTION ALERT	Avoid manually updating each session host—it's time-consuming and prone to errors. Misconfiguring scaling plans or drain mode will not address patch management needs effectively, leaving hosts vulnerable.

QUESTION 19

Answer - A) Implement MSIX App Attach for dynamic application provisioning; B) Configure FSLogix for profile management and data synchronization

Option A - Correct. MSIX App Attach enables dynamic attachment of applications to user sessions, ensuring efficient application access and management in AVD environments. Option B - Correct. FSLogix provides profile management and data synchronization capabilities, optimizing user experiences and productivity in AVD deployments. Option C - Incorrect. Azure Bastion provides secure remote access but does not directly contribute to optimizing user experiences or productivity in AVD deployments.

EXAM FOCUS	Use MSIX App Attach for seamless app delivery and FSLogix for profile management to optimize the user experience. These tools streamline application access and ensure data synchronization across sessions, boosting productivity.
CAUTION ALERT	Don't rely on Azure Bastion for user experience optimizations—it focuses on secure remote access. Ignoring FSLogix configurations can lead to profile mismatches and data inconsistencies in multi-session environments.

QUESTION 20

Answer - A) Add logout policy settings

Option A - Correct: Adding logout policy settings directly in the JSON configuration ensures that automation scripts handle user sessions according to compliance requirements.

Option B - Incorrect: While role-based application management is important, it is already implied by the "dynamic" userType and needs specific integration not outlined here. Option C - Incorrect: Ensuring logging covers security audits is necessary, but the existing "detailed" logging setting may already suffice, depending on the organization's standards. Further specifics would be defined in the logging configuration. Option D - Incorrect: The JSON needs modification to include logout policies as the scenario specifies. Option E - Incorrect: Changing userType to static contradicts the requirement for dynamic application attachment based on user roles.

EXAM FOCUS	Add logout policies in JSON configurations to enforce session management and compliance. Dynamic user environments ensure role-based application delivery, while detailed logging supports audit requirements. Validate configurations before deployment.
CAUTION ALERT	Don't omit logout policies—they're essential for session management and compliance. Misconfiguring dynamic user environments or logging settings may result in untracked changes and policy violations in AVD deployments.

QUESTION 21

Answer - C

Option C - Port 3389 is the default port used for Remote Desktop Protocol (RDP) connections. Configuring firewall rules to allow traffic on port 3389 enables RDP connections to Azure Virtual Desktop instances securely.
Option A - Port 80 is typically used for unencrypted HTTP traffic and is not suitable for RDP connections.

Option B - Port 443 is used for HTTPS traffic and is not standard for RDP connections.
Option D - Port 8080 is often used for alternative web services but is not standard for RDP connections.
Option E - Port 8443 is sometimes used for secure web services but is not the default port for RDP connections.

EXAM FOCUS	*You should configure firewall rules to allow traffic on port 3389 for RDP connections in Azure Virtual Desktop. Always verify that the port is open and not blocked by upstream firewalls. Port 3389 ensures secure remote access to session hosts. Consider network isolation strategies to minimize exposure.*
CAUTION ALERT	*Don't confuse port 3389 for RDP with ports used for HTTPS (443) or web services (80, 8080). Avoid exposing RDP to public networks without additional security measures like IP restrictions or conditional access policies to prevent unauthorized access.*

QUESTION 22

Answer - C) Enforcement of multi-factor authentication (MFA) for user sign-in; D) Automatic encryption of data at rest and in transit within AVD environments; E) Integration with Microsoft Defender for Cloud for endpoint protection and vulnerability management

Option C - Correct. Entra services enforce multi-factor authentication (MFA) to enhance user sign-in security in AVD environments. Option D - Correct. Entra services automatically encrypt data at rest and in transit within AVD environments, ensuring data security. Option E - Correct. Entra services integrate with Microsoft Defender for Cloud to provide endpoint protection and vulnerability management for AVD deployments.

Option A - Incorrect. While Azure Sentinel offers advanced threat detection, it is not specifically related to Entra services for AVD security. Option B - Incorrect. Role-based access control (RBAC) is important for access management but is not specifically a security enhancement provided by Entra services.

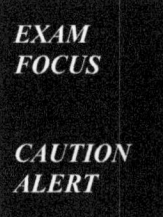

EXAM FOCUS	*You need to leverage Microsoft Entra services to enable MFA and integrate with Defender for Cloud for endpoint protection. Always enforce data encryption at rest and in transit to secure sensitive information. Entra's seamless integration strengthens AVD security posture while supporting compliance.*
CAUTION ALERT	*Don't assume Entra services automatically integrate with all Azure features like Sentinel. Avoid overlooking role-based access configurations, as they complement Entra but are not specific security enhancements provided by the service. Ensure clear implementation of Entra's features for effective threat protection.*

QUESTION 23

Answer - A) Implement Conditional Access policies with granular controls based on risk assessments; B) Define policies that allow for adaptive authentication based on user behavior and context; C) Utilize risk-based access policies to dynamically adjust security measures based on threat levels

Option A - Correct. Implementing Conditional Access policies with granular controls based on risk assessments allows for balancing security requirements with user experience. Option B - Correct. Defining policies that allow for adaptive authentication based on user behavior and context ensures a more seamless user experience while maintaining security.

Option C - Correct. Utilizing risk-based access policies enables dynamic adjustments to security measures based on changing threat levels, ensuring optimal security without overly impacting user productivity. Option D - Incorrect. While predefined access controls can minimize user disruptions, they may not necessarily balance security with user experience effectively. Option E - Incorrect. While session controls can enhance security, they are not specifically mentioned in the question as a method for balancing security with user experience.

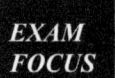

EXAM FOCUS	*Implement Conditional Access policies with granular, risk-based controls to balance security and usability. Adaptive authentication ensures seamless experiences while protecting critical resources. Always align policies with business risk assessments for effective user access management.*

| CAUTION ALERT | *Don't rely solely on predefined access controls—they may not accommodate dynamic risk scenarios. Avoid broad session control policies that overlook context such as device compliance and location. Overly strict settings can disrupt user productivity without enhancing security significantly.* |

QUESTION 24

Answer - A, B, C

A) Correct - Conditional access policies are essential for controlling who can access the virtual desktop based on compliance and risk assessment. B) Correct - Multi-factor authentication significantly increases security by adding an additional layer of user verification. C) Correct - Utilizing Azure Security Center helps in monitoring and protecting against threats in real-time. D) Incorrect - Restricting access based on geolocation might not be directly effective for securing AVD against breaches, as it is more about access management. E) Incorrect - While important, simply domain-joining all session hosts doesn't address specific security vulnerabilities in an Azure Virtual Desktop environment.

| EXAM FOCUS | *You should configure conditional access, enable MFA, and integrate Azure Security Center for comprehensive protection against breaches. Ensure a layered security approach to minimize risks and detect threats in real time. Each measure complements others to form a holistic security strategy for AVD deployments.* |
| CAUTION ALERT | *Avoid assuming geolocation restrictions alone can secure AVD. Don't rely on domain-joined hosts without implementing additional measures like MFA or role-based access control. Overlooking real-time monitoring tools like Azure Security Center can leave vulnerabilities undetected, risking breaches.* |

QUESTION 25

Answer - C) Set-MpPreference -ScanMaxCPULoadFactor 20

Option A - Incorrect: Incorrect setting name for CPU load factor.
Option B - Incorrect: Sets the CPU usage too high for performance optimization.
Option C - Correct: Correctly limits CPU usage during scans to 20%.
Option D - Incorrect: Command does not exist.
Option E - Incorrect: Incorrect command and parameter.

| EXAM FOCUS | *Use the Set-MpPreference -ScanMaxCPULoadFactor command to limit CPU usage during Defender scans. Always choose a load factor suitable for balancing performance and security (e.g., 20%). This setting ensures optimized resource allocation during heavy AVD workloads.* |
| CAUTION ALERT | *Don't confuse CPU load factor settings with unrelated parameters like REMScan or general configurations. Avoid setting load factors too high, as it could negatively impact AVD performance during simultaneous scans and user sessions. Misconfigurations can lead to degraded session responsiveness.* |

QUESTION 26

Answer - A) Define a maximum session duration for JIT access to AVD session hosts; B) Implement multi-factor authentication (MFA) for all JIT access requests; C) Configure access approval workflows with designated approvers for JIT access requests

Option A - Correct. Defining a maximum session duration helps limit the exposure of AVD session hosts to JIT access, reducing the risk of prolonged unauthorized access. Option B - Correct. Implementing MFA adds an extra layer of security to JIT access requests, enhancing authentication mechanisms.

Option C - Correct. Configuring access approval workflows with designated approvers ensures that JIT access requests are validated and authorized by authorized personnel. Option D - Incorrect. While logging and auditing are important for compliance and security monitoring, they are not specifically mentioned in the context of configuring JIT settings for optimal security as described in the question.

Option E - Incorrect. While restricting access to specific IP ranges or trusted networks is valuable, it is not directly related to configuring JIT settings for optimal security as described in the question.

EXAM FOCUS	*You should define maximum session duration, enable MFA, and implement approval workflows for JIT access. These measures ensure administrative access is strictly controlled and monitored. Use logging tools to track all activities for compliance and security analysis.*
CAUTION ALERT	*Don't forget to limit access to trusted IP ranges to further secure JIT access. Avoid lax JIT configurations without defined time limits or approvals, as this increases exposure to unauthorized access. Ensure all policies are audited regularly to maintain alignment with security goals.*

QUESTION 27

Answer - A, B, E

A) Correct - Azure Sentinel provides real-time threat detection through its SIEM capabilities, which is crucial during a cyber attack. B) Correct - Microsoft Defender for Identity focuses on securing identities, which is vital for endpoint security.
C) Incorrect - While geo-redundancy ensures resilience, it does not contribute directly to threat detection or endpoint security during an active attack. D) Incorrect - Azure Monitor is useful for performance monitoring but less effective for real-time cyber threat detection. E) Correct - EDR solutions are designed to detect and respond to endpoint threats, providing an essential layer of security during sophisticated attacks.

EXAM FOCUS	*Always integrate Azure Sentinel for real-time SIEM capabilities, deploy Defender for Identity for endpoint protection, and use EDR solutions to counter sophisticated attacks. These tools provide robust defense-in-depth strategies to detect, respond, and mitigate threats effectively in AVD environments.*
CAUTION ALERT	*Avoid assuming geo-redundancy alone secures AVD against attacks—it's a resilience feature, not a defensive strategy. Don't overlook integrating detection tools like Sentinel or EDR with active monitoring; without these, identifying real-time threats becomes challenging.*

QUESTION 28

Answer - A) Assign roles with only the permissions necessary to perform specific tasks; B) Limit administrative access to critical resources and functions

Option A - Correct. Assigning roles with only the permissions necessary to perform specific tasks ensures that users have the minimum privileges required to fulfill their job responsibilities, aligning with the least privilege principle and reducing the risk of unauthorized access. Option B - Correct. Limiting administrative access to critical resources and functions helps enforce the least privilege principle by restricting privileged access to only those who require it for their duties, minimizing the potential impact of security breaches or errors.

Option C - Incorrect. While regularly reviewing and updating role assignments is important for maintaining security, it is not directly related to the concept of least privilege in role assignment. Option D - Incorrect. While role hierarchies can help enforce access control policies, they do not inherently align with the least privilege principle, which focuses on minimizing privileges to the minimum necessary for tasks. Option E - Incorrect. While utilizing built-in Azure AD roles can provide standardized access control policies, it may not always align with the concept of least privilege, as these roles may grant broader permissions than necessary for specific tasks.

EXAM FOCUS	*Assign roles with only the minimum permissions needed for tasks to adhere to the least privilege principle. Limit administrative access strictly to critical resources. Regularly review role assignments to ensure alignment with organizational requirements while reducing the attack surface.*
CAUTION ALERT	*Avoid granting broader roles like Contributor unnecessarily—they can lead to privilege escalation risks. Don't rely on default role hierarchies without analyzing specific needs. Mismanaging role definitions increases the likelihood of unauthorized access to sensitive AVD resources.*

QUESTION 29

Answer - A) Implement MFA only for high-risk activities or privileged users; B) Offer alternative authentication methods, such as biometric or token-based authentication; C) Adjust MFA settings based on user feedback and usage patterns to minimize disruption

Option A - Correct. Implementing MFA only for high-risk activities or privileged users reduces the impact on regular user workflows while still enhancing security where it matters most. Option B - Correct. Offering alternative authentication methods allows users to choose the most convenient option while maintaining security through additional factors.

Option C - Correct. Adjusting MFA settings based on user feedback and usage patterns ensures that security measures are effective without causing unnecessary disruption to productivity. Option D - Incorrect. While providing temporary bypass options for MFA may be convenient, it can also introduce security risks and undermine the effectiveness of MFA. Option E - Incorrect. Enforcing MFA only during specific time windows or from certain locations may limit usability without providing significant security benefits.

EXAM FOCUS	*Offer biometric or token-based MFA options to enhance usability while maintaining security. Adaptive MFA policies based on risk levels ensure smoother workflows. Adjust settings based on feedback to align MFA with business operations without sacrificing user productivity.*
CAUTION ALERT	*Don't provide blanket MFA bypass options—they undermine the purpose of enhanced security. Avoid enforcing rigid MFA policies for low-risk scenarios, as they can frustrate users and lead to reduced compliance. Properly calibrate MFA triggers to balance security and user experience effectively.*

QUESTION 30

Answer - B) Enable Traffic Analytics

Option A - Incorrect: Basic configuration does not include machine learning analysis.
Option B - Correct: Enabling Traffic Analytics allows for the application of machine learning to network flow data.
Option C - Incorrect: The choice of storage account does not impact the ability to analyze data with machine learning.
Option D - Incorrect: Azure Sentinel integration is for SIEM, not directly for traffic analysis.
Option E - Incorrect: Changing the workspace does not enhance machine learning capabilities.

EXAM FOCUS	*Enable Traffic Analytics in Azure Network Watcher to apply machine learning for analyzing network flow anomalies. Traffic Analytics enhances security by detecting unusual patterns in AVD traffic and providing actionable insights. Always ensure logs are stored securely and analyzed regularly.*
CAUTION ALERT	*Don't assume enabling flow logs alone activates machine learning-based traffic analysis—Traffic Analytics must be explicitly configured. Avoid neglecting workspace integration, as it facilitates centralized analysis. Misconfigured analytics can lead to missed detection of critical security anomalies.*

QUESTION 31

Answer - A) Scalability of storage infrastructure to accommodate growing profile container sizes; B) Ability to distribute profile management tasks across multiple file servers or storage locations; D) Support for load balancing and high availability configurations for FSLogix components

Option A - Correct. Evaluating the scalability of storage infrastructure ensures that profile container sizes can accommodate growth without impacting performance. Option B - Correct. Distributing profile management tasks across multiple file servers or storage locations improves scalability and fault tolerance for FSLogix deployments. Option C - Incorrect. While user profile growth and logon/logoff activities affect performance, they may not directly relate to scalability considerations for FSLogix deployments.

Option D - Correct. Support for load balancing and high availability configurations ensures scalability and resilience for FSLogix components in large-scale AVD environments. Option E - Incorrect. While integration with Azure Monitor is valuable for performance monitoring, it may not directly address scalability considerations for FSLogix deployments.

EXAM FOCUS	*Always evaluate storage scalability for FSLogix, ensuring it can handle growing profile container sizes. Distribute profile management tasks across multiple storage locations to avoid bottlenecks. Load balancing and high availability configurations enhance fault tolerance and scalability in large AVD deployments.*
CAUTION ALERT	*Avoid relying on a single storage location for all profile containers, as it increases risks of performance degradation and downtime. Stay cautioned that user profile growth during peak logon times can impact FSLogix performance unless properly distributed.*

QUESTION 32

Answer - A) Integrate Profile Containers with Azure Blob Storage, C) Leverage Azure File Sync to synchronize Profile Containers across multiple locations, E) Utilize Azure NetApp Files for Profile Container storage.

A) Integrate Profile Containers with Azure Blob Storage - Azure Blob Storage provides scalable and cost-effective storage for Profile Containers, with redundancy and accessibility features. C) Leverage Azure File Sync to synchronize Profile Containers across multiple locations - Azure File Sync allows Profile Containers to be synchronized across multiple locations for redundancy and accessibility.

E) Utilize Azure NetApp Files for Profile Container storage - Azure NetApp Files offer high-performance storage solutions suitable for Profile Containers, ensuring optimal performance and scalability. B) Utilize OneDrive for Business as a storage solution for Profile Containers - While OneDrive for Business offers cloud storage, it may not be optimized for Profile Container storage and management. D) Implement Azure Backup for Profile Containers - Azure Backup provides data protection but may not be designed for real-time synchronization and access required for Profile Containers.

EXAM FOCUS	*You need to prioritize integration of Profile Containers with scalable solutions like Azure Blob Storage or Azure NetApp Files. Use Azure File Sync for redundancy and accessibility. These options optimize cost and ensure seamless scalability. Always assess performance impacts and backup strategies when choosing a storage solution.*
CAUTION ALERT	*Avoid using OneDrive for Business for Profile Container storage—it is not optimized for real-time access or scalability in AVD environments. Stay clear of relying solely on Azure Backup for live user profiles; backups are designed for recovery, not real-time access.*

QUESTION 33

Answer - A, B, E

A) Correct - Using Azure Monitor and Log Analytics enhances monitoring capabilities and supports compliance through detailed logs and performance metrics. B) Correct - The Standard tier of Azure Security Center offers enhanced security features including proactive threat detection.

C) Incorrect - While network segmentation is important, it does not specifically address monitoring or proactive threat detection. D) Incorrect - Azure Policy compliance standards are critical, but they are not focused on proactive threat detection. E) Correct - Azure Sentinel provides advanced SIEM capabilities, crucial for detecting threats and ensuring compliance in healthcare environments.

EXAM FOCUS	*Always integrate Azure Monitor and Log Analytics for detailed performance and compliance monitoring. Combine this with Azure Security Center Standard tier for proactive threat detection. Azure Sentinel adds advanced SIEM capabilities, ensuring thorough threat analysis and healthcare compliance.*
CAUTION ALERT	*Don't assume network segmentation alone can ensure monitoring or threat detection—it's a broader security practice. Stay cautious of omitting Sentinel or Security Center as they provide specialized compliance and monitoring capabilities essential for healthcare environments.*

QUESTION 34

Answer - A) Utilize Azure Monitor for real-time monitoring of AVD session host performance and resource utilization, B) Implement Azure Log Analytics to collect and analyze logs from AVD clients and session hosts for troubleshooting and performance optimization, C) Configure Azure Security Center to detect and remediate security threats targeting AVD clients and associated resources.

A) Utilize Azure Monitor for real-time monitoring of AVD session host performance and resource utilization - Azure Monitor provides insights into session host performance metrics, enabling proactive optimization and resource management for AVD deployments. B) Implement Azure Log Analytics to collect and analyze logs from AVD clients and session hosts for troubleshooting and performance optimization - Log Analytics centralizes log data for comprehensive analysis, facilitating efficient troubleshooting and performance tuning for AVD environments.

C) Configure Azure Security Center to detect and remediate security threats targeting AVD clients and associated resources - Security Center enhances threat detection and response capabilities, ensuring compliance with regulatory requirements and protecting AVD deployments from cyber threats. D) Leverage Azure Application Insights to track user interactions and application performance within AVD sessions for usability analysis - While Application Insights provides valuable insights, it may not directly address monitoring requirements specific to AVD client deployments. E) Use Azure Network Watcher to monitor network traffic between clients and AVD resources and identify connectivity issues - While Network Watcher monitors network traffic, it may not directly provide insights into client performance or security events within AVD sessions.

EXAM FOCUS	*Use Azure Monitor for real-time session performance tracking, Log Analytics for log analysis, and Security Center for enhanced threat detection. Together, these tools provide a comprehensive view of client activity, performance, and security compliance in AVD deployments.*
CAUTION ALERT	*Don't rely on Application Insights for client monitoring—it focuses on application performance rather than session-level metrics. Avoid neglecting Security Center's capabilities in detecting threats specifically targeting AVD environments; its absence can lead to overlooked vulnerabilities.*

QUESTION 35

Answer - C) Use Azure Automation to apply settings

Option A - Incorrect: Real-time scripting directly in the session host might not be feasible.
Option B - Incorrect: Manual adjustments are not scalable or efficient.
Option C - Correct: Azure Automation can be used to dynamically apply settings based on conditions such as network speed. Option D - Incorrect: Dynamic adjustments are supported using automation tools. Option E - Incorrect: Azure supports dynamic and conditional configurations using automation and monitoring tools.

EXAM FOCUS	*Implement dynamic multimedia redirection settings using Azure Automation. This approach allows configurations to adapt based on network conditions, enhancing user experience without compromising resource usage. Automation tools ensure scalability and consistency in applying settings across environments.*
CAUTION ALERT	*Avoid manual adjustments for dynamic conditions—they are neither scalable nor reliable for large deployments. Stay clear of scripting solutions that lack integration with Azure automation tools, as they may lead to inconsistent configurations and user disruptions.*

QUESTION 36

Answer - A, D, E

A) Correct - Azure Bastion provides secure and private access without exposing RDP connections to the public internet, crucial for securing patient data. B) Incorrect - Azure ExpressRoute provides dedicated connectivity but does not directly relate to HIPAA compliance or specific security of patient data in AVD setups.
C) Incorrect - Azure Health Data Services are specific to managing health data but do not directly impact AVD

configuration for security or compliance. D) Correct - Multi-Factor Authentication secures data access, which is a requirement under HIPAA for access control. E) Correct - Azure Private Link ensures that data exchanged between services remains on the private network, enhancing security and compliance.

EXAM FOCUS	*Deploy Azure Bastion for secure RDP connections without exposing public IPs. Use Multi-Factor Authentication to control access and Azure Private Link for secure data exchanges. Together, these measures ensure compliance and secure access in healthcare AVD environments.*
CAUTION ALERT	*Avoid assuming Azure ExpressRoute alone ensures compliance or data security—it only offers private connectivity. Don't rely on Azure Health Data Services unless specific to managing health records; for AVD, focus on securing access and transport layers through Bastion, MFA, and Private Link.*

QUESTION 37

Answer - A) Azure Network Watcher

Azure Network Watcher offers specific tools for network monitoring and troubleshooting, making it ideal for analyzing network latency and identifying potential bottlenecks affecting session stability.

Option B - Incorrect. While Azure Virtual Network provides network connectivity, Azure Network Watcher offers specific tools for network monitoring and troubleshooting. Option C - Incorrect. Azure Application Gateway optimizes app server load balancing and does not focus on network latency analysis. Option D - Incorrect. Azure Load Balancer distributes incoming network traffic and does not provide detailed network analysis. Option E - Incorrect. Azure Traffic Manager directs user traffic based on routing methods but does not analyze network latency.

EXAM FOCUS	*Use Azure Network Watcher to diagnose session timeout issues, focusing on network latency and bottlenecks. Its tools, like Connection Monitor and IP Flow Verify, provide actionable insights for resolving connectivity challenges in AVD environments.*
CAUTION ALERT	*Avoid confusing network-level issues with application or VM-level problems. Don't skip detailed latency analysis during peak hours; minor bottlenecks during high usage can significantly impact user experience. Stay alert to avoid ignoring upstream firewalls or misconfigured NSGs causing disconnections.*

QUESTION 38

Answer - C) Configuring Role-Based Access Control (RBAC) to restrict administrative privileges and access to VM resources

RBAC ensures that only authorized users have access to VM resources, mitigating risks associated with starting VMs upon user connection in sensitive environments. Option A - Incorrect. NSGs control traffic but do not directly manage VM access. Option B - Incorrect. JIT policies restrict access but do not specifically address VM startup. Option D - Incorrect. Azure Bastion provides secure access but does not manage VM access control. Option E - Incorrect. While Azure Security Center enhances security, RBAC directly controls access to VM resources.

EXAM FOCUS	*Always configure Role-Based Access Control (RBAC) to restrict administrative privileges in AVD environments. This ensures only authorized personnel can initiate or manage VM startups, mitigating security risks. Regularly review RBAC assignments for compliance with organizational policies.*
CAUTION ALERT	*Avoid relying solely on Network Security Groups or JIT policies for managing VM startup risks—while useful, they don't directly control administrative access. Stay clear of public IP exposure by implementing Bastion where secure remote access is needed. Overlooked RBAC configurations can lead to unauthorized resource management.*

QUESTION 39

Answer - A, D, E

A) Correct - Azure Bastion on a specific subnet provides a secure, private connection gateway that enhances confidentiality and security. B) Incorrect - VPN Gateway provides secure connectivity, but Azure Bastion is a more direct solution for VM access in this scenario. C) Incorrect - Azure Information Protection is crucial for data protection but not required for the secure access configuration of AVD.

D) Correct - Multi-Factor Authentication is essential for verifying user identities and securing access from various global locations. E) Correct - Conditional Access policies ensure compliance and secure access by adapting security requirements based on user location and device status.

EXAM FOCUS	Configure Azure Bastion for secure remote access, enable MFA for all users, and set Conditional Access policies tailored to user location and device compliance. These measures ensure confidentiality, secure access, and compliance for global operations.
CAUTION ALERT	Don't rely solely on Azure VPN Gateway for secure connections; Bastion is a more integrated solution for VM access. Avoid neglecting Conditional Access policies—they provide essential adaptive security tailored to global user scenarios. Ensure that MFA is universally enforced to mitigate unauthorized access risks.

QUESTION 40

Answer - C

Option A - Incorrect. The script incorrectly uses -ExcludeGroup which does not exist.
Option B - Incorrect. New-FSLogixAppMaskingRule is correct for creating a new rule.
Option C - Correct. The script should use -AssignedGroup to specify which groups the masking rule applies to, not -ExcludeGroup.
Option D - Incorrect. Although specifying a full path is best practice, it's not necessary if the executable name is unique.
Option E - Incorrect. Rules are enabled by default; -Enabled $true is unnecessary.

EXAM FOCUS	Use the -AssignedGroup parameter instead of -ExcludeGroup to correctly apply FSLogix masking rules. Specifying which groups can access certain apps ensures streamlined visibility for non-administrative staff. Verify script parameters to align with FSLogix rule configurations.
CAUTION ALERT	Avoid using unsupported parameters like -ExcludeGroup—misconfigurations can lead to rule failures. Stay cautious about not specifying the correct path to executables in the script. Misalignment between FSLogix configurations and role requirements can disrupt user access and application visibility.

QUESTION 41

Answer - C

Option A - Incorrect. The basic command does not provide enough detail for troubleshooting.
Option B - Incorrect. -SessionType is not a valid parameter for this cmdlet.
Option C - Correct. Adding -Detailed $true provides a comprehensive set of metrics, which is crucial for effective troubleshooting. Option D - Incorrect. Get-TeamsAVDStats does not exist as a valid PowerShell cmdlet.
Option E - Incorrect. Removing -Filter would broaden the scope too much, making it harder to pinpoint issues specific to Teams sessions.

EXAM FOCUS	Always remember to use PowerShell parameters like -Detailed $true for granular insights during Teams troubleshooting. Check for cmdlet updates to avoid using outdated or non-existent commands. Focus troubleshooting based on specific session types.
CAUTION ALERT	Stay cautioned not to use non-existent commands like Get-TeamsAVDStats, which will cause errors. Avoid broad queries without filtering as they may result in large, irrelevant data sets, complicating troubleshooting for Teams-specific connectivity.

QUESTION 42

Answer - A, B, E

A) Correct - Setting 'Encrypt' under FSLogix Profiles helps ensure that the profile containers are encrypted, enhancing data security. B) Correct - 'EncryptProfile' under ODFC settings ensures that Office data files are encrypted, adding an extra layer of security.

C) Incorrect - 'ProfileType' configures the type of FSLogix profile but does not pertain to security measures directly.
D) Incorrect - 'Hide' under FSLogix Apps is used to control application visibility, not to secure profile data.
E) Correct - 'PreventLoginWithFailure' ensures that users cannot log in if their profile cannot be loaded securely, which is a crucial security measure.

EXAM FOCUS	*You should enable profile and Office data encryption in FSLogix by setting Encrypt and EncryptProfile. Use PreventLoginWithFailure to enhance security by blocking logins if profiles cannot load securely. Regularly review registry changes for effectiveness.*
CAUTION ALERT	*Avoid neglecting encryption settings; they are critical for compliance and securing profile containers. Stay clear of misconfigurations like focusing on visibility settings (Hide) instead of security settings, which can lead to vulnerabilities in FSLogix profiles.*

QUESTION 43

Answer - D) Deploy AVD session hosts in proximity to user locations

Option A - Incorrect. While updating FSLogix profiles is important for user experience, it may not directly impact host pool performance or latency for users accessing AVD resources. Option B - Incorrect. QoS policies are important but may not be the primary method for minimizing latency caused by geographical distance.

Option C - Incorrect. Monitoring GPU utilization is important for graphics-intensive applications but may not directly address latency issues caused by geographical distance. Option D - Correct. Deploying AVD session hosts closer to user locations reduces latency and improves performance by minimizing the distance data needs to travel.

Option E - Incorrect. Increasing VM sizes may enhance performance but may not address latency issues caused by geographic distance between users and AVD resources.

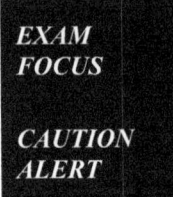

EXAM FOCUS	*Always deploy AVD session hosts geographically close to users to reduce latency and improve performance. Consider using Azure Traffic Manager for global load balancing to further optimize user experience.*
CAUTION ALERT	*Avoid assuming that increasing VM sizes or QoS policies will address geographical latency issues. Stay alert to the importance of proximity in host deployment to ensure minimal data travel distance and a smoother user experience.*

QUESTION 44

Answer - D) Azure Monitor Alerts

Option D - Azure Monitor Alerts allow you to create and manage alerts based on metrics, logs, and activity logs, enabling proactive management of AVD infrastructure by monitoring critical events and performance thresholds.

Option A - Azure Monitor Logs provide log data but not proactive alerting capabilities. Option B - Azure Policy is used for enforcing organizational standards and compliance, not for alerting. Option C - Azure Automation is used for automating tasks, not for alerting.

Option E - Azure Security Center focuses on security posture management and threat protection, not on AVD infrastructure monitoring.

EXAM FOCUS	You need to configure Azure Monitor Alerts for real-time notifications on critical events. Set thresholds thoughtfully to avoid excessive alerts. Use multiple channels (email, SMS) for timely responses to incidents in AVD deployments.
CAUTION ALERT	Stay cautious not to rely solely on logs without alert configurations; logs help in analysis but do not proactively notify administrators. Avoid overly sensitive thresholds as they can flood notifications and lead to alert fatigue.

QUESTION 45

Answer - A

A) Correct - VM2 (Windows 11 Enterprise) supports the latest desktop OS features necessary for a broad range of programming environments, and VM4 (Windows Server 2022) offers advanced server capabilities, rapid provisioning, and snapshot features essential for training labs.
B) Incorrect - VM1 does not offer the necessary capabilities for the required complex environments.
C) Incorrect - VM3 does not provide the same level of modern features as VM4, which limits its effectiveness in this scenario.
D) Incorrect - Including VM1 does not add significant value for the specified requirements.
E) Incorrect - While both VMs are strong, they lack the combined capabilities of VM2 and VM4 for handling complex software training environments efficiently.

EXAM FOCUS	Always prioritize OS compatibility with Azure Virtual Desktop features. Windows 11 Enterprise and Windows Server 2022 support advanced programming environments and modern capabilities suitable for training labs.
CAUTION ALERT	Avoid using outdated systems like Windows Server 2019 if newer versions like Server 2022 are available, as they may lack modern enhancements. Stay clear of Windows 10 Pro, which is not optimized for multi-user AVD setups.

QUESTION 46

Answer - E) Dynamic scaling with Azure Monitor

Option E - Dynamic scaling with Azure Monitor automatically adjusts AVD resource allocation based on real-time performance metrics, optimizing costs by scaling resources dynamically to meet user demands. It enables administrators to set thresholds and conditions for automatic resource adjustments, ensuring cost-effectiveness without sacrificing performance.

Option A - Manual scaling with Azure Logic Apps may require manual intervention and lacks real-time performance monitoring for automatic resource adjustments. Option B - Reserved capacity for AVD resources offers cost savings but does not provide dynamic scaling capabilities. Option C - Budget alerts In Azure Cost Management + Billing notify administrators of cost overruns but do not automatically adjust resource allocation. Option D - Scheduled scaling with Azure Automation requires predefined schedules and may not respond effectively to sudden changes in user demands, potentially leading to underutilization or overprovisioning of resources.

EXAM FOCUS	Implement dynamic scaling using Azure Monitor to optimize costs. Always configure thresholds to scale resources based on real-time demand while avoiding overprovisioning during idle periods. Use dashboards to monitor utilization.
CAUTION ALERT	Avoid relying on manual scaling; it is inefficient and prone to human error. Stay alert to over-provisioning with reserved capacity, as it can lead to unnecessary expenses. Scheduled scaling alone may not adapt to sudden user demand changes effectively.

QUESTION 47

Answer - A) Role-Based Access Control (RBAC)

Option A - Role-Based Access Control (RBAC) allows administrators to assign specific roles and permissions to users based on their responsibilities, ensuring least privilege access to AVD resources and reducing the risk of unauthorized access or data breaches.

Option B - Conditional Access policies enable conditional access based on user attributes and conditions but may not directly enforce least privilege access control for AVD resources. Option C - Group-based licensing simplifies license management but may not directly address access control for AVD resources. Option D - Azure AD Privileged Identity Management (PIM) focuses on managing elevated access but may not specifically enforce least privilege access control for AVD resources. Option E - Azure AD Identity Protection policies focus on detecting and mitigating identity-based risks but may not directly control access to AVD resources.

EXAM FOCUS	*Use Role-Based Access Control (RBAC) to enforce least privilege principles in AVD environments. Assign permissions based on role responsibilities to minimize risks and reduce unauthorized access to critical resources.*
CAUTION ALERT	*Avoid misconfiguring RBAC roles by over-assigning permissions. Stay cautious about granting overly broad access under group roles as it contradicts the least privilege principle and increases security risks.*

QUESTION 48

Answer - A, C, D

A) Correct - Windows 11 N can be a cost-effective option that meets the basic needs for educational applications.
B) Incorrect - Windows Server 2012 R2 is outdated and might not support the latest Azure Virtual Desktop features and security requirements. C) Correct - Windows 10 Enterprise multi-session offers cost efficiency by allowing multiple users to share the same virtual environment. D) Correct - Windows Server 2022 provides robust support and maintenance capabilities essential for a large educational institution. E) Incorrect - Windows 8.1 Enterprise is no longer a recommended option due to lack of support and compatibility with newer Azure Virtual Desktop features.

EXAM FOCUS	*Always select operating systems that balance cost efficiency, support for multi-user environments, and compatibility with Azure Virtual Desktop features. Windows 10 Enterprise multi-session and Server 2022 are ideal for scalable and secure remote learning setups.*
CAUTION ALERT	*Avoid using unsupported or outdated operating systems like Windows Server 2012 R2 or Windows 8.1 Enterprise, as they may fail to meet modern requirements. Stay clear of solutions without multi-user support when deploying session hosts for shared environments.*

QUESTION 49

Answer - A) Simulating failover scenarios in a non-production AVD environment
C) Documenting recovery procedures and conducting tabletop exercises

A) Simulating failover scenarios in a non-production AVD environment - Testing failover scenarios in a controlled environment ensures that recovery procedures are effective and minimize risks. C) Documenting recovery procedures and conducting tabletop exercises - Documentation and tabletop exercises help validate recovery procedures, identify gaps, and train personnel for effective response. B, D, E) While performance testing, Azure Monitor, and Azure Sentinel are valuable for AVD monitoring and testing, they are not specifically focused on testing and validating disaster recovery procedures.

EXAM FOCUS	*Always simulate failover scenarios in a non-production environment to validate disaster recovery strategies. Document recovery steps and conduct tabletop exercises to train staff and identify gaps in the process.*

| CAUTION ALERT | *Avoid skipping simulation tests or relying solely on documentation without real-world validation. Stay cautious about assuming DR procedures are effective without hands-on failover testing, which could lead to surprises during actual incidents.* |

QUESTION 50

Answer - C) Leveraging Azure Policy for enforcing application-specific configurations and security policies
D) Conducting application compatibility testing and remediation using MSIX App Attach
E) Azure Resource Manager (ARM) for deploying application updates and patches

C) Leveraging Azure Policy for enforcing application-specific configurations and security policies - Azure Policy helps enforce application-specific configurations and security policies, ensuring compliance and mitigating risks.

D) Conducting application compatibility testing and remediation using MSIX App Attach - MSIX App Attach enables organizations to test and remediate application compatibility issues, ensuring smooth operation in the AVD environment.

E) Azure Resource Manager (ARM) for deploying application updates and patches - ARM facilitates the deployment of application updates and patches, ensuring applications remain up-to-date and secure.

A, B) While Azure Advisor and Microsoft Defender Antivirus offer valuable insights and protection, they are not specifically focused on resolving application-specific issues in AVD.

| EXAM FOCUS | *Use MSIX App Attach to test application compatibility and enforce configurations with Azure Policy. Deploy updates and patches systematically with ARM to maintain application stability and productivity in AVD environments.* |
| CAUTION ALERT | *Avoid neglecting application-specific policies when troubleshooting issues in AVD environments. Stay cautious of skipping compatibility testing, as untested apps can lead to poor user experiences and productivity loss in session hosts.* |

PRACTICE TEST 4 - QUESTIONS ONLY

QUESTION 1

You are advising a multinational corporation on enhancing their AVD deployment's network resiliency and speed to improve user experience across global offices. Considerations include:
- Enhancing network reliability for consistent user experience.
- Reducing latency for real-time data processing.
- Implementing a solution that integrates smoothly with existing Azure services.

Which Azure feature would you recommend to enhance network reliability and speed in this scenario?

A) ExpressRoute
B) Azure Load Balancer
C) Azure Application Gateway
D) Content Delivery Network (CDN)
E) Virtual Network Peering

QUESTION 2

Managing a hybrid network for AVD involves addressing several challenges, particularly:
- Balancing load between on-premises and Azure resources.
- Ensuring seamless connectivity across different network segments.
- Troubleshooting connectivity issues promptly.

What tool or feature would you prioritize to manage and troubleshoot hybrid network connectivity efficiently?

A) Azure Site Recovery
B) Azure Load Balancer
C) Azure Application Gateway
D) Azure Network Watcher
E) Azure ExpressRoute

QUESTION 3

- Your task involves optimizing the performance of the Azure Virtual Desktop (AVD) service endpoints to enhance user experience.
- You need to identify the location of the service endpoints for optimization purposes.
- Your goal is to select the appropriate Log Analytics table to retrieve this information.

Which table in Log Analytics should you consult for this purpose?

A) WVDServiceLocation
B) WVDServiceHealth
C) WVDServiceMetadata
D) WVDSessionHostManagement
E) WVDSessionEvent

QUESTION 4

Your organization has implemented Azure Virtual Desktop (AVD) for remote access to applications and desktops. As part of routine maintenance, you need to generate reports on the network status and health of the AVD infrastructure. Which approach would you use to report on the network status and health in AVD environments?

A) Configure Azure Network Insights for automated network health reporting and alerts
B) Utilize Azure Monitor Workbooks to create custom dashboards for network performance monitoring
C) Export Azure Network Watcher diagnostic logs for analysis and visualization in Power BI

D) Schedule Azure Automation runbooks to collect network telemetry data and generate reports
E) Implement Azure Log Analytics queries to extract network-related metrics and trends

QUESTION 5

You are tasked with monitoring and maintaining the health of AVD host pools. Which ARM template configuration ensures that alerts are sent when usage reaches critical levels? Analyze the snippet below.

```json
{
 "type": "Microsoft.Insights/metricAlerts",
 "properties": {
 "criteria": {
 "metricName": "Percentage CPU",
 "threshold": 85,
 "timeAggregation": "Average",
 "operator": "GreaterThan"
 }
 }
}
```

A) Metric name is incorrect
B) Threshold value is too high
C) Correct alert setup
D) Missing action group
E) Time aggregation should be Total

QUESTION 6

You need to implement a cost-effective solution for managing session hosts in an Azure Virtual Desktop (AVD) environment to optimize resource utilization. The solution must meet the following requirements:
- Automatically scale session hosts based on user activity to optimize resource usage.
- Ensure that session hosts are available during peak usage hours.
- Minimize administrative overhead.
Which Azure service should you use?

A) Azure Monitor Autoscale
B) Azure Functions
C) Azure Automation with Azure Logic Apps
D) Azure Resource Manager templates
E) Azure Policy

QUESTION 7

Your organization is analyzing the licensing implications of different operating system options for Azure Virtual Desktop (AVD) deployments. As the Azure specialist, you need to recommend considerations for evaluating the licensing requirements. What factors should you highlight? Select THREE.

A) Windows 10 Multi-Session requires a Windows 10 Enterprise E3 or E5 license with Microsoft 365 E3 or E5 subscriptions for access
B) Windows Server licensing is based on the number of physical or virtual cores in the host server, with Client Access Licenses (CALs) required for each user or device accessing the server
C) Subscription-based licensing models may offer flexibility and scalability for AVD deployments, with monthly or annual payment options

D) License mobility rights may allow organizations to bring existing Windows Server licenses to Azure for AVD deployments, reducing licensing costs
E) Microsoft 365 Business Premium includes licensing for Windows 10 Multi-Session, making it a cost-effective option for AVD implementations

QUESTION 8

Your organization aims to integrate Azure Virtual Desktop (AVD) host pools seamlessly with existing IT infrastructure and workflows to ensure interoperability and efficiency. As the Azure specialist, you are tasked with identifying integration points and requirements. What aspects should you focus on? Select THREE.

A) Active Directory Integration and Group Policy Management
B) Single Sign-On (SSO) and Multi-Factor Authentication (MFA)
C) Application Compatibility and Legacy System Support
D) Monitoring and Performance Management
E) Data Migration and User Profile Management

QUESTION 9

You are configuring autoscale for host pools in an Azure Virtual Desktop (AVD) environment and need to define the scaling range. Consider the following factors:
- Current CPU utilization of session hosts.
- Number of active user sessions.
- Time of day and business hours.
- Available network bandwidth.
- Amount of available storage.
Which of these factors should be considered when defining the scaling range for autoscale? Select TWO.

A) Current CPU utilization of session hosts.
B) Number of active user sessions.
C) Time of day and business hours.
D) Available network bandwidth.
E) Amount of available storage.

QUESTION 10

You are implementing data replication strategies for Azure file shares used in AVD. Which configuration ensures data availability and disaster recovery? Evaluate this JSON snippet.

```json
{
 "type": "Microsoft.Storage/storageAccounts",
 "sku": { "name": "Standard_GRS" },
 "properties": { "accessTier": "Hot" }
}
```

A) SKU should be Standard_LRS
B) Access tier should be Cool
C) SKU and properties are configured correctly
D) Change access tier to Archive
E) Include additional redundancy options

QUESTION 11

Your organization is facing challenges with applying Windows Server licenses to session hosts in Azure Virtual Desktop (AVD). As the Azure administrator, you are responsible for troubleshooting license application issues. What are common troubleshooting steps to address these challenges? Select THREE.

A) Verify Subscription Entitlements and License Allotments
B) Review Event Logs and Diagnostic Data for Errors
C) Validate Network Connectivity to Microsoft License Servers
D) Check Session Host Configuration for License Compliance
E) Contact Microsoft Support for License Activation Assistance

QUESTION 12

You are planning a disaster recovery strategy for an Azure Virtual Desktop (AVD) infrastructure deployed across multiple Azure regions. Consider the following requirements:
- Ensure automatic failover of AVD host pools to a secondary region in case of a primary region outage.
- Minimize data loss and downtime during failover operations.
Which combination of Azure services should you implement to meet these requirements? Select TWO.

A) Azure Monitor
B) Azure Traffic Manager
C) Azure Site Recovery
D) Azure Load Balancer
E) Azure Backup

QUESTION 13

Your organization aims to automate updates and patches for Azure Virtual Desktop (AVD) images to streamline operations and ensure consistency across deployments. As the Azure specialist, you need to evaluate suitable approaches for automating image updates. Which of the following methods can be used to automate updates and patches for AVD images?

A) Azure Logic Apps Triggers
B) Azure Function App Webhooks
C) Azure Policy Compliance Checks
D) Azure Automation Update Management
E) Azure Resource Manager (ARM) Templates Deployment

QUESTION 14

Your organization aims to optimize the performance of session hosts in Azure Virtual Desktop (AVD) environments to deliver a responsive and efficient user experience. As the Azure specialist, you need to provide performance optimization tips for session hosts. What performance optimization tips should be implemented for session hosts in AVD environments? Select THREE.

A) Utilize Azure Premium SSD Storage for OS Disk
B) Configure Autoscaling Policies Based on User Demand
C) Enable GPU Acceleration for Graphics-Intensive Applications
D) Implement Network QoS Policies for Bandwidth Management
E) Optimize RDP Settings for Enhanced Connectivity

QUESTION 15

For compliance reasons, you need to configure your Compute Gallery to allow only specific users to manage images. Which PowerShell script should you use to set up Role-Based Access Control (RBAC) for the gallery?

```
New-AzRoleAssignment -ObjectId "userObjectID" -RoleDefinitionName "Contributor" -Scope "/subscriptions/subID/resourceGroups/MyResourceGroup/providers/Microsoft.Compute/galleries/MyGallery"
```

A) Correct RBAC configuration
B) RoleDefinitionName should be "Gallery Contributor"
C) ObjectId is missing
D) Scope parameter is incorrect
E) Command lacks necessary details

QUESTION 16

Data protection and encryption strategies are paramount for securing sensitive information in Azure Virtual Desktop (AVD) deployments, ensuring compliance and mitigating the risk of data breaches. As the Azure specialist, you need to recommend effective data protection and encryption strategies. What are the recommended data protection and encryption strategies for AVD deployments? Select THREE.

A) Utilize Azure Disk Encryption for VM Disk Encryption
B) Implement Azure Information Protection for Data Classification and Rights Management
C) Enable Azure Key Vault for Secure Key Management and Encryption
D) Use Azure Storage Service Encryption for Data-at-Rest Encryption
E) Implement Azure RMS for Rights Management and Document Protection

QUESTION 17

Your organization has deployed Azure Virtual Desktop (AVD) to provide remote access to applications for its employees. However, some users are experiencing performance issues, including slow application launch times and network latency. As the Azure specialist, you need to identify and resolve common performance bottlenecks to improve user experience. What are common performance bottlenecks in AVD deployments, and how can you address them? Select CORRECT answers that apply.

A) Insufficient Network Bandwidth - Implement QoS Policies and Network Optimization
B) High CPU Utilization on Host Machines - Configure Autoscaling Policies and Resource Allocation
C) Disk I/O Bottlenecks - Implement Azure Disk Storage Acceleration and Caching
D) Inadequate Memory Resources - Adjust Virtual Machine Sizes and Memory Allocation
E) Application Compatibility Issues - Utilize MSIX App Attach for Dynamic Application Delivery

QUESTION 18

You aim to optimize the performance of an Azure Virtual Desktop (AVD) environment by ensuring that all session hosts have the latest optimizations and enhancements applied. Considering the importance of performance optimization, what actions should you take to achieve this goal effectively?
- Apply consistent optimizations across all session hosts
- Streamline the optimization process for administrative efficiency
- Ensure minimal disruption to user sessions Select TWO.

A) Configure a scaling plan.
B) Implement diagnostic logging.
C) Enable drain mode.

D) Configure Azure Image Builder.
E) Manually optimize each session host.

QUESTION 19

Your role involves monitoring and maintaining an Azure Virtual Desktop (AVD) infrastructure to ensure optimal performance and user satisfaction. Critical aspects to monitor include session performance, resource utilization, and security compliance. How would you prioritize these aspects to proactively manage the AVD environment? Select TWO.

A) Monitor session performance using Azure Monitor
B) Analyze resource utilization with Azure Log Analytics
C) Implement Azure Security Center for security compliance monitoring

QUESTION 20

Automating AVD deployments often involves scripting for high availability and disaster recovery. You're using a Bicep script to deploy redundant AVD instances across multiple regions. The script must ensure instances are load-balanced, use managed identities for secure interactions, and automatically back up session data. Which Bicep resource should you focus on to implement cross-region redundancy?

```bicep
resource myResource 'Microsoft.Network/loadBalancers@2020-05-01'
```

A) Modify resource for cross-region redundancy
B) Add managed identities configuration
C) Implement automatic backup of session data
D) Resource is correctly configured for load balancing
E) Include diagnostics settings

QUESTION 21

You are configuring Azure Virtual Desktop to allow users to access resources on-premises via Remote Desktop Gateway (RD Gateway). In this configuration, which security measure should you implement to enhance authentication security? Select TWO.

A) Network Level Authentication (NLA)
B) Azure Multi-Factor Authentication (MFA)
C) Public Key Infrastructure (PKI)
D) Secure Sockets Layer (SSL)
E) Windows Hello for Business

QUESTION 22

Your organization is exploring options for integrating Microsoft Entra services with existing identity management frameworks in Azure Virtual Desktop (AVD) environments and requires guidance on best practices for seamless integration. The focus is on understanding how to integrate Entra services effectively with existing identity solutions to ensure compatibility and interoperability. What are the recommended best practices for integrating Microsoft Entra services with existing identity management frameworks in AVD environments? Select TWO.

A) Implementing Azure AD Connect for user synchronization and identity federation
B) Configuring trust relationships between on-premises Active Directory and Azure AD
C) Leveraging Azure AD Application Proxy for secure remote access to AVD resources
D) Enabling Azure AD conditional access policies to enforce security controls
E) Integrating Entra services with Azure Bastion for secure RDP access to AVD session hosts

QUESTION 23

Your organization is experiencing issues with the application of Conditional Access policies for Azure Virtual Desktop (AVD) connections, leading to access-related challenges. The focus is on troubleshooting and resolving these policy application issues effectively to ensure seamless access to AVD resources. What strategies can be employed to troubleshoot Conditional Access policy application issues in AVD environments? Select THREE.

A) Review Azure AD sign-in logs to identify policy-related errors or misconfigurations
B) Verify the scope and targeting of Conditional Access policies to ensure they cover all relevant users and scenarios
C) Check for conflicts between Conditional Access policies or with other access control mechanisms, such as network policies
D) Ensure that AVD resources are properly registered and integrated with Azure AD for policy enforcement
E) Test policy enforcement by simulating user access scenarios and analyzing the outcomes

QUESTION 24

You are tasked with ensuring high availability and disaster recovery readiness for an Azure Virtual Desktop implementation. Which actions should you prioritize? Select THREE.

A) Enable Azure Site Recovery.
B) Set up daily backups.
C) Configure redundant network connections.
D) Implement storage account failover.
E) Distribute host pools across availability zones.

QUESTION 25

In an effort to enhance security response, you need to configure Microsoft Defender Antivirus on AVD session hosts to automatically take action on detected threats. What is the correct PowerShell command to configure Defender to quarantine detected threats automatically?

```
A) Set-MpPreference -ThreatDefaultAction Quarantine
B) Set-MpPreference -ThreatDefaultAction Allow
C) Set-MpPreference -ThreatDefaultAction Block
D) Set-MpPreference -ThreatDefaultAction QuarantineAll
E) Set-MpPreference -RemediationScheduleDay Everyday
```

QUESTION 26

Your organization has deployed Azure Bastion for secure administrative access to Azure Virtual Desktop (AVD) session hosts and now wants to monitor and audit access via Azure Bastion. The focus is on understanding how to monitor and audit access activities effectively. How can access via Azure Bastion be monitored and audited effectively? Select THREE.

A) Enable Azure Bastion diagnostics logging and stream logs to Azure Monitor for analysis
B) Configure Azure Bastion session recording to capture all administrative activities on AVD session hosts
C) Implement Azure Security Center alerts for suspicious access patterns or anomalies via Azure Bastion
D) Enable RBAC role assignments for administrators to review access logs and audit trails in Azure Bastion
E) Integrate Azure Bastion with Azure Sentinel for centralized security incident detection and response

QUESTION 27

In preparation for a security audit of your AVD infrastructure, you need to demonstrate compliance with security best practices, facilitate effective incident response, and ensure data protection. What measures should you implement? Select THREE.

A) Set up Azure Policy compliance reports.

B) Enable logging and analytics with Azure Log Analytics.
C) Deploy Microsoft Defender for Cloud Apps.
D) Regularly perform vulnerability assessments.
E) Utilize data loss prevention (DLP) tools.

QUESTION 28

Your organization is tasked with auditing and maintaining role assignments in Azure Virtual Desktop (AVD) environments to ensure compliance with security policies and regulations. The focus is on understanding the best practices for auditing and maintaining role assignments. What are the best practices for auditing and maintaining role assignments in AVD environments? Select THREE.

A) Regularly review role assignments to ensure alignment with changing requirements
B) Utilize Azure Monitor to track changes and activities related to role assignments
C) Implement automated alerts for unauthorized role changes or assignments
D) Enforce separation of duties to prevent conflicts of interest in role assignments
E) Document role assignment policies and procedures for reference and accountability

QUESTION 29

Your organization has implemented Multi-Factor Authentication (MFA) for Azure Virtual Desktop (AVD) to enhance security. However, some users have encountered issues with MFA setup or lost access due to authentication failures. The focus is on MFA recovery options and procedures. What are the options for recovering from Multi-Factor Authentication issues in Azure Virtual Desktop environments? Select THREE.

A) Allow users to generate backup codes for MFA recovery in case of device loss or authentication failures
B) Provide self-service options for MFA reset or recovery through Azure AD self-service portal
C) Designate administrators or helpdesk personnel to assist users with MFA recovery processes
D) Implement temporary bypass options for MFA during recovery scenarios to restore access quickly
E) Enable Azure AD authentication methods for MFA recovery, such as email or SMS verification

QUESTION 30

As part of your responsibilities, you are to configure regular security assessments for AVD using Azure CLI to enhance proactive security measures. These assessments should include continuous monitoring and alerting configurations that adhere to industry standards for network security. Review the script below for setting up Azure Security Center monitoring and identify if it meets the requirements for comprehensive security assessments.

```bash
az security auto-provisioning-setting update --name "default" --auto-provision On
```

A) Correctly enables Security Center
B) Command should target VMs
C) Include specific AVD resources
D) Change setting to "Off"
E) Use another tool for assessments

QUESTION 31

Your organization is assessing the security implications of various FSLogix configurations for Azure Virtual Desktop (AVD) environments. The focus is on the security implications of FSLogix configurations. What security implications should be considered when configuring FSLogix for AVD environments? Select THREE.

A) Risk of data exposure and unauthorized access to user profiles stored in FSLogix containers

B) Impact of FSLogix configurations on compliance with data protection regulations and industry standards
C) Vulnerabilities in FSLogix components and potential exploitation by malicious actors
D) Compatibility of FSLogix with Azure security services such as Azure Defender for Cloud and Azure Security Center
E) Implementation of encryption and access controls for FSLogix profile containers and data

QUESTION 32

As an Azure Virtual Desktop administrator responsible for maintaining data security, you need to implement robust security measures for Profile Containers. Consider the following security best practices:
 - Restrict access to Profile Containers based on user roles and permissions.
 - Encrypt Profile Containers to protect sensitive user data from unauthorized access.
 - Regularly monitor access logs and audit trails to detect and respond to security incidents.
What are the security best practices for Profile Containers? Select THREE.

A) Enable encryption for Profile Containers using BitLocker.
B) Implement RBAC to restrict access to Profile Containers.
C) Use Azure AD conditional access policies to control access to Profile Containers.
D) Configure Profile Containers to auto-expire after a specified period.
E) Regularly audit Profile Container access and permissions.

QUESTION 33

To support remote educational staff using AVD, you need to ensure a responsive user experience, enable secure access, and maintain operational continuity. What measures are essential? Select THREE.

A) Configure Azure Application Gateway for web traffic management.
B) Deploy Azure VPN Gateway for secure remote connections.
C) Implement Azure Site Recovery across regions.
D) Utilize Azure ExpressRoute for dedicated connectivity.
E) Use Azure Traffic Manager for optimal routing.

QUESTION 34

Your organization is planning to deploy Azure Virtual Desktop (AVD) clients for remote users, requiring comprehensive documentation and training to facilitate user adoption and proficiency. Consider the following scenario:
 - The organization has users with varying levels of technical expertise, ranging from novice to advanced users.
 - Users require clear guidance on accessing AVD sessions, launching applications, and configuring settings based on their roles and responsibilities.
 - IT administrators aim to develop documentation and training materials that address the diverse needs of end-users and promote efficient usage of AVD clients.
What documentation and training strategies should you adopt for the given scenario? Select THREE.

A) Create role-based training modules tailored to different user roles and responsibilities, highlighting specific tasks and workflows in AVD sessions.
B) Develop interactive video tutorials demonstrating key features and functionalities of AVD clients, accessible through a centralized knowledge base.
C) Establish a user feedback mechanism to gather input on AVD client usage and identify areas for improvement in documentation and training materials.
D) Provide access to self-paced online courses covering AVD client deployment, configuration, and troubleshooting, with assessments to evaluate user proficiency.
E) Distribute user guides and cheat sheets outlining common tasks and troubleshooting steps for quick reference during AVD client usage.

QUESTION 35

During an audit of your Azure Virtual Desktop setup, you discover that multimedia redirection has led to unexpected bandwidth consumption. Identify the best practices for configuring redirection to optimize network usage without degrading the multimedia experience. What adjustments should be considered?
bash
Review current codec usage and adjust compression settings.
Implement QoS policies to prioritize essential traffic.

A) Increase codec compression
B) Remove multimedia redirection
C) Implement QoS for traffic management
D) No changes needed
E) Reduce session count per host

QUESTION 36

For an international corporation using AVD, there's a need to optimize for cross-continental data flows, ensure GDPR compliance, and secure sensitive corporate information. Which configurations should you employ? Select THREE.

A) Configure Azure Front Door for global load balancing.
B) Enable Azure Defender for cloud security posture management.
C) Use Azure Policy to ensure data sovereignty.
D) Implement Azure Private Link for inter-region connectivity.
E) Set up Azure ExpressRoute for reliable global connections.

QUESTION 37

You are designing session timeout configurations for Azure Virtual Desktop (AVD) users in a multinational corporation. Each geographical region has unique requirements for session duration based on local regulations. How can you ensure compliance with these regulations while maintaining optimal user productivity?

A) Implementing a policy to adjust session timeouts based on user roles
B) Configuring session duration policies using ARM templates
C) Enforcing Multi-Factor Authentication (MFA) for all AVD users
D) Deploying regional AVD host pools
E) Monitoring session activity using Azure Monitor

QUESTION 38

Understanding the impact on resource utilization and cost is crucial when configuring Start VM on Connect in Azure Virtual Desktop (AVD) environments. Consider the following scenario: Your organization aims to minimize costs while ensuring optimal user experience. What factor should you consider to achieve this balance effectively?

A) Implementing proactive monitoring and scaling strategies to adjust VM capacity based on user demand
B) Configuring session timeout policies to disconnect idle sessions and release VM resources promptly
C) Utilizing FSLogix profiles to provide persistent user settings and minimize VM startup times
D) Enforcing Multi-Factor Authentication (MFA) to enhance security and prevent unauthorized access to VMs
E) Integrating Azure Automation to automate routine tasks and optimize resource utilization across sessions

QUESTION 39

A software development company requires its AVD setup to support rapid scaling, provide robust security measures for intellectual property, and facilitate continuous integration and deployment processes. What should be implemented?

Select THREE.

A) Use Azure Scale Sets to automatically adjust VM capacity.
B) Configure Azure Bastion for secure access to development environments.
C) Apply Azure DevOps for CI/CD pipelines integration.
D) Create AzureBastionSubnet for deploying Azure Bastion.
E) Enable Azure Security Center for continuous security assessment.

QUESTION 40

You're finalizing the setup of application masking in your AVD environment and use the following script to create a rule for financial apps:

```
$FinancialApps = "Excel.exe, PowerBI.exe"
New-FSLogixAppMaskingRule -Name "FinanceApps" -FilePath $FinancialApps -AssignedUser
"AD\FinanceDept"
```

A) Split $FinancialApps = "Excel.exe, PowerBI.exe" into two separate rules.
B) Change -FilePath $FinancialApps to -FilePaths $FinancialApps to correct the parameter.
C) Ensure user "AD\FinanceDept" is correctly formatted.
D) Add -Enabled $true to activate the rule upon creation.
E) The script is correct as it stands.

QUESTION 41

Implementing Microsoft Teams on AVD requires configuring the WebRTC redirector service to ensure optimal media streaming. Which Azure CLI command correctly sets up the redirector service for Teams on AVD?

```
az avd teams config --name "WebRTCRedirector" --enable true --optimize-audio-video true
```

A) Command is correct as is.
B) Replace --enable true with --status active.
C) Add --resource-group myResourceGroup to specify the resource group.
D) Change --optimize-audio-video true to --optimize-media true.
E) Use az teams avd set --name "WebRTCRedirector" --enable true --optimize true.

QUESTION 42

For an organization focusing on rapid disaster recovery for AVD environments using FSLogix, which registry settings should be optimized to reduce recovery time and ensure data integrity? Select TWO.

```
A) HKLM\SOFTWARE\FSLogix\Profiles\BackupInterval
B) HKLM\SOFTWARE\FSLogix\Profiles\CloudCache
C) HKLM\SOFTWARE\FSLogix\Profiles\LocalCacheSize
D) HKLM\SOFTWARE\Policies\FSLogix\ODFC\CacheSize
E) HKLM\SOFTWARE\FSLogix\Profiles\RetrySync
```

QUESTION 43

You are troubleshooting intermittent access problems experienced by users in an Azure Virtual Desktop (AVD) host pool. Timely identification and resolution of these issues are critical to maintaining productivity. Which Azure CLI command can help you capture network packets for detailed analysis to diagnose the root cause of intermittent access problems effectively?

```
A) az network watcher test-connectivity
```

B) az network vnet list
C) az network watcher flow-log configure
D) az network watcher troubleshooting start
E) az network watcher packet-capture create

QUESTION 44

You are required to integrate Azure Monitor with other monitoring tools used within your organization to provide a centralized view of Azure Virtual Desktop (AVD) and other infrastructure components. When selecting the integration approach, consider:
1. The compatibility and interoperability of Azure Monitor data with other monitoring platforms and tools.
2. The real-time or batch processing requirements for integrating Azure Monitor telemetry data with external systems.
3. The security and compliance implications of sharing telemetry data across different monitoring platforms and environments.

Which approach offers seamless integration of Azure Monitor telemetry data with external monitoring tools for comprehensive AVD monitoring?

A) Utilize Azure Monitor Workbooks for data visualization.
B) Export Azure Monitor data to Azure Event Hubs.
C) Integrate Azure Monitor with Microsoft System Center Operations Manager (SCOM).
D) Use Azure Monitor Action Groups for alert notifications.
E) Enable Azure Monitor Application Insights for cross-platform monitoring.

QUESTION 45

Implement monitoring for storage usage and receive alerts when usage exceeds 80% of the quota. Provide an Azure Monitor ARM template snippet to create an alert rule.

```json
{"type": "Microsoft.Insights/metricAlerts", "properties": {"criteria": {"metricName": "Percentage Storage Used", "threshold": 80, "operator": "GreaterThan"}}}
```

A) Snippet is correct as is.
B) Add "evaluationFrequency": "PT5M", "windowSize": "PT1H" to the criteria.
C) Replace "operator": "GreaterThan" with "operator": "GreaterThanOrEqual".
D) Include "severity": 3, "actionGroups": ["storageAlerts"] in the properties.
E) Change "metricName": "Percentage Storage Used" to "metricName": "UsedCapacity".

QUESTION 46

Automation of scaling actions based on predefined rules can streamline resource management in Azure Virtual Desktop (AVD) environments. As an AVD administrator, you need to automate scaling actions to ensure efficient resource allocation and minimize manual intervention. Which tool enables administrators to automate scaling actions by defining thresholds and conditions?

A) Azure Logic Apps
B) Azure Automation
C) Azure Functions
D) Azure Policy
E) Azure Monitor

QUESTION 47

Regular security assessments and remediation are essential for identifying and mitigating vulnerabilities in Azure Virtual Desktop (AVD) environments. Which tool should be used for vulnerability assessments and remediation in AVD deployments?

A) Azure Defender
B) Azure Security Center
C) Azure Policy
D) Azure Monitor
E) Azure Sentinel

QUESTION 48

A healthcare provider is preparing to deploy Azure Virtual Desktop to handle sensitive data. The deployment must ensure data protection, compliance with health regulations, and efficient resource management. Which Windows operating systems are suitable for session hosts? Select THREE.

A) Windows 10 Pro
B) Windows Server 2019
C) Windows Server 2022
D) Windows 11 Enterprise
E) Windows Server 2016

QUESTION 49

An organization is managing backup solutions for its Azure Virtual Desktop (AVD) deployment to ensure data protection and recovery readiness. Which considerations should the organization prioritize when managing backup solutions for AVD? Select TWO.

A) Configuring Azure Backup for automatic VM backups and retention policies
B) Utilizing FSLogix for profile container backups and redirections
C) Implementing role-based access control (RBAC) for backup management permissions
D) Leveraging Azure Monitor for backup job monitoring and alerting
E) Integrating Azure Key Vault for secure storage of backup encryption keys

QUESTION 50

An organization wants to integrate application monitoring with overall management of its Azure Virtual Desktop (AVD) infrastructure. What approaches should they adopt to achieve this integration effectively? Select TWO.

A) Leveraging Azure Security Center for monitoring application security and compliance
B) Utilizing Azure DevOps for automating application deployment and monitoring
C) Implementing Azure Service Health for tracking application-related service incidents and outages
D) Integrating Azure Monitor with AVD for centralized monitoring of application performance and infrastructure health
E) Microsoft Endpoint Manager for managing application configurations and updates

PRACTICE TEST 4 - ANSWERS ONLY

QUESTION 1

Answer - A) ExpressRoute

Option A - Correct. Provides private, fast, and reliable connections to Azure services.
Option B - Incorrect. Balances internal and external traffic, not specifically for AVD.
Option C - Incorrect. Optimizes app server load balancing, not directly impacting AVD.
Option D - Incorrect. Improves global access to content, not AVD-specific.
Option E - Incorrect. Connects virtual networks, but not primarily for speed/resiliency enhancements in AVD contexts.

EXAM FOCUS	*You should prioritize private and dedicated connections using ExpressRoute for global AVD deployments. It ensures faster and more reliable network performance compared to internet-based options. Monitor bandwidth needs for future scalability.*
CAUTION ALERT	*Avoid relying solely on CDN or load balancers for AVD performance—they're not designed for internal network optimization. Stay clear of Virtual Network Peering unless your goal is inter-network communication, not latency reduction for AVD.*

QUESTION 2

Answer - D) Azure Network Watcher

Option A - Incorrect. Primarily for disaster recovery.
Option B - Incorrect. Balances load but doesn't troubleshoot connectivity.
Option C - Incorrect. Manages web traffic, not hybrid connectivity.
Option D - Correct. Provides tools for monitoring and troubleshooting network issues.
Option E - Incorrect. Provides dedicated connectivity, not troubleshooting.

EXAM FOCUS	*Always use Azure Network Watcher for hybrid connectivity troubleshooting. It offers tools like IP Flow Verify and Connection Troubleshoot, essential for diagnosing hybrid network issues. Ensure proper network topology mapping for efficient troubleshooting.*
CAUTION ALERT	*Don't confuse Azure Network Watcher with Azure Load Balancer. The latter balances traffic but does not diagnose connectivity. Avoid using tools designed solely for disaster recovery or app traffic, as they won't provide deep hybrid troubleshooting insights.*

QUESTION 3

Answer - [A]

Option A - WVDServiceLocation: This table contains information about the location of Azure Virtual Desktop service endpoints, crucial for optimizing service performance.
Option B - WVDServiceHealth: This focuses on overall service health rather than endpoint locations.
Option C - WVDServiceMetadata: This contains metadata about the service but not specific endpoint locations.
Option D - WVDSessionHostManagement: This deals with session host management rather than service endpoints.
Option E - WVDSessionEvent: This contains information about session events but not service endpoints.

EXAM FOCUS	*Keep in mind that WVDServiceLocation in Log Analytics provides endpoint location data for optimization. Using it helps ensure AVD endpoints are geographically optimized for your users' locations, enhancing performance.*
CAUTION ALERT	*Stay alert to common table missteps like choosing metadata or health tables instead of location-specific data. Misinterpreting endpoint data can lead to suboptimal configurations, resulting in unnecessary latency for your AVD deployment.*

QUESTION 4

Answer - B) Utilize Azure Monitor Workbooks to create custom dashboards for network performance monitoring

Option A - Incorrect. While Azure Network Insights may provide insights into network health, it is not specifically designed for reporting purposes in AVD environments. Option B - Correct. Azure Monitor Workbooks allow for the creation of custom dashboards tailored to monitor network performance and generate reports in AVD infrastructures.

Option C - Incorrect. While Azure Network Watcher diagnostic logs can be analyzed, exporting them for visualization in Power BI may not be the most efficient approach for network reporting in AVD setups. Option D - Incorrect. While Azure Automation runbooks can collect telemetry data, scheduling them for network reporting may not be the optimal solution compared to dedicated monitoring tools. Option E - Incorrect. While Log Analytics queries can extract network metrics, they may not provide the same level of customization and reporting capabilities as Azure Monitor Workbooks for AVD network monitoring.

EXAM FOCUS	*You should utilize Azure Monitor Workbooks for customizable dashboards tailored to AVD. These dashboards provide real-time insights and historical trends, helping administrators make informed decisions about network health and performance.*
CAUTION ALERT	*Avoid relying solely on exporting diagnostic logs to external tools for real-time monitoring. Stay cautious about overcomplicating setups with multiple tools when Workbooks can consolidate data into a single visualized source for network health insights.*

QUESTION 5

Answer - C) Correct alert setup

Option A - Incorrect: "Percentage CPU" is a valid metric for monitoring CPU usage.
Option B - Incorrect: A threshold of 85% is appropriate for critical level alerts.
Option C - Correct: This setup correctly configures an alert for high CPU usage.
Option D - Incorrect: The action group is not mandatory for alert configuration in the snippet context.
Option E - Incorrect: "Average" is the correct time aggregation for this metric.

EXAM FOCUS	*Always remember that Metric Alerts in ARM templates help you proactively monitor host pool health. Set thresholds like 85% CPU usage for optimal resource management. Test alert configurations regularly to ensure timely notifications.*
CAUTION ALERT	*Don't omit action groups if you require multi-recipient alerts or integrations with third-party systems. Avoid using improper time aggregation (e.g., Total instead of Average), as it might lead to inaccurate trigger conditions for alerts.*

QUESTION 6

Answer - [A]

Option A - Azure Monitor Autoscale: This option allows you to automatically scale resources, such as session hosts, based on predefined metrics or schedules, meeting the specified requirements and minimizing administrative overhead. Option B - Azure Functions: While Functions provide event-driven serverless compute, Azure Monitor Autoscale is more suitable for dynamically scaling resources based on demand.

Option C - Azure Automation with Azure Logic Apps: Logic Apps are used for automating workflows, but they are not specifically designed for managing resource scaling based on demand. Option D - Azure Resource Manager templates: While templates enable you to deploy and manage Azure resources, they are not specifically designed for dynamically scaling resources based on demand. Option E - Azure Policy: Policies are used for enforcing rules and standards across resources but are not designed for managing resource scaling based on demand.

| EXAM | *Make sure to configure Azure Monitor Autoscale for AVD session hosts. It dynamically adjusts resources* |

FOCUS	based on user activity, ensuring optimal utilization while keeping costs low. Always test autoscaling rules in a non-production environment.
CAUTION ALERT	Avoid manual scaling methods like Azure Logic Apps—they lack the automation and real-time responsiveness needed for fluctuating demand. Don't rely on scheduled scaling alone, as it may not adapt to unexpected changes in user activity during off-hours.

QUESTION 7

Answer - A) Windows 10 Multi-Session requires a Windows 10 Enterprise E3 or E5 license with Microsoft 365 E3 or E5 subscriptions for access; B) Windows Server licensing is based on the number of physical or virtual cores in the host server, with Client Access Licenses (CALs) required for each user or device accessing the server; D) License mobility rights may allow organizations to bring existing Windows Server licenses to Azure for AVD deployments, reducing licensing costs

Option A - Correct. Windows 10 Multi-Session requires Windows 10 Enterprise E3 or E5 licenses, along with Microsoft 365 E3 or E5 subscriptions for user access, impacting licensing costs for AVD deployments. Option B - Correct. Windows Server licensing is based on the number of cores in the host server, with additional CALs required for user or device access, which affects licensing expenses for AVD deployments. Option D - Correct. License mobility rights allow organizations to utilize existing Windows Server licenses in Azure for AVD deployments, potentially reducing licensing costs and simplifying compliance. Option C - Incorrect. While subscription-based models offer flexibility, they are not specific to the licensing requirements of Windows 10 Multi-Session or Windows Server for AVD deployments. Option E - Incorrect. While Microsoft 365 Business Premium includes licensing for Windows 10, it may not cover the specific requirements for Windows 10 Multi-Session in AVD deployments.

EXAM FOCUS	Always evaluate licensing for Windows 10 Multi-Session and Windows Server based on user requirements. Use license mobility rights for cost savings in existing environments. Highlight the need for Microsoft 365 E3/E5 for AVD deployments.
CAUTION ALERT	Stay cautious of overestimating subscription flexibility—it doesn't always apply to specific AVD configurations. Avoid assuming Microsoft 365 Business Premium covers all licensing needs, as it might not meet the requirements for multi-session AVD setups.

QUESTION 8

Answer - A) Active Directory Integration and Group Policy Management; B) Single Sign-On (SSO) and Multi-Factor Authentication (MFA); D) Monitoring and Performance Management

Option A - Correct. Active Directory integration and group policy management enable seamless user authentication and policy enforcement within AVD host pools, ensuring consistency with existing IT infrastructure. Option B - Correct. Single sign-on (SSO) and multi-factor authentication (MFA) enhance security and user experience by simplifying access to AVD resources while strengthening authentication mechanisms. Option D - Correct. Monitoring and performance management are essential for maintaining the health and efficiency of host pools, enabling proactive identification and resolution of issues. Option C - Incorrect. While application compatibility and legacy system support are important, they are primarily related to user environments and apps, rather than integration with existing IT infrastructure. Option E - Incorrect. Data migration and user profile management are relevant for user onboarding and migration but are not specific integration points for integrating AVD host pools with existing IT infrastructure.

EXAM FOCUS	You need to focus on Active Directory Integration, SSO, and Performance Management for seamless AVD host pool integration. These aspects ensure consistent policy enforcement, secure access, and reliable operation within existing IT workflows.
CAUTION ALERT	Don't confuse user environment settings (like data migration) with core integration points for IT infrastructure. Stay alert to legacy system dependencies that might disrupt integration if overlooked during planning.

QUESTION 9

Answer - [A, B]

Option A - Current CPU utilization of session hosts: Monitoring CPU utilization helps determine when to scale out (add session hosts) or scale in (remove session hosts) based on resource demand.

Option B - Number of active user sessions: Scaling should be adjusted based on the number of active user sessions to ensure that there are enough session hosts to handle user load. Option C - While the time of day and business hours may influence scaling decisions, they are not directly related to defining the scaling range for autoscale.
Option D - Available network bandwidth: Network bandwidth may impact user experience but is not directly related to defining the scaling range for autoscale. Option E - Amount of available storage: While storage availability is important, it does not directly affect the scaling range for autoscale.

EXAM FOCUS	*Consider CPU utilization and active user sessions as the primary metrics when defining autoscale ranges for host pools. These ensure optimal resource allocation while preventing over- or under-utilization in AVD environments.*
CAUTION ALERT	*Avoid assuming factors like storage availability or network bandwidth directly impact scaling rules—they influence performance but are not primary drivers for autoscale configurations. Don't overlook the importance of usage trends and business hours for fine-tuning scaling rules.*

QUESTION 10

Answer - C) SKU and properties are configured correctly

Option A - Incorrect: 'Standard_GRS' (Geo-redundant storage) is appropriate for disaster recovery.
Option B - Incorrect: The 'Hot' access tier is suitable for frequently accessed data.
Option C - Correct: This setup is appropriate for ensuring data availability and supporting disaster recovery.
Option D - Incorrect: 'Archive' is not suitable for frequently accessed AVD environments.
Option E - Incorrect: Geo-redundant storage already provides sufficient redundancy.

EXAM FOCUS	*Always configure Azure File Shares with Geo-Redundant Storage (GRS) for disaster recovery. Use the "Hot" access tier for frequently accessed data in AVD environments, ensuring both performance and redundancy without compromising cost-effectiveness.*
CAUTION ALERT	*Avoid using "Cool" or "Archive" tiers for frequently accessed AVD data—they are designed for infrequent access and may result in performance issues. Stay cautious about misconfiguring redundancy settings, as this can lead to data loss in disaster scenarios.*

QUESTION 11

Answer - A) Verify Subscription Entitlements and License Allotments; B) Review Event Logs and Diagnostic Data for Errors; C) Validate Network Connectivity to Microsoft License Servers

Option A - Correct. Verifying subscription entitlements and license allotments ensures that the organization has sufficient licenses available for assignment to session hosts within the AVD deployment. Option B - Correct. Reviewing event logs and diagnostic data helps identify specific errors or issues encountered during the license application process, aiding in targeted troubleshooting efforts. Option C - Correct. Validating network connectivity to Microsoft license servers ensures that session hosts can communicate with the licensing infrastructure for activation, addressing potential licensing-related network issues.

Option D - Incorrect. While checking session host configuration for license compliance is important, it is not a common troubleshooting step for license application issues, which typically involve verification of entitlements and communication with license servers. Option E - Incorrect. Contacting Microsoft Support is a last resort and typically unnecessary for routine license application troubleshooting, which can be resolved through internal IT processes and support resources.

EXAM FOCUS	Always verify license availability and network connectivity when troubleshooting licensing issues. Review logs for specific errors and ensure license server reachability. This can prevent delays in license activation and compliance risks.
CAUTION ALERT	Avoid assuming licenses are automatically applied—manually check configurations and compliance. Stay alert to network issues that may block server communication, and don't overlook the importance of diagnostic logs in identifying specific problems.

QUESTION 12

Answer - [B, C]

Option B - Azure Traffic Manager: Azure Traffic Manager enables DNS-based traffic routing to the closest available endpoint, facilitating automatic failover of AVD host pools to a secondary region in case of a primary region outage. Option C - Azure Site Recovery: Azure Site Recovery supports replication and failover of AVD host pools to a secondary region, minimizing data loss and downtime during failover operations.

Option A - Azure Monitor provides monitoring and analytics capabilities but does not directly support failover and disaster recovery for AVD host pools. Option D - Azure Load Balancer is a network load balancer and does not provide failover capabilities at the application level for AVD host pools. Option E - Azure Backup is primarily used for data backup and recovery and is not designed for failover and disaster recovery of AVD host pools.

EXAM FOCUS	Make sure to combine Azure Traffic Manager for routing and Azure Site Recovery for replication and failover. This ensures automatic failover with minimal data loss and downtime, meeting critical disaster recovery requirements.
CAUTION ALERT	Avoid relying solely on tools like Azure Backup or Load Balancer for disaster recovery—they are not designed for seamless failover of AVD environments. Stay cautious about latency during failover without Traffic Manager in place.

QUESTION 13

Answer - D) Azure Automation Update Management

Option A - Incorrect. Azure Logic Apps Triggers are event-driven workflows for integrating apps, data, and services, not specifically for automating updates and patches for AVD images. Option B - Incorrect. Azure Function App Webhooks allow for triggering serverless functions in response to events but are not tailored for automating updates and patches for AVD images. Option C - Incorrect. Azure Policy Compliance Checks ensure resources comply with organizational standards and requirements but do not directly automate updates and patches for AVD images. Option D - Correct. Azure Automation Update Management provides centralized control and automated patching capabilities for AVD images, ensuring they remain up-to-date with the latest updates and patches. Option E - Incorrect. While ARM templates enable infrastructure deployment and management, they are not specifically designed for automating updates and patches for AVD images.

EXAM FOCUS	Use Azure Automation Update Management to streamline patching and updates for AVD images. It ensures consistency and minimizes administrative overhead while keeping your environment compliant and up to date.
CAUTION ALERT	Don't confuse update management tasks with deployment tools like ARM templates—they are for infrastructure setup, not ongoing patching. Avoid relying on manual updates, which are time-consuming and error-prone in large-scale AVD environments.

QUESTION 14

Answer - A) Utilize Azure Premium SSD Storage for OS Disk; B) Configure Autoscaling Policies Based on User Demand; C) Enable GPU Acceleration for Graphics-Intensive Applications

Option A - Correct. Utilizing Azure Premium SSD storage for the OS disk can improve disk performance and reduce latency, enhancing overall session host performance. Option B - Correct. Configuring autoscaling policies allows session hosts to dynamically adjust resources based on user demand, optimizing resource utilization and performance. Option C - Correct. Enabling GPU acceleration is beneficial for running graphics-intensive applications on session hosts, providing improved performance for users. Option D - Incorrect. While network QoS policies can help manage bandwidth, they are not specific to optimizing performance on session hosts. Option E - Incorrect. While optimizing RDP settings can enhance connectivity, it may not directly impact session host performance.

EXAM FOCUS	*Optimize AVD performance by enabling GPU acceleration for graphics-heavy applications, using Premium SSDs for OS disks, and configuring autoscaling policies to adapt to changing user demands. These ensure responsive session hosts.*
CAUTION ALERT	*Avoid neglecting disk performance when dealing with heavy workloads—low-tier storage can bottleneck performance. Stay clear of generic settings for session hosts; tailor configurations like autoscaling and GPU to match specific workloads and user needs.*

QUESTION 15

Answer - A) Correct RBAC configuration

Option A - Correct: This PowerShell command correctly assigns the 'Contributor' role at the gallery level, allowing specified users to manage gallery resources. Option B - Incorrect: 'Contributor' is a valid role, assuming it covers the required permissions. "Gallery Contributor" might not be an actual role unless specifically created. Option C - Incorrect: 'ObjectId' is included and assumed correct. Option D - Incorrect: The scope parameter is correctly pointing to the specific Compute Gallery. Option E - Incorrect: The command includes all details necessary for setting RBAC.

EXAM FOCUS	*Ensure RBAC is configured with the appropriate role and scope using PowerShell. Validate roles like Contributor to grant the necessary permissions while maintaining security. Testing configurations after setup is crucial.*
CAUTION ALERT	*Don't assume all users need contributor access—grant permissions based on least privilege. Avoid using overly broad scopes in RBAC configurations; always assign roles at the smallest scope needed for the task, such as specific resource groups or galleries.*

QUESTION 16

Answer - A) Utilize Azure Disk Encryption for VM Disk Encryption; B) Implement Azure Information Protection for Data Classification and Rights Management; D) Use Azure Storage Service Encryption for Data-at-Rest Encryption

Option A - Correct. Utilizing Azure Disk Encryption ensures that VM disks are encrypted, protecting data at rest in AVD deployments. Option B - Correct. Implementing Azure Information Protection allows for data classification and rights management, ensuring that sensitive information is protected and accessed only by authorized users. Option C - Incorrect. While Azure Key Vault is important for secure key management, it may not be directly related to data protection and encryption strategies for AVD deployments. Option D - Correct. Using Azure Storage Service Encryption provides data-at-rest encryption for storage accounts, enhancing security for stored data in AVD environments. Option E - Incorrect. While Azure RMS offers rights management, it may not be specifically tailored for data protection and encryption in AVD deployments.

EXAM FOCUS	*Use a combination of Azure Disk Encryption, Storage Service Encryption, and Azure Information Protection for robust data protection strategies. These address compliance needs and mitigate risks of data breaches in AVD environments.*
CAUTION ALERT	*Avoid relying only on Azure Key Vault for encryption—it's for key management, not direct data encryption. Stay clear of misconfigured encryption policies, as they can expose sensitive data or fail to meet regulatory compliance requirements.*

QUESTION 17

Answer - A) Insufficient Network Bandwidth - Implement QoS Policies and Network Optimization; B) High CPU Utilization on Host Machines - Configure Autoscaling Policies and Resource Allocation; C) Disk I/O Bottlenecks - Implement Azure Disk Storage Acceleration and Caching; D) Inadequate Memory Resources - Adjust Virtual Machine Sizes and Memory Allocation

Option A - Correct. Insufficient network bandwidth can lead to performance issues in AVD deployments. Implementing Quality of Service (QoS) policies and network optimization measures can help prioritize traffic and improve performance. Option B - Correct. High CPU utilization on host machines can impact AVD performance. Configuring autoscaling policies and optimizing resource allocation can mitigate CPU bottlenecks and ensure smooth operation.

Option C - Correct. Disk I/O bottlenecks can slow down application performance. Implementing Azure Disk Storage Acceleration and caching techniques can enhance disk performance and reduce latency. Option D - Correct. Inadequate memory resources can affect AVD performance. Adjusting virtual machine sizes and memory allocation can address memory-related bottlenecks and improve performance. Option E - Incorrect. While application compatibility issues can impact performance, utilizing MSIX App Attach for dynamic application delivery may not directly address common performance bottlenecks such as network bandwidth, CPU utilization, disk I/O, and memory resources in AVD deployments.

EXAM FOCUS	*Address AVD performance bottlenecks by implementing QoS policies, autoscaling to handle CPU loads, and optimizing disk I/O with Azure Disk Storage Acceleration. Adjust VM sizes to resolve memory constraints and enhance user experiences.*
CAUTION ALERT	*Don't ignore network bandwidth limitations—lack of optimization can significantly impact user experience. Stay alert to signs of disk I/O bottlenecks, as these often go unnoticed until they cause severe performance issues during peak usage periods.*

QUESTION 18

Answer - [D, E]

Option D - Configure Azure Image Builder: This option allows you to create custom images for session hosts with pre-configured optimizations and enhancements, ensuring consistent performance across all session hosts with minimal administrative effort.

Option E - Manually optimize each session host: Alternatively, manual optimization ensures that specific optimizations and enhancements are applied to each session host, providing greater control over the optimization process.
Option A - Configuring a scaling plan is unrelated to optimizing performance and is used for dynamically adjusting the number of session hosts based on demand. Option B - Implementing diagnostic logging is used for monitoring and troubleshooting but does not involve performance optimization. Option C - Enabling drain mode is used for gracefully removing session hosts from service but does not involve performance optimization.

EXAM FOCUS	*You should use Azure Image Builder to create optimized session host images, ensuring consistent performance across your AVD environment. For targeted changes, manually optimizing session hosts is also effective but less scalable.*
CAUTION ALERT	*Avoid making optimizations directly on live session hosts during peak hours—it can disrupt user sessions. Stay cautious about skipping custom image updates, as inconsistent configurations can lead to degraded performance over time.*

QUESTION 19

Answer - A) Monitor session performance using Azure Monitor; B) Analyze resource utilization with Azure Log Analytics

Option A - Correct. Monitoring session performance with Azure Monitor helps identify and resolve performance issues, ensuring a seamless user experience in AVD deployments. Option B - Correct. Analyzing resource utilization with Azure

Log Analytics enables efficient resource allocation and capacity planning, optimizing AVD performance and cost-effectiveness. Option C - Incorrect. Azure Security Center focuses on security compliance monitoring but does not directly address performance monitoring in AVD deployments.

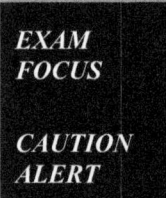	
EXAM FOCUS	Use Azure Monitor to track session performance and Log Analytics for resource utilization. These tools provide actionable insights to proactively address issues and ensure efficient operation of your AVD environment.
CAUTION ALERT	Avoid focusing solely on security monitoring when optimizing performance—ensure equal emphasis on session metrics and resource utilization. Don't confuse security compliance tasks with performance monitoring; they serve different purposes in AVD management.

QUESTION 20

Answer - A) Modify resource for cross-region redundancy

Option A - Correct: Modifying the resource to support cross-region redundancy is crucial for ensuring high availability and effective disaster recovery. Option B - Incorrect: While managed identities are critical for security, they are configured within identity management settings, not directly within the load balancer resource. Option C - Incorrect: Automatic backup of session data is vital but would typically be managed through a separate backup service or configuration, not within the load balancer. Option D - Incorrect: While the resource is configured for load balancing, it does not address the need for cross-region redundancy without modification. Option E - Incorrect: Diagnostics settings are important for monitoring and compliance but are an addition to the primary requirement of cross-region redundancy.

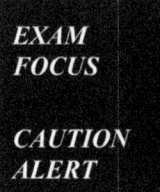	
EXAM FOCUS	Modify the Bicep script for cross-region redundancy by including region-specific load balancing configurations. This ensures high availability and disaster recovery in your AVD deployment, protecting against regional outages.
CAUTION ALERT	Don't overlook managed identity settings for secure operations—they are critical for compliance. Avoid assuming that diagnostics settings alone provide redundancy; they are supplementary for monitoring, not a substitute for proper load balancing and redundancy planning.

QUESTION 21

Answer - B,D

Option B - Implementing Azure Multi-Factor Authentication (MFA) adds an additional layer of security by requiring users to provide two or more forms of authentication before accessing resources via RD Gateway. This enhances authentication security and reduces the risk of unauthorized access. Option D - Secure Sockets Layer (SSL) provides encryption for data transmission but does not specifically address authentication security. However, SSL can be used to secure the communication between the RD Gateway and client devices, enhancing overall security.

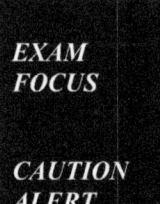	
EXAM FOCUS	You should implement Azure MFA to enhance authentication for RD Gateway by adding a second layer of user verification. Combine this with SSL for encrypted communication, ensuring a secure data exchange between endpoints. Avoid overcomplicating the setup by ensuring MFA policies cover only relevant RD Gateway connections to balance security with ease of use.
CAUTION ALERT	Stay alert when configuring SSL; it secures communication but does not inherently add authentication security. Avoid assuming SSL alone mitigates access risks. Always pair SSL with robust authentication mechanisms like MFA to ensure comprehensive protection for RD Gateway.

QUESTION 22

Answer - A) Implementing Azure AD Connect for user synchronization and identity federation; B) Configuring trust relationships between on-premises Active Directory and Azure AD

Option A - Correct. Implementing Azure AD Connect ensures user synchronization and identity federation between on-premises AD and Azure AD, facilitating seamless integration with Entra services. Option B - Correct. Configuring trust relationships between on-premises AD and Azure AD allows for secure authentication and access to AVD resources, ensuring compatibility with Entra services.

Option C - Incorrect. Azure AD Application Proxy is important for secure remote access but is not specifically related to integrating Entra services with existing identity frameworks. Option D - Incorrect. Azure AD conditional access policies enforce security controls but are not specifically related to integrating Entra services with existing identity solutions. Option E - Incorrect. While Azure Bastion provides secure RDP access, it is not directly related to integrating Entra services with existing identity management frameworks.

EXAM FOCUS	*Always remember to use Azure AD Connect for seamless user synchronization and identity federation between on-prem AD and Azure AD. This facilitates a smooth integration of Microsoft Entra services with existing identity frameworks. Configure trust relationships to ensure compatibility while avoiding unnecessary complexity in hybrid deployments.*
CAUTION ALERT	*Avoid relying solely on Azure AD Conditional Access or App Proxy for integration tasks. These features enhance security but don't replace core identity synchronization tools like Azure AD Connect. Ensure all trust configurations are well-documented and tested.*

QUESTION 23

Answer - A) Review Azure AD sign-in logs to identify policy-related errors or misconfigurations; B) Verify the scope and targeting of Conditional Access policies to ensure they cover all relevant users and scenarios; C) Check for conflicts between Conditional Access policies or with other access control mechanisms, such as network policies

Option A - Correct. Reviewing Azure AD sign-in logs helps identify policy-related errors or misconfigurations that may be causing access issues. Option B - Correct. Verifying the scope and targeting of Conditional Access policies ensures that they are applied to all relevant users and scenarios, addressing access-related challenges. Option C - Correct. Checking for conflicts between Conditional Access policies or with other access control mechanisms helps identify potential issues impacting policy enforcement and access. Option D - Incorrect. While ensuring proper registration and integration of AVD resources with Azure AD is important, it may not directly address Conditional Access policy application issues. Option E - Incorrect. While testing policy enforcement through simulated user access scenarios can be valuable, it may not specifically address troubleshooting policy application issues as described in the question.

EXAM FOCUS	*Keep in mind to review Azure AD sign-in logs for detailed error insights when troubleshooting Conditional Access policy issues. Verify the scope of policies to confirm they target all relevant users and avoid conflicts with existing access control mechanisms. Testing policy scenarios proactively ensures smooth implementation without unexpected disruptions.*
CAUTION ALERT	*Don't confuse Conditional Access policy conflicts with network-related access issues. Misconfigured network policies may mimic policy problems. Ensure policies don't overlap or contradict, as this can lead to unnecessary debugging complexities.*

QUESTION 24

Answer - A, C, E

A) Correct - Azure Site Recovery is crucial for disaster recovery, providing failover capabilities to another region.
B) Incorrect - While backups are important, they are not a direct measure for high availability and disaster recovery in terms of immediate failover capabilities. C) Correct - Redundant network connections ensure connectivity even if one line fails, essential for high availability. D) Incorrect - Storage account failover is useful but does not directly contribute to the availability of virtual desktops in disaster scenarios.
E) Correct - Distributing host pools across availability zones guards against data center failures, ensuring continuous availability.

EXAM	*You need to distribute host pools across availability zones for resilience against data center failures.*

FOCUS	Combine this with Azure Site Recovery to enable seamless failover to secondary regions during outages. Redundant network connections ensure uninterrupted access. Regularly test failover configurations to verify functionality.
CAUTION ALERT	Avoid assuming daily backups substitute for disaster recovery measures. Backups protect data but don't ensure immediate availability during disasters. Similarly, storage failover doesn't replace broader AVD availability configurations.

QUESTION 25

Answer - A) Set-MpPreference -ThreatDefaultAction Quarantine

Option A - Correct: Configures Defender to automatically quarantine detected threats.
Option B - Incorrect: Sets Defender to allow threats, which is unsafe.
Option C - Incorrect: Blocks threats but doesn't quarantine.
Option D - Incorrect: Command parameter does not exist.
Option E - Incorrect: Configures remediation schedule, not threat action.

EXAM FOCUS	Always remember to configure Defender Antivirus using Set-MpPreference -ThreatDefaultAction Quarantine to ensure threats are automatically quarantined. This action reduces manual intervention and enhances real-time threat response on AVD session hosts. Test configurations post-deployment to confirm functionality.
CAUTION ALERT	Stay cautioned about using incorrect parameters such as "Block" or "Allow," which can compromise threat management efficiency. Avoid skipping configuration reviews, as missteps can leave systems exposed.

QUESTION 26

Answer - A) Enable Azure Bastion diagnostics logging and stream logs to Azure Monitor for analysis; B) Configure Azure Bastion session recording to capture all administrative activities on AVD session hosts; C) Implement Azure Security Center alerts for suspicious access patterns or anomalies via Azure Bastion

Option A - Correct. Enabling Azure Bastion diagnostics logging and streaming logs to Azure Monitor allows for analysis of access activities and security events. Option B - Correct. Configuring Azure Bastion session recording captures all administrative activities on AVD session hosts for auditing and compliance purposes. Option C - Correct. Implementing Azure Security Center alerts enables proactive monitoring for suspicious access patterns or anomalies via Azure Bastion, enhancing security posture.

Option D - Incorrect. While RBAC role assignments are important for access control, they are not specifically mentioned in the context of monitoring and auditing access via Azure Bastion as described in the question. Option E - Incorrect. While integrating with Azure Sentinel is valuable for centralized security incident detection and response, it is not directly related to monitoring and auditing access via Azure Bastion as described in the question.

EXAM FOCUS	You should enable Azure Bastion diagnostics logging and integrate with Azure Monitor for real-time insights. Configure session recording to audit administrative activities. Use Azure Security Center to monitor anomalies proactively, ensuring compliance and enhancing security response.
CAUTION ALERT	Avoid relying solely on Azure Sentinel integration without Bastion-specific diagnostics. Sentinel is valuable for broader incident response but doesn't replace targeted monitoring directly within Bastion environments.

QUESTION 27

Answer - A, B, D

A) Correct - Azure Policy compliance reports are crucial for demonstrating adherence to security best practices during audits. B) Correct - Enabling logging and analytics facilitates effective incident response by providing detailed insight into security events. C) Incorrect - Microsoft Defender for Cloud Apps is useful for app-level security but is not specifically targeted at incident response or compliance reporting. D) Correct - Regular vulnerability assessments are vital for identifying and mitigating risks, essential for security audits. E) Incorrect - While DLP is important for data protection, it does not directly contribute to the audit requirements mentioned.

EXAM FOCUS	*Make sure to regularly perform vulnerability assessments as part of your security audit preparations. Use Azure Policy compliance reports to demonstrate adherence to best practices and Azure Log Analytics for incident response visibility. This comprehensive approach simplifies audits and strengthens your security posture.*
CAUTION ALERT	*Don't overlook the importance of maintaining up-to-date vulnerability assessments. Relying solely on DLP tools or app-specific defenses can leave broader infrastructure gaps, impacting audit readiness.*

QUESTION 28

Answer - A) Regularly review role assignments to ensure alignment with changing requirements; B) Utilize Azure Monitor to track changes and activities related to role assignments; C) Implement automated alerts for unauthorized role changes or assignments

Option A - Correct. Regularly reviewing role assignments ensures that they remain aligned with changing organizational requirements and security policies, helping maintain compliance and security. Option B - Correct. Utilizing Azure Monitor allows organizations to track changes and activities related to role assignments, enabling proactive identification of potential security issues or unauthorized changes. Option C - Correct. Implementing automated alerts for unauthorized role changes or assignments helps organizations quickly detect and respond to security incidents, reducing the risk of unauthorized access or data breaches. Option D - Incorrect. While enforcing separation of duties is important for security, it is not directly related to auditing and maintaining role assignments. Option E - Incorrect. While documenting role assignment policies and procedures is important for reference and accountability, it is not directly related to auditing and maintaining role assignments.

EXAM FOCUS	*Always remember to regularly review role assignments and implement Azure Monitor to track changes for proactive oversight. Use automated alerts to identify unauthorized modifications immediately. Maintaining alignment with organizational needs ensures compliance and prevents privilege escalation risks.*
CAUTION ALERT	*Avoid neglecting role reviews or relying exclusively on separation of duties without activity tracking. Overlooking unauthorized changes can result in security breaches and compliance violations.*

QUESTION 29

Answer - A) Allow users to generate backup codes for MFA recovery in case of device loss or authentication failures; B) Provide self-service options for MFA reset or recovery through Azure AD self-service portal; C) Designate administrators or helpdesk personnel to assist users with MFA recovery processes

Option A - Correct. Allowing users to generate backup codes for MFA recovery provides a reliable method for regaining access in case of device loss or authentication failures. Option B - Correct. Providing self-service options for MFA reset or recovery through the Azure AD self-service portal empowers users to resolve authentication issues independently. Option C - Correct. Designating administrators or helpdesk personnel to assist users with MFA recovery processes ensures that users receive prompt assistance and guidance when needed. Option D - Incorrect. While implementing temporary bypass options for MFA during recovery scenarios may restore access quickly, it can also introduce security risks and undermine the effectiveness of MFA. Option E - Incorrect. While enabling Azure AD authentication methods for MFA recovery can be convenient, it may not provide sufficient security for sensitive access recovery scenarios.

EXAM FOCUS	*Keep in mind to enable backup codes for MFA recovery to mitigate risks from device loss or authentication failures. Provide users with self-service recovery options through the Azure AD portal to reduce downtime. Designate support staff for prompt assistance in more complex cases.*

| CAUTION ALERT | Don't confuse temporary MFA bypass options as secure recovery measures. While convenient, they introduce risks that undermine MFA's purpose. Always prioritize secure, user-friendly recovery processes. |

QUESTION 30

Answer - A) Correctly enables Security Center

Option A - Correct: This command enables Azure Security Center, providing continuous security assessments.
Option B - Incorrect: Targeting VMs is managed within Security Center policies.
Option C - Incorrect: Auto-provisioning applies generally and does not require specific resources to be named.
Option D - Incorrect: Turning it "Off" would disable the security monitoring.
Option E - Incorrect: Azure Security Center is suitable for this purpose.

| EXAM FOCUS | Make sure to use Azure Security Center's auto-provisioning feature to enable comprehensive security monitoring. It simplifies compliance with industry standards by automating assessments and ensuring continuous oversight of your AVD environment. |
| CAUTION ALERT | Avoid disabling or skipping the auto-provisioning setup. Failing to enable it can leave significant security gaps, undermining your proactive monitoring efforts. |

QUESTION 31

Answer - A) Risk of data exposure and unauthorized access to user profiles stored in FSLogix containers; B) Impact of FSLogix configurations on compliance with data protection regulations and industry standards; C) Vulnerabilities in FSLogix components and potential exploitation by malicious actors

Option A - Correct. Assessing the risk of data exposure and unauthorized access to user profiles stored in FSLogix containers is crucial for maintaining data security. Option B - Correct. Understanding the impact of FSLogix configurations on compliance with data protection regulations ensures regulatory compliance and data privacy. Option C - Correct. Identifying vulnerabilities in FSLogix components and potential exploitation by malicious actors is essential for mitigating security risks and ensuring system integrity. Option D - Incorrect. While compatibility with Azure security services is important, it may not directly relate to the security implications of FSLogix configurations. Option E - Incorrect. While encryption and access controls are important security measures, they may not cover all security implications of FSLogix configurations.

| EXAM FOCUS | You should prioritize encrypting FSLogix profile containers and limit access through role-based permissions. Monitor configurations against compliance requirements and assess potential vulnerabilities. This approach protects user data, ensures regulatory alignment, and secures FSLogix from unauthorized modifications. |
| CAUTION ALERT | Avoid assuming FSLogix profiles are inherently secure. Without encryption and robust access control, sensitive user data may be exposed. Regularly update FSLogix configurations to mitigate risks from exploitation or compatibility gaps. |

QUESTION 32

Answer - B) Implement RBAC to restrict access to Profile Containers, C) Use Azure AD conditional access policies to control access to Profile Containers, E) Regularly audit Profile Container access and permissions.

B) Implement RBAC to restrict access to Profile Containers - Role-Based Access Control (RBAC) ensures that only authorized users have access to Profile Containers based on their assigned roles and permissions. C) Use Azure AD conditional access policies to control access to Profile Containers - Conditional access policies allow administrators to enforce access controls based on specific conditions, enhancing security for Profile Containers. E) Regularly audit Profile Container access and permissions - Auditing access logs and permissions helps identify unauthorized access attempts and ensure compliance with security policies. A) Enable encryption for Profile Containers using BitLocker - BitLocker encryption may not be suitable for Profile Containers as it encrypts entire volumes rather than specific user data. D) Configure Profile Containers to auto-expire after a specified period - Auto-expiration may disrupt user workflows and is not a common security practice for Profile Containers.

EXAM FOCUS	Always remember to use RBAC for Profile Containers to enforce access control based on roles. Combine this with conditional access policies to enhance security and audit access logs regularly to detect anomalies. A layered approach ensures comprehensive protection for sensitive user data.
CAUTION ALERT	Don't confuse BitLocker encryption with Profile Container encryption needs. BitLocker encrypts the disk, not specific profile data. Use dedicated FSLogix encryption methods for granular and effective security of user profiles.

QUESTION 33

Answer - B, D, E

A) Incorrect - Azure Application Gateway manages web traffic but does not directly enhance responsiveness or secure access for AVD. B) Correct - Azure VPN Gateway ensures secure and private connections for remote users, crucial for security. C) Incorrect - Site Recovery is essential for continuity but not directly for user experience or secure access. D) Correct - ExpressRoute provides dedicated connectivity, reducing latency and improving the responsiveness of the AVD environment. E) Correct - Azure Traffic Manager improves responsiveness by routing users to the nearest or most responsive AVD host pool.

EXAM FOCUS	Make sure to use Azure VPN Gateway for secure user access, ExpressRoute for low-latency dedicated connections, and Traffic Manager for optimal user routing. This combination supports seamless connectivity, robust security, and efficient resource allocation for remote educational staff.
CAUTION ALERT	Avoid relying solely on application-level solutions like Azure Application Gateway for AVD responsiveness. These tools do not directly address secure access or connection reliability essential for remote user experience.

QUESTION 34

Answer - A) Create role-based training modules tailored to different user roles and responsibilities, B) Develop interactive video tutorials demonstrating key features and functionalities of AVD clients, E) Distribute user guides and cheat sheets outlining common tasks and troubleshooting steps for quick reference during AVD client usage.

A) Create role-based training modules tailored to different user roles and responsibilities - Role-based training modules cater to the diverse needs of users, providing targeted guidance on AVD client usage based on their roles and responsibilities within the organization. B) Develop interactive video tutorials demonstrating key features and functionalities of AVD clients - Interactive video tutorials offer engaging learning experiences, helping users grasp complex concepts and functionalities of AVD clients effectively.

E) Distribute user guides and cheat sheets outlining common tasks and troubleshooting steps for quick reference during AVD client usage - User guides and cheat sheets serve as handy references for users, offering step-by-step instructions and tips for efficient usage and troubleshooting of AVD clients. C) Establish a user feedback mechanism to gather input on AVD client usage and identify areas for improvement in documentation and training materials - While user feedback is valuable, it may not directly address the immediate need for comprehensive documentation and training strategies for AVD client deployment. D) Provide access to self-paced online courses covering AVD client deployment, configuration, and troubleshooting, with assessments to evaluate user proficiency - While online courses offer in-depth learning opportunities, they may not suit users seeking quick guidance and reference materials for AVD client usage.

EXAM FOCUS	You can create tailored role-based training modules, provide interactive tutorials, and distribute user-friendly guides to meet varying technical expertise. This structured approach fosters user proficiency, boosts confidence, and ensures seamless adoption of AVD technologies.

CAUTION ALERT	*Stay alert when assuming advanced training suits all users. Novice users benefit from simple, step-by-step guidance. Avoid overlooking the importance of quick reference materials like cheat sheets for resolving common issues effectively.*

QUESTION 35

Answer - C) Implement QoS for traffic management

Option A - Incorrect: Simply increasing compression might degrade the multimedia experience. Option B - Incorrect: Removing multimedia redirection is not necessary and removes the benefits of enhanced user experience. Option C - Correct: Implementing Quality of Service (QoS) policies can effectively manage bandwidth without impacting core functionalities, ensuring essential traffic is prioritized. Option D - Incorrect: The current issue indicates that adjustments are necessary to manage bandwidth usage effectively. Option E - Incorrect: Reducing the session count per host might not address the specific issue of bandwidth consumption by multimedia content.

EXAM FOCUS	*Keep in mind to implement QoS policies for multimedia traffic to prioritize critical network usage. Adjust codec settings strategically to balance compression and quality, ensuring bandwidth efficiency while maintaining user satisfaction with multimedia experiences in AVD.*
CAUTION ALERT	*Avoid drastic measures like disabling multimedia redirection entirely. This negates user experience enhancements. Instead, optimize network configurations to address bandwidth consumption without impacting the user experience negatively.*

QUESTION 36

Answer - C, D, E

A) Incorrect - Azure Front Door improves global application performance but does not directly address data security or compliance. B) Incorrect - Azure Defender is important for security but does not specifically manage data compliance like GDPR in an AVD scenario. C) Correct - Azure Policy can enforce rules that ensure data remains in specific regions, complying with GDPR. D) Correct - Azure Private Link secures data transfer between regions without exposing data to the public internet, aiding GDPR compliance.
E) Correct - Azure ExpressRoute provides dedicated network connections that enhance data security and reliability for global operations.

EXAM FOCUS	*Use Azure Policy to enforce GDPR-compliant data localization rules. Combine it with Private Link to secure inter-region data flows and ExpressRoute for reliable global connectivity. This ensures data security, sovereignty, and efficient operations across international boundaries.*
CAUTION ALERT	*Stay cautioned against assuming Azure Front Door can ensure compliance. While it optimizes global traffic, data protection and security compliance require dedicated tools like Azure Policy and Private Link for robust governance and privacy adherence.*

QUESTION 37

Answer - D) Deploying regional AVD host pools

Deploying regional AVD host pools allows for the customization of session timeout configurations based on geographical regulations while maintaining optimal user productivity.

Option A - Incorrect. While adjusting session timeouts based on user roles can be useful, it does not directly address regional regulatory compliance. Option B - Incorrect. ARM templates are for deploying Azure resources and do not directly manage session duration policies. Option C - Incorrect. While MFA enhances security, it does not specifically address session duration configurations for different regions. Option E - Incorrect. Azure Monitor helps in monitoring but does not directly impact session duration policies based on geographical regions.

EXAM FOCUS	You need to deploy regional AVD host pools to tailor session timeout policies to local regulations while maintaining performance. This approach ensures compliance without disrupting productivity and facilitates efficient resource management tailored to user needs.
CAUTION ALERT	Avoid applying uniform timeout policies across regions without considering local legal and operational requirements. Such oversight can lead to non-compliance and decreased user satisfaction in specific jurisdictions.

QUESTION 38

Answer - B) Configuring session timeout policies to disconnect idle sessions and release VM resources promptly

Configuring session timeout policies helps minimize costs by disconnecting idle sessions and releasing VM resources promptly, ensuring efficient resource utilization while maintaining user experience.
Option A - Incorrect. While monitoring and scaling are important, session timeouts directly impact resource release.
Option C - Incorrect. FSLogix profiles enhance user experience but do not directly address resource utilization.
Option D - Incorrect. MFA enhances security but does not directly impact resource utilization.
Option E - Incorrect. While automation optimizes tasks, it may not directly impact resource utilization related to session management.

EXAM FOCUS	Configure session timeout policies to promptly release resources after idle periods. Pair this with autoscaling strategies to meet peak demands efficiently. This minimizes costs and maximizes resource utilization without compromising the user experience.
CAUTION ALERT	Don't overlook idle session management. Allowing sessions to linger unnecessarily leads to wasted resources and increased costs. Implement session policies that balance productivity with operational efficiency.

QUESTION 39

Answer - A, B, D

A) Correct - Azure Scale Sets allow for automatic scaling of VMs to meet the demands of development workloads, crucial for rapid scaling needs. B) Correct - Azure Bastion provides a secure and controlled access point to development VMs, safeguarding intellectual property.
C) Incorrect - Azure DevOps is integral for CI/CD but does not directly relate to the configuration needs of Azure Bastion or VM scaling in Azure Virtual Desktop. D) Correct - A specific subnet, AzureBastionSubnet, is necessary for deploying Azure Bastion, ensuring it is correctly integrated into the network architecture.
E) Incorrect - While Azure Security Center is important for security, it does not directly address the setup requirements specified for scalability and secure access.

EXAM FOCUS	Leverage Azure Scale Sets for rapid VM scaling, Azure Bastion for secure development access, and dedicate AzureBastionSubnet for a robust network setup. These ensure operational agility, intellectual property protection, and scalability for CI/CD workflows in AVD environments.
CAUTION ALERT	Avoid assuming Azure DevOps integration is a substitute for AVD-specific configurations like Bastion or scaling solutions. Development pipelines enhance processes but don't inherently support the infrastructure's scalability or security.

QUESTION 40

Answer - B

Option A - Incorrect. Multiple applications can be included in a single rule, but the syntax used is incorrect.
Option B - Correct. The correct parameter for specifying multiple files in FSLogix is -FilePaths, not -FilePath.
Option C - Incorrect. The user format "AD\FinanceDept" is already correct.

Option D - Incorrect. Rules are enabled by default, so this addition is unnecessary.
Option E - Incorrect. The parameter for multiple file paths needs correction.

EXAM FOCUS	Ensure you use the correct FSLogix parameter -FilePaths for multiple applications. Validate the rule configuration to guarantee proper assignment and activation. Consistent syntax and thorough testing prevent misconfigurations that could disrupt AVD operations.
CAUTION ALERT	Don't misinterpret user formatting as the root issue when scripts fail. Errors like incorrect parameters (-FilePath vs. -FilePaths) are often overlooked but can critically impact the functionality of FSLogix application masking rules.

QUESTION 41

Answer - C

Option A - Incorrect. The command lacks the specification of the resource group.
Option B - Incorrect. --enable true is correct, and --status active is not a valid parameter.
Option C - Correct. Including --resource-group is necessary to specify where the AVD environment is hosted.
Option D - Incorrect. The parameter --optimize-audio-video true is correct for this context.
Option E - Incorrect. The correct command uses az avd, not az teams avd.

EXAM FOCUS	Include --resource-group to ensure the command targets the correct AVD environment, especially in multi-tenant or resource-dense environments. Validate parameters like --enable and --optimize-audio-video against the CLI documentation. Testing commands in isolated environments before production deployment ensures compatibility with your specific setup.
CAUTION ALERT	Avoid assuming alternatives like --status active or az teams avd are correct; these parameters and commands do not apply here. Misconfiguring the WebRTC redirector can severely impact Teams performance, leading to poor user experience. Always confirm valid parameters before implementation.

QUESTION 42

Answer - B, E

A) Incorrect - 'BackupInterval' is not a recognized FSLogix registry setting for managing backups or recovery.
B) Correct - The 'CloudCache' setting enables the use of multiple storage locations, helping in disaster recovery by maintaining profile availability across locations. C) Incorrect - 'LocalCacheSize' manages the size of the local cache but does not impact disaster recovery directly. D) Incorrect - 'CacheSize' under ODFC settings adjusts the cache size for Office documents but is not directly related to rapid recovery settings.
E) Correct - 'RetrySync' is crucial for ensuring that if an initial sync fails, FSLogix retries, which is vital for maintaining data integrity during recovery scenarios.

EXAM FOCUS	Use CloudCache for high availability by distributing profile storage across multiple locations. Combine it with RetrySync to retry failed synchronization attempts, ensuring data consistency during failures. Test disaster recovery scenarios with these settings to confirm they meet your organization's failover and recovery standards under real-world conditions.
CAUTION ALERT	Avoid assuming non-relevant settings like BackupInterval or LocalCacheSize assist in disaster recovery. These settings impact backups and local cache management but do not provide redundancy. Misinterpreting their role can lead to insufficient preparation for recovery during storage failures.

QUESTION 43

Answer - E) az network watcher packet-capture create

Option A - Incorrect. az network watcher test-connectivity tests connectivity but does not capture network packets for detailed analysis. Option B - Incorrect. az network vnet list lists virtual networks but does not capture network packets for detailed analysis.

Option C - Incorrect. az network watcher flow-log configure configures flow logs but does not capture network packets for detailed analysis. Option D - Incorrect. az network watcher troubleshooting start initiates troubleshooting but may not capture network packets for detailed analysis.Option E - Correct. az network watcher packet-capture create captures network packets, allowing for detailed analysis of intermittent access problems.

EXAM FOCUS	*Utilize az network watcher packet-capture create for capturing detailed packet data in scenarios involving intermittent connectivity issues. Packet capture provides deep insights into traffic patterns, allowing precise root cause analysis. Configure filters to focus on specific traffic for efficient data collection, reducing noise and enhancing the troubleshooting process.*
CAUTION ALERT	*Do not confuse general connectivity commands like test-connectivity or flow-log configure with packet-level diagnostics. While they offer useful insights, they lack the granular analysis needed for identifying intermittent issues. Using the wrong tool may delay resolution and negatively impact AVD user productivity.*

QUESTION 44

Answer - B) Export Azure Monitor data to Azure Event Hubs

Option B - Exporting Azure Monitor data to Azure Event Hubs allows seamless integration with other monitoring tools and platforms by streaming telemetry data for AVD and other Azure services.

Option A - Azure Monitor Workbooks are used for data visualization but do not facilitate integration with external monitoring tools. Option C - Integrating Azure Monitor with SCOM may not provide seamless integration with other monitoring tools outside the Microsoft ecosystem. Option D - Azure Monitor Action Groups are used for alert notifications, not for integration with external monitoring tools. Option E - Azure Monitor Application Insights focuses on application-level monitoring, not integration with external monitoring tools.

EXAM FOCUS	*Exporting Azure Monitor data to Event Hubs ensures real-time telemetry streaming to external platforms. This approach enables integration with third-party tools for enhanced analytics and reporting. Configure Event Hubs with appropriate throughput units to handle high volumes of data from AVD infrastructure while ensuring compliance with security requirements.*
CAUTION ALERT	*Avoid relying on visualization tools like Workbooks or alerting mechanisms like Action Groups for telemetry integration. These tools focus on Azure-native monitoring and reporting but lack support for external system compatibility. Misusing them can lead to incomplete insights or failure to meet compliance requirements.*

QUESTION 45

Answer - D

Option A - Incorrect. The snippet sets a condition but lacks specifics for action on alert. Option B - Incorrect. While specifying frequency and window size is helpful, it does not fully address alert actions. Option C - Incorrect. "GreaterThanOrEqual" might trigger too many alerts at exactly 80%, which could be normal fluctuation.

Option D - Correct. Adding "severity" and linking to an "actionGroups" ensures that appropriate actions are taken when the alert is triggered, and that it's treated with a correct level of urgency. Option E - Incorrect. "UsedCapacity" might not be the correct metric name depending on the context and how metrics are named in Azure Monitor.

EXAM FOCUS	*Add severity and link to actionGroups in alert configurations to ensure timely action when alerts are triggered. Use severity levels strategically to categorize alerts based on criticality, improving operational responses. Always test your alert rules in non-production environments to confirm they trigger correctly and provide actionable insights.*
CAUTION ALERT	*Avoid omitting key details like severity or actionGroups. These omissions can result in either no action being taken on critical alerts or inappropriate prioritization, leading to operational inefficiencies.*

Misconfigured alerts can create noise or fail to escalate critical issues properly.

QUESTION 46

Answer - B) Azure Automation

Option B - Azure Automation allows administrators to define rules and conditions for scaling actions in AVD environments, automating resource adjustments based on predefined criteria. It supports runbooks and workflows for executing tasks at scale, reducing manual intervention and ensuring consistent resource management.

Option A - Azure Logic Apps is a workflow automation platform but may not provide the necessary flexibility for scaling actions in AVD environments. Option C - Azure Functions is a serverless compute service and may not be specifically tailored for scaling actions in AVD environments. Option D - Azure Policy enforces organizational standards and compliance but does not directly automate scaling actions in AVD environments. Option E - Azure Monitor focuses on monitoring and alerting but may require additional configuration for automating scaling actions.

EXAM FOCUS	*Use Azure Automation for scaling AVD resources based on predefined rules. Leverage runbooks to automate routine tasks and scaling operations, reducing manual intervention. Define thresholds and conditions carefully to avoid over- or under-scaling, which could lead to resource inefficiencies or degraded performance in high-demand scenarios.*
CAUTION ALERT	*Avoid mistaking Azure Logic Apps or Azure Functions for scaling automation. While useful for workflows and serverless operations, they lack the flexibility and resource management capabilities of Azure Automation in scaling AVD environments. Misuse can lead to unnecessary complexity or inefficiencies.*

QUESTION 47

Answer - B) Azure Security Center

Option B - Azure Security Center provides vulnerability assessments, security recommendations, and remediation guidance for AVD environments, helping administrators identify and address security gaps to reduce the risk of security incidents and data breaches. Option A - Azure Defender offers threat protection but may not specialize in vulnerability assessments and remediation for AVD deployments.

Option C - Azure Policy focuses on governance and compliance but may not provide vulnerability assessment capabilities. Option D - Azure Monitor monitors Azure resources but may not offer dedicated vulnerability assessment features for AVD environments. Option E - Azure Sentinel offers security information and event management (SIEM) but may not specifically focus on vulnerability assessments and remediation in AVD deployments.

EXAM FOCUS	*Use Azure Security Center for proactive vulnerability assessments and remediation in AVD. Regularly review its recommendations to address security gaps and maintain compliance. Integrate it with Azure Defender for extended threat detection capabilities, ensuring a secure and resilient AVD environment. Test remediation steps in isolated environments before broad implementation.*
CAUTION ALERT	*Avoid relying solely on tools like Azure Policy or Azure Sentinel for vulnerability management. While valuable, these tools lack dedicated assessment and remediation features. Misinterpreting their capabilities may result in unaddressed security risks or non-compliance in critical AVD deployments.*

QUESTION 48

Answer - B, C, D

A) Incorrect - Windows 10 Pro is not suitable for environments where stringent compliance and data protection are required. B) Correct - Windows Server 2019 is well-suited for healthcare environments needing stability and compliance with health regulations. C) Correct - Windows Server 2022 offers advanced security features that are crucial for protecting sensitive healthcare data. D) Correct - Windows 11 Enterprise provides modern security features and efficient resource management, suitable for healthcare settings. E) Incorrect - While Windows Server 2016 is generally secure, it does not offer the same level of advanced security features as newer versions.

EXAM FOCUS	*Choose Windows Server 2019/2022 or Windows 11 Enterprise for session hosts in compliance-sensitive environments like healthcare. These OS versions offer advanced security, enhanced resource management, and compatibility with Azure Virtual Desktop, making them ideal for regulated industries requiring data protection and modern features.*
CAUTION ALERT	*Avoid using Windows 10 Pro or older server versions like Windows Server 2016 for session hosts. They lack the advanced security features and compliance readiness required for sensitive environments. Missteps here could lead to regulatory violations or security vulnerabilities.*

QUESTION 49

Answer - A) Configuring Azure Backup for automatic VM backups and retention policies
B) Utilizing FSLogix for profile container backups and redirections

A) Configuring Azure Backup for automatic VM backups and retention policies - Azure Backup ensures regular backups of AVD VMs and provides retention policies for data protection. B) Utilizing FSLogix for profile container backups and redirections - FSLogix enables backup and redirection of user profiles, ensuring data availability and user continuity. C, D, E) While RBAC, Azure Monitor, and Azure Key Vault are important for backup management and security, they are not directly related to managing backup solutions for AVD.

EXAM FOCUS	*Configure Azure Backup for VM snapshots and FSLogix for user profile backups to ensure comprehensive recovery strategies. Regularly test backup processes to confirm they meet RTO (Recovery Time Objective) and RPO (Recovery Point Objective) requirements. Use Azure Monitor to track backup job status and set alerts for failures to maintain operational continuity.*
CAUTION ALERT	*Avoid neglecting FSLogix for profile data protection. Relying solely on Azure Backup can leave user-specific data vulnerable, disrupting business continuity during recovery. Mismanagement of backups can lead to data loss or extended downtime in AVD environments.*

QUESTION 50

Answer - B) Utilizing Azure DevOps for automating application deployment and monitoring
D) Integrating Azure Monitor with AVD for centralized monitoring of application performance and infrastructure health

B) Utilizing Azure DevOps for automating application deployment and monitoring - Azure DevOps enables organizations to automate application deployment and monitoring processes, ensuring efficiency and consistency. D) Integrating Azure Monitor with AVD for centralized monitoring of application performance and infrastructure health - Integrating Azure Monitor with AVD provides centralized monitoring of application performance and infrastructure health, facilitating proactive issue identification and resolution.

A, C, E) While Azure Security Center, Azure Service Health, and Microsoft Endpoint Manager offer valuable capabilities, they are not specifically focused on integrating application monitoring with overall AVD management.

EXAM FOCUS	*Integrate Azure Monitor with AVD for real-time application and infrastructure performance insights. Use Azure DevOps to automate deployment pipelines, ensuring consistent monitoring configurations. Centralized monitoring facilitates proactive issue detection and resolution, improving overall system reliability and end-user experience in AVD deployments.*
CAUTION ALERT	*Avoid assuming Azure Security Center or Service Health provide centralized app monitoring. While valuable for security and incident tracking, they lack the comprehensive application performance insights required for managing AVD infrastructures. Misuse could lead to fragmented monitoring processes.*

PRACTICE TEST 5 - QUESTIONS ONLY

QUESTION 1

As the IT manager for a multinational corporation, you are tasked with optimizing network speed for AVD to support remote desktops across various regions. Your objectives are to:
- Deploy a solution that minimizes latency and maximizes bandwidth.
- Ensure a smooth user experience for employees in different geographical locations.
- Consider the impact of network configuration on overall performance.

What best practice would you prioritize to optimize network speed for remote desktops in this scenario?

A) Implement QoS policies on AVD traffic
B) Increase bandwidth limits at peak times
C) Deploy regional AVD host pools
D) Consolidate network traffic through a central hub
E) Enable Multi-Factor Authentication (MFA)

QUESTION 2

In a scenario where you must optimize VPNs and ExpressRoute for an AVD setup to support remote development teams, you need to:
- Ensure low latency and high throughput.
- Maintain secure and encrypted channels.
- Provide flexible and scalable connectivity solutions.

Which configuration approach would you recommend for setting up ExpressRoute with redundancy and high availability?

A) Single ExpressRoute circuit with multiple peering locations
B) Multiple ExpressRoute circuits with single peering location
C) Dual ExpressRoute circuits with redundant peering locations
D) ExpressRoute Direct with dynamic routing
E) VPN Gateway with ExpressRoute failover

QUESTION 3

- Your objective is to analyze user session patterns to optimize resource allocation in an Azure Virtual Desktop (AVD) environment.
- You need to track the usage patterns of user sessions to make informed decisions.
- Your task involves selecting the appropriate Log Analytics table for this analysis.

To track the usage patterns of user sessions in an Azure Virtual Desktop environment, which table in Log Analytics should you query?

A) WVDUserSessions
B) WVDSessionEvent
C) WVDSessionHostManagement
D) WVDAuditLogs
E) WVDServiceHealth

QUESTION 4

Your organization relies heavily on Azure Virtual Desktop (AVD) for remote work scenarios, and any network downtime can severely impact business operations. As the IT administrator, you are tasked with implementing preventive measures to avoid network downtime in AVD environments. Which measures would you prioritize to prevent network downtime effectively? Select TWO.

A) Implement Azure Load Balancer for distributing incoming traffic across multiple AVD session hosts
B) Configure Azure Traffic Manager for automatic failover and traffic rerouting during network disruptions
C) Deploy Azure Bastion as a secure gateway for remote desktop connections to AVD session hosts
D) Utilize Azure Application Gateway for SSL termination and web application firewall (WAF) protection
E) Set up Azure Front Door for global HTTP load balancing and DDoS protection for AVD resources

QUESTION 5

While integrating a new session host into an existing environment, you use a Bicep script to automate the deployment. Identify errors or optimizations in the script below.

```bicep
resource newSessionHost 'Microsoft.DesktopVirtualization/sessionHosts@2020-09-01-preview' = {
  name: 'sessionHost1',
  location: 'eastus',
  properties: {
    osVersion: 'Windows 10 Enterprise',
    disallowPublicIpAddress: true,
    maxSessionLimit: 15
  }
}
```

A) API version is outdated
B) 'osVersion' property is incorrectly specified
C) 'disallowPublicIpAddress' should be false
D) 'maxSessionLimit' is incorrectly set
E) Script is correctly configured

QUESTION 6

You are tasked with optimizing infrastructure costs for an Azure Virtual Desktop (AVD) environment containing a host pool with 10 pooled session hosts. The solution must meet the following requirements:
- Start session hosts at 7:00 AM.
- Shut down session hosts at 5:00 PM.
- Only be in effect Monday to Friday.
- Minimize administrative effort.
What should you configure? Select TWO.

A) Microsoft Sentinel playbook
B) Scaling plan
C) Azure Blueprint
D) Azure Automation with Azure Logic Apps
E) Azure Policy

QUESTION 7

Your organization is reviewing case studies on operating system selection for specific business needs in Azure Virtual Desktop (AVD) deployments. As the Azure architect, you need to provide insights into these scenarios. What considerations should you discuss? Select THREE.

A) A software development company opts for Windows Server to leverage Remote Desktop Services (RDS) for centralized application development environments

B) A financial institution selects Windows 10 Multi-Session for enhanced security features and compliance with industry regulations
C) An architecture firm chooses Windows Server for its scalability and resource efficiency in handling large CAD software deployments
D) A healthcare organization decides on Windows 10 Multi-Session for seamless integration with Microsoft Teams and other collaboration tools
E) A customer support center adopts Windows Server for its cost-effective licensing options and support for legacy applications

QUESTION 8

Your organization seeks to learn from successful implementations of Azure Virtual Desktop (AVD) host pool architectures to inform its own deployment strategy. As the Azure architect, you are tasked with analyzing case studies and identifying key insights. What factors should you consider in these case studies? Select THREE.

A) Industry Vertical and Use Case Scenarios
B) Performance Metrics and User Feedback
C) Scalability Challenges and Growth Trajectory
D) Cost Analysis and Return on Investment (ROI)
E) Best Practices and Lessons Learned

QUESTION 9

You are implementing autoscale for host pools in an Azure Virtual Desktop (AVD) environment and need to integrate Azure services to trigger scaling actions. Consider the following options:
- Azure Monitor.
- Azure Logic Apps.
- Azure Functions.
- Azure Resource Manager templates.
- Azure Sentinel.

Which of these Azure services can be effectively integrated with autoscale to trigger scaling actions? Select THREE.

A) Azure Monitor.
B) Azure Logic Apps.
C) Azure Functions.
D) Azure Resource Manager templates.
E) Azure Sentinel.

QUESTION 10

Security best practices are paramount when managing storage for AVD. Analyze this Bicep script for creating a secured storage account. What security enhancements are recommended?

```bicep
resource secureStorage 'Microsoft.Storage/storageAccounts@2021-06-01' = {
  name: 'SecuredStorage',
  location: 'westus2',
  sku: { name: 'Standard_RAGRS' },
  properties: {
    supportsHttpsTrafficOnly: true,
    networkAcls: {
      bypass: 'AzureServices',
      defaultAction: 'Deny'
    }
  }
}
```

A) Enable MFA for access control
B) Set networkAcls defaultAction to Allow
C) Disable supportsHttpsTrafficOnly
D) Configuration is already secure
E) Change location to eastus

QUESTION 11

Your organization is focused on maintaining compliance in licensing for session hosts deployed in Azure Virtual Desktop (AVD). As the Azure specialist, you are tasked with ensuring adherence to best practices. What are recommended strategies for maintaining compliance in licensing? Select THREE.

A) Regular Audits and Reviews of License Usage and Allocation
B) Automation of License Assignment and Renewal Processes
C) Implementation of Role-Based Access Control (RBAC) for License Management
D) Integration with Azure Policy for Enforcement of Licensing Policies
E) Training and Awareness Programs for End Users on Licensing Policies

QUESTION 12

You are designing a disaster recovery strategy for an Azure Virtual Desktop (AVD) environment to ensure high availability and data resilience. Consider the following factors:
- Implement automatic failover of AVD host pools to a secondary Azure region.
- Ensure minimal data loss and downtime during failover operations.
Which Azure service should you incorporate into the strategy to achieve these objectives?

A) Azure Active Directory
B) Azure Traffic Manager
C) Azure Backup
D) Azure Monitor
E) Azure Site Recovery

QUESTION 13

Your organization is required to maintain comprehensive documentation and compliance with regulatory requirements in the management of Azure Virtual Desktop (AVD) images. As the Azure specialist, you need to identify the documentation and compliance requirements relevant to image management. Which of the following measures are necessary to fulfill documentation and compliance requirements in AVD image management? Select TWO.

A) Documenting Image Configuration Settings and Changes
B) Retaining Audit Logs of Image Modifications
C) Implementing Multi-Factor Authentication (MFA) for Image Access
D) Conducting Periodic Security Assessments of Image Repositories
E) Ensuring Encryption of Image Data at Rest and in Transit

QUESTION 14

Your organization is encountering issues during the creation of session hosts from golden images in Azure Virtual Desktop (AVD), leading to delays and disruptions in deployment processes. As the Azure specialist, you need to troubleshoot creation issues and identify potential solutions. What troubleshooting steps should be taken to address creation issues from golden images in AVD? Select THREE.

A) Check Azure Resource Manager (ARM) Template Configuration
B) Validate Image Generalization Process for Golden Image
C) Review Network Connectivity and Subnet Configuration

D) Verify Azure Active Directory (Azure AD) Integration Settings
E) Monitor Azure Service Health for Platform Issues

QUESTION 15

To enhance security, your AVD deployment must utilize images from the Compute Gallery that comply with the latest security standards. What is the best practice for ensuring your images meet these standards?

```json
{"action": "Review and update images quarterly", "method": "Automated patch management tools", "compliance": "Regular audits and version control"}
```

A) Best practice correctly identified
B) JSON format is inappropriate for this setting
C) Action should be bi-annual
D) Method should involve manual reviews
E) Compliance lacks specific standards

QUESTION 16

Auditing and compliance monitoring are essential components of maintaining a secure Azure Virtual Desktop (AVD) environment, ensuring adherence to regulatory requirements and identifying security incidents proactively. As the Azure specialist, you need to identify the auditing and compliance monitoring features available for AVD environments. What auditing and compliance monitoring features does Azure Virtual Desktop offer? Select THREE.

A) Azure Monitor Logs for Activity Logging and Analysis
B) Integration with Azure Sentinel for Security Incident Detection
C) Azure Security Center Compliance Score for Regulatory Compliance Assessment
D) Built-in Reporting and Dashboarding Capabilities for Compliance Monitoring
E) Integration with Microsoft Defender for Cloud for Threat Intelligence and Detection

QUESTION 17

Your organization is interested in learning from successful case studies of performance tuning in Azure Virtual Desktop (AVD) deployments to improve its own implementation. As the Azure specialist, you're tasked with gathering insights from relevant case studies. Which areas should you focus on when studying successful performance tuning case studies for AVD deployments? Select THREE.

A) Optimization Techniques for Remote Display Protocols and Multimedia Redirection
B) Resource Allocation Strategies for Different User Profiles and Workloads
C) Integration of Third-Party Performance Monitoring Tools with Azure Monitor
D) Implementation of User Experience (UX) Testing and Feedback Mechanisms
E) Leveraging Azure Bastion for Secure Remote Access and Management

QUESTION 18

You're troubleshooting performance issues in an Azure Virtual Desktop (AVD) environment and suspect that outdated Azure Virtual Desktop agents may be contributing to the problem. To verify this suspicion, what action should you take?
- Identify the version of Azure Virtual Desktop agents on session hosts
- Confirm whether outdated agents are causing performance degradation
- Ensure minimal disruption to user sessions

A) Review diagnostic logs.
B) Analyze network traffic.
C) Monitor CPU usage on session hosts.

D) Verify the Azure Virtual Desktop agent version on session hosts.
E) Check Azure Monitor metrics.

QUESTION 19

You are troubleshooting performance issues in an Azure Virtual Desktop (AVD) deployment. Critical points to consider include network bandwidth optimization, virtual machine (VM) configurations, and application compatibility. How would you prioritize these points to identify and resolve performance issues effectively? Select TWO.

A) Analyze network bandwidth utilization with Azure Network Watcher
B) Review VM configurations and adjust resource allocation if necessary
C) Utilize Azure Application Insights to identify application compatibility issues

QUESTION 20

In your role, you are ensuring that automation scripts for AVD not only deploy environments but also enforce compliance with data protection regulations. Scripts should encrypt user data, restrict access based on user roles, and log all access attempts for auditing. What is a critical PowerShell command to enforce encryption of user data in AVD environments?

```powershell
Set-AzAVDEncryption -ResourceGroupName "RG1" -HostPoolName "HP1" -Encrypt $true
```

A) Command correctly enforces encryption
B) Include command to restrict access based on roles
C) Add logging of all access attempts
D) Command should specify encryption type
E) Add parameters for compliance auditing

QUESTION 21

You are configuring Azure Virtual Desktop to allow remote access for users via Remote Desktop Protocol (RDP). You need to ensure that firewall rules permit traffic for RDP connections. Which port should you allow in the firewall rules?

A) 80
B) 443
C) 3389
D) 8080
E) 8443

QUESTION 22

Your organization is experiencing issues with Microsoft Entra services in Azure Virtual Desktop (AVD) environments and needs to troubleshoot and manage these issues effectively to ensure uninterrupted service delivery. The focus is on identifying common problems with Entra services and implementing appropriate troubleshooting measures. What steps should be taken to troubleshoot and manage issues with Microsoft Entra in AVD environments? Select THREE.

A) Reviewing Azure AD Connect synchronization logs for errors and warnings
B) Checking Azure AD sign-in logs for authentication failures and anomalies
C) Monitoring Azure AD health status for service disruptions and outages
D) Reviewing Entra service status in the Azure portal for performance issues
E) Analyzing AVD session host event logs for Entra-related errors and warnings

QUESTION 23

Your organization is committed to maintaining a robust security posture for Azure Virtual Desktop (AVD) environments and regularly monitoring and revising Conditional Access policies to address emerging security threats. The focus is on proactive management of security measures to adapt to evolving risks effectively. How can Conditional Access policies be monitored and revised based on new security threats in AVD environments? Select THREE.

A) Monitor Azure AD logs for suspicious sign-in activities or policy violations
B) Stay informed about security advisories and updates from Microsoft and other trusted sources
C) Conduct regular security assessments and risk evaluations to identify potential gaps or vulnerabilities
D) Collaborate with Azure security engineers to analyze threat intelligence and adjust policy settings accordingly
E) Implement automated alerts and notifications for policy violations or unauthorized access attempts

QUESTION 24

In configuring Azure Virtual Desktop for a highly regulated industry, compliance and security are paramount. What steps should you take to meet these requirements? Select CORRECT answers that apply.

A) Encrypt all data at rest and in transit.
B) Use private endpoints for all network connections.
C) Regularly audit user access and activities.
D) Integrate with Azure Policy.
E) All users must use VPNs.

QUESTION 25

Troubleshooting common issues with Defender Antivirus in AVD often involves ensuring that antivirus definitions are up-to-date. What is the best PowerShell command to force an update of the Defender antivirus definitions?

```
A) Update-MpSignature
B) Get-MpSignature
C) Force-MpUpdate
D) Update-MpPreference -SignatureUpdate
E) Check-MpUpdate
```

QUESTION 26

Your organization is reviewing its administrative access policies for Azure Virtual Desktop (AVD) session hosts and wants to implement best practices for administrative access. The focus is on ensuring secure and efficient access management. What are the best practices for administrative access to AVD session hosts? Select THREE.

A) Implement Just-In-Time (JIT) access for temporary and time-bound administrative access
B) Enforce multi-factor authentication (MFA) for all administrative access to AVD session hosts
C) Configure role-based access control (RBAC) to limit administrative privileges based on job roles
D) Utilize Azure Bastion for secure RDP/SSH access to AVD session hosts without exposing public IP addresses
E) Regularly review and update access permissions to align with organizational changes and security policies

QUESTION 27

To optimize the security posture of your AVD setup amidst increasing remote work demands, it is essential to ensure robust access control, mitigate network threats, and integrate with enterprise security operations. Which initiatives should you prioritize? Select THREE.

A) Implement multi-factor authentication (MFA).
B) Configure Azure Firewall with threat intelligence.
C) Establish VPN connectivity for secure remote access.

D) Integrate AVD with corporate Security Information and Event Management (SIEM) systems.
E) Apply network micro-segmentation strategies.

QUESTION 28

Your organization is facing common challenges in RBAC implementation in Azure Virtual Desktop (AVD) environments and seeks solutions to overcome these challenges. The focus is on understanding common challenges and their solutions in RBAC implementation. What are the common challenges in RBAC implementation in AVD environments, and how can they be addressed? Select CORRECT answers that apply.

A) Complexity in defining granular roles and permissions
B) Role sprawl due to excessive role creation and assignment
C) Difficulty in aligning role assignments with changing organizational needs
D) Lack of visibility into role assignments and access permissions
E) Inadequate user training and awareness on role-based access control

QUESTION 29

Your organization has implemented Multi-Factor Authentication (MFA) for Azure Virtual Desktop (AVD) to enhance security. However, there is a need to monitor and evaluate the effectiveness of MFA measures over time. The focus is on reporting and monitoring MFA effectiveness. How can you effectively monitor and evaluate the effectiveness of Multi-Factor Authentication (MFA) measures for Azure Virtual Desktop? Select THREE.

A) Review MFA usage reports and logs in Azure Active Directory to track authentication attempts and success rates
B) Implement Azure Monitor alerts for suspicious or failed MFA authentication events to detect potential security incidents
C) Conduct regular user surveys or feedback sessions to assess satisfaction and compliance with MFA requirements
D) Analyze user support tickets and helpdesk requests related to MFA setup or authentication issues to identify trends and areas for improvement
E) Perform periodic security audits and assessments to evaluate overall MFA effectiveness and identify potential vulnerabilities

QUESTION 30

In a hybrid environment, you are tasked with setting up secure connections between on-premises infrastructure and AVD to ensure data security and compliance with regulatory requirements. The setup must include encrypted communication channels and robust authentication mechanisms. Evaluate the Azure CLI script below intended for creating a hybrid connection and assess if it adequately secures the connection against potential security breaches.
bash
```
az network vpn-connection create --name "HybridConnection" --resource-group "HybridResources" --vnet-gateway1 "HybridGateway" --shared-key "abc123"
```

A) Script is correct for hybrid connection
B) Specify on-premises gateway
C) Shared-key should be stronger
D) Add encryption protocol
E) Change resource group for better organization

QUESTION 31

Your organization is troubleshooting common configuration issues related to FSLogix in Azure Virtual Desktop (AVD) environments. The focus is on troubleshooting common FSLogix configuration issues. What common FSLogix configuration issues may occur in AVD environments, and how can they be addressed? Select THREE.

A) Profile container bloat due to excessive user data storage and disk space utilization
B) Inconsistent application settings and configurations across user sessions and environments
C) Profile corruption or loss resulting from FSLogix service failures or unexpected interruptions
D) Performance degradation due to excessive disk I/O operations and profile disk fragmentation
E) Compatibility issues with legacy applications and plugins not fully supported by FSLogix

QUESTION 32

As an Azure Virtual Desktop administrator troubleshooting issues with Profile Containers, you need to identify common problems and solutions. Consider the following:
- Identify common installation pitfalls and their resolutions.
- Validate the integrity and functionality of Profile Containers post-installation.
- Implement monitoring and alerting systems to detect Profile Container issues proactively.
What are the troubleshooting techniques for Profile Containers? Select THREE.

A) Analyze event logs for Profile Container-related errors.
B) Utilize FSLogix diagnostic tools to identify performance bottlenecks.
C) Test Profile Container functionality by creating and accessing user profiles.
D) Monitor storage usage and performance metrics for Profile Containers.
E) Use PowerShell scripts to automate Profile Container maintenance tasks.

QUESTION 33

An AVD deployment for a government agency requires strict access controls, audit capabilities, and protection against external threats. What should be configured? Select THREE.

A) Enable Multi-Factor Authentication (MFA) with Azure AD.
B) Use Azure Firewall to govern inbound and outbound traffic.
C) Implement Azure Information Protection for data classification.
D) Configure Azure Audit Logs with retention policies.
E) Integrate Microsoft Defender for Identity.

QUESTION 34

As an Azure Virtual Desktop administrator, you encounter challenges optimizing client performance and user experience in diverse usage scenarios. Consider the following scenario:
- Users access AVD sessions from a variety of devices, including laptops, tablets, and thin clients, each with different hardware capabilities.
- Some users require access to resource-intensive applications, while others prioritize seamless connectivity and responsiveness for daily tasks.
- IT administrators aim to implement strategies to optimize client performance and user experience across diverse usage scenarios effectively.
How can you optimize client performance and user experience for the given scenario? Select TWO.

A) Implement Azure Bastion for secure RDP access to AVD instances without exposing them to the public internet.
B) Configure FSLogix Profile Containers to provide a consistent user experience across different devices and sessions.
C) Leverage Azure AD Conditional Access policies to enforce multi-factor authentication (MFA) based on user roles.
D) Utilize Azure Network Watcher to monitor network traffic between clients and AVD resources and identify connectivity issues.
E) Deploy GPU-accelerated virtual machines (VMs) for users requiring high-definition multimedia applications.

QUESTION 35

You are responsible for diagnosing issues with multimedia redirection in a hybrid Azure Virtual Desktop environment.

Users report intermittent performance degradation, especially during peak hours. To troubleshoot, you decide to implement monitoring for multimedia traffic to identify bottlenecks. Evaluate the following PowerShell command designed to monitor network traffic related to multimedia redirection:

```powershell
Get-AzNetworkWatcherFlowLogStatus -Location "East US" -TargetResourceId "resource-id"
```

A) Command correctly monitors multimedia traffic
B) Command should include specific multimedia filters
C) Location parameter is incorrect
D) TargetResourceId should specify the AVD instance
E) Monitoring is not possible with this command

QUESTION 36

A technology firm requires its Azure Virtual Desktop to be configured for scalable deployments, protection against cyber threats, and to ensure only authorized personnel can modify configurations. What measures should you implement? Select THREE.

A) Use Azure Automation to scale VMs based on demand.
B) Deploy Azure Sentinel for monitoring and threat detection.
C) Configure role-based access control (RBAC) on the Azure portal.
D) Implement Azure Active Directory Conditional Access.
E) Set up Azure Security Center for overall security management.

QUESTION 37

You are troubleshooting session timeout issues in an Azure Virtual Desktop (AVD) environment where users intermittently lose connectivity. You suspect network-related issues. Which Azure CLI command can assist you in capturing network traffic for analysis to identify potential causes of session disruptions?

```
A) az network watcher packet-capture create
B) az network vnet list
C) az network watcher flow-log configure
D) az network watcher troubleshooting start
E) az network watcher test-connectivity
```

QUESTION 38

Troubleshooting common issues with Start VM on Connect requires a comprehensive understanding of Azure Virtual Desktop (AVD) environments. Consider the following scenario: Users report delays in accessing their desktop environments after logging in. What troubleshooting step is essential to identify and resolve this issue effectively?

A) Reviewing Azure Activity Logs to identify any recent changes or events affecting desktop provisioning
B) Analyzing network performance metrics to detect potential bottlenecks or connectivity issues
C) Checking FSLogix profile status to ensure user settings and configurations are loading correctly
D) Reviewing Azure Resource Manager (ARM) templates to verify correct configuration and deployment settings
E) Monitoring Azure Bastion logs for any authentication failures or access attempts to VMs

QUESTION 39

For a media company deploying AVD for video editors working remotely, ensuring low latency, high bandwidth, and secure access to editing tools is essential. What configurations are crucial? Select THREE.

A) Implement Azure ExpressRoute for enhanced network performance.
B) Deploy Azure Bastion for secure and private access to editing VMs.

C) Configure Azure Media Services for optimized media streaming.
D) Create a dedicated AzureBastionSubnet for Bastion deployment.
E) Set up Azure Front Door for global traffic management.

QUESTION 40

A PowerShell script is written to implement FSLogix application masking for a project management tool only for the project management team. The script is as follows:
```
$App = "Project.exe"
New-FSLogixAppMaskingRule -Name "PMTools" -FilePath $App -AssignedUser "AD\PMTeam"
```
Identify the correct measure to enhance the script's effectiveness.

A) Replace -FilePath $App with -FilePaths $App as it may involve multiple files.
B) Replace New-FSLogixAppMaskingRule with Set-FSLogixAppMaskingRule since the rule may already exist.
C) Add -Enabled $true to make sure the rule is active.
D) Use -AssignedUserGroup "AD\PMTeam" instead of -AssignedUser to apply it to the group.
E) The script is correctly formulated.

QUESTION 41

Security is a priority when integrating Microsoft Teams into AVD, especially in regulated industries. What configuration in a Bicep template ensures that Teams communications are routed through secured channels only?
```
resource teamsSecurity 'Microsoft.Network/virtualNetworks/subnets' = { name: 'secureTeamsChannel' properties: { enforcePrivateLink: true } }
```

A) Configuration is correct.
B) Add secureTrafficOnly: true under properties.
C) Replace enforcePrivateLink: true with forceTunneling: true.
D) Include protocol: "HTTPS" to specify secure protocols.
E) Change the resource type to 'Microsoft.Teams/securitySettings'.

QUESTION 42

You are configuring an AVD setup for a design firm that needs to ensure high performance, manage large graphic files within FSLogix profiles, and maintain user settings consistency. Which registry settings should be adjusted? Select THREE.

A) HKLM\SOFTWARE\FSLogix\Profiles\VHDLocations
B) HKLM\SOFTWARE\FSLogix\Profiles\Size
C) HKLM\SOFTWARE\FSLogix\Profiles\DynamicVHDAllocation
D) HKLM\SOFTWARE\Policies\FSLogix\ODFC\DiskType
E) HKLM\SOFTWARE\FSLogix\Profiles\ProfileType

QUESTION 43

You are responsible for monitoring and maintaining the performance of Azure Virtual Desktop (AVD) host pools. You need to identify common performance issues and implement appropriate measures to optimize performance. Which tool allows you to analyze performance metrics in real-time and identify potential performance bottlenecks effectively?

A) Azure Health Monitor
B) Azure Resource Graph
C) Azure Monitor Metrics Explorer
D) Azure Network Watcher
E) Azure Advisor

QUESTION 44

To adhere to compliance requirements and best practices, you need to implement effective data retention and analysis strategies for Azure Virtual Desktop (AVD) telemetry data. In formulating the strategy, consider:
1. The regulatory requirements and industry standards governing data retention periods for AVD telemetry data.
2. The volume and growth rate of AVD telemetry data, influencing storage and analysis costs.
3. The trade-offs between long-term data retention for historical analysis and the need for real-time insights into AVD performance.

What is the recommended approach for balancing compliance requirements and cost-effective data retention and analysis for AVD telemetry data?

A) Configure Azure Monitor Logs retention policies for AVD.
B) Store AVD telemetry data in Azure Blob Storage for long-term retention.
C) Implement Azure Monitor Workbooks for real-time data analysis.
D) Use Azure Data Explorer for ad-hoc querying of AVD metrics.
E) Integrate AVD telemetry with Azure Log Analytics for advanced analytics.

QUESTION 45

Develop a strategy for ensuring user data compliance in AVD, focusing on data retention and governance. Draft an ARM template snippet to enforce retention policies for Azure Blob Storage used for user data backups.
JSON

```json
{"type": "Microsoft.Storage/storageAccounts/managementPolicies", "properties": {"policy": {"rules": [{"name": "RetentionPolicy", "enabled": true, "type": "Lifecycle", "definition": {"actions": {"baseBlob": {"delete": {"daysAfterModificationGreaterThan": 365}}}}}]}}}
```

A) Snippet is correct as is.
B) Replace "type": "Lifecycle" with "type": "DataRetention".
C) Modify "daysAfterModificationGreaterThan": 365 to "daysAfterCreationGreaterThan": 365.
D) Include "filters": {"blobTypes": ["blockBlob"]} in the "definition".
E) Change "enabled": true to "isEnabled": true.

QUESTION 46

Scaling actions in Azure Virtual Desktop (AVD) environments can impact user experience and productivity. As an AVD administrator, you need to consider various factors when implementing scaling strategies to minimize disruptions and ensure seamless user access. Which factor should administrators prioritize to minimize disruptions and ensure seamless user access during scaling operations?

A) Network latency and bandwidth constraints
B) Cost implications of resource scaling
C) Compatibility of applications with scaled resources
D) Availability of Azure Bastion for remote access
E) Impact on Azure Active Directory (Azure AD) authentication

QUESTION 47

Compliance with industry standards and regulations is a top priority for Azure Virtual Desktop (AVD) environments to ensure data protection and regulatory compliance. Which regulatory compliance standard should be considered when assessing AVD deployments?

A) GDPR (General Data Protection Regulation)
B) HIPAA (Health Insurance Portability and Accountability Act)
C) SOX (Sarbanes-Oxley Act)

D) PCI DSS (Payment Card Industry Data Security Standard)
E) ISO/IEC 27001 (Information Security Management System)

QUESTION 48

A multinational corporation is upgrading its Azure Virtual Desktop infrastructure to enhance global collaboration among employees. The key requirements are support for multi-lingual setups, high-performance computing, and advanced security features. Which Windows operating systems should be deployed? Select THREE.

A) Windows 11 Enterprise
B) Windows 10 Enterprise multi-session
C) Windows Server 2022
D) Windows Server 2016
E) Windows 8.1 Pro

QUESTION 49

An organization is conducting documentation and training on disaster recovery plans for its Azure Virtual Desktop (AVD) environment to ensure preparedness and response effectiveness. Which actions should the organization prioritize to enhance documentation and training efforts for AVD disaster recovery? Select THREE.

A) Developing comprehensive runbooks detailing step-by-step recovery procedures
B) Conducting tabletop exercises to simulate disaster scenarios and validate response procedures
C) Providing role-specific training on AVD disaster recovery roles and responsibilities
D) Leveraging Azure Resource Manager templates for automated recovery environment provisioning
E) Implementing Azure Information Protection for sensitive data classification and protection

QUESTION 50

A company wants to customize application performance alerts in its Azure Virtual Desktop (AVD) environment to better suit its operational needs. What options should they consider for customizing these alerts effectively? Select THREE.

A) Utilizing Azure Policy for creating custom policies to trigger alerts based on application performance thresholds
B) Configuring custom log alerts in Azure Monitor to notify stakeholders of application performance issues
C) Implementing Azure Automation for triggering automated actions based on predefined application performance metrics
D) Leveraging Azure Log Analytics to create custom queries for monitoring specific application performance metrics
E) Microsoft 365 Security Center for setting up custom alert policies to detect anomalous application behavior

PRACTICE TEST 5 - ANSWERS ONLY

QUESTION 1

Answer - C) Deploy regional AVD host pools

Option A - Incorrect. QoS is important but not the primary method for speed optimization.
Option B - Incorrect. May help but not as effective as geographical optimization.
Option C - Correct. Reduces latency by locating resources closer to users.
Option D - Incorrect. May increase latency due to centralized processing.
Option E - Incorrect. Enhances security but does not impact network speed.

EXAM FOCUS	Deploying regional AVD host pools minimizes latency by placing resources closer to users, improving performance in distributed setups. You should evaluate user locations and traffic patterns to optimize resource placement effectively. Ensure proper network configuration for each region to maximize bandwidth and reduce inter-regional latency.
CAUTION ALERT	Avoid centralizing all resources in one hub; this increases latency for distant users, degrading user experience. Stay clear of unrelated measures like increasing bandwidth at peak times, as they do not address geographical performance bottlenecks.

QUESTION 2

Answer - C) Dual ExpressRoute circuits with redundant peering locations

Option A - Incorrect. Does not provide redundancy.
Option B - Incorrect. Lacks redundancy in circuit setup.
Option C - Correct. Offers redundancy and high availability.
Option D - Incorrect. Focuses on direct routing, not redundancy.
Option E - Incorrect. VPN failover is not as reliable as dual circuits.

EXAM FOCUS	Redundant circuits with separate peering locations ensure high availability and low latency in AVD setups. You need to design ExpressRoute with failover paths to handle outages without disrupting connectivity. Validate routing tables to ensure all traffic flows securely and efficiently during failovers.
CAUTION ALERT	Avoid relying on a single ExpressRoute circuit or peering location, as this creates a single point of failure. Also, do not consider VPN failovers as equivalent to dual circuits—they are less reliable and may introduce latency.

QUESTION 3

Answer - [B]

Option B - WVDSessionEvent: This table contains detailed logs of session events, including session start and end times, which can help track usage patterns.
Option A - WVDUserSessions: While it may seem relevant, it typically does not contain detailed event information.
Option C - WVDSessionHostManagement: This deals with session host details rather than session events.
Option D - WVDAuditLogs: This focuses on broader audit logs rather than session-specific events.
Option E - WVDServiceHealth: This provides overall service health information, not session event logs.

EXAM FOCUS	Use WVDSessionEvent in Log Analytics to analyze session patterns, as it provides detailed logs of user activity, including session start and end times. These insights are crucial for optimizing resource allocation and managing user loads effectively. Always filter by relevant metrics to avoid overwhelming data.
CAUTION ALERT	Stay alert to differences between WVDSessionEvent and similar tables like WVDUserSessions, which lacks detailed event logs. Do not use general tables like WVDAuditLogs or WVDServiceHealth for session-

specific analysis—they do not provide actionable insights for resource planning.

QUESTION 4

Answer - A) Implement Azure Load Balancer for distributing incoming traffic across multiple AVD session hosts; B) Configure Azure Traffic Manager for automatic failover and traffic rerouting during network disruptions

Option A - Correct. Implementing Azure Load Balancer helps distribute incoming traffic across multiple AVD session hosts, reducing the risk of network downtime due to single points of failure. Option B - Correct. Configuring Azure Traffic Manager for automatic failover and traffic rerouting ensures continuous service availability during network disruptions, minimizing downtime in AVD environments.

Option C - Incorrect. While Azure Bastion enhances remote desktop connections, it may not directly prevent network downtime in AVD setups. Option D - Incorrect. Azure Application Gateway focuses on web traffic management and security but may not address network downtime prevention for AVD infrastructures. Option E - Incorrect. Azure Front Door provides HTTP load balancing and DDoS protection but may not be tailored specifically for preventing network downtime in AVD deployments.

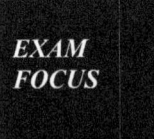	
EXAM FOCUS	*Implement Azure Load Balancer to distribute traffic across session hosts, reducing risks of overload or single-point failures. Use Traffic Manager for automatic failover during network disruptions. These tools ensure service continuity in AVD environments. Regularly test failover configurations to verify their effectiveness.*
CAUTION ALERT	*Avoid assuming tools like Azure Bastion or Application Gateway directly address network downtime. While valuable for specific tasks, they do not provide load balancing or failover capabilities. Stay clear of overcomplicating your setup with tools unsuited to AVD downtime prevention.*

QUESTION 5

Answer - A) API version is outdated

Option A - Correct: The API version '2020-09-01-preview' is outdated and should be updated.
Option B - Incorrect: 'osVersion' property is specified correctly for the session host.
Option C - Incorrect: Setting 'disallowPublicIpAddress' to true is a security best practice.
Option D - Incorrect: The 'maxSessionLimit' of 15 is appropriate for the configuration.
Option E - Incorrect: Due to the outdated API version, the entire script is not correctly configured.

EXAM FOCUS	*Update API versions in your Bicep scripts to align with the latest Azure standards, ensuring compatibility and access to the newest features. You should validate all properties and test deployment in a staging environment to catch potential issues before production deployment.*
CAUTION ALERT	*Avoid using outdated API versions, as they can lead to deployment failures or missing features. Do not set disallowPublicIpAddress to false; it compromises security. Misconfigured properties like maxSessionLimit could degrade performance.*

QUESTION 6

Answer - [B, D]

Option B - Scaling plan: Allows you to automatically start and stop session hosts based on a predefined schedule, meeting the specified requirements and minimizing administrative effort.
Option D - Azure Automation with Azure Logic Apps: Logic Apps can be used to trigger the start and stop actions for session hosts based on the specified schedule, fulfilling the requirements efficiently.
Option A - Microsoft Sentinel playbook: Sentinel is a SIEM tool and is not used for infrastructure cost optimization.
Option C - Azure Blueprint: Blueprints are used for governance and compliance, not for managing session host

schedules.

Option E - Azure Policy: Policies are used for enforcing rules and standards across resources but are not designed for managing session host schedules based on demand.

EXAM FOCUS	*Use a scaling plan to automate start and stop actions for AVD session hosts based on schedules, reducing costs. Combine this with Azure Automation and Logic Apps for custom workflows. Ensure configurations match operational hours to avoid unnecessary charges or downtime during peak hours.*
CAUTION ALERT	*Avoid tools like Sentinel, Blueprints, or Policies for cost optimization—they are not designed for schedule-based scaling. Misusing these tools can result in inefficiencies or compliance violations without addressing the root issue of cost optimization.*

QUESTION 7

Answer - A) A software development company opts for Windows Server to leverage Remote Desktop Services (RDS) for centralized application development environments; B) A financial institution selects Windows 10 Multi-Session for enhanced security features and compliance with industry regulations; C) An architecture firm chooses Windows Server for its scalability and resource efficiency in handling large CAD software deployments

Option A - Correct. Windows Server is often chosen by software development companies for leveraging RDS in centralized development environments, facilitating collaboration and version control. Option B - Correct. Financial institutions prioritize security and compliance, making Windows 10 Multi-Session an attractive option due to its built-in security features and alignment with industry regulations.

Option C - Correct. Architecture firms require scalable solutions for handling resource-intensive CAD software, making Windows Server an optimal choice for its resource efficiency and scalability in AVD deployments. Option D - Incorrect. While Windows 10 Multi-Session may integrate well with Microsoft Teams, it may not be the sole criterion for selecting an OS for AVD deployments in a healthcare organization. Option E - Incorrect. While Windows Server may offer cost-effective licensing and support for legacy applications, other factors such as security and regulatory compliance may also influence OS selection for AVD deployments in customer support centers.

EXAM FOCUS	*Select the OS based on specific use cases: Windows Server for centralized RDS environments, Windows 10 Multi-Session for security and compliance, and scalable setups for resource-intensive workloads. You should analyze organizational needs and software compatibility when making OS decisions for AVD deployments.*
CAUTION ALERT	*Avoid making assumptions based solely on licensing cost. While Windows Server might appear cost-effective, failing to consider regulatory compliance or scalability can lead to mismatched solutions. Always prioritize organizational needs over general cost savings.*

QUESTION 8

Answer - A) Industry Vertical and Use Case Scenarios; B) Performance Metrics and User Feedback; E) Best Practices and Lessons Learned

Option A - Correct. Industry vertical and use case scenarios provide context for understanding how different organizations leverage AVD host pools to address specific business needs and challenges. Option B - Correct. Performance metrics and user feedback offer insights into the usability and effectiveness of AVD deployments, helping identify areas for improvement and optimization.

Option E - Correct. Best practices and lessons learned from successful implementations serve as valuable resources for guiding decision-making and avoiding common pitfalls in AVD host pool architectures. Option C - Incorrect. While scalability challenges and growth trajectory are important considerations, they are not exclusive to case studies and may vary depending on organizational context. Option D - Incorrect. While cost analysis and ROI are critical for evaluating the success of AVD deployments, they are not specific factors typically highlighted in case studies of host pool architectures.

Page | 145

EXAM FOCUS	*When analyzing case studies, focus on industry-specific challenges, performance metrics, and best practices. Consider lessons learned from scalability and user feedback to inform architecture decisions. Prioritize scenarios that closely align with your organizational goals and resource demands for maximum relevance.*
CAUTION ALERT	*Do not overlook critical insights by focusing solely on cost or ROI metrics. Case studies often emphasize user experience and operational strategies, which are crucial for successful AVD deployments. Stay clear of generic lessons that may not apply to your specific use case.*

QUESTION 9

Answer - [A, B, C]

Option A - Azure Monitor: Provides metrics and alerts that can trigger autoscaling actions based on predefined conditions. Option B - Azure Logic Apps: Can be used to create workflows that trigger scaling actions in response to specific events or conditions. Option C - Azure Functions: Can be integrated with autoscale to execute custom scripts or actions in response to scaling events.

Option D - Azure Resource Manager templates: While useful for deploying and managing resources, they are not typically integrated with autoscale for triggering scaling actions. Option E - Azure Sentinel: A security information and event management (SIEM) service, not directly related to autoscaling AVD session hosts.

EXAM FOCUS	*Integrate Azure Monitor for metrics-based autoscaling, Logic Apps for workflows, and Functions for custom actions. These tools together enable proactive scaling responses based on usage trends. Ensure configurations align with operational thresholds to avoid over-scaling or resource shortages.*
CAUTION ALERT	*Avoid assuming tools like ARM templates or Sentinel are autoscale-friendly—they do not offer direct triggers for scaling. Misusing such tools could delay scaling actions or complicate workflows unnecessarily.*

QUESTION 10

Answer - D) Configuration is already secure

Option A - Incorrect: MFA is not directly configurable via storage account settings but should be enforced where possible.
Option B - Incorrect: The 'Deny' default action is a secure setup, only allowing specified traffic.
Option C - Incorrect: 'supportsHttpsTrafficOnly' set to true enhances security.
Option D - Correct: The current configuration aligns with security best practices.
Option E - Incorrect: The location 'westus2' is a valid choice and does not impact security.

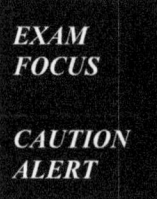

EXAM FOCUS	*The Bicep script is secure as configured, with HTTPS traffic enforced and default action set to deny. Ensure networkAcls are appropriately defined to allow only trusted sources. Regularly review access controls and integrate identity solutions like Azure AD for added protection.*
CAUTION ALERT	*Avoid altering security-enhancing configurations like supportsHttpsTrafficOnly or defaultAction: Deny. Misconfiguring these settings could expose sensitive data or weaken defenses against unauthorized access. Always validate scripts for compliance and best practices.*

QUESTION 11

Answer - A) Regular Audits and Reviews of License Usage and Allocation; B) Automation of License Assignment and Renewal Processes; D) Integration with Azure Policy for Enforcement of Licensing Policies

Option A - Correct. Regular audits and reviews of license usage and allocation help identify any discrepancies or non-compliance issues, allowing for corrective actions to be taken.

Option B - Correct. Automation of license assignment and renewal processes streamlines administrative tasks and reduces the likelihood of manual errors or oversights in license management, contributing to compliance. Option D - Correct. Integration with Azure Policy enables organizations to enforce licensing policies across the AVD environment, ensuring consistent compliance and adherence to regulatory requirements.

Option C - Incorrect. While RBAC is important for access control and governance, it is not directly related to maintaining compliance in licensing for session hosts within AVD deployments. Option E - Incorrect. Training and awareness programs for end users focus on education about licensing policies but do not directly contribute to maintaining compliance in license management processes.

EXAM FOCUS	*You should conduct regular license audits to catch discrepancies early, automate license assignments for efficiency, and use Azure Policy for enforcement to ensure consistent compliance. Always maintain detailed records to support audits and regulatory checks. Leverage tools like Azure Cost Management for proactive tracking of license usage.*
CAUTION ALERT	*Avoid assuming RBAC alone can enforce licensing compliance; it primarily controls access. Do not overlook Azure Policy as a critical enforcement tool for maintaining consistent licensing across session hosts, as manual processes often lead to non-compliance.*

QUESTION 12

Answer - [E]

Option E - Azure Site Recovery: Azure Site Recovery provides disaster recovery as a service and supports automatic failover of AVD host pools to a secondary Azure region, ensuring minimal data loss and downtime during failover operations.

Option A - Azure Active Directory is an identity and access management service and is not directly related to failover and disaster recovery of AVD host pools. Option B - Azure Traffic Manager provides DNS-based traffic routing but does not directly support failover and disaster recovery for AVD host pools. Option C - Azure Backup is primarily used for data backup and recovery and is not designed for failover and disaster recovery of AVD host pools. Option D - Azure Monitor provides monitoring and analytics capabilities but does not directly support failover and disaster recovery for AVD host pools.

EXAM FOCUS	*Incorporate Azure Site Recovery to automate failover and replication for AVD environments. This ensures data resilience and high availability across regions. You need to configure recovery plans that align with organizational RTO/RPO goals and test them regularly to verify readiness for real-world scenarios.*
CAUTION ALERT	*Stay clear of relying solely on Azure Traffic Manager or Azure Backup for disaster recovery. Traffic Manager only handles DNS routing, and Backup is designed for data restoration, not failover automation. Misusing these tools can result in incomplete disaster recovery plans.*

QUESTION 13

Answer - A) Documenting Image Configuration Settings and Changes; B) Retaining Audit Logs of Image Modifications

Option A - Correct. Documenting image configuration settings and changes provides transparency and traceability, essential for compliance and auditing purposes. Option B - Correct. Retaining audit logs of image modifications allows for accountability and monitoring of changes, supporting compliance with regulatory requirements.

Option C - Incorrect. While MFA enhances security, it is not directly related to fulfilling documentation and compliance requirements in AVD image management. Option D - Incorrect. Periodic security assessments are important for overall security posture but do not specifically address documentation and compliance requirements in AVD image management. Option E - Incorrect. Ensuring encryption of image data enhances security but is not solely focused on fulfilling documentation and compliance requirements in AVD image management.

EXAM	*Document image configurations and changes thoroughly for traceability and compliance. Retain audit logs*

FOCUS	*for all modifications to ensure accountability and facilitate compliance reporting. You need to use automation to streamline these processes while maintaining security standards for your image repositories.*
CAUTION ALERT	*Avoid assuming encryption or MFA alone satisfies compliance requirements. While these enhance security, they do not address documentation and traceability needs. Neglecting detailed configuration records can result in audit failures and non-compliance with regulatory standards.*

QUESTION 14

Answer - A) Check Azure Resource Manager (ARM) Template Configuration; B) Validate Image Generalization Process for Golden Image; C) Review Network Connectivity and Subnet Configuration

Option A - Correct. Checking the ARM template configuration ensures that the deployment settings are correctly defined, preventing potential issues during creation. Option B - Correct. Validating the image generalization process confirms that the golden image is properly prepared for deployment, reducing errors during creation.

Option C - Correct. Reviewing network connectivity and subnet configuration ensures that session hosts can communicate with required resources and services, resolving potential connectivity issues. Option D - Incorrect. While Azure AD integration is essential for user authentication, it is not directly related to creation issues from golden images. Option E - Incorrect. Monitoring Azure Service Health is important for platform-wide issues but may not provide specific insights into creation issues from golden images.

EXAM FOCUS	*Validate the golden image preparation process to confirm it's properly generalized. Check ARM template configurations for deployment consistency and review network settings to ensure connectivity to critical resources. Test image deployment in a non-production environment to identify and resolve issues proactively.*
CAUTION ALERT	*Avoid overlooking the generalization process. Deploying non-generalized images can lead to duplicate SID conflicts, causing deployment failures. Don't assume Azure AD integration or platform health alone addresses creation issues—they are not directly tied to golden image preparation.*

QUESTION 15

Answer - A) Best practice correctly identified

Option A - Correct: The described actions, methods, and compliance strategies are best practices for managing secure and compliant images in a Compute Gallery.
Option B - Incorrect: JSON is used here to represent the policy and is appropriate for illustrating the answer.
Option C - Incorrect: Quarterly reviews are adequate and more frequent than bi-annual, providing timely updates.
Option D - Incorrect: Automated tools are preferred for scalability and consistency over manual reviews.
Option E - Incorrect: Regular audits and version control are specific enough for general security compliance standards.

EXAM FOCUS	*You need to use automated patching tools and conduct quarterly reviews to maintain compliance with security standards for AVD images. Ensure all updates are documented, and version control is implemented to streamline audit processes. Regularly test images in staging environments before deploying to production.*
CAUTION ALERT	*Avoid relying on manual patching processes—they are time-intensive and prone to errors. Also, don't underestimate the importance of quarterly reviews; less frequent updates, such as bi-annual, may result in outdated security configurations, exposing your environment to vulnerabilities.*

QUESTION 16

Answer - A) Azure Monitor Logs for Activity Logging and Analysis; C) Azure Security Center Compliance Score for Regulatory Compliance Assessment; D) Built-in Reporting and Dashboarding Capabilities for Compliance Monitoring

Option A - Correct. Azure Monitor Logs provide activity logging and analysis capabilities, allowing administrators to track user actions and detect security incidents in AVD deployments.

Option B - Incorrect. While integration with Azure Sentinel is valuable for security incident detection, it may not be a specific feature offered by Azure Virtual Desktop for auditing and compliance monitoring. Option C - Correct. Azure Security Center Compliance Score assesses AVD environments against regulatory compliance standards, helping organizations identify and address compliance gaps.

Option D - Correct. Azure Virtual Desktop offers built-in reporting and dashboarding capabilities for compliance monitoring, providing insights into security posture and regulatory adherence. Option E - Incorrect. While integration with Microsoft Defender for Cloud is important for threat intelligence, it may not be directly related to auditing and compliance monitoring features in Azure Virtual Desktop.

EXAM FOCUS	*Use Azure Monitor Logs for activity tracking, Security Center Compliance Score for regulatory assessments, and built-in dashboards for compliance visibility. Combine these tools to create a comprehensive monitoring strategy tailored to your AVD environment. Conduct regular reviews of logs and compliance reports.*
CAUTION ALERT	*Don't rely solely on Sentinel or Defender for Cloud for compliance. While they provide valuable insights, they are primarily focused on threat intelligence and incident detection, not auditing and compliance monitoring. Neglecting built-in AVD features can lead to gaps in visibility.*

QUESTION 17

Answer - A) Optimization Techniques for Remote Display Protocols and Multimedia Redirection; B) Resource Allocation Strategies for Different User Profiles and Workloads; D) Implementation of User Experience (UX) Testing and Feedback Mechanisms

Option A - Correct. Successful case studies often highlight optimization techniques for remote display protocols and multimedia redirection, which are crucial for improving AVD performance. Option B - Correct. Resource allocation strategies tailored to different user profiles and workloads play a key role in optimizing AVD performance and ensuring a smooth user experience.

Option C - Incorrect. While integrating third-party performance monitoring tools may be beneficial, it may not be a primary focus area highlighted in successful case studies of performance tuning in AVD deployments. Option D - Correct. Implementation of user experience (UX) testing and feedback mechanisms helps identify performance issues from the end-user perspective and guides performance tuning efforts in AVD deployments. Option E - Incorrect. While leveraging Azure Bastion for secure remote access is important, it may not be a primary focus area highlighted in successful case studies of performance tuning in AVD deployments.

EXAM FOCUS	*Focus on optimizing remote display protocols and multimedia redirection to enhance user experience. Tailor resource allocation strategies to match diverse workloads, and incorporate user experience feedback mechanisms to identify performance bottlenecks. These strategies are frequently highlighted in successful case studies for performance tuning.*
CAUTION ALERT	*Avoid focusing on generic tools like Azure Bastion for performance tuning—it's primarily for secure access, not optimization. Similarly, third-party tools are helpful but should complement, not replace, Azure-native features like Monitor and built-in optimization techniques.*

QUESTION 18

Answer - [D]

Option D - Verify the Azure Virtual Desktop agent version on session hosts: This action directly confirms whether outdated Azure Virtual Desktop agents are present on session hosts, helping to determine their impact on performance issues. Option A - Reviewing diagnostic logs may provide insights into performance issues but may not directly indicate the status of Azure Virtual Desktop agents.

Option B - Analyzing network traffic helps diagnose network-related performance issues but does not specifically

address the status of Azure Virtual Desktop agents. Option C - Monitoring CPU usage on session hosts can help identify resource utilization issues but does not directly confirm whether Azure Virtual Desktop agents are outdated.
Option E - Checking Azure Monitor metrics provides overall system performance data but does not specifically indicate the version of Azure Virtual Desktop agents installed on session hosts.

EXAM FOCUS	*Always verify the version of Azure Virtual Desktop agents on session hosts to confirm they're up to date. You should establish a regular update process for agents and review version release notes to understand performance improvements or bug fixes. Use automation tools to streamline agent updates across hosts.*
CAUTION ALERT	*Don't confuse performance monitoring tools like Azure Monitor with agent version verification. While helpful for general diagnostics, they won't identify outdated agents. Neglecting regular updates can lead to compatibility issues or degraded performance in AVD environments.*

QUESTION 19

Answer - A) Analyze network bandwidth utilization with Azure Network Watcher; B) Review VM configurations and adjust resource allocation if necessary

Option A - Correct. Analyzing network bandwidth utilization with Azure Network Watcher helps identify potential bottlenecks and optimize network performance for AVD deployments. Option B - Correct. Reviewing VM configurations and adjusting resource allocation ensures efficient resource utilization, enhancing AVD performance and responsiveness. Option C - Incorrect. Azure Application Insights focuses on application performance monitoring but does not directly address network or VM configuration issues in AVD deployments.

EXAM FOCUS	*Start by analyzing network bandwidth utilization with Azure Network Watcher to identify potential bottlenecks. Then review VM configurations to ensure optimal resource allocation. Address these areas systematically to resolve performance issues and enhance overall AVD efficiency. Always consider workload-specific optimizations.*
CAUTION ALERT	*Avoid assuming application monitoring tools like Application Insights will address network or VM issues. They are useful for application diagnostics but irrelevant for infrastructure-level performance optimization. Neglecting foundational areas like bandwidth and VM sizing can lead to incomplete resolutions.*

QUESTION 20

Answer - A) Command correctly enforces encryption

Option A - Correct: The command directly addresses the requirement to encrypt user data, which is essential for compliance with data protection regulations.

Option B - Incorrect: Restricting access based on user roles is crucial but would involve additional RBAC or identity management configurations, not covered by this command. Option C - Incorrect: Logging access attempts is necessary for auditing but would be configured in security monitoring or log management tools. Option D - Incorrect: While specifying the type of encryption could be necessary, the given command assumes the default or most applicable encryption type is used. Option E - Incorrect: Parameters for compliance auditing are important, but the focus here is on enforcing data encryption directly.

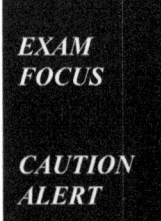

EXAM FOCUS	*Use the Set-AzAVDEncryption command to enforce data encryption for AVD environments. Combine this with role-based access controls and logging mechanisms to ensure comprehensive compliance with data protection regulations. Regularly audit encryption settings and access logs to maintain security and meet regulatory requirements.*
CAUTION ALERT	*Don't neglect access control and auditing when enforcing encryption. While the command addresses encryption directly, failing to implement RBAC or log monitoring may leave gaps in compliance. Misconfigured encryption settings can also result in unprotected data if not validated post-deployment.*

QUESTION 21

Answer - C

Option C - Port 3389 is the default port used for Remote Desktop Protocol (RDP) connections. Configuring firewall rules to allow traffic on port 3389 enables RDP connections to Azure Virtual Desktop instances securely.
Option A - Port 80 is typically used for unencrypted HTTP traffic and is not suitable for RDP connections.
Option B - Port 443 is used for HTTPS traffic and is not standard for RDP connections.
Option D - Port 8080 is often used for alternative web services but is not standard for RDP connections.
Option E - Port 8443 is sometimes used for secure web services but is not the default port for RDP connections.

EXAM FOCUS	*You need to ensure port 3389 is open in firewall rules to enable RDP connections for AVD securely. Test connectivity after configuration to confirm proper access. Avoid exposing port 3389 to the public internet; use VPN or private endpoints to secure connections.*
CAUTION ALERT	*Avoid confusing RDP port 3389 with other commonly used ports like 443 or 8443. Misconfiguring the firewall to open unnecessary ports can lead to security vulnerabilities, compromising the AVD environment.*

QUESTION 22

Answer - A) Reviewing Azure AD Connect synchronization logs for errors and warnings; B) Checking Azure AD sign-in logs for authentication failures and anomalies; E) Analyzing AVD session host event logs for Entra-related errors and warnings

Option A - Correct. Reviewing Azure AD Connect synchronization logs helps identify synchronization errors that may impact Entra services. Option B - Correct. Checking Azure AD sign-in logs allows for the detection of authentication failures and anomalies related to Entra services. Option E - Correct. Analyzing AVD session host event logs helps identify Entra-related errors and warnings that may affect service availability.

Option C - Incorrect. While monitoring Azure AD health status is important, it is not specifically related to troubleshooting Entra service issues in AVD environments. Option D - Incorrect. Reviewing Entra service status in the Azure portal may provide insights into performance issues but is not the primary method for troubleshooting Entra-related problems.

EXAM FOCUS	*Review Azure AD Connect sync logs for synchronization errors, sign-in logs for authentication failures, and AVD session host event logs for Entra-related issues. You should correlate these logs to pinpoint root causes and resolve them quickly. Use the Azure portal to monitor overall health for better visibility.*
CAUTION ALERT	*Avoid relying solely on Azure AD health monitoring or the Entra service status page for troubleshooting. While helpful, these do not provide detailed insights into synchronization errors or session host-specific issues, which are critical for effective resolution.*

QUESTION 23

Answer - A) Monitor Azure AD logs for suspicious sign-in activities or policy violations; B) Stay informed about security advisories and updates from Microsoft and other trusted sources; D) Collaborate with Azure security engineers to analyze threat intelligence and adjust policy settings accordingly

Option A - Correct. Monitoring Azure AD logs allows for detecting suspicious sign-in activities or policy violations, providing insights into potential security threats. Option B - Correct. Staying informed about security advisories and updates from trusted sources helps organizations stay proactive in addressing emerging security threats.

Option C - Incorrect. While conducting regular security assessments and risk evaluations is important, it may not specifically address monitoring and revising Conditional Access policies based on new security threats. Option D - Correct. Collaborating with Azure security engineers to analyze threat intelligence enables organizations to adjust policy settings effectively in response to evolving security threats.

Option E - Incorrect. While implementing automated alerts and notifications can enhance security monitoring, it may not directly address the revision of Conditional Access policies based on new security threats as described in the question.

EXAM FOCUS: Monitor Azure AD logs for unusual sign-ins, and stay updated with Microsoft security advisories to address new threats. Collaborate with security engineers to refine Conditional Access policies. Proactively adjust policies based on analyzed threat intelligence to minimize security risks in your AVD environment.

CAUTION ALERT: Avoid neglecting real-time monitoring and collaboration with experts. Conditional Access policies need continuous updates to counter emerging threats. Relying solely on static configurations without adjustments can leave your AVD vulnerable to evolving security risks.

QUESTION 24

Answer - A, B, C, D

A) Correct - Encrypting data at rest and in transit is fundamental in meeting compliance requirements for data security.
B) Correct - Using private endpoints enhances security by ensuring that network traffic between Azure services remains on the Microsoft backbone network, not the public internet.
C) Correct - Regular auditing is necessary for compliance, ensuring that all access and activities are monitored and recorded.
D) Correct - Integration with Azure Policy helps enforce organizational standards and regulatory compliance across Azure resources.
E) Incorrect - While using VPNs can add a layer of security, it is not specifically required for Azure Virtual Desktop environments from a compliance perspective.

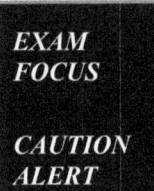

EXAM FOCUS: You should encrypt data at rest and in transit, use private endpoints for secure network connections, and regularly audit user activities for compliance. Integrating Azure Policy helps enforce standards across resources consistently. Implement these practices to align with highly regulated industry requirements.

CAUTION ALERT: Avoid relying solely on VPNs for security compliance in AVD. While useful, VPNs are not mandatory or sufficient for ensuring full regulatory compliance. Neglecting private endpoints or encryption can expose data to unauthorized access or breaches.

QUESTION 25

Answer - A) Update-MpSignature

Option A - Correct: This command directly initiates an update of the antivirus definitions, ensuring that the latest security measures are in place.
Option B - Incorrect: Retrieves the current signature version but does not update it.
Option C - Incorrect: This command does not exist in PowerShell.
Option D - Incorrect: Incorrect syntax and command for updating signatures.
Option E - Incorrect: This command does not exist in PowerShell.

EXAM FOCUS: Use Update-MpSignature in PowerShell to update Defender antivirus definitions. Automate this command via scripts or scheduled tasks to ensure definitions are always current. Regularly verify updates to maintain optimal security for AVD session hosts.

CAUTION ALERT: Avoid confusing commands like Get-MpSignature or Force-MpUpdate, which do not initiate updates. Using incorrect commands can delay updates, leaving your AVD environment vulnerable to the latest threats. Always validate command syntax before implementation.

QUESTION 26

Answer - A) Implement Just-In-Time (JIT) access for temporary and time-bound administrative access; B) Enforce multi-factor authentication (MFA) for all administrative access to AVD session hosts; C) Configure role-based access control (RBAC) to limit administrative privileges based on job roles

Option A - Correct. Implementing JIT access enhances security by providing temporary and time-bound administrative access to AVD session hosts. Option B - Correct. Enforcing MFA adds an extra layer of security to administrative access, reducing the risk of unauthorized access. Option C - Correct. Configuring RBAC helps limit administrative privileges based on job roles, minimizing the potential impact of security breaches. Option D - Incorrect. While Azure Bastion is a secure option for RDP/SSH access, it is not the only best practice for administrative access to AVD session hosts as described in the question.

Option E - Incorrect. While regularly reviewing and updating access permissions is important, it is not specifically mentioned in the context of best practices for administrative access to AVD session hosts as described in the question.

EXAM FOCUS	*Implement Just-In-Time (JIT) access for temporary admin tasks, enforce MFA for all admin accounts, and use RBAC to align privileges with job roles. Regularly review access settings to prevent privilege escalation and unauthorized access to AVD session hosts.*
CAUTION ALERT	*Avoid assuming Azure Bastion alone fulfills best practices for admin access. While useful for secure connections, it is not a substitute for JIT, MFA, or RBAC. Misconfigured admin access policies can lead to unnecessary risks and operational inefficiencies.*

QUESTION 27

Answer - A, B, D

A) Correct - Implementing MFA is crucial for robust access control, providing an additional layer of security for remote access. B) Correct - Configuring Azure Firewall with threat intelligence helps mitigate network threats by blocking malicious traffic and activities.

C) Incorrect - While VPN connectivity is important for secure access, it does not directly address the integration with enterprise security operations or the broader scope of network threats. D) Correct - Integrating AVD with corporate SIEM systems enhances security operations by allowing real-time monitoring and response to security incidents.
E) Incorrect - Network micro-segmentation is beneficial for limiting lateral movement within networks but does not directly address robust access control or integration with security operations.

EXAM FOCUS	*You need to implement MFA for strong access control, configure Azure Firewall with threat intelligence to mitigate threats, and integrate AVD with SIEM tools for enterprise-grade security monitoring. These measures ensure robust protection for AVD environments under increased remote work demands.*
CAUTION ALERT	*Avoid over-relying on VPN connectivity or micro-segmentation alone for comprehensive security. While helpful, these measures do not address broader security integration or proactive threat management. Neglecting MFA or SIEM integration leaves critical gaps in AVD defenses.*

QUESTION 28

Answer - A) Complexity in defining granular roles and permissions; B) Role sprawl due to excessive role creation and assignment; C) Difficulty in aligning role assignments with changing organizational needs; D) Lack of visibility into role assignments and access permissions

Option A - Correct. Complexity in defining granular roles and permissions can be addressed by conducting thorough role analysis and collaborating with stakeholders to ensure roles are accurately defined and scoped. Option B - Correct. Role sprawl due to excessive role creation and assignment can be mitigated by implementing role hierarchy structures and regularly reviewing and consolidating roles. Option C - Correct. Difficulty in aligning role assignments with changing organizational needs can be addressed by establishing a robust role management process that includes regular reviews and updates based on evolving requirements.

Option D - Correct. Lack of visibility into role assignments and access permissions can be overcome by implementing centralized role management tools and regular auditing and reporting mechanisms to track role assignments and permissions. Option E - Incorrect. While user training and awareness are important for successful RBAC implementation, they are not directly related to the challenges of RBAC implementation described in the question.

EXAM FOCUS	*Define granular roles collaboratively with stakeholders to avoid excessive role creation. Regularly review and consolidate roles to prevent sprawl, and use centralized tools for visibility into role assignments. Establish a clear process for aligning roles with evolving organizational needs.*
CAUTION ALERT	*Avoid neglecting periodic reviews of RBAC roles, as outdated configurations can lead to unauthorized access. Overcomplicating RBAC by creating too many roles without clear scopes results in inefficiency and increased management overhead. Use centralized tools for better control.*

QUESTION 29

Answer - A) Review MFA usage reports and logs in Azure Active Directory to track authentication attempts and success rates; B) Implement Azure Monitor alerts for suspicious or failed MFA authentication events to detect potential security incidents; D) Analyze user support tickets and helpdesk requests related to MFA setup or authentication issues to identify trends and areas for improvement

Option A - Correct. Reviewing MFA usage reports and logs in Azure Active Directory provides insights into authentication attempts, success rates, and potential security threats. Option B - Correct. Implementing Azure Monitor alerts for suspicious or failed MFA authentication events enables proactive detection and response to potential security incidents.

Option C - Incorrect. While conducting user surveys or feedback sessions can provide valuable insights, it may not capture comprehensive data on MFA effectiveness or security incidents. Option D - Correct. Analyzing user support tickets and helpdesk requests related to MFA setup or authentication issues helps identify trends and areas for improvement in MFA implementation and user experience. Option E - Incorrect. While performing periodic security audits and assessments is important, it may not provide real-time visibility into MFA effectiveness or ongoing security threats.

EXAM FOCUS	*Review MFA usage reports in Azure AD to analyze success rates and trends. Use Azure Monitor alerts for failed or suspicious MFA attempts and track user support tickets to identify setup or authentication issues. This ensures ongoing improvements in MFA effectiveness and user experience.*
CAUTION ALERT	*Avoid relying solely on periodic security audits or user surveys for MFA evaluation. These methods may miss real-time issues or patterns. Neglecting automated monitoring tools can lead to delays in detecting and addressing potential vulnerabilities or user friction points.*

QUESTION 30

Answer - B) Specify on-premises gateway

Option A - Incorrect: The script is incomplete without specifying the on-premises connection endpoint.
Option B - Correct: The on-premises gateway must be specified to complete the hybrid connection.
Option C - Incorrect: While security is crucial, the key strength is a separate concern from establishing the connection.
Option D - Incorrect: Encryption is important but configuring it requires additional parameters not shown.
Option E - Incorrect: Resource group naming is organizational and does not impact the technical configuration of the connection.

EXAM FOCUS	*Specify the on-premises gateway when creating a hybrid VPN connection. Use a strong shared key and configure encryption protocols for secure communication. Always validate configurations for compliance with data protection standards before deploying connections in production.*
CAUTION ALERT	*Avoid incomplete scripts that omit critical parameters like the on-premises gateway. Failing to define encryption protocols or using weak shared keys exposes hybrid connections to potential breaches. Validate all configurations to ensure secure and compliant setups.*

QUESTION 31

Answer - A) Profile container bloat due to excessive user data storage and disk space utilization; B) Inconsistent application settings and configurations across user sessions and environments; C) Profile corruption or loss resulting from FSLogix service failures or unexpected interruptions

Option A - Correct. Profile container bloat can lead to performance issues and increased disk space utilization, requiring regular maintenance and cleanup. Option B - Correct. Inconsistent application settings across user sessions can cause usability issues and impact productivity, requiring synchronization mechanisms or standardized configurations.

Option C - Correct. Profile corruption or loss due to FSLogix service failures or interruptions can result in data loss and user profile inconsistencies, necessitating backup and recovery procedures. Option D - Incorrect. While performance degradation due to disk I/O operations is a concern, it may not be specific to FSLogix configuration issues. Option E - Incorrect. While compatibility issues with legacy applications are relevant, they may not be considered common configuration issues specific to FSLogix in AVD environments.

EXAM FOCUS	*You should monitor profile containers regularly and implement quotas to prevent bloat. Use standardized configurations for consistent application settings and set up backups to recover from service failures. Always validate that FSLogix services are running correctly post-deployment.*
CAUTION ALERT	*Avoid overlooking regular profile maintenance. Stay cautioned against relying on manual cleanup processes, as they can lead to inconsistencies. Automated monitoring tools can save significant troubleshooting time.*

QUESTION 32

Answer - A) Analyze event logs for Profile Container-related errors, C) Test Profile Container functionality by creating and accessing user profiles, D) Monitor storage usage and performance metrics for Profile Containers.

A) Analyze event logs for Profile Container-related errors - Event logs provide valuable insights into any errors or issues encountered during Profile Container operations, aiding in troubleshooting efforts. C) Test Profile Container functionality by creating and accessing user profiles - Testing user profile creation and access helps verify the integrity and functionality of Profile Containers post-installation.

D) Monitor storage usage and performance metrics for Profile Containers - Monitoring storage usage and performance metrics allows administrators to identify any anomalies or performance issues with Profile Containers. B) Utilize FSLogix diagnostic tools to identify performance bottlenecks - While FSLogix diagnostic tools can help diagnose performance issues, they may not be specific to Profile Container-related problems. E) Use PowerShell scripts to automate Profile Container maintenance tasks - PowerShell scripts can automate maintenance tasks but may not directly address troubleshooting issues with Profile Containers.

EXAM FOCUS	*Always remember to use event logs for diagnostic insights and validate Profile Container functionality by simulating user scenarios. Regular storage monitoring can proactively catch issues. You can consider using both manual and automated checks for holistic troubleshooting.*
CAUTION ALERT	*Stay clear of assuming all errors are FSLogix-specific. Profile issues might stem from storage misconfigurations or network connectivity. Always validate each layer of the setup independently.*

QUESTION 33

Answer - A, B, D

A) Correct - MFA adds a layer of security, ensuring that only authorized users access the AVD environment, essential for government agencies.
B) Correct - Azure Firewall controls traffic, protecting against external threats and unauthorized access.
C) Incorrect - While Azure Information Protection classifies and protects data, it does not directly relate to access control or external threat protection in an AVD context.

D) Correct - Azure Audit Logs, especially with appropriate retention policies, are crucial for monitoring, auditing, and compliance in governmental setups.

E) Incorrect - Defender for Identity protects against identity-based attacks but is not specifically required for the access control or auditing needs stated.

EXAM FOCUS	*Make sure MFA is enabled for all users to add a critical security layer. Configure Azure Firewall with strict inbound and outbound rules for better governance. Retain audit logs long enough for compliance and analysis.*
CAUTION ALERT	*Avoid assuming that data classification directly addresses security threats. Stay cautioned about configuring audit policies incorrectly, as improper retention can lead to compliance issues.*

QUESTION 34

Answer - B) Configure FSLogix Profile Containers to provide a consistent user experience across different devices and sessions, D) Utilize Azure Network Watcher to monitor network traffic between clients and AVD resources and identify connectivity issues.

B) Configure FSLogix Profile Containers to provide a consistent user experience across different devices and sessions - FSLogix Profile Containers ensure a seamless user experience by maintaining consistent user profiles across different devices and sessions, enhancing usability and productivity.

D) Utilize Azure Network Watcher to monitor network traffic between clients and AVD resources and identify connectivity issues - Monitoring network traffic helps identify and address connectivity issues affecting client performance and user experience, ensuring smooth AVD sessions for users. A) Implement Azure Bastion for secure RDP access to AVD instances without exposing them to the public internet - While Azure Bastion enhances access security, it may not directly optimize client performance and user experience across diverse usage scenarios.

C) Leverage Azure AD Conditional Access policies to enforce multi-factor authentication (MFA) based on user roles - While Conditional Access policies enhance security, they may not directly address performance optimization and user experience for AVD clients. E) Deploy GPU-accelerated virtual machines (VMs) for users requiring high-definition multimedia applications - While GPU-accelerated VMs enhance performance for multimedia applications, they may not directly optimize client performance and user experience for diverse usage scenarios.

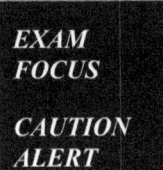	
EXAM FOCUS	*You need to prioritize FSLogix Profile Containers for consistent user experience and monitor network traffic for bottlenecks using tools like Azure Network Watcher. Consider the needs of diverse devices and allocate resources accordingly.*
CAUTION ALERT	*Stay alert to underestimating the impact of weak network performance. Avoid overlooking lightweight VM options for users who do not need resource-intensive applications.*

QUESTION 35

Answer - A) Command correctly monitors multimedia traffic

Option A - Correct: This command is appropriate for starting the diagnosis by checking the flow log status, which can help identify network traffic issues.

Option B - Incorrect: While specific filters could enhance the diagnosis, the basic command setup is correct for initial monitoring. Option C - Incorrect: The location parameter should match the deployment region, and "East US" is a typical setting.

Option D - Incorrect: The TargetResourceId should indeed specify the resource, and assuming "resource-id" is a placeholder for the actual ID, this would be correct. Option E - Incorrect: Network traffic monitoring is possible with Azure Network Watcher, which includes flow log status.

| EXAM | *Keep in mind that the Get-AzNetworkWatcherFlowLogStatus command is an initial diagnostic tool. You* |

FOCUS	can further enhance it with specific filters for multimedia traffic analysis. Ensure deployment regions match the correct location.
CAUTION ALERT	Avoid assuming this command alone is enough for in-depth analysis. Stay cautioned against using incorrect resource IDs, as it can lead to misleading diagnostics.

QUESTION 36

Answer - A, B, C

A) Correct - Azure Automation allows for scaling of VMs based on real-time demand, ensuring scalability of the AVD environment. B) Correct - Azure Sentinel provides advanced monitoring and threat detection capabilities, protecting against cyber threats. C) Correct - RBAC ensures that only authorized personnel have the necessary permissions to modify configurations, enhancing security.

D) Incorrect - While Azure AD Conditional Access is crucial for securing access, it does not directly pertain to VM modification permissions or scalability. E) Incorrect - Azure Security Center is essential for security management but does not directly ensure scalability or specific access to configuration settings.

EXAM FOCUS	You need to leverage Azure Automation for dynamic scaling. Always implement RBAC for secure modifications and deploy Azure Sentinel for real-time threat detection. Use layered security approaches for maximum protection.
CAUTION ALERT	Stay cautioned about relying solely on Azure Security Center for scalability. Avoid granting broad permissions in RBAC roles; this can lead to security vulnerabilities.

QUESTION 37

Answer - A) az network watcher packet-capture create

The "az network watcher packet-capture create" command captures network packets for analysis, helping to identify potential causes of session disruptions related to network issues.

Option B - Incorrect. "az network vnet list" command lists virtual networks but does not capture network traffic for analysis. Option C - Incorrect. "az network watcher flow-log configure" command configures flow logs for traffic but does not capture packet data for analysis.

Option D - Incorrect. "az network watcher troubleshooting start" initiates a troubleshooting session but does not capture packet data for analysis. Option E - Incorrect. "az network watcher test-connectivity" command tests connectivity but does not capture packet data for analysis.

EXAM FOCUS	You should use the az network watcher packet-capture create command for detailed traffic analysis. It's essential to identify session disruptions by capturing and analyzing real-time packet flows.
CAUTION ALERT	Stay clear of using commands like test-connectivity for in-depth troubleshooting. Avoid capturing packets without filtering, as it can result in excessive and irrelevant data.

QUESTION 38

Answer - A) Reviewing Azure Activity Logs to identify any recent changes or events affecting desktop provisioning

Reviewing Azure Activity Logs helps identify recent changes or events affecting desktop provisioning, enabling efficient troubleshooting and resolution of delays in accessing desktop environments.

Option B - Incorrect. While network performance is important, it may not directly relate to desktop provisioning delays.
Option C - Incorrect. FSLogix profiles impact user settings but may not cause delays in accessing desktop environments.
Option D - Incorrect. ARM templates affect deployment but are not directly related to desktop access delays.

Option E - Incorrect. Azure Bastion logs may reveal access issues but are not specific to desktop provisioning delays.

EXAM FOCUS	Always remember to review Azure Activity Logs for recent changes affecting desktop provisioning. This can provide direct insights into the root causes of delays. Consider correlating logs with other metrics for better context.
CAUTION ALERT	Avoid neglecting Activity Logs in favor of network metrics alone. Stay cautioned against assuming FSLogix profiles or ARM templates are the sole culprits without evidence.

QUESTION 39

Answer - A, B, D

A) Correct - Azure ExpressRoute provides direct, private connectivity that enhances network performance, crucial for video editing tasks requiring high bandwidth. B) Correct - Azure Bastion offers a secure method to access remote desktops, crucial for protecting access to sensitive editing tools and content.

C) Incorrect - Azure Media Services is critical for media handling but does not impact the configuration of AVD in terms of network performance or secure access. D) Correct - A dedicated subnet, AzureBastionSubnet, is required for Bastion, ensuring that it functions correctly within the network. E) Incorrect - Azure Front Door improves content delivery across global regions but is not specific to enhancing AVD configurations for low latency or secure access in this context.

EXAM FOCUS	You need to deploy Azure ExpressRoute for low-latency network performance and use Azure Bastion for secure VM access. Configure a dedicated subnet for Bastion to avoid conflicts and ensure secure connectivity.
CAUTION ALERT	Stay cautioned against relying on Azure Media Services for network optimization—it is not designed for AVD performance. Avoid misconfiguring the AzureBastionSubnet, as it may lead to connectivity issues.

QUESTION 40

Answer - D

Option A - Incorrect. The script currently only specifies one application, so -FilePath is appropriate.

Option B - Incorrect. There is no indication the rule already exists; New-FSLogixAppMaskingRule is appropriate for creating a new rule. Option C - Incorrect. Rules are enabled by default; this addition is unnecessary. Option D - Correct. - AssignedUserGroup should be used to specify a group, not -AssignedUser, which is intended for individual user accounts. Option E - Incorrect. There is an error in specifying the user group versus individual users.

EXAM FOCUS	Always remember to use -AssignedUserGroup for group assignments in FSLogix rules. It simplifies management for large teams. Ensure the rules align with organizational policies and user access requirements.
CAUTION ALERT	Avoid assuming -AssignedUser can apply to groups. Stay alert to unnecessary additions like -Enabled $true, as rules are enabled by default, which might lead to script inefficiencies.

QUESTION 41

Answer - B

Option A - Incorrect. While the configuration enforces private links, it doesn't explicitly secure all traffic.
Option B - Correct. Adding secureTrafficOnly: true ensures that all communications are conducted over secured channels only. Option C - Incorrect. forceTunneling: true is more related to network routing than security per se.
Option D - Incorrect. While specifying protocols is good, it's not relevant to the resource type in question.
Option E - Incorrect. The resource type 'Microsoft.Network/virtualNetworks/subnets' is correct for network configurations related to Teams.

EXAM FOCUS	You should ensure secureTrafficOnly: true is added in the Bicep template to enforce secure communication for Microsoft Teams in AVD. This configuration safeguards sensitive data. Always validate templates by comparing against official security guidelines to prevent misconfigurations.
CAUTION ALERT	Stay clear of mistaking forceTunneling for enforcing security. It primarily addresses routing and not secure communication. Misconfiguring protocol: HTTPS can result in partial protection, so validate every parameter carefully.

QUESTION 42

Answer - A, B, C

A) Correct - 'VHDLocations' needs to be set to manage where user profile disks are stored, crucial for handling large files efficiently. B) Correct - Adjusting 'Size' ensures that the container is large enough to handle graphic files without performance degradation.

C) Correct - 'DynamicVHDAllocation' helps in managing disk space efficiently, which is key when dealing with large file sizes typical in design work. D) Incorrect - 'DiskType' under ODFC does not directly impact performance or file management within FSLogix profiles. E) Incorrect - 'ProfileType' determines the type of profile but does not specifically address performance or file management needs in this context.

EXAM FOCUS	Make sure VHDLocations points to a scalable storage location, and DynamicVHDAllocation is enabled to optimize disk usage. Configure Size appropriately for large graphic files. These settings ensure high performance and support design workloads effectively. Test changes in staging environments.
CAUTION ALERT	Avoid overlooking dynamic allocation settings, as static configurations can cause unnecessary disk space usage. Stay cautioned against incorrect paths for VHDLocations, which may lead to profile errors or inaccessible user data in production.

QUESTION 43

Answer - D) Azure Network Watcher

Option A - Incorrect. While Azure Health Monitor provides insights into the health of Azure services, Azure Network Watcher offers more specific tools for analyzing performance metrics and identifying potential bottlenecks in AVD host pools.

Option B - Incorrect. Azure Resource Graph provides insights into Azure resources but may not offer real-time analysis of performance metrics for AVD host pools. Option C - Incorrect. Azure Monitor Metrics Explorer visualizes metrics but may not provide real-time analysis of performance metrics for AVD host pools.

Option D - Correct. Azure Network Watcher offers network diagnostics, including real-time monitoring and troubleshooting, making it an effective tool for identifying common performance issues in AVD host pools. Option E - Incorrect. Azure Advisor provides recommendations for Azure resources but may not offer real-time analysis of performance metrics for AVD host pools.

EXAM FOCUS	You should utilize Azure Monitor Metrics Explorer for real-time analysis and historical insights into AVD host pool performance. Combine it with alerts to identify and resolve bottlenecks proactively. Cross-reference metrics with session logs for comprehensive diagnostics.
CAUTION ALERT	Avoid relying solely on Azure Health Monitor for in-depth analysis. While useful for general health insights, it lacks the granularity needed for specific performance issues. Always validate data sources in Metrics Explorer for consistency.

QUESTION 44

Answer - A) Configure Azure Monitor Logs retention policies for AVD

Option A - Configuring Azure Monitor Logs retention policies for AVD allows you to define the duration for retaining log data, ensuring compliance with data retention requirements while enabling historical analysis. Option B - Storing AVD telemetry data in Azure Blob Storage may offer long-term retention but lacks built-in analytics capabilities.

Option C - Azure Monitor Workbooks are used for data visualization, not for data retention and analysis. Option D - Azure Data Explorer is suitable for ad-hoc querying but may not provide cost-effective long-term data retention. Option E - Integrating AVD telemetry with Azure Log Analytics offers advanced analytics but may not provide customizable retention policies for AVD-specific data.

EXAM FOCUS	*Always configure Azure Monitor Logs retention policies for AVD telemetry. Set durations that align with regulatory needs to balance compliance, cost, and analytics. Use Azure Monitor Workbooks to visualize trends and identify anomalies efficiently while maintaining retention standards.*
CAUTION ALERT	*Avoid storing telemetry in Blob Storage without analyzing the cost vs. benefit. Blob Storage is great for archival but lacks integrated analytics. Stay alert to over-retention, which increases costs without adding proportional business value.*

QUESTION 45

Answer - D

Option A - Incorrect. The snippet sets a policy but may not specify the blob type, which can be crucial for targeting specific data.

Option B - Incorrect. "Lifecycle" is the correct type for Azure Blob Storage management policies. Option C - Incorrect. "daysAfterModificationGreaterThan" is typically the correct setting for retention policies based on last modification, not creation.

Option D - Correct. Including "filters" with "blobTypes" ["blockBlob"] ensures that the retention policy is correctly applied to the intended type of blob storage, which is essential for managing compliance effectively. Option E - Incorrect. The property for enabling a rule in the JSON snippet is "enabled", not "isEnabled".

EXAM FOCUS	*You should include filters with blobTypes: ["blockBlob"] in the ARM template to target specific data types for retention policies. Use lifecycle rules to optimize data management, and validate compliance by regularly auditing retention policies against industry standards.*
CAUTION ALERT	*Avoid assuming a generic template will meet your needs. Misconfigured rules can lead to excessive storage costs or data loss. Validate lifecycle configurations and ensure the targeted blobs align with your compliance and operational requirements.*

QUESTION 46

Answer - A) Network latency and bandwidth constraints

Option A - Network latency and bandwidth constraints can significantly impact user experience in AVD environments, especially during scaling operations. Prioritizing network optimization can help minimize disruptions and ensure seamless user access, enhancing productivity and satisfaction.

Option B - Cost implications are important but may not directly affect user experience unless resource scaling affects service availability or performance. Option C - Compatibility of applications with scaled resources is essential but may not directly address user experience during scaling operations.

Option D - Azure Bastion provides secure remote access to VMs but is not directly related to user experience during resource scaling. Option E - Azure AD authentication is crucial for user access but may not be significantly impacted by resource scaling actions.

EXAM	*You need to prioritize minimizing network latency and ensuring sufficient bandwidth during scaling*

FOCUS	operations. Proactively monitor network health and implement load balancing to maintain optimal user experiences. Consider scaling during non-peak hours to avoid disruptions.
CAUTION ALERT	Avoid focusing solely on cost when planning scaling actions. Stay cautious about underestimating the impact of poor network performance on user productivity. Proactively test scaling configurations in staging before applying them to production environments.

QUESTION 47

Answer - E) ISO/IEC 27001 (Information Security Management System)

Option E - ISO/IEC 27001 is an internationally recognized standard for information security management systems, providing a framework for implementing and maintaining security controls to protect sensitive data in AVD environments and ensuring compliance with regulatory requirements.

Option A - GDPR focuses on data protection and privacy for individuals within the European Union but may not apply universally to AVD deployments. Option B - HIPAA regulates the use and disclosure of protected health information (PHI) but may not be applicable to all AVD deployments. Option C - SOX focuses on financial reporting and internal controls but may not directly relate to AVD deployments. Option D - PCI DSS sets security standards for payment card transactions but may not apply to all AVD deployments.

EXAM FOCUS	Always align your AVD deployments with ISO/IEC 27001 for comprehensive security and compliance frameworks. Map its controls to industry-specific standards (e.g., GDPR, HIPAA) as needed. Use Azure Policy to enforce ISO compliance and streamline audits effectively.
CAUTION ALERT	Avoid overlooking ISO/IEC 27001 even if other frameworks (e.g., GDPR) are in focus. Stay alert to differences in regional regulations, and ensure your deployment adheres to both global and local compliance requirements for holistic security.

QUESTION 48

Answer - A, B, C

A) Correct - Windows 11 Enterprise supports multi-lingual setups and offers the latest security and performance enhancements. B) Correct - Windows 10 Enterprise multi-session allows for cost-effective, high-performance computing environments suitable for collaboration. C) Correct - Windows Server 2022 offers advanced security features necessary for protecting corporate data across global offices.

D) Incorrect - Windows Server 2016, while stable, does not provide the latest enhancements in security and performance required for a global corporate environment. E) Incorrect - Windows 8.1 Pro is outdated and does not meet the modern requirements for security or performance.

EXAM FOCUS	Deploy Windows 11 Enterprise for advanced security and multilingual support. Use Windows 10 Enterprise multi-session for shared environments. Windows Server 2022 offers robust server-side performance. Test all configurations for compatibility with your AVD workloads before deployment.
CAUTION ALERT	Avoid using outdated OS versions like Windows 8.1 or unsupported older servers. They lack modern security and performance features required for high-demand AVD setups. Stay cautious with licensing requirements to avoid non-compliance issues.

QUESTION 49

Answer - A) Developing comprehensive runbooks detailing step-by-step recovery procedures
B) Conducting tabletop exercises to simulate disaster scenarios and validate response procedures
C) Providing role-specific training on AVD disaster recovery roles and responsibilities

A) Developing comprehensive runbooks detailing step-by-step recovery procedures - Detailed runbooks ensure clarity and consistency in AVD disaster recovery procedures.

B) Conducting tabletop exercises to simulate disaster scenarios and validate response procedures - Tabletop exercises help identify gaps in recovery plans and train personnel for effective response. C) Providing role-specific training on AVD disaster recovery roles and responsibilities - Role-specific training ensures that personnel understand their roles and responsibilities during disaster recovery.

D, E) While Azure Resource Manager templates and Azure Information Protection are valuable for automation and data protection, they are not directly related to documentation and training on AVD disaster recovery plans.

EXAM FOCUS	*Make sure disaster recovery plans include detailed runbooks, role-specific training, and tabletop exercises to validate procedures. Use Azure Resource Manager templates for quick recovery provisioning and regular reviews to ensure the plan reflects current infrastructure.*
CAUTION ALERT	*Avoid relying solely on automated recovery tools. Stay clear of skipping live training exercises, as they are critical for ensuring staff readiness. Overlooked gaps in documentation can lead to significant delays during actual recovery scenarios.*

QUESTION 50

Answer - B) Configuring custom log alerts in Azure Monitor to notify stakeholders of application performance issues
C) Implementing Azure Automation for triggering automated actions based on predefined application performance metrics
D) Leveraging Azure Log Analytics to create custom queries for monitoring specific application performance metrics.

B) Configuring custom log alerts in Azure Monitor to notify stakeholders of application performance issues - Custom log alerts in Azure Monitor allow organizations to configure alerts based on specific application performance metrics, ensuring timely notification of issues.

C) Implementing Azure Automation for triggering automated actions based on predefined application performance metrics - Azure Automation enables organizations to automate actions based on predefined application performance metrics, enhancing operational efficiency.

D) Leveraging Azure Log Analytics to create custom queries for monitoring specific application performance metrics - Azure Log Analytics enables the creation of custom queries for monitoring specific application performance metrics, providing flexibility in performance monitoring.

A, E) While Azure Policy and Microsoft 365 Security Center offer valuable capabilities, they are not specifically focused on customizing application performance alerts in AVD.

EXAM FOCUS	*Configure custom alerts in Azure Monitor for application performance thresholds. Use Log Analytics for detailed queries and automate actions with Azure Automation. Regularly update alert rules to reflect operational changes and align thresholds with business objectives.*
CAUTION ALERT	*Avoid generic alert rules that don't align with specific operational needs. Stay cautious about alert fatigue from too many irrelevant alerts; they can obscure critical issues. Test your configurations to ensure accurate alerting before going live.*

PRACTICE TEST 6 - QUESTIONS ONLY

QUESTION 1

As a desktop administrator, you're tasked with configuring virtual network connectivity for a new AVD setup within a multinational corporation. Considerations include:
- Ensuring secure and isolated access for different departments.
- Integrating with existing on-premises AD DS.
- Utilizing Azure RBAC for granular control.

Which PowerShell cmdlet would you use to create and configure the virtual network necessary for this setup?

```
A) New-AzVirtualNetwork
B) Set-AzVirtualNetworkSubnetConfig
C) New-AzVirtualNetworkGateway
D) Get-AzVirtualNetwork
E) Add-AzVirtualNetworkPeering
```

QUESTION 2

You are tasked with configuring RDP Shortpath in Azure Virtual Desktop (AVD) to improve end-user experience. Your organization prioritizes seamless remote access for employees, especially for those working from home due to the pandemic. However, ensuring secure connectivity while optimizing performance poses a challenge. Additionally, the IT department must balance the need for efficient resource utilization with the demand for high-quality user experiences. How would you address these challenges when configuring RDP Shortpath in AVD?

A) Implement Azure Bastion for secure RDP access
B) Configure Azure Firewall to control RDP traffic
C) Enable RDP Shortpath via Group Policy settings
D) Utilize Azure AD Conditional Access policies
E) Deploy FSLogix to manage user profiles

QUESTION 3

- You are responsible for maintaining security standards in an Azure Virtual Desktop (AVD) environment.
- You need to ensure that only authorized users can access the AVD resources securely.
- Your task involves selecting the appropriate Log Analytics table to monitor and analyze security-related events.

Which table should you query to access detailed logs of security events, such as unauthorized access attempts and security policy violations?

```
A) WVDConnections
B) WVDSecurityEvents
C) WVDAuditLogs
D) WVDServiceMetadata
E) WVDAgentHealth
```

QUESTION 4

Your organization is planning the storage solution for Azure Virtual Desktop (AVD) user data to ensure optimal performance and cost-effectiveness. As the IT administrator, you need to consider various factors when planning storage solutions for AVD. Which factors should be considered in this planning process? Select CORRECT answers that apply.

A) Storage type (e.g., Premium SSD, Standard SSD, Standard HDD)
B) Performance requirements (e.g., IOPS, throughput)

C) Data redundancy and high availability
D) Scalability and elasticity of storage
E) Cost considerations (e.g., storage tiers, data transfer costs)

QUESTION 5

As an Azure administrator, you are tasked with setting up a new storage account optimized for AVD environments. You must use the Azure CLI to create the account. Identify the correct command to use.
bash
```
az storage account create --name MyStorageAccount --resource-group MyResourceGroup --location eastus --sku Standard_LRS --kind StorageV2
```

A) Command is correct
B) Incorrect location parameter
C) Incorrect SKU for AVD
D) Kind parameter is not suitable for AVD
E) Resource group does not exist

QUESTION 6

You are responsible for managing session hosts in an Azure Virtual Desktop (AVD) environment to optimize costs. The solution must meet the following requirements:
- Automatically start session hosts at 8:00 AM and shut them down at 6:00 PM.
- Only be in effect Monday to Friday.
- Minimize manual intervention and administrative effort.
Which Azure service should you leverage to achieve this? Select TWO.

A) Azure Monitor Alerts
B) Azure Automation with Azure Functions
C) Azure Resource Manager templates
D) Azure Automation with Azure Runbooks
E) Azure Virtual Machine Scale Sets

QUESTION 7

Your organization is exploring the licensing models available for Azure Virtual Desktop (AVD) deployments and needs to understand the options in detail. As the Azure specialist, you are tasked with providing an overview of these models. Which options should you include? Select THREE.

A) Per User Subscription
B) Per Device Subscription
C) Consumption-based Pricing
D) Enterprise Agreement (EA)
E) Bring Your Own License (BYOL)

QUESTION 8

Your organization is planning to deploy Azure Virtual Desktop (AVD) and needs to ensure optimal performance for end users. As the Azure specialist, you are tasked with evaluating methods to calculate and optimize performance. Which methods should you consider? Select THREE.

A) Load Testing and Benchmarking
B) Resource Utilization Monitoring and Analysis
C) User Experience Monitoring and Feedback

D) Performance Profiling and Optimization
E) Capacity Planning and Forecasting

QUESTION 9

You are responsible for optimizing resource utilization in an Azure Virtual Desktop (AVD) environment by implementing autoscale for host pools. Consider the following requirements:
- Ensure seamless scalability to accommodate fluctuating user demands.
- Automatically adjust resource allocation based on predefined performance thresholds.
- Minimize costs associated with overprovisioning resources.
Which of the following options should you prioritize to meet these requirements?

A) Implement a static scaling configuration for each host pool.
B) Utilize Azure Cost Management to monitor resource usage.
C) Configure autoscale rules based on CPU and memory utilization.
D) Schedule regular maintenance windows for scaling operations.
E) Implement network traffic shaping to control resource consumption.

QUESTION 10

You are configuring host pools for Azure Virtual Desktop to ensure optimal performance and security. Using PowerShell, how would you enforce the use of session hosts with GPUs for high-demand applications?

```powershell
New-AzAVDHostPool -Name "HighPerfHosts" -PreferredAppGroupType "Desktop" -CustomRdpProperty "use:gpu=True"
```

A) Correct configuration
B) CustomRdpProperty is incorrect
C) PreferredAppGroupType should be 'RemoteApp'
D) Missing location parameter
E) All are incorrect

QUESTION 11

Your organization is planning to create a golden image manually for Azure Virtual Desktop (AVD) to streamline deployment and ensure consistency across session hosts. As the Azure administrator, you need to understand the steps involved in this process. What are the critical steps for creating a golden image manually? Select CORRECT answers that apply.

A) Prepare Base Virtual Machine with Desired Configuration
B) Install and Configure Applications and Customizations
C) Sysprep and Generalize the Virtual Machine
D) Capture Virtual Machine Image in Azure
E) Verify Image Deployment and Accessibility

QUESTION 12

You are responsible for configuring a disaster recovery strategy for an Azure Virtual Desktop (AVD) infrastructure. Consider the following requirements:
- Ensure failover of AVD host pools to a secondary Azure region in case of a primary region failure.
- Minimize data loss and downtime during failover operations.
Which Azure service should you utilize to meet these requirements?

A) Azure Backup

B) Azure Traffic Manager
C) Azure Site Recovery
D) Azure Load Balancer
E) Azure Blob Storage

QUESTION 13

Your organization is exploring best practices for applying updates to Azure Virtual Desktop (AVD) images to ensure efficient management and minimal disruptions. As the Azure specialist, you need to identify key best practices for updating OS and applications in AVD images. Which of the following are considered best practices for applying updates to AVD images? Select TWO.

A) Implementing Automated Testing Workflows
B) Utilizing Ring-Based Deployment Strategies
C) Applying Updates During Off-Peak Hours
D) Leveraging Differential Image Updates
E) Enforcing Least Privilege Access Controls for Update Processes

QUESTION 14

Your organization is planning to implement image storage for Azure Virtual Desktop (AVD) environments and is exploring different options available in Azure. As the Azure specialist, you need to identify the options for storing images in Azure that align with AVD requirements. What are the options for storing images in Azure for AVD environments? Select THREE.

A) Azure Blob Storage
B) Azure Managed Disks
C) Azure Files
D) Azure Shared Image Gallery
E) Azure Data Lake Storage

QUESTION 15

You are tasked with designing an advanced networking solution for AVD to enhance performance across distributed geographical locations. Which Azure CLI command correctly sets up global VNET peering?

```bash
az network vnet peering create --name myVNetPeering --resource-group myResourceGroup --vnet-name myVNet --remote-vnet remoteVNetId --allow-vnet-access
```

A) Command is correct
B) Incorrect parameter --allow-vnet-access
C) Should include --allow-forwarded-traffic
D) --remote-vnet should be --remote-vnet-name
E) Missing subscription parameter

QUESTION 16

Your organization is facing key compliance challenges in Azure Virtual Desktop (AVD) deployments due to regulatory requirements and industry standards. As the Azure specialist, you need to address these challenges effectively. What are the key compliance challenges in AVD deployments? Select THREE.

A) Ensuring Data Sovereignty and Residency Compliance
B) Managing User Access Controls and Permissions
C) Maintaining Audit Trails for Regulatory Compliance

D) Securing Data Encryption and Protection Measures
E) Implementing Continuous Monitoring and Incident Response

QUESTION 17

Your organization is seeking to reduce costs in its Azure Virtual Desktop (AVD) deployment while maintaining optimal performance and user experience. As the Azure specialist, you need to implement cost optimization strategies. Which methods can you employ to reduce costs in AVD deployments? Select THREE.

A) Implementing Schedule-Based Auto-Shutdown for VMs
B) Utilizing Azure Hybrid Benefit for Windows Server Licenses
C) Enabling Azure Cost Management and Billing Alerts
D) Implementing Azure Policy for Resource Tagging and Management
E) Utilizing Reserved Instances for predictable workload

QUESTION 18

You are tasked with implementing a business continuity solution for an Azure Virtual Desktop (AVD) infrastructure. The solution must ensure the replication of session host virtual machines to a secondary location while minimizing administrative effort. What solution should you recommend given the following requirements and challenges:
- Efficient replication of session host virtual machines
- Minimization of administrative overhead
- Ensuring business continuity in case of primary location failure?

A) Azure Data Explorer
B) Azure Data Factory
C) Azure Site Recovery
D) Azure Traffic Manager
E) Azure Backup

QUESTION 19

Your organization is planning a disaster recovery strategy for its Azure Virtual Desktop (AVD) infrastructure. The focus is on ensuring minimal downtime and data loss in case of disruptions. Critical considerations include failover mechanisms, data backup, and recovery procedures. How would you design a robust disaster recovery plan to meet these requirements effectively? Select TWO.

A) Implement Azure Site Recovery (ASR) for automated failover
B) Utilize Azure Backup for data backup and recovery
C) Configure Azure Traffic Manager for DNS-based failover
D) Deploy Azure Blob Storage for long-term data retention
E) Set up Azure Log Analytics for real-time monitoring and analysis

QUESTION 20

As an Azure administrator, you are tasked with setting up monitoring for AVD to ensure optimal performance and proactive issue resolution. You need to monitor CPU usage, memory consumption, and disk I/O operations, and integrate alerts with Azure Monitor and Azure Security Center for enhanced incident response. Which Azure CLI command would you use to create diagnostic settings to send logs and metrics to both Azure Monitor and a storage account for long-term retention?

```
A) az monitor diagnostic-settings create
B) az monitor metrics alert create
C) az monitor log-profiles create
```

D) az security alert create
E) az monitor autoscale create

QUESTION 21

You are configuring Azure Virtual Desktop for a company that requires secure access to on-premises resources via Remote Desktop Protocol (RDP). You need to ensure that the appropriate network protocol is used for RDP connections. Which protocol should you configure to provide the highest level of security?

A) TLS
B) IPsec
C) SSH
D) SSL/TLS
E) SMB

QUESTION 22

Your organization is planning to design a role-based access control (RBAC) system for Azure Virtual Desktop (AVD) to ensure granular access management. The focus is on defining roles and permissions effectively to meet security and operational requirements. Which best practices should be considered when defining roles and permissions in an RBAC system for AVD? Select THREE.

A) Use built-in Azure AD roles for common AVD tasks
B) Define custom roles tailored to specific AVD functions
C) Assign permissions based on least privilege principle
D) Regularly review and update role assignments
E) Implement role hierarchy to streamline access management

QUESTION 23

Your organization is planning to implement multi-factor authentication (MFA) in Azure Virtual Desktop (AVD) environments to enhance security. The focus is on understanding the steps involved in setting up MFA effectively for AVD. What steps are required to set up multi-factor authentication for Azure Virtual Desktop (AVD)? Select THREE.

A) Enable Azure Multi-Factor Authentication for AVD users in Azure AD
B) Configure Conditional Access policies to require MFA for AVD connections
C) Integrate Azure AD with a supported MFA provider
D) Enforce MFA for RDP access to AVD resources
E) Install and configure the Azure MFA Extension for NPS (Network Policy Server)

QUESTION 24

Your organization is expanding its Azure Virtual Desktop (AVD) infrastructure to support a globally dispersed workforce. You need to ensure minimal latency and high data sovereignty compliance. What configurations are essential? Select THREE.

A) Implement a content delivery network (CDN).
B) Establish host pools in each major region.
C) Enforce local data storage policies.
D) Utilize Azure ExpressRoute.
E) Configure regional Azure Active Directory.

QUESTION 25

You are tasked with setting up secure network communication for AVD using PowerShell. Evaluate this script that configures a Network Security Group (NSG) with a rule to allow RDP access only from a specific IP range.

```powershell
New-AzNetworkSecurityGroup -Name "AVDNSG" -ResourceGroupName "AVDResources"
New-AzNetworkSecurityRuleConfig -Name "AllowRDP" -Access Allow -Protocol Tcp -Direction Inbound -Priority 100 -SourceAddressPrefix "203.0.113.0/24" -SourcePortRange "*" -DestinationAddressPrefix "*" -DestinationPortRange 3389 -NetworkSecurityGroup "AVDNSG"
```

A) Correct configuration
B) SourceAddressPrefix should be broader
C) DestinationPortRange should include more ports
D) NSG name does not follow naming conventions
E) Priority should be lower to take precedence

QUESTION 26

Your organization is planning to enhance the security of Azure Virtual Desktop (AVD) by implementing Windows Threat Protection features. The focus is on understanding an overview of Windows Threat Protection features suitable for AVD. Which Windows Threat Protection features are suitable for AVD? Select THREE.

A) Windows Defender Antivirus
B) Windows Defender Application Guard
C) Windows Defender Application Control
D) Windows Defender Exploit Guard
E) Windows Defender Credential Guard

QUESTION 27

As part of enhancing the security for a multinational corporation's AVD deployment, it is critical to ensure secure data transmission, implement stringent access controls, and integrate advanced malware protection. Which steps should be prioritized? Select THREE.

A) Enable Azure Multi-Factor Authentication.
B) Use Azure Private Link for data transmission.
C) Deploy Azure Application Gateway with WAF.
D) Integrate Microsoft Defender for Identity.
E) Implement Azure Bastion for secure access.

QUESTION 28

Your organization is planning the implementation of Conditional Access for Azure Virtual Desktop (AVD) to ensure secure access based on user roles and locations. The focus is on understanding the key considerations for planning Conditional Access. What are the key considerations for planning Conditional Access based on user roles and locations in AVD environments? Select THREE.

A) Define user roles and groups in Azure AD for role-based access control
B) Configure conditional access policies to enforce access based on user roles and locations
C) Implement multi-factor authentication (MFA) for additional security
D) Utilize Azure Bastion for secure RDP access to virtual desktops
E) Enable session controls to limit access based on device compliance status

QUESTION 29

Your organization is deploying Azure Virtual Desktop (AVD) session hosts and wants to ensure optimal security configurations. The focus is on configuring session hosts for optimal security. What are essential security configurations to apply to Azure Virtual Desktop session hosts? Select THREE.

A) Enable NLA for RDP connections
B) Implement Windows Defender Antivirus and real-time protection
C) Configure Windows Firewall to restrict inbound traffic to necessary ports
D) Enable BitLocker encryption for data volumes on session hosts
E) Install and configure Microsoft Defender for Cloud on session hosts

QUESTION 30

As an Azure Virtual Desktop administrator, you are tasked with implementing secure management practices. You need to deploy role-based access controls (RBAC) to restrict access based on job roles and ensure that administrative activities are logged and auditable. Review the PowerShell script below that sets RBAC policies and logs for a new AVD deployment. Does this script correctly implement the necessary security controls?

```powershell
Set-AzRoleAssignment -SignInName admin@contoso.com -RoleDefinitionName "Virtual Desktop Administrator" -Scope "/subscriptions/sub-id"
Start-AzOperationalInsightsWorkspace -WorkspaceName "AVDLogs" -Location "East US"
```

A) Correctly sets RBAC and logs
B) Missing logging of administrative actions
C) Incorrect role definition for administrative access
D) Workspace for logs is incorrectly configured
E) SignInName should be linked to Azure AD roles

QUESTION 31

You are tasked with installing and configuring FSLogix for an Azure Virtual Desktop (AVD) environment in a multinational corporation. The deployment must accommodate various user environments and applications efficiently. You encounter the following challenges:
1. Accommodating different user environments, including those with heavy application requirements.
2. Ensuring seamless access to applications for remote users.
3. Minimizing user profile management overhead.

A) Run the FSLogix installer on each virtual machine
B) Configure FSLogix profiles using Group Policy
C) Customize FSLogix settings in the registry
D) Utilize Azure Automation for FSLogix deployment
E) Implement FSLogix policies via Azure Policy

QUESTION 32

As an Azure Virtual Desktop administrator tasked with configuring Office Containers for multi-session use, you need to ensure optimal performance and resource utilization. Consider the following scenario:
- The solution should accommodate multiple users concurrently accessing Office applications without performance degradation.
- Resource allocation must be optimized to ensure equitable distribution among users.
- Office Containers should be configured to minimize conflicts and compatibility issues between user sessions.
What are the best practices for configuring Office Containers for multi-session use? Select THREE.

A) Enable Office Container pooling to share resources among sessions.
B) Configure Office Containers to store user settings centrally.
C) Implement session-based licensing for Office applications.

D) Utilize FSLogix Office 365 Containers for seamless application provisioning.
E) Enable multi-session support for Office applications within Containers.

QUESTION 33

You are tasked with configuring AVD for a legal firm that requires high data confidentiality, secure client access, and reliable disaster recovery options. What configurations should you prioritize? Select THREE.

A) Implement Azure Bastion for secure access.
B) Enable Azure Disk Encryption.
C) Configure Azure Site Recovery for each host pool.
D) Use Azure AD Conditional Access.
E) Set up Azure Backup for daily data backups.

QUESTION 34

Your organization is planning to enable and configure device redirection in Azure Virtual Desktop (AVD) to enhance user productivity and flexibility. Consider the following scenario:
- The organization has a Bring Your Own Device (BYOD) policy allowing employees to access AVD sessions from their personal devices.
- Users require seamless access to local peripherals such as printers, USB drives, and smart card readers during AVD sessions.
- IT administrators aim to implement device redirection while mitigating security risks and ensuring optimal performance.
Which considerations should you prioritize when enabling and configuring device redirection for the given scenario? Select THREE.

A) Implement role-based access control (RBAC) policies to restrict device redirection based on user roles and responsibilities.
B) Enable multi-factor authentication (MFA) for device redirection to enhance access security and prevent unauthorized device access.
C) Utilize Azure AD Conditional Access policies to enforce device compliance requirements before allowing redirection.
D) Configure Group Policy settings to manage device redirection behavior and permissions for AVD users.
E) Implement network Quality of Service (QoS) policies to prioritize traffic for redirected devices, ensuring optimal performance.

QUESTION 35

As an Azure Virtual Desktop admin, you are tasked with integrating Universal Print to streamline printing services across your organization. You need to ensure the integration supports centralized management and scales efficiently. Consider the PowerShell script below that registers a new printer and assigns it to a group:

```powershell
New-AzUniversalPrintPrinter -Name "MainOfficePrinter" -Location "BuildingA" -Group "AllUsers"
```

A) Correct implementation for Universal Print
B) Printer should not be assigned to a group
C) Location attribute is not supported
D) The command lacks necessary printer drivers installation
E) The script does not activate Universal Print

QUESTION 36

For a software development company using AVD, you need to ensure robust source code security, facilitate secure developer access, and allow for scalable resource allocation. What configurations should you implement? Select THREE.

A) Enable Azure Bastion for secure access to development environments.
B) Deploy Azure Kubernetes Service (AKS) for containerized application scaling.
C) Implement Azure Key Vault for managing application secrets.
D) Use Azure Scale Sets for dynamically scaling VMs.
E) Configure Azure AD Conditional Access policies for developer authentication.

QUESTION 37

You are tasked with optimizing user experience and resource utilization in an Azure Virtual Desktop (AVD) environment by implementing the Start VM on Connect feature. Which scenario best illustrates the benefits of using Start VM on Connect?

A) Ensuring that virtual machines (VMs) are only started when users connect to minimize costs
B) Providing users with faster access to their desktops and applications upon login
C) Automatically shutting down idle VMs to conserve resources and reduce expenses
D) Enforcing stricter security policies by requiring users to authenticate before VM startup
E) Distributing workloads evenly across available VMs to optimize performance

QUESTION 38

In the context of deploying applications to Azure Virtual Desktop (AVD), which method provides the most flexibility and isolation for application delivery, ensuring compatibility and performance across various user environments?

A) MSIX App Attach
B) MSI deployment
C) PowerShell script execution
D) Azure Marketplace integration
E) FSLogix profile containerization

QUESTION 39

A multinational corporation plans to use Azure Virtual Desktop for their global sales team. The requirements are for secure data access, compliance with international trade laws, and minimal downtime. What configurations should you implement? Select THREE.

A) Deploy Azure Bastion with a dedicated AzureBastionSubnet.
B) Set up Azure Site Recovery across multiple regions.
C) Configure Azure AD Conditional Access based on geographical locations.
D) Implement Azure Policy for compliance governance.
E) Enable Azure ExpressRoute for improved network reliability.

QUESTION 40

As an Azure administrator, you are tasked to configure OneDrive on AVD to support multiple session environments efficiently. Implement the PowerShell script below:
```
$TenantId = "123456"
Set-ODSettings -TenantId $TenantId -EnableMultiSession $true -OptimizePerformance $true
```
What adjustment should be made?

A) Add -SessionType "Shared" to the script.
B) Replace -EnableMultiSession $true with -MultiSessionEnabled $true.

C) Change -OptimizePerformance $true to -PerformanceOptimization $true.
D) No changes needed.
E) Replace $TenantId with the actual tenant GUID.

QUESTION 41

As an Azure desktop administrator, you are tasked with deploying Microsoft 365 Apps using MSIX app attach in an AVD environment. Which PowerShell script correctly sets up MSIX app attach for Microsoft 365 Apps to ensure optimal performance?

```
New-AVDMSIXPackage -Path "\\server\share\Office365.msix" -DynamicMount $true
```

A) Script is correct as is.
B) Replace -DynamicMount $true with -AttachOnDemand $true.
C) Add -EnableBackgroundUpdates $true for update management.
D) Include -UserGroup "AVDUsers" to specify the user group.
E) Change -Path to the UNC path where the MSIX package is stored.

QUESTION 42

For a global media company using AVD, ensuring quick access to large video editing files, maintaining high availability, and securing sensitive media content are priorities with FSLogix. Which settings should be adjusted? Select THREE.

A) HKLM\SOFTWARE\FSLogix\Profiles\CloudCache
B) HKLM\SOFTWARE\FSLogix\Profiles\CloudCacheLocations
C) HKLM\SOFTWARE\FSLogix\Profiles\Encrypt
D) HKLM\SOFTWARE\FSLogix\Profiles\VHDLocations
E) HKLM\SOFTWARE\FSLogix\Profiles\LargeFileHandlingMode

QUESTION 43

You are responsible for monitoring the session health and stability of Azure Virtual Desktop (AVD) for a multinational corporation. The company has recently migrated to AVD, and you need to ensure smooth operations. Which tool would you use to monitor session health and stability effectively?

A) Azure Monitor Logs
B) Azure Automation
C) Azure Policy
D) Azure Security Center
E) Azure Monitor Alerts

QUESTION 44

As part of your role as an Azure Virtual Desktop (AVD) administrator, you need to configure diagnostic settings for troubleshooting and monitoring AVD infrastructure. You must consider:
1. The types of diagnostic data required for effective troubleshooting and monitoring, including performance metrics and audit logs.
2. The destination for exporting diagnostic logs, ensuring accessibility and compliance with organizational policies.
3. The impact of diagnostic settings on AVD performance and cost, optimizing for efficiency and resource utilization.
Which destination is most suitable for exporting diagnostic logs to ensure accessibility and compliance for AVD infrastructure?

A) Azure Event Hubs
B) Azure Blob Storage
C) Azure Monitor Logs

D) Azure Log Analytics
E) Azure Storage Queue

QUESTION 45

As an AVD administrator, you need to schedule updates during off-peak hours to minimize disruption. Provide a PowerShell script that sets the update window to start at 2 AM.

```
$updateSchedule = New-AzAutomationSchedule -Name "OffPeakUpdates" -StartTime "2:00 AM" -WeekInterval 1 -ResourceGroupName "AVDResourceGroup"
```

A) Script is correct as is.
B) Add -ForUpdateManagement $true to specify that the schedule is for update management.
C) Change -WeekInterval 1 to -Frequency "Weekly".
D) Replace New-AzAutomationSchedule with Set-AzVmAutoUpdateSchedule.
E) Include -TimeZone "UTC" to ensure time accuracy.

QUESTION 46

As an Azure Virtual Desktop (AVD) administrator, you are responsible for monitoring network performance to ensure optimal user experience. You need to select the appropriate tool for monitoring network performance in AVD environments. Which tool should you choose for this task?

A) Azure Monitor
B) Azure Network Watcher
C) Azure Resource Graph
D) Azure Log Analytics
E) Azure Diagnostics

QUESTION 47

A company recently migrated its entire workforce to Azure Virtual Desktop (AVD) to enable remote work. However, the finance department has raised concerns about escalating costs associated with the AVD deployment. The IT team needs to implement strategies to reduce operational costs while maintaining optimal performance. What measures should the IT team take to address the finance department's concerns? Select CORRECT answers that apply.

A) Implementing Azure Cost Management tools
B) Rightsizing virtual machine instances
C) Enabling auto-scaling based on demand
D) Using FSLogix to manage user profiles
E) Optimizing network bandwidth

QUESTION 48

For a tech startup focusing on software development, Azure Virtual Desktop is being deployed to enhance development agility, support continuous integration/delivery (CI/CD), and ensure compatibility with various development tools. Which operating systems should you deploy on session hosts? Select THREE.

A) Windows 11 Enterprise
B) Windows 10 Enterprise multi-session
C) Windows Server 2022
D) Windows Server 2019
E) Windows 10 Pro

QUESTION 49

A company is tasked with managing AVD licenses and ensuring compliance with licensing agreements. Which strategies should the company prioritize to effectively manage AVD licenses and ensure compliance? Select TWO.

A) Utilizing Azure Policy for license enforcement and compliance monitoring
B) Implementing RBAC policies to control access to AVD resources based on licensing status
C) Conducting regular audits to track license usage and compliance
D) Leveraging Azure Cost Management for cost optimization and license tracking
E) Integrating Azure Active Directory with AVD for centralized license management

QUESTION 50

A company is planning to implement effective log management practices in its Azure Virtual Desktop (AVD) environment to ensure compliance and facilitate troubleshooting. What are some best practices they should consider for log management? Select THREE.

A) Implementing centralized logging using Azure Monitor Logs for aggregation and analysis
B) Enabling diagnostic settings in AVD to collect logs and metrics for monitoring and troubleshooting
C) Utilizing Azure Log Analytics workspaces for long-term log retention and analysis
D) Implementing RBAC controls to restrict access to log data based on role and responsibility
E) Configuring log rotation and archival policies to manage log retention and storage costs

PRACTICE TEST 6 - ANSWERS ONLY

QUESTION 1

Answer - A) New-AzVirtualNetwork

Option A - Correct. This cmdlet creates a new virtual network, essential for initial setup.
Option B - Incorrect. This configures subnets, used after creating the network.
Option C - Incorrect. Creates a gateway, not the initial network.
Option D - Incorrect. Retrieves information, doesn't configure.
Option E - Incorrect. Adds peering, not for initial setup.

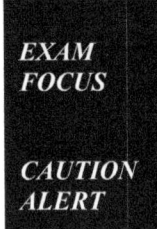

Always remember to use New-AzVirtualNetwork for creating the initial virtual network in AVD setups. Ensure subnet planning aligns with department isolation requirements, integrates with on-premises AD DS, and allows Azure RBAC for granular access control. Validate network security group rules for proper connectivity.

Avoid confusing subnet configuration (Set-AzVirtualNetworkSubnetConfig) with virtual network creation. Subnets come after the network setup. Stay cautious of over-permissioning when assigning Azure RBAC roles.

QUESTION 2

Answer - C) Enable RDP Shortpath via Group Policy settings

Option A - Incorrect. Azure Bastion provides secure RDP/SSH access but is not directly related to configuring RDP Shortpath.
Option B - Incorrect. Azure Firewall controls network traffic but does not configure RDP Shortpath.
Option C - Correct. Enabling RDP Shortpath via Group Policy settings is the recommended approach.
Option D - Incorrect. Conditional Access policies enhance security but do not configure RDP Shortpath.
Option E - Incorrect. FSLogix manages user profiles but is not involved in configuring RDP Shortpath.

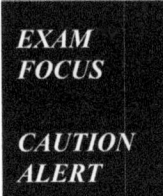

You should enable RDP Shortpath via Group Policy to optimize performance and connectivity for remote users. Validate that firewalls and network configurations support UDP traffic, as Shortpath relies on it. Test configurations in a controlled environment before deploying organization-wide.

Avoid relying on Azure Bastion or Conditional Access policies for configuring RDP Shortpath—they serve different purposes. Stay alert to blocked UDP ports, as they will prevent Shortpath from functioning effectively.

QUESTION 3

Answer - [B]

Option B - WVDSecurityEvents: This table contains detailed logs of security events, including unauthorized access attempts and policy violations, making it essential for monitoring security in the AVD environment.
Option A - WVDConnections: This table provides information about user connections but does not focus specifically on security events.
Option C - WVDAuditLogs: While it contains audit logs, it may not capture detailed security-related events.
Option D - WVDServiceMetadata: This contains metadata about the AVD service rather than security event logs.
Option E - WVDAgentHealth: This deals with agent health status, not security events.

EXAM FOCUS — *Make sure to query WVDSecurityEvents to analyze detailed logs of unauthorized access attempts and policy violations in AVD. Regular monitoring of this table provides actionable insights to enhance security. You can also set alerts for critical events to proactively address issues.*

CAUTION ALERT	*Avoid assuming WVDConnections or WVDAuditLogs covers security events comprehensively—they focus on session details and audit activities, respectively. Stay cautious about using incomplete data sources for security monitoring.*

QUESTION 4

Answer - A) Storage type (e.g., Premium SSD, Standard SSD, Standard HDD); B) Performance requirements (e.g., IOPS, throughput); C) Data redundancy and high availability; D) Scalability and elasticity of storage; E) Cost considerations (e.g., storage tiers, data transfer costs)

Option A - Correct. Storage type selection is crucial for meeting performance requirements and balancing cost-effectiveness in AVD deployments. Option B - Correct. Performance requirements, including IOPS and throughput, should be assessed to ensure adequate storage performance for AVD workloads.

Option C - Correct. Data redundancy and high availability are essential for maintaining data integrity and minimizing downtime in AVD environments. Option D - Correct. Scalability and elasticity of storage solutions enable seamless expansion and contraction of storage resources to accommodate changing AVD demands. Option E - Correct. Cost considerations play a significant role in storage planning, including selecting appropriate storage tiers and managing data transfer costs to optimize AVD infrastructure spending.

EXAM FOCUS	*Always consider storage type, performance requirements (IOPS), redundancy, scalability, and cost optimization when planning AVD storage solutions. Premium SSDs are ideal for high performance, while Standard HDDs suit cost-sensitive workloads. Factor in data transfer costs to avoid hidden expenses.*
CAUTION ALERT	*Avoid neglecting redundancy and scalability in storage planning. Stay clear of overspending on Premium SSDs for workloads that don't require high IOPS. Cost considerations should include storage tiers and unexpected transfer charges.*

QUESTION 5

Answer - A) Command is correct

Option A - Correct: The command is correctly set up for creating a storage account in Azure.
Option B - Incorrect: The location 'eastus' is valid.
Option C - Incorrect: 'Standard_LRS' is a suitable SKU for general purposes in AVD.
Option D - Incorrect: 'StorageV2' is the correct kind for this setup.
Option E - Incorrect: Existence of the resource group cannot be determined from the command itself.

EXAM FOCUS	*You need to use az storage account create with parameters like --sku Standard_LRS and --kind StorageV2 for AVD environments. This setup ensures optimized performance and compatibility. Validate resource group existence beforehand to avoid deployment failures.*
CAUTION ALERT	*Avoid assuming the location parameter is incorrect if it matches your region. Stay cautious of using unsupported SKUs or storage kinds, as these can lead to performance issues in AVD environments.*

QUESTION 6

Answer - [B, D]

Option B - Azure Automation with Azure Functions: Functions can be scheduled to start and stop session hosts at the specified times, meeting the requirements and minimizing manual intervention.
Option D - Azure Automation with Azure Runbooks: Runbooks can automate tasks such as starting and stopping session hosts based on a schedule, fulfilling the requirements efficiently.
Option A - Azure Monitor Alerts: Alerts notify you of potential issues but are not specifically designed for managing session host schedules based on demand.

Option C - Azure Resource Manager templates: While templates enable you to deploy and manage Azure resources, they are not specifically designed for managing session host schedules based on demand.

Option E - Azure Virtual Machine Scale Sets: While Scale Sets can help with scaling resources, they are not specifically designed for managing session host schedules based on demand.

EXAM FOCUS	*Leverage Azure Automation with Runbooks and Azure Functions to automate session host scheduling in AVD. Schedule start and stop times to minimize costs and administrative overhead. Configure weekday-specific tasks to meet business hours without impacting resource availability.*
CAUTION ALERT	*Avoid relying on Azure Monitor Alerts or Scale Sets for time-based session management—they are not designed for this purpose. Stay alert to improperly configured schedules, which can lead to unnecessary costs or downtime.*

QUESTION 7

Answer - A) Per User Subscription; B) Per Device Subscription; D) Enterprise Agreement (EA)

Option A - Correct. Per User Subscription model charges based on the number of users accessing AVD, providing flexibility for organizations with varying user counts.

Option B - Correct. Per Device Subscription model charges based on the number of devices accessing AVD, suitable for scenarios where multiple users share a single device. Option D - Correct. Enterprise Agreement (EA) offers customized licensing terms and volume discounts for larger organizations, providing cost savings and flexibility for AVD deployments. Option C - Incorrect. Consumption-based pricing is not typically associated with AVD licensing models and may not be applicable in this context. Option E - Incorrect. Bring Your Own License (BYOL) is not a common licensing model for AVD deployments, as it typically refers to using existing software licenses in Azure.

EXAM FOCUS	*Make sure to evaluate Per User, Per Device, and Enterprise Agreement licensing models for AVD. Choose Per User for flexible user counts, Per Device for shared devices, and EA for large organizations needing volume discounts. Consider BYOL only when specifically applicable.*
CAUTION ALERT	*Avoid assuming that consumption-based pricing or BYOL is a standard licensing model for AVD. Stay cautious of licensing misalignment with actual usage, which can lead to compliance or cost issues.*

QUESTION 8

Answer - A) Load Testing and Benchmarking; B) Resource Utilization Monitoring and Analysis; D) Performance Profiling and Optimization

Option A - Correct. Load testing and benchmarking help assess system performance under simulated workloads, identifying potential bottlenecks and areas for optimization. Option B - Correct. Resource utilization monitoring and analysis enable tracking of system resources such as CPU, memory, and network usage, providing insights into performance metrics and areas for improvement.

Option D - Correct. Performance profiling and optimization involve analyzing application behavior and performance characteristics to identify inefficiencies and optimize resource usage. Option C - Incorrect. While user experience monitoring and feedback are important, they are not direct methods for calculating and optimizing performance in AVD deployments. Option E - Incorrect. Capacity planning and forecasting focus on predicting future resource requirements but do not directly address performance calculation and optimization methods.

EXAM FOCUS	*You should perform load testing, monitor resource utilization, and conduct performance profiling to optimize AVD. Regularly analyze CPU, memory, and network usage under peak loads. Use profiling to fine-tune applications and resources for improved efficiency.*
CAUTION ALERT	*Avoid relying solely on user feedback or capacity planning for performance optimization. Stay alert to neglecting periodic performance tests, as resource needs may evolve over time, leading to potential bottlenecks.*

QUESTION 9

Answer - [C]

Option C - Configure autoscale rules based on CPU and memory utilization: This allows for dynamic adjustment of resources based on performance metrics, ensuring seamless scalability and cost optimization.
Option A - Implementing a static scaling configuration does not allow for dynamic adjustment based on performance metrics and may lead to overprovisioning.

Option B - While Azure Cost Management is important for monitoring costs, it does not directly address the requirement for dynamic resource adjustment. Option D - Scheduling maintenance windows for scaling operations may be necessary but does not meet the requirement for real-time adjustment based on performance metrics.
Option E - Network traffic shaping can control resource consumption but is not directly related to autoscaling based on performance thresholds.

EXAM FOCUS	*Configure autoscale rules based on CPU and memory thresholds to dynamically adjust AVD host pool resources. This minimizes overprovisioning costs and ensures optimal performance during user demand fluctuations. Monitor scaling events to fine-tune thresholds.*
CAUTION ALERT	*Avoid static scaling configurations—they lack adaptability to real-time changes. Stay cautious about setting thresholds too low or too high, as this can result in either resource exhaustion or unnecessary expenses.*

QUESTION 10

Answer - B) CustomRdpProperty is incorrect

Option A - Incorrect: The command as it is does not correctly enforce GPU usage.
Option B - Correct: 'CustomRdpProperty "use:gpu=True"' is not the correct way to enforce GPU usage in AVD.
Option C - Incorrect: 'PreferredAppGroupType "Desktop"' is appropriate for this scenario.
Option D - Correct: Location parameter is indeed missing which is essential for the deployment.
Option E - Incorrect: Not all elements are incorrect.

EXAM FOCUS	*Always use accurate parameters like CustomRdpProperty in PowerShell commands to enforce GPU usage in AVD host pools. Validate syntax and ensure GPU-enabled VMs are available. Adding the location parameter is essential for successful deployments.*
CAUTION ALERT	*Avoid omitting essential parameters like location in deployment commands. Stay alert to incorrect CustomRdpProperty syntax, as it can lead to GPU settings not being applied, causing performance issues for high-demand applications.*

QUESTION 11

Answer - A) Prepare Base Virtual Machine with Desired Configuration; B) Install and Configure Applications and Customizations; C) Sysprep and Generalize the Virtual Machine; D) Capture Virtual Machine Image in Azure

Option A - Correct. Before creating a golden image, it's essential to prepare a base virtual machine with the desired configuration, including operating system settings and software prerequisites. Option B - Correct. Installing and configuring applications and customizations ensure that the golden image includes all necessary software and settings required for end-user productivity.

Option C - Correct. Sysprepping and generalizing the virtual machine prepares it for image capture by removing unique identifiers and configurations, allowing for deployment on multiple devices. Option D - Correct. Capturing the virtual machine image in Azure involves creating a managed image or a snapshot to serve as the golden image template for provisioning session hosts within the AVD deployment.

Option E - Incorrect. While verifying image deployment and accessibility are important steps, they come after capturing the image and deploying session hosts and are not directly part of the golden image creation process.

EXAM FOCUS	*Always remember to Sysprep the base VM to remove unique identifiers before creating the image. You should ensure all required software and configurations are installed to streamline deployment. Use managed images for consistent provisioning across AVD session hosts and minimal setup errors.*
CAUTION ALERT	*Avoid skipping Sysprep, as it can lead to deployment issues. Stay clear of including unnecessary software in the golden image—it increases image size and can affect performance. Test captured images thoroughly before deploying to production.*

QUESTION 12

Answer - [C]

Option C - Azure Site Recovery: Azure Site Recovery supports replication and failover of AVD host pools to a secondary region, minimizing data loss and downtime during failover operations. Option A - Azure Backup is primarily used for data backup and recovery, not for failover and disaster recovery of AVD host pools.

Option B - Azure Traffic Manager provides DNS-based traffic routing but does not directly support failover and disaster recovery for AVD host pools. Option D - Azure Load Balancer is a network load balancer and does not provide failover capabilities at the application level for AVD host pools. Option E - Azure Blob Storage is a storage service and is not directly related to failover and disaster recovery of AVD host pools.

EXAM FOCUS	*Make sure to use Azure Site Recovery for seamless failover and replication of AVD host pools across regions. Enable continuous replication and regular failover drills to minimize data loss and downtime. Configure secondary region resources in advance to ensure quick recovery.*
CAUTION ALERT	*Avoid assuming Azure Traffic Manager or Load Balancer can replicate session hosts—they are limited to DNS-based or network-level traffic routing. Stay cautious of neglecting secondary region setup, as this can delay recovery in a real failure.*

QUESTION 13

Answer - B) Utilizing Ring-Based Deployment Strategies; D) Leveraging Differential Image Updates

Option A - Incorrect. While automated testing workflows are beneficial, they are not specifically a best practice for applying updates to AVD images. Option B - Correct. Utilizing ring-based deployment strategies involves deploying updates to a subset of users or devices before broader deployment, allowing for controlled testing and mitigation of potential issues.

Option C - Incorrect. While applying updates during off-peak hours can minimize user impact, it is not necessarily a best practice specific to AVD image updates. Option D - Correct. Leveraging differential image updates involves deploying only the changes between versions, reducing deployment time and resource consumption. Option E - Incorrect. Enforcing least privilege access controls is essential for security but is not specifically a best practice for applying updates to AVD images.

EXAM FOCUS	*You should implement ring-based deployments for AVD updates to minimize impact and catch issues early. Always leverage differential updates to reduce deployment time and resource consumption. Automate update validation processes to streamline management and ensure minimal disruption to users.*
CAUTION ALERT	*Avoid deploying updates to all session hosts simultaneously—it increases downtime risk. Stay cautious of using outdated or incompatible software versions in your AVD image updates, as they can lead to application failures or degraded user experience.*

QUESTION 14

Answer - A) Azure Blob Storage; B) Azure Managed Disks; C) Azure Files

Option A - Correct. Azure Blob Storage is a scalable storage solution suitable for storing VHD/VHDX images used in AVD deployments.

Option B - Correct. Azure Managed Disks provide persistent, high-performance storage for virtual machine images, including those used in AVD environments. Option C - Incorrect. While Azure Files is suitable for file sharing, it is not typically used for storing virtual machine images in AVD environments.

Option D - Correct. Azure Shared Image Gallery allows you to centrally manage custom images across Azure subscriptions, facilitating image sharing and distribution in AVD deployments. Option E - Incorrect. Azure Data Lake Storage is designed for big data analytics and data lake scenarios, not specifically for storing virtual machine images in AVD deployments.

EXAM FOCUS	*You need to utilize Azure Shared Image Gallery for centralized image management, Blob Storage for flexible image handling, and Managed Disks for persistent storage. Shared Image Gallery allows you to replicate images across regions efficiently, enhancing performance and scalability.*
CAUTION ALERT	*Avoid using Azure Files or Data Lake for VM image storage—they are not designed for this purpose. Stay alert to selecting storage options that don't meet AVD requirements, such as unsupported disk types or unoptimized regional replication settings.*

QUESTION 15

Answer - A) Command is correct

Option A - Correct: The command accurately configures global VNET peering for Azure Virtual Desktop.
Option B - Incorrect: The parameter '--allow-vnet-access' is correctly used here to enable access between the VNets.
Option C - Incorrect: '--allow-forwarded-traffic' is not necessary for basic peering setup.
Option D - Incorrect: '--remote-vnet' correctly specifies the ID of the remote VNet, which is required.
Option E - Incorrect: Subscription parameter is not required if operating within the context of the current subscription.

EXAM FOCUS	*Always validate global VNET peering commands by specifying --allow-vnet-access for seamless connectivity. Ensure the remote VNet ID is correct and matches the configuration requirements. Use a dedicated resource group to manage dependencies efficiently.*
CAUTION ALERT	*Avoid omitting key parameters like --remote-vnet in VNET peering commands—it can cause configuration failures. Stay clear of unnecessary settings like --allow-forwarded-traffic unless explicitly required by your network design.*

QUESTION 16

Answer - A) Ensuring Data Sovereignty and Residency Compliance; C) Maintaining Audit Trails for Regulatory Compliance; D) Securing Data Encryption and Protection Measures

Option A - Correct. Ensuring data sovereignty and residency compliance involves meeting regulatory requirements regarding where data is stored and processed in AVD deployments. Option B - Incorrect. While managing user access controls is important, it may not be a key compliance challenge specific to AVD deployments.

Option C - Correct. Maintaining audit trails for regulatory compliance involves tracking and documenting activities to demonstrate compliance with regulatory requirements in AVD environments. Option D - Correct. Securing data encryption and protection measures is crucial for compliance with data protection regulations in AVD deployments. Option E - Incorrect. While implementing continuous monitoring and incident response is important for security, it may not be directly related to compliance challenges in AVD deployments.

EXAM FOCUS	*Make sure to prioritize compliance with data sovereignty and encryption requirements. Maintain audit trails for all activities in AVD deployments. Implement robust access policies to restrict data access based on regulatory mandates and security guidelines.*
CAUTION ALERT	*Avoid neglecting region-specific compliance rules, such as GDPR or HIPAA, depending on your organization's data residency. Stay cautious of inadequate encryption measures, as they can lead to non-*

compliance and data breaches.

QUESTION 17

Answer - A) Implementing Schedule-Based Auto-Shutdown for VMs; B) Utilizing Azure Hybrid Benefit for Windows Server Licenses; C) Enabling Azure Cost Management and Billing Alerts

Option A - Correct. Implementing schedule-based auto-shutdown for VMs allows for cost savings by automatically shutting down VMs during non-business hours or low usage periods. Option B - Correct. Utilizing Azure Hybrid Benefit for Windows Server Licenses enables organizations to use existing on-premises Windows Server licenses to reduce costs on Azure VMs.

Option C - Correct. Enabling Azure Cost Management and billing alerts helps monitor and manage costs effectively, providing insights into usage patterns and potential cost-saving opportunities. Option D - Incorrect. While Azure Policy can help with resource management, it may not directly impact cost optimization strategies in AVD deployments. Option E - Incorrect. While utilizing reserved instances can provide cost savings for predictable workloads, it may not address broader cost optimization strategies such as auto-shutdown and license optimization in AVD deployments.

EXAM FOCUS	*Utilize cost-saving strategies like auto-shutdown schedules, Azure Hybrid Benefit, and billing alerts. These ensure you minimize resource wastage while maintaining performance. Reserved Instances can help for predictable workloads but may not suit dynamic usage.*
CAUTION ALERT	*Avoid ignoring Hybrid Benefit—it's a significant cost saver if you have eligible licenses. Stay clear of over-committing with Reserved Instances unless you are confident about your usage patterns; it may lead to unnecessary expenses.*

QUESTION 18

Answer - [C]

Option C - Azure Site Recovery: Azure Site Recovery provides efficient replication of session host virtual machines to a secondary location with minimal administrative effort, ensuring business continuity in case of primary location failure.

Option A - Azure Data Explorer is a data analysis service and is not designed for replicating session host virtual machines. Option B - Azure Data Factory is an ETL (extract, transform, load) service and does not address the replication of session host virtual machines for business continuity. Option D - Azure Traffic Manager is a DNS-based traffic load balancer and does not offer session host virtual machine replication capabilities.
 Option E - Azure Backup is used for data backup and recovery, not for replicating session host virtual machines.

EXAM FOCUS	*Always implement Azure Site Recovery to ensure efficient replication and failover of session hosts. Automate replication to minimize manual effort and test failover scenarios regularly to ensure business continuity. Use ASR's reporting features for monitoring readiness.*
CAUTION ALERT	*Avoid relying on Azure Backup or Traffic Manager for VM replication—they don't address session host continuity. Stay cautious of untested failover plans; ensure periodic drills to validate recovery strategies and minimize downtime during real incidents.*

QUESTION 19

Answer - A) Implement Azure Site Recovery (ASR) for automated failover; B) Utilize Azure Backup for data backup and recovery

Option A - Correct. Azure Site Recovery (ASR) provides automated failover capabilities, enabling rapid recovery and minimal downtime in AVD environments. Option B - Correct. Azure Backup ensures data protection and facilitates recovery operations, enhancing the resilience of AVD deployments.

Option C - Incorrect. Azure Traffic Manager is used for DNS-based traffic routing and load balancing but does not directly address failover and recovery in AVD environments. Option D - Incorrect. While Azure Blob Storage is suitable for long-term data retention, it is not specifically designed for disaster recovery purposes in AVD environments. Option E - Incorrect. Azure Log Analytics offers monitoring and analysis capabilities but is not a primary component of disaster recovery plans for AVD deployments.

EXAM FOCUS	*You need to combine Azure Site Recovery for automated failover with Azure Backup for comprehensive disaster recovery. Site Recovery handles VM replication and failover, while Backup ensures critical data is protected and retrievable. Regularly validate your recovery plans for effectiveness.*
CAUTION ALERT	*Avoid using Traffic Manager or Blob Storage as standalone disaster recovery solutions—they are limited in scope. Stay alert to neglecting off-site backup storage or failing to align your strategy with specific recovery time and point objectives (RTO/RPO).*

QUESTION 20

Answer - A) az monitor diagnostic-settings create

Option A - Correct: This command allows for the creation of diagnostic settings that can route logs and metrics to Azure Monitor and a designated storage account, facilitating both real-time and long-term analysis.

Option B - Incorrect: This command sets up alerts based on metrics but does not configure the storage or routing of performance data. Option C - Incorrect: Log profiles are for archiving activity logs, not for detailed performance metrics.

Option D - Incorrect: This command is specific to Azure Security Center alerts and does not cover the broader diagnostic scope required. Option E - Incorrect: Autoscale settings are for scaling resources, not for monitoring or logging.

EXAM FOCUS	*Use az monitor diagnostic-settings create to send AVD logs and metrics to Azure Monitor and storage for analysis and retention. Integrate alerts with Azure Monitor to enable proactive incident resolution. Ensure you configure long-term storage for compliance and historical insights.*
CAUTION ALERT	*Avoid assuming that metric alerts (az monitor metrics alert create) cover diagnostics—they don't capture full logs. Stay cautious of misconfigured diagnostic settings, as they can result in incomplete monitoring or missed critical metrics.*

QUESTION 21

Answer - D

Option D - SSL/TLS (Secure Sockets Layer/Transport Layer Security) provides encryption and secure communication for RDP connections, ensuring the highest level of security. Configuring Azure Virtual Desktop to use SSL/TLS for RDP connections enhances data protection and confidentiality, meeting the company's security requirements for accessing on-premises resources securely.

Option A - TLS (Transport Layer Security) is a cryptographic protocol used for securing internet communications but is not specifically designed for RDP connections. Option B - IPsec (Internet Protocol Security) is a suite of protocols used for secure internet communications but is not specific to RDP connections. Option C - SSH (Secure Shell) is a protocol used for secure remote access to systems but is not typically used for RDP connections.
Option E - SMB (Server Message Block) is a file sharing protocol and is not used for securing RDP connections.

EXAM FOCUS	*Always configure SSL/TLS for secure RDP communication in Azure Virtual Desktop to ensure encrypted data transmission and compliance with security standards. Validate certificate configurations to avoid connectivity issues. Implement best practices to safeguard RDP from unauthorized access.*
CAUTION ALERT	*Avoid using non-encrypted protocols like SMB or standard TLS alone for RDP connections—they don't ensure the required security levels. Stay cautious of misconfigured certificates, which can expose RDP sessions to vulnerabilities.*

QUESTION 22

Answer - A) Use built-in Azure AD roles for common AVD tasks; B) Define custom roles tailored to specific AVD functions; C) Assign permissions based on least privilege principle; D) Regularly review and update role assignments

Option A - Correct. Using built-in Azure AD roles for common AVD tasks simplifies role management and ensures consistency. Option B - Correct. Defining custom roles tailored to specific AVD functions allows for fine-grained access control tailored to organizational needs. Option C - Correct. Assigning permissions based on the least privilege principle minimizes the risk of unauthorized access and data breaches.

Option D - Correct. Regularly reviewing and updating role assignments ensures alignment with changing organizational requirements and minimizes security risks. Option E - Incorrect. While role hierarchy can streamline access management, it is not a common best practice for RBAC in AVD environments.

EXAM FOCUS	*You should define roles in RBAC using the least privilege principle and tailor custom roles for AVD-specific tasks. Regularly review roles to align with organizational changes. Leverage built-in Azure roles for common tasks to simplify management. Automate role assignments where feasible.*
CAUTION ALERT	*Avoid over-granting permissions when creating roles. Stay clear of ignoring role reviews, as outdated assignments can lead to security risks. Avoid relying on hierarchical role structures—they can complicate access management unnecessarily.*

QUESTION 23

Answer - A) Enable Azure Multi-Factor Authentication for AVD users in Azure AD; B) Configure Conditional Access policies to require MFA for AVD connections; C) Integrate Azure AD with a supported MFA provider

Option A - Correct. Enabling Azure Multi-Factor Authentication for AVD users in Azure AD is a fundamental step in implementing MFA for AVD environments. Option B - Correct. Configuring Conditional Access policies to require MFA for AVD connections ensures that MFA is enforced for accessing AVD resources.

Option C - Correct. Integrating Azure AD with a supported MFA provider allows organizations to leverage third-party MFA solutions for AVD environments. Option D - Incorrect. While enforcing MFA for RDP access to AVD resources may be a valid security measure, it is not specifically mentioned in the question as a step for setting up MFA for AVD. Option E - Incorrect. Installing and configuring the Azure MFA Extension for NPS may be relevant for other scenarios, but it is not directly related to setting up MFA for AVD as described in the question.

EXAM FOCUS	*Make sure to enable MFA for AVD users in Azure AD and enforce Conditional Access policies for enhanced security. Integrate Azure AD with a supported MFA provider for seamless implementation. Use analytics to monitor MFA usage and identify potential anomalies.*
CAUTION ALERT	*Avoid skipping Conditional Access policies—they ensure MFA enforcement effectively. Stay cautious about misconfigured MFA providers or incomplete integrations, which can weaken authentication mechanisms and lead to unauthorized access.*

QUESTION 24

Answer - B, C, D

A) Incorrect - A CDN is more suitable for static content delivery and does not directly impact AVD performance.
B) Correct - Establishing host pools in each major region reduces latency by serving users from the nearest data center.
C) Correct - Enforcing local data storage policies ensures compliance with data sovereignty laws.
D) Correct - Azure ExpressRoute provides more reliable and faster connectivity than typical internet connections, enhancing performance for global users.
E) Incorrect - Azure Active Directory configuration is not region-specific and does not directly impact data sovereignty or latency.

EXAM FOCUS	*Deploy AVD host pools in geographically distributed regions to reduce latency for global users. Use Azure ExpressRoute for reliable connectivity and enforce local storage policies for compliance with data sovereignty regulations. Monitor traffic flows for optimization.*
CAUTION ALERT	*Avoid relying on a CDN for AVD performance—it's unsuitable for dynamic workloads. Stay cautious about neglecting to enforce local data policies, as this can lead to compliance violations and potential legal ramifications.*

QUESTION 25

Answer - A) Correct configuration

Option A - Correct: The script correctly sets up an NSG to allow RDP access from a specific IP range on the standard port, following best practices for secure remote access.

Option B - Incorrect: A broader IP range would reduce the security effectiveness of the rule. Option C - Incorrect: Limiting the destination port range to 3389 (RDP) enhances security by restricting access to the necessary service only.

Option D - Incorrect: The NSG name "AVDNSG" is appropriately descriptive for Azure Virtual Desktop. Option E - Incorrect: Priority 100 is typically adequate to ensure the rule is evaluated properly without interfering with other potential rules.

EXAM FOCUS	*Always configure NSGs to restrict RDP access to specific IP ranges and necessary ports. Use New-AzNetworkSecurityRuleConfig to define precise rules. Validate rule priorities to prevent unintended access. Regularly audit NSG configurations for alignment with security requirements.*
CAUTION ALERT	*Avoid setting broad IP ranges or open port configurations—they weaken the security posture. Stay cautious of overlapping NSG rules, as they can cause unexpected connectivity issues or leave critical ports inadvertently exposed.*

QUESTION 26

Answer - A) Windows Defender Antivirus; C) Windows Defender Application Control; D) Windows Defender Exploit Guard

Option A - Correct. Windows Defender Antivirus provides real-time protection against viruses, malware, and other threats on AVD session hosts. Option C - Correct. Windows Defender Application Control helps prevent unauthorized applications from running on AVD session hosts, enhancing security. Option D - Correct. Windows Defender Exploit Guard helps protect AVD session hosts from common exploit techniques and vulnerabilities, strengthening defenses against cyber threats.

Option B - Incorrect. While Windows Defender Application Guard is a security feature, it is not specifically mentioned in the context of Windows Threat Protection features suitable for AVD as described in the question. Option E - Incorrect. While Windows Defender Credential Guard is a valuable security feature, it is not specifically mentioned in the context of Windows Threat Protection features suitable for AVD as described in the question.

EXAM FOCUS	*Implement Windows Defender Antivirus for real-time protection, Application Control for controlling executable integrity, and Exploit Guard to mitigate common attack vectors. Regularly update threat definitions and configure alerting for proactive incident response in AVD environments.*
CAUTION ALERT	*Avoid relying solely on antivirus tools—combine multiple layers of Windows Threat Protection features for comprehensive security. Stay clear of misconfigured Application Control policies, which may inadvertently block necessary applications.*

QUESTION 27

Answer - A, B, E

A) Correct - Multi-Factor Authentication ensures stringent access control by requiring more than one form of verification. B) Correct - Azure Private Link provides secure and private data transmission by keeping data within the Azure network.

C) Incorrect - While Azure Application Gateway with WAF protects against web-based attacks, it does not directly relate to secure data transmission or access control for AVD environments. D) Incorrect - Defender for Identity focuses on protecting identity infrastructure, not directly enhancing malware protection or data transmission security in AVD.
E) Correct - Azure Bastion provides secure and seamless RDP and SSH access to virtual machines, enhancing access control without exposing the VMs to the public internet.

EXAM FOCUS	*You need to enable MFA for robust access controls, use Azure Private Link for secure data transmission, and deploy Azure Bastion for seamless and secure access to AVD session hosts. Ensure regular reviews of access policies for alignment with security practices.*
CAUTION ALERT	*Avoid assuming Application Gateway with WAF or Defender for Identity are enough for AVD-specific security needs. Stay cautious of exposing session hosts directly to the internet—this is mitigated by Private Link and Bastion deployments.*

QUESTION 28

Answer - A) Define user roles and groups in Azure AD for role-based access control; B) Configure conditional access policies to enforce access based on user roles and locations; E) Enable session controls to limit access based on device compliance status

Option A - Correct. Defining user roles and groups in Azure AD allows for role-based access control, enabling administrators to assign access permissions based on user roles and responsibilities. Option B - Correct. Configuring conditional access policies to enforce access based on user roles and locations ensures that access to AVD resources is restricted to authorized users in specific contexts, enhancing security.

Option C - Incorrect. While implementing MFA enhances security, it is not directly related to planning Conditional Access based on user roles and locations. Option D - Incorrect. While Azure Bastion provides secure RDP access to virtual desktops, it is not directly related to planning Conditional Access based on user roles and locations. Option E - Correct. Enabling session controls to limit access based on device compliance status helps enforce security policies and ensure that only compliant devices can access AVD resources.

EXAM FOCUS	*Define roles and groups in Azure AD to establish a solid foundation for Conditional Access. Enforce location-based policies to restrict access to specific regions and devices. Use session controls to ensure device compliance before granting access to AVD resources.*
CAUTION ALERT	*Avoid using generic Conditional Access policies—they don't offer sufficient granularity for AVD-specific scenarios. Stay alert to ignoring session controls, as non-compliant devices can increase the risk of data breaches.*

QUESTION 29

Answer - A) Enable NLA for RDP connections; C) Configure Windows Firewall to restrict inbound traffic to necessary ports; D) Enable BitLocker encryption for data volumes on session hosts

Option A - Correct. Enabling Network Level Authentication (NLA) for RDP connections enhances security by requiring users to authenticate before establishing a session. Option B - Incorrect. While Windows Defender Antivirus is important, it may not directly relate to configuring session hosts for optimal security.

Option C - Correct. Configuring Windows Firewall helps restrict inbound traffic to necessary ports, reducing the attack surface.

Option D - Correct. Enabling BitLocker encryption for data volumes on session hosts ensures data protection in case of unauthorized access or theft. Option E - Incorrect. While Microsoft Defender for Cloud provides advanced threat protection, it may not be directly related to configuring session hosts for optimal security.

EXAM FOCUS	*You should enable NLA for RDP connections to secure session authentication. Configure Windows Firewall to limit inbound traffic to essential ports, and apply BitLocker encryption for protecting session host data. Regularly monitor compliance to ensure ongoing security effectiveness.*
CAUTION ALERT	*Avoid leaving default RDP settings active—they often lack adequate security controls. Stay cautious of unencrypted data volumes on session hosts, as they are vulnerable to unauthorized access or theft, compromising data integrity.*

QUESTION 30

Answer - A) Correctly sets RBAC and logs

Option A - Correct: The script assigns the correct role for AVD administration and initiates a workspace for logging, covering both access control and auditing requirements.
Option B - Incorrect: Logging is initiated with the operational insights workspace.
Option C - Incorrect: "Virtual Desktop Administrator" is a valid role for managing AVD.
Option D - Incorrect: The workspace configuration is correct for the given region.
Option E - Incorrect: SignInName correctly identifies the administrator by their Azure AD login, appropriate for RBAC assignments.

EXAM FOCUS	*Always assign RBAC roles using Azure AD and log administrative actions using Azure Monitor. Use the "Virtual Desktop Administrator" role for AVD management. Configure Operational Insights workspaces to centralize logs for audit purposes. Ensure proper role definitions and logging retention.*
CAUTION ALERT	*Avoid misconfiguring RBAC roles—they can result in unauthorized access. Stay alert to incomplete log setups, as missing logs can hinder auditing. Ensure the administrator's SignInName is correctly linked to their Azure AD account for proper RBAC enforcement.*

QUESTION 31

Answer - B) Configure FSLogix profiles using Group Policy

Option A - Incorrect. Running the installer manually on each VM is impractical and increases management overhead.
Option B - Correct. Group Policy allows centralized configuration and management of FSLogix profiles, suitable for diverse user environments.
Option C - Incorrect. Direct registry customization lacks centralized control and is error-prone.
Option D - Incorrect. Azure Automation is more suited for automated tasks, not FSLogix deployment.
Option E - Incorrect. Azure Policy is not designed for FSLogix configuration.

EXAM FOCUS	*You should use Group Policy to configure FSLogix profiles centrally for scalability and efficiency. This approach reduces profile management overhead and ensures a consistent setup for diverse user environments. Validate all FSLogix policies for compatibility with applications.*
CAUTION ALERT	*Avoid manual configuration or registry edits—they increase the chance of errors and lack centralized control. Stay cautious of misaligned Group Policy settings, as they can cause profile inconsistencies across session hosts.*

QUESTION 32

Answer - A) Enable Office Container pooling to share resources among sessions, D) Utilize FSLogix Office 365 Containers for seamless application provisioning, E) Enable multi-session support for Office applications within Containers.

A) Enable Office Container pooling to share resources among sessions - Pooling resources ensures efficient resource utilization and equitable distribution among multiple user sessions. D) Utilize FSLogix Office 365 Containers for seamless application provisioning - FSLogix Containers provide a seamless user experience by virtualizing Office applications within Containers, reducing conflicts and compatibility issues.

E) Enable multi-session support for Office applications within Containers - Enabling multi-session support allows multiple users to concurrently access Office applications within the same Container, optimizing resource utilization. B) Configure Office Containers to store user settings centrally - While centralizing user settings can simplify management, it may not directly address multi-session use or resource optimization.

C) Implement session-based licensing for Office applications - Session-based licensing may not be directly related to configuring Office Containers for multi-session use and resource optimization.

EXAM FOCUS	*Always enable multi-session support for Office Containers and use FSLogix Office 365 Containers for resource optimization. Ensure pooling is configured to allocate resources equitably among users. Test configurations thoroughly in a multi-session environment to prevent compatibility issues.*
CAUTION ALERT	*Avoid centralized user settings storage unless necessary—it may not optimize multi-session performance. Stay cautious of inadequate resource allocation policies, as they can lead to degraded performance in high-demand environments.*

QUESTION 33

Answer - A, B, D

A) Correct - Azure Bastion provides secure and private access without exposing RDP and SSH to the internet, enhancing data confidentiality. B) Correct - Azure Disk Encryption secures data at rest, crucial for maintaining client information confidentiality.

C) Incorrect - While Azure Site Recovery is important for disaster recovery, it does not directly enhance data confidentiality or secure client access. D) Correct - Azure AD Conditional Access allows for fine-grained security controls over who can access the AVD environment, ensuring secure client access. E) Incorrect - Azure Backup is essential for data preservation but does not directly address the specific requirements of secure access or confidentiality.

EXAM FOCUS	*Make sure to deploy Azure Bastion for secure RDP/SSH access, enable Azure Disk Encryption for data at rest, and configure Conditional Access for secure client connectivity. These measures ensure confidentiality and security while meeting legal compliance requirements.*
CAUTION ALERT	*Avoid relying solely on Azure Backup or Site Recovery for secure access—they do not directly enhance data confidentiality. Stay alert to misconfiguring Conditional Access policies, which can leave the AVD environment vulnerable to unauthorized access.*

QUESTION 34

Answer - A) Implement role-based access control (RBAC) policies to restrict device redirection based on user roles and responsibilities, C) Utilize Azure AD Conditional Access policies to enforce device compliance requirements before allowing redirection, D) Configure Group Policy settings to manage device redirection behavior and permissions for AVD users.

A) Implement role-based access control (RBAC) policies to restrict device redirection based on user roles and responsibilities - RBAC policies help enforce granular access controls, ensuring that only authorized users can redirect devices based on their roles and responsibilities within the organization. C) Utilize Azure AD Conditional Access policies to enforce device compliance requirements before allowing redirection - Conditional Access policies enhance security by verifying device compliance before permitting redirection, mitigating risks associated with non-compliant or compromised devices.

D) Configure Group Policy settings to manage device redirection behavior and permissions for AVD users - Group Policy settings provide centralized management of device redirection settings, allowing administrators to define policies tailored to organizational requirements and compliance standards.

B) Enable multi-factor authentication (MFA) for device redirection to enhance access security and prevent unauthorized device access - While MFA enhances overall access security, it may not directly address device redirection-specific considerations related to user roles, compliance, and management. E) Implement network Quality of Service (QoS) policies to prioritize traffic for redirected devices, ensuring optimal performance - While QoS policies optimize network performance, they may not directly relate to device redirection policies and security considerations.

EXAM FOCUS	*Configure Group Policy to manage device redirection, enforce Conditional Access to verify device compliance, and implement RBAC to restrict redirection based on roles. Regularly audit device redirection settings to ensure alignment with security and productivity goals.*
CAUTION ALERT	*Avoid enabling unrestricted device redirection—it increases security risks. Stay cautious of misconfigured Conditional Access policies or neglected RBAC settings, which can allow unauthorized devices to access sensitive AVD resources.*

QUESTION 35

Answer - A) Correct implementation for Universal Print

Option A - Correct: The script correctly registers a printer with Universal Print and assigns it to a user group, allowing centralized management and easy accessibility.

Option B - Incorrect: Assigning printers to groups is a recommended practice for managing access controls efficiently.
Option C - Incorrect: The location attribute helps in identifying the physical location of the printer, supported by Universal Print for better management. Option D - Incorrect: Printer drivers are typically managed on the client or session host; this script is focused on registration and assignment.

Option E - Incorrect: The command implicitly activates Universal Print by registering a printer under its management.

EXAM FOCUS	*You should use Universal Print to centralize printer management and assign printers to user groups for efficient access control. Ensure printers are registered correctly with attributes like location for easier identification and troubleshooting. Monitor usage for optimization.*
CAUTION ALERT	*Avoid neglecting group assignment in Universal Print—it simplifies access and controls. Stay cautious about not setting a clear naming or location structure, as it can make printer management and troubleshooting challenging in large environments.*

QUESTION 36

Answer - A, C, E

A) Correct - Azure Bastion provides secure and seamless access to virtual desktops over SSL, crucial for protecting development environments.
B) Incorrect - While AKS is important for scaling containerized applications, it does not directly enhance security or access management within an AVD setup. C) Correct - Azure Key Vault secures application secrets, crucial for source code and credential security in software development. D) Incorrect - Azure Scale Sets are effective for scaling but the primary need is secure access and source code security, not general VM scaling. E) Correct - Azure AD Conditional Access ensures that only authenticated and authorized developers can access the AVD environment, securing developer access.

EXAM FOCUS	*Enable Azure Bastion for secure access, use Key Vault for managing application secrets, and enforce Conditional Access for secure authentication. These configurations ensure source code security, robust access control, and scalable development environments in AVD setups.*
CAUTION ALERT	*Avoid assuming Azure Kubernetes Service (AKS) or Scale Sets can address all security concerns—they focus on application scaling. Stay cautious of storing application secrets outside of Key Vault, as this*

increases vulnerability risks.

QUESTION 37

Answer - B) Providing users with faster access to their desktops and applications upon login

Start VM on Connect accelerates user access by initiating VM startup upon login, enhancing user experience. Option A - Incorrect. Start VM on Connect doesn't determine VM startup behavior but improves user experience by reducing login times.

Option C - Incorrect. Shutting down idle VMs is unrelated to the Start VM on Connect feature. Option D - Incorrect. While authentication is important, it doesn't directly relate to VM startup upon user connection. Option E - Incorrect. Even workload distribution is not the primary function of the Start VM on Connect feature.

EXAM FOCUS	*Start VM on Connect is ideal for improving login times and minimizing VM idle states, enhancing both user experience and resource utilization. Ensure users are aware of potential startup delays during the first login and configure alerts for VM status monitoring.*
CAUTION ALERT	*Avoid relying on Start VM on Connect as a cost-cutting solution alone—it doesn't automatically manage idle VM shutdowns. Stay cautious of improper VM scheduling configurations, which can cause delays during high-demand periods or peak workloads.*

QUESTION 38

Answer - A) MSIX App Attach
MSIX App Attach enables dynamically attaching a packaged application to a user session, ensuring compatibility and performance across different user environments while maintaining isolation and flexibility.

Option B - MSI deployment: While MSI deployment is commonly used, it lacks the flexibility and isolation provided by MSIX App Attach. Option C - PowerShell script execution: PowerShell scripts may offer automation but do not provide the level of isolation and flexibility required for application delivery in AVD. Option D - Azure Marketplace integration: While Azure Marketplace offers various applications, it does not address the flexibility and isolation concerns of application deployment in AVD. Option E - FSLogix profile containerization: FSLogix profiles manage user settings but do not directly address application delivery.

EXAM FOCUS	*You need to use MSIX App Attach for its flexibility in dynamically delivering applications with isolation and compatibility across various environments. It ensures seamless deployment and reduced conflicts while maintaining high performance for AVD users.*
CAUTION ALERT	*Avoid using traditional MSI deployments for dynamic AVD environments—they lack flexibility. Stay clear of improperly packaged MSIX applications, as they can result in compatibility issues or failures during dynamic attachment processes.*

QUESTION 39

Answer - A, B, C

A) Correct - Azure Bastion provides secure and controlled access, ensuring data security for the global team.
B) Correct - Azure Site Recovery enhances business continuity and minimizes downtime by replicating VMs across regions. C) Correct - Azure AD Conditional Access can enforce policies based on user location, helping comply with international trade laws.
D) Incorrect - While Azure Policy is crucial for governance, it does not directly address the specific needs of minimal downtime or secure access configuration.
E) Incorrect - Azure ExpressRoute improves network reliability but is more about performance enhancement than compliance or secure remote access in this scenario.

EXAM FOCUS	*Deploy Azure Bastion for secure access, configure Site Recovery for cross-region failover, and use Conditional Access to enforce location-based security policies. These configurations provide robust security and compliance while ensuring minimal downtime for global teams.*
CAUTION ALERT	*Avoid using Azure Policy or ExpressRoute as standalone solutions—they do not directly address secure access or disaster recovery needs. Stay cautious of incomplete Conditional Access setups that fail to restrict access based on geographical requirements.*

QUESTION 40

Answer - B

Option A - Incorrect. The parameter -SessionType "Shared" does not exist in this context.
Option B - Correct. The correct parameter for enabling multisession is -MultiSessionEnabled.
Option C - Incorrect. -OptimizePerformance $true is the correct usage.
Option D - Incorrect. There is a parameter mistake.
Option E - Incorrect. $TenantId is correctly used as a variable that should be defined by the admin.

EXAM FOCUS	*Make sure to use the correct parameter -MultiSessionEnabled when configuring OneDrive for AVD. This setting ensures OneDrive functions efficiently in multi-session environments. Regularly update and optimize performance settings to align with changing user demands.*
CAUTION ALERT	*Avoid using incorrect parameter names like -EnableMultiSession—this will result in configuration errors. Stay alert to overlooked performance optimizations, as they can lead to degraded user experiences in multi-session environments.*

QUESTION 41

Answer - B

Option A - Incorrect. The parameter for on-demand attachment should be -AttachOnDemand.

Option B - Correct. The -AttachOnDemand $true parameter optimally manages resources by only mounting the app when needed. Option C - Incorrect. While enabling background updates is important, the flag used does not exist in this context. Option D - Incorrect. User groups are managed through different configuration settings.

Option E - Incorrect. The -Path parameter is correctly specified; it should point to the UNC path where the MSIX package is located.

EXAM FOCUS	*Always remember to use -AttachOnDemand for efficient MSIX app attach management. It optimizes resource allocation by only mounting apps when required. Ensure the UNC path is correct and accessible to avoid deployment failures. Test app compatibility thoroughly.*
CAUTION ALERT	*Avoid using -DynamicMount, as it is not a valid parameter for on-demand attachment. Stay alert to incorrect file paths or insufficient permissions, which can cause MSIX app attach to fail during user sessions.*

QUESTION 42

Answer - A, B, C

A) Correct - 'CloudCache' enables using multiple storage locations to provide redundancy and quick access, crucial for handling large media files across global locations. B) Correct - 'CloudCacheLocations' specifies the actual storage locations used by CloudCache, essential for ensuring high availability and quick data retrieval.

C) Correct - 'Encrypt' ensures the security of sensitive media content, which is paramount for protecting intellectual property in the media industry. D) Incorrect - While 'VHDLocations' determines where virtual hard disks are stored, it's less about speed and security than specifying storage paths. E) Incorrect - 'LargeFileHandlingMode' is not a standard registry setting within FSLogix, thus not applicable here.

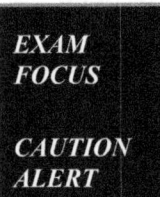	You should configure CloudCache and CloudCacheLocations for redundancy and performance when handling large media files. Encryption settings are vital for protecting sensitive media content. Regularly monitor CloudCache health for high availability.
	Avoid relying solely on VHDLocations for performance; it's for defining storage paths, not optimization. Stay clear of missing encryption settings—they are critical for intellectual property protection in the media industry.

QUESTION 43

Answer - A) Azure Monitor Logs

Option A - Azure Monitor Logs provide comprehensive monitoring capabilities, including session health and stability metrics for AVD. This tool allows you to collect, analyze, and act on telemetry data from AVD deployments.

Option B - Azure Automation is primarily used for automating repetitive tasks and configurations and is not focused on monitoring session health. Option C - Azure Policy is used to enforce and govern organizational standards and compliance, not for monitoring session health. Option D - Azure Security Center focuses on security posture management and threat protection, not specifically for monitoring session health.

Option E - Azure Monitor Alerts are used to set up alerts based on metrics, logs, and activity logs, but they do not provide detailed session health and stability monitoring.

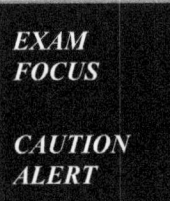	Use Azure Monitor Logs for detailed session health monitoring. Set up alerts for critical metrics to proactively address performance or stability issues. Integrate with Log Analytics to analyze trends and identify recurring problems.
	Avoid relying solely on Azure Monitor Alerts—they don't provide detailed insights into session health. Stay cautious about neglecting session performance telemetry, as it's crucial for ensuring a smooth user experience in AVD deployments.

QUESTION 44

Answer - B) Azure Blob Storage

Option B - Azure Blob Storage is the most suitable destination for exporting diagnostic logs because it provides a scalable and cost-effective solution, ensuring accessibility and compliance for AVD infrastructure.

Option A - Azure Event Hubs are more suitable for real-time telemetry streaming, not long-term log storage.
Option C - Azure Monitor Logs store log data primarily for monitoring and analytics, not for long-term log retention.
Option D - Azure Log Analytics is used for analyzing log data, not as a storage destination for diagnostic logs.
Option E - Azure Storage Queue is designed for message queuing, not for storing diagnostic logs.

EXAM FOCUS	You need to export diagnostic logs to Azure Blob Storage for scalable, cost-effective, and compliant storage. Ensure you capture performance metrics, audit logs, and error diagnostics. Regularly review log retention policies to balance compliance and cost.
CAUTION ALERT	Avoid exporting logs to unsupported destinations like Azure Storage Queue—it's not meant for long-term log storage. Stay alert to potential cost overruns if diagnostic settings capture excessive or irrelevant data without proper filtering.

QUESTION 45

Answer - C

Option A - Incorrect. The script does not specify the correct parameter to indicate the frequency of the updates.
Option B - Incorrect. The -ForUpdateManagement parameter does not exist in the New-AzAutomationSchedule cmdlet.
Option C - Correct. Changing -WeekInterval 1 to -Frequency "Weekly" correctly specifies that the updates should occur weekly, which is a necessary adjustment for correct scheduling.
Option D - Incorrect. Set-AzVmAutoUpdateSchedule is not a valid cmdlet for creating a schedule in Azure Automation.
Option E - Incorrect. While specifying the time zone is important, the primary issue is with the frequency of the updates, not the time zone.

EXAM FOCUS	*Replace -WeekInterval with -Frequency "Weekly" to correctly define the schedule for updates. Ensure the timezone is UTC or relevant to your region for accurate scheduling. Leverage Azure Automation to manage update execution efficiently.*
CAUTION ALERT	*Avoid using deprecated or incorrect cmdlet parameters like -WeekInterval for defining update schedules. Stay cautious of omitting timezone configurations, which can lead to unintended update times affecting end-user sessions.*

QUESTION 46

Answer - B) Azure Network Watcher

Option B - Azure Network Watcher is specifically designed for monitoring and diagnosing network performance in Azure environments, including AVD. It provides insights into network topology, traffic flows, and connectivity issues, enabling administrators to optimize network performance and troubleshoot connectivity problems effectively.

Option A - Azure Monitor focuses on monitoring various Azure services but may not provide detailed network performance metrics required for AVD environments. Option C - Azure Resource Graph allows querying Azure resources but may not offer specialized network monitoring capabilities required for AVD environments.

Option D - Azure Log Analytics provides insights into resource usage and performance but may not specialize in network performance monitoring. Option E - Azure Diagnostics captures diagnostic data from Azure services but may not focus specifically on network performance monitoring in AVD environments.

EXAM FOCUS	*Use Azure Network Watcher for network performance diagnostics in AVD environments. It provides tools like connection monitors and flow logs, enabling detailed insights into network latency and throughput issues. Integrate findings with Azure Monitor for holistic analysis.*
CAUTION ALERT	*Avoid assuming Azure Monitor or Log Analytics will suffice for network performance—they are not designed for granular network diagnostics. Stay clear of overlooking periodic network topology checks to ensure continued compliance with performance baselines.*

QUESTION 47

Answer - A) Implementing Azure Cost Management tools
B) Rightsizing virtual machine instances
C) Enabling auto-scaling based on demand
E) Optimizing network bandwidth

A) Implementing Azure Cost Management tools - Azure Cost Management tools provide insights into AVD costs and help identify areas for optimization. B) Rightsizing virtual machine instances - Rightsizing VM instances ensures that resources are allocated efficiently, minimizing unnecessary costs.

C) Enabling auto-scaling based on demand - Auto-scaling allows resources to be dynamically adjusted according to workload, optimizing cost-efficiency.

E) Optimizing network bandwidth - Optimizing network bandwidth can reduce data transfer costs associated with AVD usage. D) Using FSLogix to manage user profiles - While FSLogix improves user experience and management, it's not directly related to reducing operational costs.

EXAM FOCUS	*Implement Azure Cost Management to monitor usage trends and identify cost-saving opportunities. Rightsize VM instances based on user demand and enable auto-scaling to optimize resource usage dynamically. Minimize bandwidth usage through compression and QoS policies.*
CAUTION ALERT	*Avoid keeping oversized VM instances running during low-demand periods—it's a significant cost factor. Stay alert to underutilized resources or overly aggressive scaling rules that could compromise user experience or lead to unnecessary expenses.*

QUESTION 48

Answer - A, B, C

A) Correct - Windows 11 Enterprise supports the latest development tools and is compatible with various software requirements for agile development. B) Correct - Windows 10 Enterprise multi-session is ideal for software development teams, allowing multiple developers to access environments simultaneously for CI/CD processes.

C) Correct - Windows Server 2022 provides robust infrastructure for development environments, supporting advanced CI/CD workflows and tool compatibility. D) Incorrect - While Windows Server 2019 is capable, it does not offer the same level of performance optimization as Windows Server 2022 for cutting-edge development tools. E) Incorrect - Windows 10 Pro does not support the multi-session environment needed for agile software development teams.

EXAM FOCUS	*Deploy Windows 11 Enterprise for advanced development features, Windows 10 Enterprise multi-session for shared environments, and Windows Server 2022 for robust CI/CD support. Regularly update these systems to ensure compatibility with the latest development tools and frameworks.*
CAUTION ALERT	*Avoid deploying outdated systems like Windows 10 Pro, which lack multi-session capabilities. Stay cautious of mismatched operating system versions within the AVD environment, as it can cause compatibility issues with development tools.*

QUESTION 49

Answer - A) Utilizing Azure Policy for license enforcement and compliance monitoring
C) Conducting regular audits to track license usage and compliance

A) Utilizing Azure Policy for license enforcement and compliance monitoring - Azure Policy enables organizations to define and enforce policies for AVD license usage, ensuring compliance with licensing agreements. C) Conducting regular audits to track license usage and compliance - Regular audits help identify any discrepancies or non-compliance issues, allowing corrective actions to be taken.

B, D, E) While RBAC policies, Azure Cost Management, and Azure Active Directory integration are important for access control, cost optimization, and centralized management, they are not specifically tailored for managing AVD licenses and ensuring compliance.

EXAM FOCUS	*Utilize Azure Policy to enforce license compliance rules and automate monitoring. Conduct regular audits to identify and address potential compliance issues. Maintain detailed license usage logs for transparency and readiness in case of external audits.*
CAUTION ALERT	*Avoid neglecting periodic compliance checks—they are vital for staying aligned with licensing agreements. Stay clear of over-assigning licenses to users or resources, which can result in unnecessary costs or non-compliance penalties.*

QUESTION 50

Answer - A) Implementing centralized logging using Azure Monitor Logs for aggregation and analysis
B) Enabling diagnostic settings in AVD to collect logs and metrics for monitoring and troubleshooting
C) Utilizing Azure Log Analytics workspaces for long-term log retention and analysis

A) Implementing centralized logging using Azure Monitor Logs for aggregation and analysis - Centralized logging using Azure Monitor Logs allows for aggregation and analysis of logs from various AVD components, enabling efficient troubleshooting and compliance.

B) Enabling diagnostic settings in AVD to collect logs and metrics for monitoring and troubleshooting - Enabling diagnostic settings ensures the collection of logs and metrics from AVD components, facilitating proactive monitoring and troubleshooting.

C) Utilizing Azure Log Analytics workspaces for long-term log retention and analysis - Azure Log Analytics workspaces provide long-term log retention and analysis capabilities, enabling historical insights and compliance reporting.

D, E) While implementing RBAC controls and configuring log rotation are important considerations, they are not specific to log management practices in AVD.

EXAM FOCUS	*Centralize logging with Azure Monitor Logs to aggregate data from all AVD components. Use Log Analytics workspaces for detailed analysis and long-term retention. Enable diagnostic settings to capture performance metrics and system events for compliance and troubleshooting.*
CAUTION ALERT	*Avoid inconsistent log collection configurations across AVD components—it complicates analysis. Stay alert to improper log retention policies that can lead to unnecessary costs or gaps in compliance-related data for audit purposes.*

PRACTICE TEST 7 - QUESTIONS ONLY

QUESTION 1

Your role involves enhancing security for an AVD implementation by planning virtual network designs that protect against external threats while ensuring reliable connectivity. You need to:
• Implement MFA for secure access.
• Design a network topology that supports Azure Bastion.
• Ensure JIT access for admin tasks.
Which Azure service should you prioritize configuring to meet these requirements?

A) Azure Firewall
B) Azure VPN Gateway
C) Azure Network Security Group
D) Azure Application Gateway
E) Azure Bastion

QUESTION 2

Your organization requires strict Quality of Service (QoS) policies to ensure optimal performance for Azure Virtual Desktop (AVD) users. The finance department heavily relies on AVD to access critical financial applications, necessitating consistent and reliable network performance. However, managing bandwidth allocation and prioritizing traffic based on application type presents a significant challenge. How would you design QoS policies to meet the demands of the finance department while ensuring overall AVD performance?

A) Allocate dedicated bandwidth for finance department users
B) Prioritize network traffic for financial applications
C) Implement ExpressRoute for dedicated connectivity
D) Enable Azure Traffic Manager for load balancing
E) Configure VM scale sets for resource optimization

QUESTION 3

- As part of optimizing resource utilization in an Azure Virtual Desktop (AVD) environment, you need to identify underutilized session hosts.
- Your goal is to allocate resources efficiently and minimize costs.
- Your task involves selecting the appropriate Log Analytics table to analyze session host performance.

Which table should you query to retrieve performance metrics and identify underutilized session hosts based on CPU and memory usage?

A) `WVDPerformanceCounters`
B) `WVDSessionHostUtilization`
C) `WVDHostRegistrations`
D) `WVDAgentHealth`
E) `WVDServiceHealth`

QUESTION 4

Your organization is evaluating different Azure storage options for hosting user data in Azure Virtual Desktop (AVD) environments. As the IT specialist, you need to compare the performance and cost implications of these options to make an informed decision. Which Azure storage options should you compare for AVD user data? Select CORRECT answers that apply.

A) Azure Blob Storage

B) Azure Files
C) Azure Disk Storage
D) Azure Data Lake Storage
E) Azure NetApp Files

QUESTION 5

You need to configure file shares in Azure for a high-traffic AVD environment. Your task includes setting up the share with appropriate access and scalability settings. Review this PowerShell snippet for potential issues.

```powershell
New-AzRmStorageShare -StorageAccountName "AVDStorage" -Name "AVDFiles" -Quota 512 -EnabledProtocol "SMB"
```

A) Quota too low for high-traffic
B) Incorrect protocol for AVD
C) Command syntax is incorrect
D) Storage account name is inappropriate
E) Command is correctly configured

QUESTION 6

You are managing session hosts in an Azure Virtual Desktop (AVD) environment and need to implement a cost-effective solution to optimize resource usage. The solution must meet the following requirements:
- Automatically start session hosts at 9:00 AM and shut them down at 7:00 PM.
- Ensure that session hosts are active every day of the week.
- Minimize manual intervention and administrative effort.
Which Azure service should you use to achieve this? Select TWO.

A) Azure Monitor Alerts
B) Azure Automation with Azure Runbooks
C) Azure Virtual Machine Scale Sets
D) Azure Automation with Azure Logic Apps
E) Azure Resource Manager templates

QUESTION 7

Your organization is planning to deploy Azure Virtual Desktop (AVD) for different use cases, each with unique requirements and budget constraints. As the Azure architect, you need to determine the most cost-effective licensing model for these scenarios. What factors should you consider? Select THREE.

A) User Density and Concurrent Access
B) Application Workload and Resource Consumption
C) Geographical Distribution and Data Sovereignty
D) Long-Term Growth and Scalability Requirements
E) Budget Allocation and Financial Forecasting

QUESTION 8

Your organization is evaluating tools and metrics to assess the performance of Azure Virtual Desktop (AVD) deployments. As the Azure administrator, you need to select appropriate options. Which tools and metrics should you prioritize? Select THREE.

A) Azure Monitor and Performance Counters
B) Network Latency and Bandwidth Utilization

C) User Logon Times and Session Duration
D) Application Response Times and Launch Latency
E) CPU Usage and Memory Consumption

QUESTION 9

You are configuring autoscale for host pools in an Azure Virtual Desktop (AVD) environment and need to determine the appropriate scaling thresholds. Consider the following factors:
- User login activity throughout the day.
- CPU and memory utilization during peak usage hours.
- Network latency and throughput.
- Available storage capacity.
- Number of active user sessions.

Which of these factors should be used as criteria for defining scaling thresholds? Select TWO.

A) User login activity throughout the day.
B) CPU and memory utilization during peak usage hours.
C) Network latency and throughput.
D) Available storage capacity.
E) Number of active user sessions.

QUESTION 10

As part of compliance, you need to ensure all session hosts in a host pool are using FSLogix for profile management. Which Azure CLI command ensures FSLogix is used across the deployment?

```bash
az avd hostpool update --name MyHostPool --resource-group MyGroup --set customRdpProperties="useFsLogix=true"
```

A) Command is correct
B) Incorrect property name
C) FSLogix cannot be set via CLI
D) Syntax error in command
E) Command requires additional parameters

QUESTION 11

Your organization is embarking on the creation of a golden image manually for Azure Virtual Desktop (AVD). As the Azure specialist, you are responsible for ensuring adherence to best practices during the image creation process. What are recommended best practices for golden image creation? Select THREE.

A) Minimize Image Size and Complexity
B) Include Latest Security Updates and Patches
C) Utilize Unmanaged Disks for Image Storage
D) Avoid Hardcoding Configuration Settings
E) Document Image Configuration and Versioning

QUESTION 12

You are tasked with implementing a disaster recovery strategy for an Azure Virtual Desktop (AVD) environment. Consider the following requirements:
- Enable automatic failover of AVD host pools to a secondary Azure region in case of a primary region outage.
- Minimize downtime and ensure business continuity during failover operations.

Which combination of Azure services should you use to achieve these objectives? Select TWO.

A) Azure Traffic Manager
B) Azure Site Recovery
C) Azure Backup
D) Azure Load Balancer
E) Azure Blob Storage

QUESTION 13

Your organization is seeking to automate the update processes for Azure Virtual Desktop (AVD) images to enhance efficiency and consistency. As the Azure specialist, you need to evaluate suitable tools and services for automating update processes. Which of the following tools and services can be used to automate update processes for AVD images?

A) Azure Logic Apps
B) Azure Functions
C) Azure Automation State Configuration
D) Azure Update Management
E) Azure DevOps Pipelines

QUESTION 14

Your organization is concerned about security best practices for image storage in Azure Virtual Desktop (AVD) deployments to protect sensitive data and prevent unauthorized access. As the Azure specialist, you need to identify security best practices for image storage. What are the security best practices for image storage in AVD deployments? Select THREE.

A) Implement Role-Based Access Control (RBAC) to Restrict Access
B) Encrypt Data at Rest and in Transit
C) Enable Azure Security Center Recommendations for Image Storage
D) Regularly Audit and Monitor Access to Image Storage Resources
E) Implement Multi-Factor Authentication (MFA) for Image Management Operations

QUESTION 15

Implementing high-availability for AVD involves setting up redundant network connections. Using PowerShell, how would you configure a failover group between two Azure regions?

```powershell
New-AzLoadBalancer -ResourceGroupName "HA-RG" -Name "HaLoadBalancer" -Location "East US" -Sku "Standard" -FrontendIpConfiguration $config
```

A) Command is correctly configured
B) Missing failover group setup
C) Sku should be "Basic"
D) Incorrect Location
E) $config needs to be defined

QUESTION 16

Your organization needs to align Azure Virtual Desktop (AVD) operations with regulatory frameworks such as GDPR and HIPAA to ensure the protection of sensitive data and maintain compliance. As the Azure specialist, you need to implement measures to achieve alignment effectively. How can AVD operations be aligned with GDPR, HIPAA, etc.? Select THREE.

A) Implement Data Access Controls and Encryption
B) Conduct Regular Compliance Assessments and Audits
C) Ensure User Consent and Data Subject Rights Management
D) Enable Secure Data Retention and Deletion Policies
E) Establish Data Breach Notification Procedures and Incident Response Plans

QUESTION 17

Your organization is concerned about effectively monitoring and managing costs in its Azure Virtual Desktop (AVD) deployment to ensure budget compliance. As the Azure specialist, you need to identify suitable tools for cost monitoring and management. Which tools can you use for monitoring and managing Azure costs in AVD deployments? Select TWO.

A) Azure Cost Management and Billing
B) Azure Log Analytics for Performance Monitoring
C) Azure Security Center for Threat Detection
D) Azure Monitor for Resource Monitoring
E) Azure Advisor for Cost Optimization Recommendations

QUESTION 18

In the context of managing an Azure Virtual Desktop (AVD) environment, you need to implement a solution for efficient load balancing and failover across multiple session hosts. Considering this scenario, what approach should you take to achieve the desired outcome?
- Ensure seamless user experience during session host failures
- Minimize downtime and disruption to user sessions
- Streamline administrative tasks for managing session host availability Select TWO.

A) Azure Traffic Manager
B) Azure Load Balancer
C) Azure Application Gateway
D) Azure Front Door
E) Azure Load Balancer Standard

QUESTION 19

Your organization is reviewing its disaster recovery plan for Azure Virtual Desktop (AVD) environments to ensure compliance with industry regulations. Key considerations include data sovereignty, encryption standards, and audit trails for recovery operations. How would you enhance the disaster recovery plan to meet these regulatory requirements effectively? Select TWO.

A) Implement Azure Key Vault for centralized key management
B) Configure Azure Policy for compliance enforcement
C) Utilize Azure AD Privileged Identity Management (PIM) for access control
D) Deploy Azure Firewall for network security and compliance
E) Set up Azure Security Center for threat detection and compliance monitoring

QUESTION 20

You need to customize AVD performance reports to meet different stakeholder needs, including IT management and compliance teams. Each report should include data on login times, session durations, and active user counts, and must be automatically generated weekly. How would you configure Azure Monitor to generate these customized reports and ensure they meet the specified requirements?

A) Use Azure Monitor Workbooks

B) Configure Azure Logic Apps
C) Implement Azure Automation runbooks
D) Deploy Azure Functions
E) Set up Azure Monitor insights

QUESTION 21

You need to configure Azure Virtual Desktop to optimize network performance and reduce latency for users accessing resources over a managed network connection. Which optimization technique should you implement to achieve this goal?

A) Enable Quality of Service (QoS)
B) Implement TCP/IP Offload Engine (TOE)
C) Enable RDP Shortpath for managed networks
D) Configure Network Load Balancing
E) Enable Dynamic Host Configuration Protocol (DHCP) relay agent

QUESTION 22

Your organization is evaluating the impact of role-based access control (RBAC) on security and operational efficiency in Azure Virtual Desktop (AVD) environments. The focus is on understanding the benefits and challenges associated with implementing RBAC to make informed decisions. How does RBAC impact security and operational efficiency in AVD environments? Select THREE.

A) Enhances security by enforcing fine-grained access control
B) Improves operational efficiency by automating access management tasks
C) Reduces security risks by minimizing excessive privileges
D) Increases complexity of access management but strengthens security posture
E) Streamlines operational workflows by delegating access management responsibilities

QUESTION 23

Your organization is implementing multi-factor authentication (MFA) for Azure Virtual Desktop (AVD) connections to enhance security measures. The focus is on understanding the impact of MFA on user access and security in AVD environments. What are the potential impacts of implementing multi-factor authentication (MFA) on user access and security in Azure Virtual Desktop (AVD) environments? Select THREE.

A) Enhanced security through additional authentication factors
B) Increased user friction due to additional authentication steps
C) Improved user awareness of security best practices
D) Reduced risk of unauthorized access to AVD resources
E) Potential compatibility issues with legacy applications or devices

QUESTION 24

You are configuring AVD for a financial services firm that requires extremely high security and compliance standards. Which of the following measures would you prioritize to secure the desktop environment? Select CORRECT answers that apply.

A) Enable role-based access control (RBAC).
B) Configure end-to-end encryption.
C) Set up a virtual network firewall.
D) Implement Azure Sentinel.
E) Audit and log all user sessions.

QUESTION 25

As part of your Azure Virtual Desktop deployment, you need to automate the setup of VM network interfaces to include advanced threat protection. Review this Azure CLI script and identify the necessary modification to enable Azure Defender for VMs on the network interface.

```bash
az network nic create --name "AVDVMNic" --resource-group "AVDResources" --network-security-group "AVDNSG" --enable-accelerated-networking true --location "eastus2"
```

A) Script is correct
B) Add --enable-vm-protection true
C) Replace --enable-accelerated-networking with --enable-nsg-flow-logging
D) Include --tags "Security:AzureDefender"
E) None of the modifications are needed

QUESTION 26

Your organization is deploying Azure Virtual Desktop (AVD) and wants to implement Windows Defender Application Control to enhance security. The focus is on understanding the steps to implement Windows Defender Application Control. What are the steps to implement Windows Defender Application Control? Select TWO.

A) Create and configure Code Integrity policies for AVD session hosts
B) Enable Windows Defender Application Control in audit mode for initial testing and validation
C) Define and enforce AppLocker rules to allow or deny applications based on file and publisher attributes
D) Deploy Windows Defender Application Control policies using Group Policy or Microsoft Endpoint Manager
E) Monitor Windows Defender Application Control events and alerts for policy violations and security incidents

QUESTION 27

To meet regulatory compliance and ensure high security for AVD in a healthcare organization, which configurations are essential to protect patient data, provide secure access, and ensure data recovery capabilities? Select THREE.

A) Configure encrypted storage with Azure Disk Encryption.
B) Implement Azure ExpressRoute for dedicated connectivity.
C) Set up conditional access policies with Azure AD.
D) Enable Azure Site Recovery for disaster recovery.
E) Use network security groups (NSGs) to control traffic.

QUESTION 28

Your organization is implementing device compliance policies in Azure Virtual Desktop (AVD) environments to enhance security and ensure that only compliant devices can access resources. The focus is on understanding the process of implementing device compliance policies. What are the steps involved in implementing device compliance policies in AVD environments? Select THREE.

A) Define device compliance requirements based on organizational security policies
B) Configure compliance policies in Microsoft Intune to assess device compliance status
C) Deploy Azure Monitor to track compliance status and security events
D) Remediate non-compliant devices by applying conditional access policies
E) Enable automated alerts for non-compliant devices to facilitate prompt action

QUESTION 29

Your organization is enforcing security baselines and group policies for Azure Virtual Desktop (AVD) session hosts to meet compliance requirements. The focus is on applying security baselines and group policies. Which security baselines and group policies should be applied to Azure Virtual Desktop session hosts to enhance security? Select THREE.

A) Enforce password complexity requirements and account lockout policies through Group Policy
B) Apply Windows Defender Firewall rules to block suspicious inbound and outbound traffic
C) Implement AppLocker rules to control which applications can run on session hosts
D) Configure Windows Update policies to ensure timely installation of security patches and updates
E) Enable Windows Defender Credential Guard to protect against credential theft attacks

QUESTION 30

Implement Azure AD Privileged Identity Management (PIM) to manage, control, and monitor access within your Azure Virtual Desktop environments. You need to ensure that Just-In-Time (JIT) access is configured for enhanced security. Evaluate the Azure CLI command below for setting up PIM with JIT for a group of administrators.

```bash
az ad sp create-for-rbac --name "JIT-PIM" --role "Desktop Virtualization User" --scopes /subscriptions/sub-id --years 1
```

A) Correct setup for JIT-PIM
B) Role should be "Desktop Virtualization Administrator"
C) JIT setup requires additional parameters
D) Scopes parameter is incorrectly set
E) Time bound parameter is unnecessary

QUESTION 31

You are configuring FSLogix for a healthcare organization's AVD deployment, aiming to enhance performance and data security. The organization requires a solution that addresses the following concerns:
1. Optimizing FSLogix settings to minimize login times for clinicians accessing patient records.
2. Ensuring secure access to FSLogix profiles while adhering to HIPAA compliance.
3. Streamlining FSLogix configuration across multiple AVD host pools.

A) Enable Profile Containers with VHDX disk format
B) Implement Kerberos authentication for FSLogix access
C) Encrypt FSLogix profiles with BitLocker
D) Utilize Azure Key Vault for FSLogix profile encryption keys
E) Configure FSLogix settings via Azure Policy

QUESTION 32

As an Azure Virtual Desktop administrator tasked with customizing Office Containers for optimal performance, you need to consider various factors to enhance user experience. Consider the following scenario:
- User productivity must be maximized by optimizing application load times and responsiveness.
- Office Containers should be tailored to meet specific user requirements and preferences.
- Customizations should be implemented without compromising security or stability.
How can Office Containers be customized for optimal performance? Select THREE.

A) Implement selective application virtualization within Office Containers.
B) Configure Office Containers to utilize GPU acceleration for graphics-intensive tasks.
C) Customize Office Container profiles to preload frequently used applications.
D) Utilize Azure AD conditional access policies to optimize Office application access.
E) Enable OneDrive integration within Office Containers for seamless file access.

QUESTION 33

For a retail company using AVD during high traffic events like Black Friday, you need to ensure system scalability, maintain low latency, and provide secure transaction processing. Which measures should you implement? Select THREE.

A) Scale out session hosts using Azure Automation.
B) Implement Azure Front Door for global traffic management.
C) Enable Azure Firewall with application rules.
D) Configure Azure Traffic Manager for optimal routing.
E) Use Azure ExpressRoute for consistent network performance.

QUESTION 34

Your organization is evaluating the security risks associated with device redirection in Azure Virtual Desktop (AVD) deployments. Consider the following scenario:
- The organization deals with sensitive data and operates in a regulated industry with strict compliance requirements.
- Users often connect to AVD sessions from unmanaged devices outside the corporate network, posing potential security threats.
- IT administrators aim to identify and mitigate security risks associated with device redirection while ensuring compliance with regulatory standards.

What security risks are associated with device redirection in the given scenario, and how can they be mitigated? Select THREE.

A) Risk: Data leakage due to unauthorized access to redirected devices. Mitigation: Implement Azure AD Conditional Access policies to enforce device compliance and access controls before allowing redirection.
B) Risk: Malware infection from compromised USB drives or peripherals. Mitigation: Configure Group Policy settings to restrict device redirection from untrusted sources and implement endpoint protection measures.
C) Risk: Unauthorized access to sensitive resources through redirected smart card readers. Mitigation: Utilize role-based access control (RBAC) policies to restrict smart card redirection based on user roles and responsibilities.
D) Risk: Network eavesdropping and data interception during device redirection sessions. Mitigation: Enable network encryption and secure tunneling protocols for device redirection traffic, such as Remote Desktop Protocol (RDP) over TLS.
E) Risk: Insider threats exploiting device redirection for unauthorized data exfiltration. Mitigation: Implement logging and monitoring mechanisms to track device redirection activities and detect suspicious behavior in real-time.

QUESTION 35

In configuring printing preferences for AVD, you need to balance performance and quality. You've decided to set up a print policy that defaults to black-and-white printing to conserve color resources. Review the JSON configuration you plan to implement:

```json
{
 "defaultColorMode": "BlackAndWhite",
 "qualitySettings": "Standard"
}
```

A) Configuration optimizes resource use
B) Color mode setting is incorrect
C) Quality should be set to high
D) JSON structure is invalid
E) Policy lacks user-specific settings

QUESTION 36

In a consulting firm utilizing AVD, there's a need to maintain client confidentiality, ensure high data availability, and provide secure communication channels. What measures should you employ? Select THREE.

A) Configure Azure Information Protection for data classification and encryption.
B) Implement Azure Site Recovery to ensure data availability during outages.
C) Use Azure ExpressRoute for private network connections.
D) Deploy Azure VPN Gateway for secure remote access.
E) Set up Azure Active Directory for secure identity management.

QUESTION 37

You are configuring the Start VM on Connect feature for a large Azure Virtual Desktop (AVD) deployment. What is a critical consideration when managing the Start VM on Connect feature to ensure efficiency and cost-effectiveness?

A) Implementing auto-scaling to dynamically adjust VM capacity based on user demand
B) Enabling session pre-launch to reduce user wait times during login
C) Monitoring user activity to optimize VM startup times and resource allocation
D) Enforcing strict RBAC policies to control access to VM startup settings
E) Deploying FSLogix to manage user profiles and session persistence

QUESTION 38

When choosing a method for deploying apps to Azure Virtual Desktop (AVD), what factor should be considered to ensure optimal performance and user experience?

A) Application compatibility with user environments
B) Cost-effectiveness of deployment method
C) Integration with Azure Active Directory for user authentication
D) Utilization of Azure Bastion for secure application access
E) Automation capabilities for deployment tasks

QUESTION 39

An AVD setup for a government agency must ensure ultra-high security for sensitive data, allow only authorized devices to connect, and maintain rigorous audit trails. What should be configured? Select THREE.

A) Implement Azure Bastion for all remote access.
B) Use Azure Firewall with strict rules to control network traffic.
C) Enable device compliance policies with Azure AD Conditional Access.
D) Configure Azure Monitor and Azure Log Analytics for auditing.
E) Create a new subnet named AzureBastionSubnet for deployment.

QUESTION 40

You need to ensure data compliance and security when configuring OneDrive within AVD. Which Azure CLI script would properly set up OneDrive to enforce MFA and restrict file sync to the AVD environment?
az storage fs file create --account-name myaccount --sas-token $token -require-mfa $true --only-in-avd $true

A) Script is correct.
B) Replace --only-in-avd $true with --sync-group "AVDUsers".
C) Change -require-mfa $true to --require-mfa $true.
D) Add --encrypt-files $true to enhance security.
E) Replace az storage fs with az onedrive config.

QUESTION 41

You are configuring Microsoft 365 Apps for AVD and need to ensure that your configuration adheres to company security policies which require that all data must be encrypted at rest. What is the best PowerShell command to achieve this when setting up OneDrive within Microsoft 365 Apps?
Set-OneDriveConfig -EncryptData $true

A) Command is correct.
B) Add -StorageType "AzureBlob" to specify storage type.
C) Replace -EncryptData $true with -EnableEncryption $true.
D) Include -AADIntegration $true for better Azure AD integration.
E) Change to Set-M365AppConfig -EncryptDataStorage $true.

QUESTION 42

An insurance company needs to optimize its AVD setup for handling sensitive client data, ensuring compliance with financial regulations, and facilitating rapid disaster recovery. Which FSLogix settings should be configured? Select THREE.

A) HKLM\SOFTWARE\FSLogix\Profiles\CloudCache
B) HKLM\SOFTWARE\FSLogix\Profiles\Encrypt
C) HKLM\SOFTWARE\FSLogix\Profiles\CloudCacheLocations
D) HKLM\SOFTWARE\FSLogix\Profiles\BackupInterval
E) HKLM\SOFTWARE\FSLogix\Profiles\LocalCacheSize

QUESTION 43

As part of your role as an Azure Virtual Desktop (AVD) administrator, you need to troubleshoot session drops and lag experienced by users in a remote work environment. What tool or service would you utilize for effective troubleshooting?

A) Azure Monitor Metrics Explorer
B) Azure Resource Graph
C) Azure Log Analytics
D) Azure Monitor Workbooks
E) Azure Security Center

QUESTION 44

In order to facilitate effective troubleshooting and performance analysis of your Azure Virtual Desktop (AVD) environment, you need to manage log retention policies. Considerations include:
1. Regulatory requirements and organizational policies governing data retention periods for AVD diagnostic logs.
2. The impact of log retention on storage costs and availability of historical data for analysis.
3. The need for balancing compliance requirements with operational efficiency in log retention management.
What is the recommended approach for managing log retention policies to balance compliance and operational efficiency in AVD environments?

A) Set a fixed retention period for all diagnostic logs.
B) Apply different retention periods based on log severity and importance.
C) Implement a data lifecycle management solution for automated log retention.
D) Archive diagnostic logs to long-term storage for historical analysis.
E) Purge diagnostic logs after a predetermined period to minimize storage costs.

QUESTION 45

Automate the deployment of updates across AVD session hosts using Azure Automation. Write the Azure CLI command

to create a new update deployment to a specific host pool.
```
az automation update-management deployment create --name "AVDUpdates" --resource-group "AVDResourceGroup" --hosts "HostPool1" --schedule "Weekly"
```

A) Command is correct.
B) Replace --hosts "HostPool1" with --target "HostPool1".
C) Add --duration "2h" to define how long the update window is open.
D) Change --schedule "Weekly" to --schedule-id $(az automation schedule show --name "OffPeakUpdates" --resource-group "AVDResourceGroup" --query id -o tsv).
E) Include --type "VM" to specify the type of resource being updated.

QUESTION 46

In an Azure Virtual Desktop (AVD) deployment, users are experiencing intermittent connectivity issues, impacting productivity. As the AVD administrator, you need to troubleshoot network connectivity issues to identify and resolve the root cause. Which step should be prioritized in the troubleshooting process?

A) Reviewing Azure Monitor logs
B) Analyzing network traffic with Azure Network Watcher
C) Checking Virtual Network Gateway status
D) Reviewing Active Directory Domain Services (AD DS) logs
E) Inspecting Azure Bastion configurations

QUESTION 47

An organization is experiencing unpredictable usage patterns with its Azure Virtual Desktop (AVD) deployment, leading to budgetary challenges. The IT department needs to identify cost-effective measures while ensuring scalability and performance. What actions should the IT department prioritize to address the budgetary challenges caused by unpredictable usage patterns? Select TWO.

A) A company with a fixed budget for AVD operations
B) An organization experiencing unpredictable usage patterns
C) A business with limited storage resources for AVD profiles
D) A company aiming to enhance user experience with FSLogix
E) An enterprise requiring additional security measures for AVD resources

QUESTION 48

A non-profit organization requires an Azure Virtual Desktop setup that prioritizes cost-effectiveness, accessibility from older devices, and ease of management. Which Windows operating systems should be selected for the session hosts? Select THREE.

A) Windows 11 N
B) Windows 10 Enterprise multi-session
C) Windows Server 2022
D) Windows Server 2019
E) Windows 8.1 Enterprise

QUESTION 49

An organization is required to audit usage and licenses in its Azure Virtual Desktop (AVD) environment to ensure compliance with licensing agreements. Which actions should the organization take to effectively audit AVD usage and licenses? Select TWO.

A) Configuring Azure Monitor to track AVD resource utilization and license usage

B) Implementing Azure AD reporting to monitor user sign-ins and license assignments
C) Utilizing Power BI for visualizing license consumption and usage trends
D) Enforcing JIT access control to AVD resources based on licensing entitlements
E) Integrating Azure Security Center with AVD for license compliance assessments

QUESTION 50

An organization needs to configure log collection and storage mechanisms for its Azure Virtual Desktop (AVD) environment to comply with regulatory requirements and facilitate efficient log analysis. What options should they consider for achieving this goal effectively? Select THREE.

A) Leveraging Azure Blob Storage for storing log data with built-in redundancy and scalability
B) Enabling Azure Monitor Logs integration with AVD for centralized log collection and analysis
C) Configuring Azure Storage Lifecycle Management to automate log retention and archival processes
D) Implementing Azure Event Hubs for real-time log ingestion and processing
E) Utilizing Azure Data Lake Storage for storing structured and unstructured log data with granular access controls

PRACTICE TEST 7 - ANSWERS ONLY

QUESTION 1

Answer - E) Azure Bastion

Option A - Incorrect. Provides broad security but not specific to access.
Option B - Incorrect. Focuses on connectivity, not admin access security.
Option C - Incorrect. Controls traffic, not access.
Option D - Incorrect. Manages web traffic, not secure admin access.
Option E - Correct. Provides secure and seamless RDP/SSH access, aligning with JIT and MFA needs.

EXAM FOCUS	*Always use Azure Bastion for secure admin access. It ensures seamless RDP/SSH connectivity without exposing VMs to the public internet. You should combine this with MFA and JIT access to fortify security. Ensure network topology supports Bastion deployment zones.*
CAUTION ALERT	*Avoid relying on NSG or Azure Firewall for admin access—they're not designed for seamless admin connections. Stay alert to public IP configurations; exposing VMs to the internet increases the risk of breaches.*

QUESTION 2

Answer - B) Prioritize network traffic for financial applications

Option A - Incorrect. Allocating dedicated bandwidth may not efficiently utilize resources and could impact other users.
Option B - Correct. Prioritizing network traffic for financial applications ensures consistent performance for critical tasks.
Option C - Incorrect. ExpressRoute provides dedicated connectivity but does not directly address QoS policies.
Option D - Incorrect. Azure Traffic Manager is for load balancing and does not configure QoS policies.
Option E - Incorrect. VM scale sets optimize resource usage but do not address QoS policies.

EXAM FOCUS	*You need to prioritize QoS policies by application type for critical tasks like financial operations. This approach ensures bandwidth allocation aligns with application importance. Use Azure Monitor to validate traffic prioritization effectiveness.*
CAUTION ALERT	*Don't allocate dedicated bandwidth without considering dynamic needs; it may waste resources. Stay clear of confusing Azure Traffic Manager with QoS—it's for load balancing and does not manage application-level traffic priorities.*

QUESTION 3

Answer - [A]

Option A - WVDPerformanceCounters: This table contains performance metrics for session hosts, including CPU and memory usage, enabling you to identify underutilized hosts for resource optimization.
Option B - WVDSessionHostUtilization: While it may seem relevant, this table does not exist, and performance metrics are typically stored in WVDPerformanceCounters.

Option C - WVDHostRegistrations: This table deals with host registration details, not performance metrics.
Option D - WVDAgentHealth: This deals with agent health status, not session host utilization.
Option E - WVDServiceHealth: This provides overall service health information, not host-specific performance metrics.

EXAM FOCUS	*Always remember to query WVDPerformanceCounters for CPU and memory usage data. It provides actionable insights into resource utilization. You should create alerts for thresholds to optimize underutilized session hosts dynamically.*

CAUTION ALERT	*Avoid selecting tables that sound performance-related but do not exist, such as WVDSessionHostUtilization. Stay clear of querying tables like WVDAgentHealth, as they focus on host agent health and not resource utilization.*

QUESTION 4

Answer - B) Azure Files; C) Azure Disk Storage; D) Azure Data Lake Storage; E) Azure NetApp Files

Option A - Incorrect. Azure Blob Storage is primarily designed for unstructured data, such as documents and images, and may not be suitable for hosting user profiles or application data in AVD environments. Option B - Correct. Azure Files provides SMB-based file storage, making it a suitable option for hosting user profiles and shared application data in AVD deployments.

Option C - Correct. Azure Disk Storage offers block-level storage for virtual machines, including AVD session hosts, and can be used for hosting user data disks or OS disks in AVD setups. Option D - Correct. Azure Data Lake Storage is optimized for big data analytics and may be suitable for storing large volumes of structured or unstructured data generated by AVD workloads. Option E - Correct. Azure NetApp Files offers high-performance file storage with advanced features like snapshots and replication, making it suitable for demanding AVD use cases requiring high IOPS and low latency.

EXAM FOCUS	*Compare Azure Files for SMB-based profile storage and Azure Disk Storage for session host disks. Azure NetApp Files provides high IOPS for demanding workloads. Always evaluate Data Lake Storage for analytic workloads and compliance needs.*
CAUTION ALERT	*Avoid relying on Azure Blob Storage for structured user data—it's designed for unstructured data. Stay cautious when selecting Azure Data Lake Storage for general storage—it's best suited for specific analytics workloads.*

QUESTION 5

Answer - E) Command is correctly configured

Option A - Incorrect: A 512 GB quota is generally sufficient for initial setup but may need adjustment based on actual usage.
Option B - Incorrect: 'SMB' is the correct protocol for file shares used with AVD.
Option C - Incorrect: The command syntax is correct.
Option D - Incorrect: 'AVDStorage' is a valid storage account name.
Option E - Correct: The command is configured appropriately for setting up file shares.

EXAM FOCUS	*Always confirm quota settings meet high-traffic demands. The given command is correctly configured with SMB protocol, ensuring compatibility with AVD. Regularly review quota requirements based on actual usage patterns to avoid future capacity issues.*
CAUTION ALERT	*Avoid setting quotas too low for expected workloads. Stay clear of configuring NFS protocol for AVD—it's not supported for Windows-based environments. Double-check the storage account location for optimal performance.*

QUESTION 6

Answer - [B, C]

Option B - Azure Automation with Azure Runbooks: Runbooks can be used to schedule the start and stop actions for session hosts at the specified times, fulfilling the requirements efficiently.
Option C - Azure Virtual Machine Scale Sets: Scale Sets can automatically adjust the number of session hosts based on a schedule, meeting the specified requirements and minimizing manual intervention.

Option A - Azure Monitor Alerts: Alerts notify you of potential issues but are not specifically designed for managing session host schedules based on demand. Option D - Azure Automation with Azure Logic Apps: While Logic Apps can automate workflows, they are not specifically designed for managing resource schedules based on demand.

Option E - Azure Resource Manager templates: While templates enable you to deploy and manage Azure resources, they are not specifically designed for managing session host schedules based on demand.

EXAM FOCUS	*Use Azure Automation with Runbooks to define specific schedules for starting and stopping session hosts. Complement this with VM Scale Sets for dynamic scaling based on demand patterns to optimize costs and ensure availability.*
CAUTION ALERT	*Avoid manual intervention for host management—it's inefficient and prone to errors. Stay clear of assuming Azure Monitor Alerts can handle scaling; they only provide notifications and lack automation capabilities for resource management.*

QUESTION 7

Answer - A) User Density and Concurrent Access; B) Application Workload and Resource Consumption; D) Long-Term Growth and Scalability Requirements

Option A - Correct. User density and concurrent access impact licensing costs, as models like Per User or Per Device Subscription are based on user counts and device access. Option B - Correct. Application workload and resource consumption influence licensing costs, especially for models like Consumption-based Pricing that align with usage metrics.

Option D - Correct. Long-term growth and scalability requirements affect licensing decisions, as options like Enterprise Agreement (EA) offer flexibility and cost savings for expanding deployments over time. Option C - Incorrect. While geographical distribution and data sovereignty may influence deployment considerations, they are not directly related to licensing models for AVD. Option E - Incorrect. Budget allocation and financial forecasting are important but are secondary considerations to factors directly impacting licensing costs and scalability.

EXAM FOCUS	*Evaluate Per User vs. Per Device Subscription based on density and concurrent access needs. For scalability, Enterprise Agreements are cost-efficient. Include workload resource consumption and long-term user growth in your licensing strategy.*
CAUTION ALERT	*Avoid neglecting the impact of user density when choosing licenses—it directly influences costs. Stay alert to licensing models not aligned with your workload usage, such as Consumption-based Pricing, which may lead to unpredictable costs.*

QUESTION 8

Answer - A) Azure Monitor and Performance Counters; B) Network Latency and Bandwidth Utilization; D) Application Response Times and Launch Latency

Option A - Correct. Azure Monitor and performance counters provide insights into various performance metrics such as CPU usage, memory utilization, and disk I/O, enabling proactive monitoring and troubleshooting. Option B - Correct. Monitoring network latency and bandwidth utilization helps assess network performance and identify potential connectivity issues impacting AVD user experience.

Option D - Correct. Measuring application response times and launch latency allows administrators to evaluate application performance within AVD sessions, identifying areas for optimization. Option C - Incorrect. While user logon times and session duration are important metrics, they are more focused on user experience monitoring rather than performance evaluation.

Option E - Incorrect. While CPU usage and memory consumption are critical performance metrics, they are encompassed within Azure Monitor and performance counters, making option A more comprehensive.

EXAM FOCUS	*Use Azure Monitor for aggregated insights and Performance Counters for specific resource metrics. Always include network latency and application response times for comprehensive performance evaluation in AVD.*
CAUTION ALERT	*Avoid relying solely on user experience metrics like logon times for performance optimization—they're not indicative of overall system health. Stay clear of overloading Azure Monitor with unnecessary metrics—it increases analysis complexity.*

QUESTION 9

Answer - [B, E]

Option B - CPU and memory utilization during peak usage hours: These metrics directly reflect the resource demands of user sessions and are essential for determining when to scale resources. Option E - Number of active user sessions: The number of active sessions directly impacts resource utilization and is a key factor for defining scaling thresholds.

Option A - While user login activity provides insights into session starts, it may not accurately reflect resource demands and is less relevant for scaling decisions. Option C - Network latency and throughput are important for user experience but are not direct indicators of resource demand for scaling. Option D - Available storage capacity is important for overall system health but does not directly influence scaling thresholds based on resource demand.

EXAM FOCUS	*Define scaling thresholds based on CPU/memory utilization and the number of active user sessions. These metrics are reliable indicators of resource demand. Always test scaling rules in a controlled environment before applying them to production.*
CAUTION ALERT	*Don't use non-critical metrics like storage capacity for autoscale decisions—it does not reflect real-time resource usage. Stay cautious about using only user login activity; it's insufficient for comprehensive scaling decisions.*

QUESTION 10

Answer - A) Command is correct

Option A - Correct: This is a valid command to update host pool properties to use FSLogix.
Option B - Incorrect: The property name is assumed correct in this context for educational purposes.
Option C - Incorrect: FSLogix settings can be manipulated via CLI as part of custom RDP properties.
Option D - Incorrect: There's no syntax error provided the CLI version supports the commands.
Option E - Incorrect: No additional parameters are necessary for this specific command.

EXAM FOCUS	*The command is correct for enabling FSLogix across host pools via custom RDP properties. Ensure that FSLogix is configured properly on session hosts to avoid user profile management issues. Validate CLI syntax compatibility with your Azure version.*
CAUTION ALERT	*Avoid misconfiguring custom RDP properties; incorrect properties may render FSLogix ineffective. Stay alert to using outdated CLI versions, as they might not support certain commands or properties required for FSLogix deployment.*

QUESTION 11

Answer - A) Minimize Image Size and Complexity; B) Include Latest Security Updates and Patches; D) Avoid Hardcoding Configuration Settings

Option A - Correct. Minimizing image size and complexity reduces deployment time and storage requirements while improving performance and manageability of session hosts within the AVD environment. Option B - Correct. Including the latest security updates and patches ensures that the golden image is secure and compliant with security standards, minimizing vulnerabilities and risks.

Option D - Correct. Avoiding hardcoding configuration settings promotes flexibility and scalability by allowing dynamic configuration changes without modifying the golden image, facilitating easier maintenance and updates. Option C - Incorrect. Utilizing unmanaged disks for image storage is not a best practice, as managed disks offer additional management features, scalability, and security benefits for golden image storage in Azure.

Option E - Incorrect. While documenting image configuration and versioning is important for tracking changes and troubleshooting, it is not directly related to best practices for golden image creation but rather for image management and governance.

EXAM FOCUS	*Always remember to include latest security patches and avoid hardcoding settings in your golden image. This practice ensures flexibility and easier updates. Minimizing image size also improves deployment time and performance. Test the image before production deployment to avoid errors in dynamic environments.*
CAUTION ALERT	*Avoid using unmanaged disks for image storage—they lack the scalability and security of managed disks. Stay clear of skipping documentation for configurations and versioning, as this oversight can lead to troubleshooting difficulties or non-compliance with organizational standards.*

QUESTION 12

Answer - [A, B]

Option A - Azure Traffic Manager: Azure Traffic Manager enables DNS-based traffic routing to the closest available endpoint, facilitating automatic failover of AVD host pools to a secondary region in case of a primary region outage.
Option B - Azure Site Recovery: Azure Site Recovery supports replication and failover of AVD host pools to a secondary region, ensuring minimal downtime and business continuity during failover operations.

Option C - Azure Backup is primarily used for data backup and recovery and is not designed for failover and disaster recovery of AVD host pools. Option D - Azure Load Balancer is a network load balancer and does not provide failover capabilities at the application level for AVD host pools. Option E - Azure Blob Storage is a storage service and is not directly related to failover and disaster recovery of AVD host pools.

EXAM FOCUS	*You should use Azure Site Recovery for replication and failover and Azure Traffic Manager for routing. This combination ensures seamless failover and business continuity. Ensure configurations align with regional policies and test failover setups regularly to identify potential gaps.*
CAUTION ALERT	*Don't confuse Azure Backup with disaster recovery—it's for data recovery, not failover. Stay alert to relying solely on Load Balancer, as it only manages network traffic and lacks the application-level failover required for AVD host pools.*

QUESTION 13

Answer - D) Azure Update Management; E) Azure DevOps Pipelines

Option A - Incorrect. Azure Logic Apps are primarily used for workflow automation and integration, not specifically for automating update processes for AVD images.

Option B - Incorrect. Azure Functions provide serverless computing but are not tailored for automating update processes for AVD images. Option C - Incorrect. Azure Automation State Configuration focuses on managing the state of resources but is not specifically designed for automating update processes for AVD images.

Option D - Correct. Azure Update Management provides centralized control and automated patching capabilities for AVD images, streamlining update processes and ensuring consistency. Option E - Correct. Azure DevOps Pipelines enable continuous integration and deployment, allowing for automated update processes for AVD images through pipeline automation.

EXAM FOCUS	*Always consider Azure Update Management for centralized patching and Azure DevOps Pipelines for automation. These tools ensure consistency across updates while minimizing manual intervention.*

CAUTION ALERT	*Regularly monitor update schedules to avoid user session interruptions during peak hours.* *Avoid using Azure Functions for updates—they are not designed for comprehensive update processes. Stay cautious when depending solely on Logic Apps, as they are suited for workflows rather than managing AVD image updates.*

QUESTION 14

Answer - A) Implement Role-Based Access Control (RBAC) to Restrict Access; B) Encrypt Data at Rest and in Transit; D) Regularly Audit and Monitor Access to Image Storage Resources

Option A - Correct. Implementing RBAC helps control access to image storage resources based on user roles and responsibilities, reducing the risk of unauthorized access. Option B - Correct. Encrypting data at rest and in transit adds an extra layer of security to image storage, protecting sensitive information from unauthorized access.

Option C - Incorrect. While Azure Security Center provides recommendations for overall security posture, it may not specifically focus on image storage best practices for AVD deployments. Option D - Correct. Regularly auditing and monitoring access to image storage resources helps detect and mitigate potential security breaches or unauthorized activities. Option E - Incorrect. While MFA is essential for securing access to Azure resources, it may not be specific to image storage operations in AVD deployments.

EXAM FOCUS	*You should enforce RBAC to restrict access and implement encryption at rest and in transit to safeguard image storage. Conduct regular audits and enable Azure Monitor to track access and detect anomalies. Ensure that security configurations comply with organizational and regulatory requirements.*
CAUTION ALERT	*Avoid neglecting access control policies, as they are critical for protecting sensitive data. Stay cautious of relying only on Azure Security Center recommendations, as they provide broad insights but may not cover specific AVD storage nuances.*

QUESTION 15

Answer - B) Missing failover group setup

Option A - Incorrect: The command creates a load balancer but does not configure a failover group.

Option B - Correct: This setup does not include the necessary configuration for a failover group which is crucial for high availability. Option C - Incorrect: "Standard" SKU is suitable for high availability as it supports Availability Zones. Option D - Incorrect: "East US" can be a correct location depending on the organization's needs. Option E - Correct: The variable '$config' needs to be defined or elaborated on for the command to be functional.

EXAM FOCUS	*Always define a failover group when configuring high availability. This ensures seamless redirection of traffic during failures. Use the Standard SKU for load balancers, as it supports availability zones, improving resiliency and performance in multi-region deployments.*
CAUTION ALERT	*Avoid using Basic SKU for high availability—it lacks advanced features like zone redundancy. Stay clear of incomplete configurations where variables like $config are not properly defined, as this can lead to deployment failures.*

QUESTION 16

Answer - A) Implement Data Access Controls and Encryption; B) Conduct Regular Compliance Assessments and Audits; C) Ensure User Consent and Data Subject Rights Management

Option A - Correct. Implementing data access controls and encryption helps protect sensitive data and aligns with GDPR and HIPAA requirements for data security in AVD deployments. Option B - Correct. Conducting regular compliance assessments and audits ensures ongoing compliance with GDPR, HIPAA, and other regulatory frameworks in AVD environments.

Option C - Correct. Ensuring user consent and data subject rights management aligns with GDPR requirements for managing personal data privacy in AVD deployments. Option D - Incorrect. While enabling secure data retention and deletion policies is important, it may not be specifically related to aligning AVD operations with GDPR and HIPAA.

Option E - Incorrect. While establishing data breach notification procedures is crucial, it may not be directly related to aligning AVD operations with GDPR and HIPAA.

EXAM FOCUS	*Implement data access controls and encryption to meet compliance standards like GDPR and HIPAA. Ensure that user consent management is part of your strategy and conduct regular compliance audits to verify adherence. These practices are foundational for maintaining regulatory compliance in AVD.*
CAUTION ALERT	*Don't overlook secure data retention policies, but understand they may not directly address compliance frameworks. Avoid assuming data breach notification procedures alone ensure compliance—they must be part of a broader regulatory alignment strategy.*

QUESTION 17

Answer - A) Azure Cost Management and Billing; E) Azure Advisor for Cost Optimization Recommendations

Option A - Correct. Azure Cost Management and Billing provide comprehensive tools for monitoring and managing costs in AVD deployments, including budgeting, forecasting, and reporting.

Option B - Incorrect. While Azure Log Analytics is useful for performance monitoring, it may not specifically focus on cost monitoring and management in AVD deployments. Option C - Incorrect. Azure Security Center focuses on threat detection and response, which is important for security but may not directly address cost monitoring and management in AVD deployments.

Option D - Incorrect. Azure Monitor primarily focuses on resource monitoring and metrics collection, which may not cover cost-related aspects in AVD deployments. Option E - Correct. Azure Advisor provides cost optimization recommendations based on Azure best practices and usage patterns, helping organizations identify opportunities to reduce costs in AVD deployments.

EXAM FOCUS	*Utilize Azure Cost Management and Billing to track expenses and set budgets for AVD. Complement this with Azure Advisor to identify cost-saving opportunities like resizing VMs or eliminating underused resources. Regularly review these insights to ensure budget compliance and avoid unnecessary expenditures.*
CAUTION ALERT	*Avoid relying on Azure Monitor for cost tracking—it's not optimized for budget management. Stay clear of confusing Azure Security Center with cost tools—it focuses on threat management and doesn't address financial aspects.*

QUESTION 18

Answer - [B, C]

Option B - Azure Load Balancer: Azure Load Balancer provides efficient load balancing and failover capabilities across multiple session hosts, ensuring seamless user experience and minimal downtime during session host failures. Option C - Azure Application Gateway: Azure Application Gateway offers layer 7 load balancing and web application firewall capabilities, complementing Azure Load Balancer for enhanced session host availability and performance.

Option A - Azure Traffic Manager is a DNS-based traffic load balancer and does not provide session host-specific load balancing and failover capabilities. Option D - Azure Front Door is a global content delivery network (CDN) service and is not designed for session host load balancing. Option E - Azure Load Balancer Standard provides load balancing for virtual machines and network resources but does not specifically address session host load balancing for Azure Virtual Desktop environments.

EXAM	*Use Azure Load Balancer for efficient distribution and failover across session hosts, ensuring minimal*

FOCUS	downtime. Combine this with Azure Application Gateway for advanced layer 7 load balancing to optimize session host availability and performance. Test configurations thoroughly in a production-like environment.
CAUTION ALERT	Avoid relying on Traffic Manager for session host-specific load balancing—it's DNS-based and not designed for this purpose. Stay cautious of overloading the configuration with services like Front Door, which is not intended for session-level load balancing in AVD deployments.

QUESTION 19

Answer - A) Implement Azure Key Vault for centralized key management; B) Configure Azure Policy for compliance enforcement

Option A - Correct. Azure Key Vault provides centralized key management, ensuring compliance with encryption standards and regulatory requirements in AVD environments.

Option B - Correct. Azure Policy enables organizations to enforce compliance standards and regulatory requirements effectively across AVD deployments. Option C - Incorrect. Azure AD Privileged Identity Management (PIM) focuses on managing access to Azure resources but does not directly address encryption standards or regulatory compliance in AVD environments.

Option D - Incorrect. Azure Firewall offers network security features but is not specifically designed for compliance enforcement in AVD environments. Option E - Incorrect. While Azure Security Center provides threat detection and compliance monitoring, it is not a primary component of disaster recovery plans for AVD deployments.

EXAM FOCUS	Use Azure Key Vault to manage encryption keys centrally, ensuring compliance with encryption standards. Combine this with Azure Policy to enforce compliance rules across resources, reducing risks of regulatory violations. These measures are essential for protecting sensitive data in AVD environments.
CAUTION ALERT	Don't assume Azure Firewall addresses compliance—it focuses on network security. Stay cautious of relying solely on Azure Security Center for compliance monitoring—it must be complemented by tools like Key Vault and Azure Policy to ensure full alignment with regulations.

QUESTION 20

Answer - A) Use Azure Monitor Workbooks

Option A - Correct: Azure Monitor Workbooks provide the customization needed for creating detailed, recurring reports that can be tailored to different audience needs.

Option B - Incorrect: Logic Apps could automate some tasks but are not primarily used for data reporting. Option C - Incorrect: Automation runbooks are great for managing resources but less so for custom report generation. Option D - Incorrect: Azure Functions could technically extract and process data but would require significant setup for reporting. Option E - Incorrect: Monitor insights offer built-in solutions that aren't as customizable for specific reporting needs as Workbooks.

EXAM FOCUS	Leverage Azure Monitor Workbooks for tailored performance reports. These provide flexibility to customize data like logon times and session durations and automate weekly report generation. Workbooks ensure stakeholders receive relevant insights aligned with their needs, boosting operational transparency.
CAUTION ALERT	Avoid relying solely on Logic Apps for report customization—they are workflow-centric, not designed for granular report generation. Stay clear of overcomplicating solutions with Azure Functions, which require significant setup and are not inherently optimized for AVD performance reporting.

QUESTION 21

Answer - C

Option C - Enabling RDP Shortpath for managed networks optimizes network performance and reduces latency for Azure Virtual Desktop users accessing resources over managed network connections. RDP Shortpath improves connection speed and responsiveness, enhancing user experience by prioritizing RDP traffic over managed networks. Option A - Quality of Service (QoS) prioritizes network traffic to improve performance but may not specifically address latency reduction for Azure Virtual Desktop connections over managed networks.

Option B - TCP/IP Offload Engine (TOE) offloads TCP/IP processing to network adapters to improve network performance but does not specifically optimize latency for Azure Virtual Desktop connections. Option D - Network Load Balancing distributes incoming network traffic across multiple servers but is not specifically designed to reduce latency for Azure Virtual Desktop connections over managed networks.

Option E - Dynamic Host Configuration Protocol (DHCP) relay agent forwards DHCP messages between clients and servers but does not optimize network performance or reduce latency for Azure Virtual Desktop connections.

EXAM FOCUS	*You should enable RDP Shortpath for managed networks to reduce latency and optimize network performance. This feature bypasses the relay server for supported connections, improving speed. Test connectivity post-implementation to ensure users experience reduced latency and responsiveness.*
CAUTION ALERT	*Avoid confusing QoS with RDP Shortpath—they serve different purposes. QoS prioritizes traffic but does not reduce latency. Stay clear of assuming that Network Load Balancing or TCP/IP Offload Engine can address Azure Virtual Desktop-specific latency issues.*

QUESTION 22

Answer - A) Enhances security by enforcing fine-grained access control; C) Reduces security risks by minimizing excessive privileges; D) Increases complexity of access management but strengthens security posture

Option A - Correct. RBAC enhances security by enforcing fine-grained access control, limiting access to resources based on roles and permissions. Option C - Correct. RBAC reduces security risks by minimizing excessive privileges, ensuring that users have access only to the resources they need.

Option D - Correct. While RBAC may increase the complexity of access management, it strengthens the overall security posture of AVD environments by enforcing granular access controls. Option B - Incorrect. While RBAC can improve operational efficiency by automating access management tasks, its primary impact is on security rather than operational efficiency.

Option E - Incorrect. While RBAC can streamline operational workflows by delegating access management responsibilities, its primary impact is on security rather than operational efficiency.

EXAM FOCUS	*Always consider RBAC for fine-grained access control in AVD environments. RBAC reduces risks by enforcing the principle of least privilege. Regularly audit role assignments to maintain efficiency and security. Focus on roles that align closely with user responsibilities to streamline management.*
CAUTION ALERT	*Stay cautious of over-complicating RBAC configurations—it may increase administrative complexity. Avoid assuming that RBAC automation directly translates to operational efficiency; it primarily enhances security by restricting unnecessary access.*

QUESTION 23

Answer - A) Enhanced security through additional authentication factors; B) Increased user friction due to additional authentication steps; D) Reduced risk of unauthorized access to AVD resources

Option A - Correct. Implementing MFA enhances security by requiring additional authentication factors beyond passwords. Option B - Correct. While MFA enhances security, it may also increase user friction due to additional authentication steps, impacting user experience.

Option C - Incorrect. While implementing MFA may raise user awareness of security best practices, it is not directly related to the impact of MFA on user access and security in AVD environments as described in the question. Option D - Correct. Implementing MFA reduces the risk of unauthorized access to AVD resources by adding an extra layer of authentication.

Option E - Incorrect. While potential compatibility issues with legacy applications or devices are a concern, they are not specifically mentioned in the question as impacts of implementing MFA in AVD environments.

EXAM FOCUS	*Implement MFA for Azure Virtual Desktop to enhance security by adding an extra layer of authentication. Educate users about its benefits to mitigate friction. Monitor compatibility with legacy systems or applications during testing to avoid disruptions in user workflows.*
CAUTION ALERT	*Avoid overlooking the potential user friction caused by MFA. While MFA enhances security, it may slow down workflows. Stay alert for compatibility issues with older applications or devices that may not fully support modern authentication mechanisms.*

QUESTION 24

Answer - A, B, C, E

A) Correct - RBAC ensures that only authorized personnel have access to specific resources, crucial for compliance in financial services.
B) Correct - End-to-end encryption protects data from being intercepted during transmission.
C) Correct - A virtual network firewall will help protect against network-based threats.
D) Incorrect - While Azure Sentinel is important for security monitoring, the question specifically asks about securing the desktop environment, which is directly addressed by other options.
E) Correct - Auditing and logging all user sessions is essential for tracking activities and maintaining security compliance.

EXAM FOCUS	*You need to enable end-to-end encryption, RBAC, and audit logging to secure financial environments. Prioritize setting up a virtual firewall to protect against network-based threats. Test your configurations periodically to ensure compliance with stringent industry standards.*
CAUTION ALERT	*Don't confuse Azure Sentinel with direct desktop security measures—it's a monitoring tool. Avoid assuming audit logging is optional in high-security environments; it's essential for compliance and forensic purposes. Stay clear of skipping RBAC implementation—it's foundational for role security.*

QUESTION 25

Answer - B) Add --enable-vm-protection true

Option A - Incorrect: The script does not enable Azure Defender for VMs by default.

Option B - Correct: Adding --enable-vm-protection true explicitly enables Azure Defender for VMs, providing advanced threat protection. Option C - Incorrect: NSG flow logging is unrelated to enabling Defender for VMs. Option D - Incorrect: While tagging is good for organization and billing, it does not impact security settings.

Option E - Incorrect: The original script does not enable Azure Defender, which is necessary for comprehensive threat protection in this scenario.

EXAM FOCUS	*You should include --enable-vm-protection true in the Azure CLI command to activate Azure Defender for VMs. This ensures comprehensive threat protection by monitoring vulnerabilities and network threats. Always verify protection status post-configuration to confirm successful deployment.*
CAUTION ALERT	*Avoid relying solely on NSG configurations without enabling Azure Defender. Stay clear of omitting advanced threat protection in critical environments—it is key for detecting and mitigating risks. Avoid assuming that default settings enable full protection—they often require manual activation.*

QUESTION 26

Answer - A) Create and configure Code Integrity policies for AVD session hosts; D) Deploy Windows Defender Application Control policies using Group Policy or Microsoft Endpoint Manager

Option A - Correct. Creating and configuring Code Integrity policies is a prerequisite for implementing Windows Defender Application Control on AVD session hosts. Option D - Correct. Deploying Windows Defender Application Control policies using Group Policy or Microsoft Endpoint Manager ensures consistent enforcement of security policies across AVD session hosts.

Option B - Incorrect. While enabling audit mode is a step in the implementation process, it is not sufficient for full deployment of Windows Defender Application Control policies as described in the question. Option C - Incorrect. While AppLocker is related to application control, it is not specifically mentioned in the context of implementing Windows Defender Application Control as described in the question. Option E - Incorrect. While monitoring events and alerts is important for security, it is not directly related to the steps to implement Windows Defender Application Control as described in the question.

EXAM FOCUS	*Always configure Code Integrity policies for Windows Defender Application Control on session hosts. Use Microsoft Endpoint Manager for consistent deployment across the environment. Start with audit mode to test policy effectiveness before full enforcement to avoid user disruptions.*
CAUTION ALERT	*Avoid skipping the audit phase—it helps identify potential application conflicts. Don't assume AppLocker rules are interchangeable with Windows Defender Application Control; while related, they address different use cases. Ensure Group Policy is correctly configured to apply security policies organization-wide.*

QUESTION 27

Answer - A, C, D

A) Correct - Encrypted storage is essential for protecting sensitive patient data.
B) Incorrect - While Azure ExpressRoute provides dedicated connectivity, it is more about performance and less about direct compliance or security of patient data.

C) Correct - Conditional access policies ensure that only authenticated and authorized users can access specific resources, crucial for healthcare regulations. D) Correct - Azure Site Recovery ensures data recovery capabilities, critical in maintaining data availability and compliance in healthcare. E) Incorrect - NSGs are important for traffic control but are not directly related to data protection or secure access specific to healthcare requirements.

EXAM FOCUS	*Always encrypt storage with Azure Disk Encryption to protect sensitive healthcare data. Combine this with conditional access policies and Azure Site Recovery to ensure secure access and data availability during disasters. Regularly review these configurations for compliance alignment.*
CAUTION ALERT	*Avoid relying solely on NSGs for regulatory compliance—they are not sufficient for protecting healthcare data. Stay cautious of assuming Azure ExpressRoute is a compliance measure—it ensures connectivity but doesn't directly address data security.*

QUESTION 28

Answer - A) Define device compliance requirements based on organizational security policies; B) Configure compliance policies in Microsoft Intune to assess device compliance status; D) Remediate non-compliant devices by applying conditional access policies

Option A - Correct. Defining device compliance requirements based on organizational security policies establishes the criteria for assessing device compliance status. Option B - Correct. Configuring compliance policies in Microsoft Intune allows organizations to assess device compliance status and enforce compliance requirements. Option C - Incorrect. While Azure Monitor can track compliance status and security events, it is not directly involved in implementing device

Page | 219

compliance policies.

Option D - Correct. Remediating non-compliant devices by applying conditional access policies helps enforce security policies and ensure that only compliant devices can access AVD resources. Option E - Incorrect. While enabling automated alerts for non-compliant devices is important for prompt action, it is not directly related to the process of implementing device compliance policies.

EXAM FOCUS	*Define device compliance policies in Microsoft Intune to enforce security standards. Use conditional access to restrict non-compliant devices from accessing resources. Regularly update compliance requirements to reflect evolving organizational security policies.*
CAUTION ALERT	*Don't skip device remediation steps for non-compliant devices—it's crucial for maintaining a secure environment. Stay clear of assuming Azure Monitor is a substitute for compliance policies—it's a complementary tool for monitoring, not enforcement.*

QUESTION 29

Answer - A) Enforce password complexity requirements and account lockout policies through Group Policy; C) Implement AppLocker rules to control which applications can run on session hosts; D) Configure Windows Update policies to ensure timely installation of security patches and updates

Option A - Correct. Enforcing password complexity requirements and account lockout policies through Group Policy helps prevent unauthorized access and enhance account security. Option B - Incorrect. While applying Windows Defender Firewall rules is important, it may not cover all aspects of security policy enforcement.

Option C - Correct. Implementing AppLocker rules controls which applications can run on session hosts, reducing the risk of malware and unauthorized software execution. Option D - Correct. Configuring Windows Update policies ensures that session hosts receive timely security patches and updates to mitigate vulnerabilities. Option E - Incorrect. While Windows Defender Credential Guard enhances credential protection, it may not be directly applicable to securing session hosts in all scenarios.

EXAM FOCUS	*Enforce password complexity and account lockout policies via Group Policy. Implement AppLocker rules to control application execution and configure Windows Update to automate security patches. These measures strengthen session host security while reducing administrative overhead.*
CAUTION ALERT	*Avoid assuming firewall rules alone are sufficient for host security—they are a component of a broader strategy. Stay cautious of skipping timely updates; unpatched vulnerabilities are a major risk. Don't overlook AppLocker—it's crucial for preventing unauthorized or malicious application execution.*

QUESTION 30

Answer - C) JIT setup requires additional parameters

Option A - Incorrect: The command creates a service principal but does not configure JIT.

Option B - Incorrect: While "Desktop Virtualization Administrator" is a more privileged role, the scenario does not specify the level needed. Option C - Correct: JIT access requires configuration through Azure AD PIM, not just RBAC creation. Option D - Incorrect: The scopes parameter is correctly set to apply the role assignment to the specified subscription. Option E - Incorrect: Time bounding is a part of PIM but the command does not establish JIT or enforce any real-time access restrictions.

EXAM FOCUS	*Use Azure AD Privileged Identity Management (PIM) to configure JIT access for admins, ensuring permissions are active only when needed. Properly define additional parameters for JIT setup, including approval workflows, to enhance security and prevent excessive privilege exposure.*
CAUTION ALERT	*Avoid creating service principals without PIM enforcement—it does not meet JIT requirements. Don't confuse RBAC creation with PIM—it's only a step in setting up JIT access. Ensure that JIT configurations include proper time restrictions and approval mechanisms to meet security standards effectively.*

QUESTION 31

Answer - D) Utilize Azure Key Vault for FSLogix profile encryption keys

Option A - Incorrect. Profile Containers with VHDX format doesn't directly address security or compliance requirements. Option B - Incorrect. Kerberos authentication is not specific to FSLogix and may not address HIPAA compliance concerns. Option C - Incorrect. BitLocker encrypts disks, not FSLogix profiles, and lacks centralized key management.

Option D - Correct. Azure Key Vault provides secure and centralized management of encryption keys, aligning with HIPAA requirements. Option E - Incorrect. Azure Policy isn't used for managing encryption keys.

	*You should utilize Azure Key Vault for centralized and secure management of encryption keys for FSLogix profiles. This setup aligns with compliance requirements like HIPAA, ensuring data security and regulatory adherence. Verify key management configurations post-implementation.*
	Avoid assuming that BitLocker encryption is sufficient for FSLogix profiles—it secures disks, not profile containers. Stay cautious about directly configuring encryption without centralized key management, as this may compromise security and compliance.

QUESTION 32

Answer - B) Configure Office Containers to utilize GPU acceleration for graphics-intensive tasks, C) Customize Office Container profiles to preload frequently used applications, E) Enable OneDrive integration within Office Containers for seamless file access.

B) Configure Office Containers to utilize GPU acceleration for graphics-intensive tasks - GPU acceleration enhances the performance of graphics-intensive Office applications, improving user experience and productivity. C) Customize Office Container profiles to preload frequently used applications - Preloading frequently used applications reduces load times, improving overall application responsiveness and user satisfaction.

E) Enable OneDrive integration within Office Containers for seamless file access - Integrating OneDrive allows users to access and save files seamlessly within Office applications, enhancing productivity without compromising security. A) Implement selective application virtualization within Office Containers - While selective application virtualization may optimize resource usage, it may not directly enhance performance or responsiveness for Office applications. D) Utilize Azure AD conditional access policies to optimize Office application access - Conditional access policies focus on controlling access rather than directly enhancing performance within Office Containers.

	*Enable GPU acceleration for Office Containers to improve performance in graphics-heavy tasks. Preload commonly used applications to reduce load times, and integrate OneDrive for seamless file access. These steps significantly enhance user experience while maintaining security.*
	Avoid overcomplicating configurations with unnecessary features like selective application virtualization—it may not directly impact Office performance. Stay clear of confusing conditional access policies with performance enhancements; they focus on access security, not optimization.

QUESTION 33

Answer - A, D, E

A) Correct - Scaling out session hosts automatically during peak traffic times ensures the AVD environment can handle increased load, maintaining scalability.

B) Incorrect - Azure Front Door manages web traffic and application delivery at the edge, which is more about managing incoming web traffic than specifically enhancing AVD performance during peak times. C) Incorrect - Azure Firewall secures network boundaries but does not directly contribute to scalability or latency improvements for AVD. D) Correct - Azure Traffic Manager improves AVD responsiveness by routing traffic efficiently, reducing latency.

E) Correct - Azure ExpressRoute provides private, dedicated, high-throughput network connections, ensuring low latency and secure transactions.

EXAM FOCUS	*Always implement Azure Traffic Manager for optimized traffic routing during peak events. Use Azure Automation to scale session hosts dynamically and deploy ExpressRoute for consistent, low-latency network performance. Test these configurations pre-event to ensure readiness.*
CAUTION ALERT	*Avoid relying on Azure Firewall or Azure Front Door for traffic scalability—they address security and content delivery, not AVD performance. Ensure that scaling configurations are properly automated to handle demand surges efficiently.*

QUESTION 34

Answer - A) Risk: Data leakage due to unauthorized access to redirected devices. Mitigation: Implement Azure AD Conditional Access policies to enforce device compliance and access controls before allowing redirection, B) Risk: Malware infection from compromised USB drives or peripherals. Mitigation: Configure Group Policy settings to restrict device redirection from untrusted sources and implement endpoint protection measures, D) Risk: Network eavesdropping and data interception during device redirection sessions. Mitigation: Enable network encryption and secure tunneling protocols for device redirection traffic, such as Remote Desktop Protocol (RDP) over TLS.

A) Risk: Data leakage due to unauthorized access to redirected devices. Mitigation: Implement Azure AD Conditional Access policies to enforce device compliance and access controls before allowing redirection - Conditional Access policies ensure that only compliant devices can access redirected resources, reducing the risk of data leakage from unauthorized devices. B) Risk: Malware infection from compromised USB drives or peripherals. Mitigation: Configure Group Policy settings to restrict device redirection from untrusted sources and implement endpoint protection measures - Group Policy settings help control which devices can be redirected, minimizing the risk of malware infection from unauthorized or compromised peripherals.

D) Risk: Network eavesdropping and data interception during device redirection sessions. Mitigation: Enable network encryption and secure tunneling protocols for device redirection traffic, such as Remote Desktop Protocol (RDP) over TLS - Network encryption safeguards data transmitted during device redirection sessions, preventing unauthorized interception and eavesdropping. C) Risk: Unauthorized access to sensitive resources through redirected smart card readers. Mitigation: Utilize role-based access control (RBAC) policies to restrict smart card redirection based on user roles and responsibilities - RBAC policies ensure that only authorized users can access sensitive resources through redirected smart card readers, reducing the risk of unauthorized access.

E) Risk: Insider threats exploiting device redirection for unauthorized data exfiltration. Mitigation: Implement logging and monitoring mechanisms to track device redirection activities and detect suspicious behavior in real-time - Logging and monitoring help identify and mitigate insider threats by providing visibility into device redirection activities and detecting anomalous behavior indicative of unauthorized data exfiltration.

EXAM FOCUS	*Implement Conditional Access policies for device compliance before allowing redirection. Use Group Policy to restrict untrusted device redirection and enable RDP over TLS for encrypted traffic. Monitor redirection logs to identify and mitigate risks.*
CAUTION ALERT	*Avoid assuming that Group Policy settings alone suffice for securing device redirection—combine them with Conditional Access. Stay cautious about allowing unmanaged devices without enforcing compliance policies to prevent data leakage and malware risks.*

QUESTION 35

Answer - A) Configuration optimizes resource use

Option A - Correct: Setting the default color mode to Black and White and quality to Standard balances performance with resource use, appropriate for a general user base.

Option B - Incorrect: The color mode setting is correct for conserving color ink or toner.

Option C - Incorrect: High quality is not necessary for all documents and can significantly consume more resources.
Option D - Incorrect: The JSON structure is valid and correctly formatted for policy definitions.
Option E - Incorrect: This general setting is a starting point; user-specific settings can be configured additionally as needed.

EXAM FOCUS	*You can set print policies to balance performance and resource use effectively. Configuring the default color mode to Black and White and using Standard quality is optimal for most users while conserving printer resources.*
CAUTION ALERT	*Avoid setting high-quality printing as default unless necessary—it consumes more resources and increases operational costs. Ensure the JSON configuration is well-tested and complements any additional user-specific settings that might be required.*

QUESTION 36

Answer - A, B, D

A) Correct - Azure Information Protection ensures sensitive client data is classified and encrypted, maintaining confidentiality. B) Correct - Azure Site Recovery enhances data availability, ensuring business continuity during outages.
C) Incorrect - While Azure ExpressRoute provides private connectivity, it's more about performance improvement rather than securing communication channels specifically.

D) Correct - Azure VPN Gateway provides a secure connection for remote access, protecting data in transit and ensuring secure communications. E) Incorrect - Azure Active Directory is crucial for identity management but does not directly address data availability or the specific requirement of securing communication channels.

EXAM FOCUS	*Configure Azure Information Protection for encryption and classification of sensitive data. Deploy Azure Site Recovery for data availability during outages, and implement Azure VPN Gateway for secure communication channels.*
CAUTION ALERT	*Avoid assuming Azure ExpressRoute is a substitute for VPN Gateway—it focuses on dedicated connectivity, not securing data transmission. Stay cautious about missing data classification policies, as they are essential for maintaining confidentiality and compliance.*

QUESTION 37

Answer - C) Monitoring user activity to optimize VM startup times and resource allocation

Monitoring user activity allows for informed decisions regarding VM startup times and resource allocation, enhancing efficiency and cost-effectiveness.
Option A - Incorrect. Auto-scaling adjusts VM capacity but is not directly related to the Start VM on Connect feature.
Option B - Incorrect. Session pre-launch reduces login times but is not part of the Start VM on Connect configuration.
Option D - Incorrect. RBAC policies control access but do not directly optimize VM startup times.
Option E - Incorrect. FSLogix manages user profiles but does not directly impact the Start VM on Connect feature.

EXAM FOCUS	*You need to monitor user activity and VM startup times to optimize the Start VM on Connect feature. This approach minimizes resource wastage and ensures cost-effectiveness while maintaining user satisfaction with reduced wait times during login.*
CAUTION ALERT	*Avoid confusing Start VM on Connect with auto-scaling—they serve distinct purposes. Stay cautious of implementing the feature without monitoring user activity patterns, as this can lead to inefficient resource allocation and unnecessary costs.*

QUESTION 38

Answer - A) Application compatibility with user environments

Ensuring application compatibility with user environments is crucial to maintain optimal performance and user experience in AVD deployments. Option B - Cost-effectiveness of deployment method: While cost is important, it is secondary to ensuring optimal performance and user experience.

Option C - Integration with Azure Active Directory: While important for authentication, it does not directly impact application performance. Option D - Utilization of Azure Bastion: Azure Bastion provides secure access but does not affect application compatibility. Option E - Automation capabilities for deployment tasks: While automation is valuable, it does not directly address application compatibility.

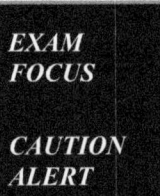	
EXAM FOCUS	*Ensure application compatibility with user environments when deploying apps to Azure Virtual Desktop. Test applications in sandboxed environments to identify potential issues and choose methods like MSIX App Attach for seamless, flexible deployments.*
CAUTION ALERT	*Avoid focusing solely on cost-effectiveness without considering performance. Stay clear of prioritizing automation capabilities over compatibility, as the user experience depends significantly on how well applications integrate with AVD environments.*

QUESTION 39

Answer - A, C, D

A) Correct - Azure Bastion secures remote access by providing a gateway that does not expose VMs directly to the internet. B) Incorrect - Azure Firewall is essential for network security but not specified for device authorization or audit requirements.

C) Correct - Device compliance policies in Azure AD Conditional Access ensure that only authorized devices can access the network, meeting security protocols. D) Correct - Azure Monitor and Log Analytics provide comprehensive logging and auditing capabilities necessary for governmental compliance. E) Incorrect - Creating a new subnet is a prerequisite for Bastion but does not directly enhance security or compliance.

EXAM FOCUS	*Implement Azure Bastion for secure, internet-free VM access. Use Conditional Access policies to allow only authorized, compliant devices, and enable Azure Monitor with Log Analytics to track and audit activities for compliance requirements.*
CAUTION ALERT	*Avoid relying solely on Azure Firewall for compliance—it secures traffic but doesn't enforce device policies. Stay cautious about skipping detailed auditing configurations, as rigorous audit trails are critical for regulatory adherence in government setups.*

QUESTION 40

Answer - C

Option A - Incorrect. There is a syntax error.
Option B - Incorrect. The --sync-group parameter is not relevant here.
Option C - Correct. The correct flag for requiring MFA should be --require-mfa $true.
Option D - Incorrect, though encryption is recommended.
Option E - Incorrect. az onedrive config is not a valid command.

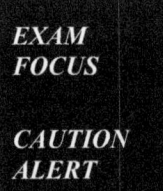	
EXAM FOCUS	*Configure OneDrive with CLI scripts to enforce MFA and restrict syncing to AVD environments. Correct CLI flags for requiring MFA and restricting sync locations to prevent unauthorized data access and ensure compliance with organizational policies.*
CAUTION ALERT	*Avoid missing proper syntax for CLI commands, such as incorrect flags for MFA enforcement. Stay clear of assuming encryption is automatically enabled—it needs explicit configuration. Test your setup to ensure that OneDrive settings align with compliance requirements.*

QUESTION 41

Answer - E

Option A - Incorrect. The flag -EncryptData $true is not correctly named.
Option B - Incorrect. Specifying storage type here is irrelevant to encryption.
Option C - Incorrect. The correct PowerShell syntax for enabling encryption isn't specified.
Option D - Incorrect. Azure AD integration is unrelated to data encryption here.
Option E - Correct. The correct command and parameter for setting encryption for Microsoft 365 Apps data at rest within AVD is Set-M365AppConfig -EncryptDataStorage $true.

EXAM FOCUS	*You need to ensure encryption settings are configured using the Set-M365AppConfig -EncryptDataStorage $true command. Always confirm the exact PowerShell command syntax, especially when aligning with compliance policies for Microsoft 365 Apps in AVD.*
CAUTION ALERT	*Stay alert to misnaming PowerShell flags like -EncryptData $true, as it can result in ineffective configurations. Avoid assuming that Azure AD integration directly impacts encryption settings—it is related to authentication.*

QUESTION 42

Answer - A, B, C

A) Correct - 'CloudCache' allows for using multiple storage locations, which is critical for rapid recovery and data availability. B) Correct - 'Encrypt' ensures that sensitive client data is protected, addressing compliance and security concerns.

C) Correct - 'CloudCacheLocations' specifies the actual cloud storage locations, enhancing data redundancy and supporting disaster recovery strategies. D) Incorrect - 'BackupInterval' does not exist within FSLogix's standard configuration settings. E) Incorrect - 'LocalCacheSize' impacts performance but is not directly linked to compliance or disaster recovery.

EXAM FOCUS	*Configure FSLogix CloudCache and Encrypt settings to enhance data security and recovery. Use CloudCacheLocations to define storage redundancies for compliance and disaster recovery. Test configurations to ensure performance is not impacted.*
CAUTION ALERT	*Stay clear of assuming BackupInterval exists in FSLogix—it's a non-standard setting. Avoid configuring only LocalCacheSize for performance without addressing compliance and recovery needs with proper encryption and multiple cache locations.*

QUESTION 43

Answer - C) Azure Log Analytics

Option C - Azure Log Analytics provides powerful query capabilities and insights into log data collected from various sources, including AVD deployments. It allows you to analyze log data to identify and troubleshoot session drops and lag effectively.

Option A - Azure Monitor Metrics Explorer is used to visualize and analyze metric data, which may not provide detailed insights into session drops and lag. Option B - Azure Resource Graph is used for querying Azure resource metadata and relationships, not specifically tailored for troubleshooting session issues. Option D - Azure Monitor Workbooks provides customizable dashboards for visualizing and analyzing data, but it may not offer specialized insights into session health.

Option E - Azure Security Center focuses on security posture management and threat protection, rather than troubleshooting session drops and lag.

EXAM FOCUS	*Use Azure Log Analytics for detailed session drop and lag analysis in AVD environments. Combine query-based insights with Azure Monitor logs for identifying network and session performance issues effectively.*

CAUTION ALERT	Avoid relying solely on Azure Monitor Metrics Explorer, as it lacks detailed log query capabilities. Do not confuse Azure Security Center as a tool for performance troubleshooting—it focuses on security posture management.

QUESTION 44

Answer - C) Implement a data lifecycle management solution for automated log retention.

Option C - Implementing a data lifecycle management solution enables automated management of log retention, allowing for compliance with regulatory requirements while optimizing storage costs and operational efficiency.

Option A - Setting a fixed retention period may not align with varying compliance requirements and log importance.
Option B - Applying different retention periods manually may be inefficient and prone to errors.
Option D - Archiving to long-term storage may introduce complexity and increase costs without automation.
Option E - Purging logs may lead to data loss and hinder historical analysis.

EXAM FOCUS	You should implement data lifecycle management for automated retention of AVD logs, balancing compliance needs and operational efficiency. Define retention periods based on regulatory needs and cost considerations, and regularly audit configurations.
CAUTION ALERT	Avoid setting a fixed retention period without understanding compliance requirements—it may lead to data loss or over-retention costs. Stay cautious about manual log retention configurations, as they are prone to errors and inefficiencies.

QUESTION 45

Answer - D

Option A - Incorrect. The command lacks the correct identifier for associating the update deployment with the existing schedule. Option B - Incorrect. The correct flag for specifying hosts in Azure Automation is not --target. Option C - Incorrect. The duration is important but not the primary missing element.

Option D - Correct. Using --schedule-id with a specific lookup for the schedule ID ensures that the update deployment is linked to the correct schedule created for off-peak updates.
Option E - Incorrect. The --type "VM" is unnecessary in this context as the update management deployment inherently targets the session hosts in AVD.

EXAM FOCUS	Use --schedule-id with specific Azure CLI commands to link update deployments with existing schedules. Properly automate update deployments to minimize manual interventions and ensure alignment with off-peak hours for AVD session hosts.
CAUTION ALERT	Avoid assuming that generic --schedule parameters are sufficient. Ensure you retrieve and use the correct schedule ID to avoid deploying updates at incorrect times, which can disrupt user sessions or waste resources.

QUESTION 46

Answer - C) Checking Virtual Network Gateway status

Option C - Checking Virtual Network Gateway status is crucial in troubleshooting network connectivity issues in AVD environments as it serves as the gateway for network traffic between on-premises networks and Azure resources. Ensuring the gateway's availability and proper configuration is essential for resolving connectivity issues effectively.

Option A - Reviewing Azure Monitor logs may provide insights into overall system health but may not directly address network connectivity issues.

Option B - Analyzing network traffic with Azure Network Watcher is valuable but may be secondary to verifying the status of the Virtual Network Gateway. Option D - Reviewing AD DS logs may help identify authentication issues but may not directly relate to network connectivity problems.

Option E - Inspecting Azure Bastion configurations is important for remote access but may not be directly related to intermittent connectivity issues.

EXAM FOCUS	Prioritize checking the Virtual Network Gateway status during AVD network troubleshooting to resolve connectivity issues. The gateway serves as a critical component for connecting on-premises networks to Azure resources.
CAUTION ALERT	Stay cautious about overlooking gateway status—many intermittent network issues stem from misconfigured or unavailable gateways. Avoid starting with Azure Monitor or AD DS logs unless gateway issues are ruled out.

QUESTION 47

Answer - B) An organization experiencing unpredictable usage patterns
E) An enterprise requiring additional security measures for AVD resources

B) An organization experiencing unpredictable usage patterns - Azure Cost Management tools can help monitor usage and spending, allowing adjustments to be made in response to fluctuating demands. E) An enterprise requiring additional security measures for AVD resources - Utilizing Azure Cost Management tools can ensure cost-efficient implementation of security measures while maintaining budgetary constraints.

A, C, D) While Azure Cost Management tools can be beneficial in various scenarios, they are most critical in situations where usage patterns are unpredictable or additional security measures are required.

EXAM FOCUS	Use Azure Cost Management tools to monitor usage patterns and identify cost-saving opportunities. Implement auto-scaling for unpredictable usage to ensure scalability while controlling costs. Review usage reports regularly to stay within budget.
CAUTION ALERT	Avoid neglecting Azure tools like Cost Management for budgeting and optimization. Stay cautious about over-provisioning resources during high usage—use demand-based scaling to optimize resource utilization and reduce wastage.

QUESTION 48

Answer - B, C, D

A) Incorrect - Windows 11 N is cost-effective but may not support older devices.
B) Correct - Windows 10 Enterprise multi-session is cost-effective and allows multiple users to share the same resources.
C) Correct - Windows Server 2022 offers modern management features while being efficient on resources.
D) Correct - Windows Server 2019 supports older devices and is easier to manage compared to newer versions.
E) Incorrect - Windows 8.1 Enterprise is outdated and may not integrate well with current Azure services.

EXAM FOCUS	You can consider Windows 10 Enterprise multi-session for multi-user environments, Windows Server 2022 for modern management, and Windows Server 2019 for compatibility with older devices, balancing cost and accessibility needs for AVD.
CAUTION ALERT	Avoid choosing outdated options like Windows 8.1 Enterprise, as they may lack support for modern Azure services. Stay alert to compatibility issues when selecting newer OS versions like Windows 11 N for older hardware in cost-sensitive environments.

QUESTION 49

Answer - A) Configuring Azure Monitor to track AVD resource utilization and license usage
B) Implementing Azure AD reporting to monitor user sign-ins and license assignments

A) Configuring Azure Monitor to track AVD resource utilization and license usage - Azure Monitor provides insights into resource utilization and license consumption, facilitating auditing and compliance monitoring. B) Implementing Azure AD reporting to monitor user sign-ins and license assignments - Azure AD reporting offers visibility into user activities and license assignments, enabling organizations to track usage and ensure compliance.

C, D, E) While Power BI, JIT access control, and Azure Security Center are valuable for reporting, access control, and security assessments, they are not specifically focused on auditing AVD usage and licenses.

EXAM FOCUS	*Utilize Azure Monitor to track AVD license usage and Azure AD reporting for monitoring user sign-ins and assignments. Regularly review these reports to ensure compliance with licensing agreements and adjust resource allocations accordingly.*
CAUTION ALERT	*Avoid relying on tools like Azure Security Center, which focuses on threat detection and not license auditing. Stay cautious about incomplete tracking—both resource usage and license assignments need to be monitored for full compliance visibility.*

QUESTION 50

Answer - A) Leveraging Azure Blob Storage for storing log data with built-in redundancy and scalability
B) Enabling Azure Monitor Logs integration with AVD for centralized log collection and analysis
E) Utilizing Azure Data Lake Storage for storing structured and unstructured log data with granular access controls

A) Leveraging Azure Blob Storage for storing log data with built-in redundancy and scalability - Azure Blob Storage provides a cost-effective solution for storing log data with built-in redundancy and scalability, ensuring data durability and availability.

B) Enabling Azure Monitor Logs integration with AVD for centralized log collection and analysis - Azure Monitor Logs integration with AVD enables centralized log collection and analysis, simplifying management and enhancing visibility.

E) Utilizing Azure Data Lake Storage for storing structured and unstructured log data with granular access controls - Azure Data Lake Storage offers the flexibility to store structured and unstructured log data with granular access controls, facilitating secure storage and analysis.

C, D) While configuring Azure Storage Lifecycle Management and implementing Azure Event Hubs are viable options, they are not specifically tailored for log collection and storage in AVD.

EXAM FOCUS	*Combine Azure Blob Storage for scalable log storage, Azure Monitor Logs for centralized analysis, and Azure Data Lake Storage for structured and unstructured data. These tools ensure compliance and facilitate efficient log management.*
CAUTION ALERT	*Avoid neglecting redundancy when using Azure Blob Storage—ensure proper configurations for compliance. Do not confuse Azure Event Hubs as a primary tool for AVD log storage—it's better suited for real-time telemetry and ingestion tasks.*

PRACTICE TEST 8 - QUESTIONS ONLY

QUESTION 1

As part of the AVD deployment team, you are integrating on-premises networks with Azure virtual networks to support remote work scenarios. Key considerations include:
• Maintaining low latency and high resilience.
• Ensuring consistent identity management through Azure AD.
• Using RBAC to control access based on user roles.
Which configuration should be implemented first to achieve a seamless integration?

A) Azure ExpressRoute
B) VPN Gateway
C) Azure AD Connect
D) Virtual Network Peering
E) Network Security Groups

QUESTION 2

You have implemented RDP Shortpath in Azure Virtual Desktop (AVD) to reduce latency and improve end-user experience. However, some users are reporting issues with audio and video quality during remote sessions. The marketing department frequently conducts virtual meetings and presentations, relying heavily on multimedia content. Ensuring smooth audio and video playback while maintaining the benefits of RDP Shortpath presents a dilemma. How would you address these challenges while maximizing the benefits of RDP Shortpath for the marketing department?

A) Increase network bandwidth allocation for multimedia streaming
B) Optimize codec settings for audio and video compression
C) Disable RDP Shortpath for multimedia-intensive sessions
D) Implement Webrtc for multimedia redirection
E) Upgrade AVD client devices to support multimedia playback

QUESTION 3

- Your organization has strict compliance requirements for data retention in an Azure Virtual Desktop (AVD) environment.
- You need to ensure that logs related to user activities are retained for the required duration to meet compliance standards.
- Your task involves selecting the appropriate Log Analytics table containing user activity logs for retention purposes.

Which table should you query to access and retain detailed logs of user activities, including session start and end times and application usage?

A) WVDUserActivityLogs
B) WVDSessionEvent
C) WVDAuditLogs
D) WVDUserSessions
E) WVDServiceHealth

QUESTION 4

Your organization must ensure data security and compliance when planning storage solutions for Azure Virtual Desktop (AVD) user data. As the Azure administrator, you need to address specific considerations related to data security and compliance in AVD storage. Which considerations should you prioritize in this context? Select CORRECT answers that apply.

A) Encryption at rest and in transit
B) Role-based access control (RBAC) for data access
C) Data residency and regulatory requirements
D) Auditing and logging of data access and modifications
E) Integration with Azure Active Directory for user authentication

QUESTION 5

Implementing secure access to Azure file shares is critical. Assume you are configuring access using RBAC and Azure AD credentials. What adjustments should be made to this ARM template snippet?

```json
{
 "type": "Microsoft.Storage/storageAccounts/fileServices/shares",
 "apiVersion": "2019-06-01",
 "properties": {
 "enabledProtocols": "SMB",
 "rootSquashType": "NoRootSquash"
 }
}
```

A) Update API version
B) Change enabledProtocols to NFS
C) Add an RBAC role assignment
D) Remove rootSquashType for SMB
E) No changes needed

QUESTION 6

You need to implement a cost-effective solution for managing session hosts in an Azure Virtual Desktop (AVD) environment to optimize resource utilization. The solution must meet the following requirements:
- Dynamically scale session hosts based on user demand to ensure optimal resource usage.
- Ensure that session hosts are available during peak usage hours.
- Minimize administrative overhead.
Which Azure service should you use to fulfill these requirements? Select THREE.

A) Azure Functions
B) Azure Monitor Alerts
C) Azure Automation with Azure Logic Apps
D) Azure Resource Manager templates
E) Azure Virtual Machine Scale Sets

QUESTION 7

Your organization is navigating legal and compliance considerations in Azure Virtual Desktop (AVD) deployments, particularly regarding licensing agreements. As the Azure specialist, you need to address these concerns. What should you highlight? Select THREE.

A) Regulatory Requirements and Compliance Standards
B) Software Asset Management (SAM) and License Audits
C) End-User Agreements and Acceptable Use Policies
D) Data Privacy and Protection Regulations
E) Contractual Obligations and Vendor Relationships

QUESTION 8

Your organization encounters performance issues in its Azure Virtual Desktop (AVD) environment and needs to troubleshoot effectively. As the Azure specialist, you are responsible for addressing these challenges. Which case scenarios should you consider for performance troubleshooting? Select THREE.

A) Application Crashes and Hangs
B) Slow Login and Profile Loading Times
C) High Network Latency and Packet Loss
D) Disk I/O Bottlenecks and Storage Latency
E) Excessive CPU Utilization and Memory Leaks

QUESTION 9

You are tasked with configuring autoscale for host pools in an Azure Virtual Desktop (AVD) environment to ensure optimal performance and cost efficiency. Consider the following requirements:
- Dynamically adjust the number of session hosts based on user activity to maintain performance.
- Scale resources down during periods of low demand to minimize costs.
- Implement predictive scaling to anticipate resource needs and proactively adjust capacity.
Which combination of actions should you take to meet these requirements? Select THREE.

A) Set up autoscale rules based on CPU and memory utilization.
B) Schedule recurring scaling events during off-peak hours.
C) Utilize Azure Advisor recommendations to optimize resource utilization.
D) Implement predictive analytics to forecast resource demands.
E) Configure alerts for abnormal resource usage patterns.

QUESTION 10

You're tasked with automating the configuration changes across multiple host pools using ARM templates. The goal is to standardize the max session limit. What modification is necessary in this snippet?

```json
{ "properties": { "maxSessionLimit": "25" } }
```

A) Change maxSessionLimit to an integer
B) Correct as is
C) Add type and location
D) Include a deployment script
E) Syntax error in JSON

QUESTION 11

Your organization is considering creating a golden image manually for Azure Virtual Desktop (AVD) and wants to ensure access to the necessary tools and resources for image creation. What tools and resources are needed for manual image creation? Select THREE.

A) Azure Portal or Azure CLI for VM Management
B) Sysprep Tool for Image Generalization
C) Azure Storage Account for Image Storage
D) Desired State Configuration (DSC) for Configuration Management
E) Windows Assessment and Deployment Kit (Windows ADK) for Image Customization

QUESTION 12

You are designing a disaster recovery strategy for an Azure Virtual Desktop (AVD) environment to ensure high availability and data resilience. Consider the following factors:
- Implement automatic failover of AVD host pools to a secondary Azure region.
- Minimize data loss and downtime during failover operations.
Which Azure service should you incorporate into the strategy to achieve these objectives?

A) Azure Traffic Manager
B) Azure Site Recovery
C) Azure Backup
D) Azure Monitor
E) Azure Blob Storage

QUESTION 13

Your organization prioritizes security considerations when updating operating systems and applications in Azure Virtual Desktop (AVD) images to mitigate potential vulnerabilities and risks. As the Azure specialist, you need to identify key security considerations for updating OS and applications in AVD images. Which of the following security considerations are important when updating OS and applications in AVD images? Select TWO.

A) Validating Digital Signatures of Updates
B) Implementing Role-Based Access Controls (RBAC) for Update Repositories
C) Scanning Images for Known Vulnerabilities
D) Encrypting Image Data During Updates
E) Enforcing Multi-Factor Authentication (MFA) for Update Processes

QUESTION 14

Your organization is looking to optimize costs associated with image storage in Azure Virtual Desktop (AVD) deployments without compromising performance or reliability. As the Azure specialist, you need to identify cost management strategies for image storage. What cost management strategies should be implemented for image storage in AVD deployments? Select THREE.

A) Utilize Azure Blob Storage Cool Tier for Infrequently Accessed Images
B) Implement Azure Storage Account Reservations for Predictable Workloads
C) Leverage Azure Hybrid Benefit for Image Storage Licensing Costs
D) Implement Azure Policy for Tagging and Cost Allocation
E) Monitor and Optimize Storage Consumption with Azure Cost Management and Billing

QUESTION 15

Advanced routing for AVD can significantly improve network efficiency. Which ARM template snippet correctly defines route tables for optimized traffic management?

```json
{ "type": "Microsoft.Network/routeTables", "properties": { "routes": [ { "name": "defaultRoute", "properties": { "addressPrefix": "0.0.0.0/0", "nextHopType": "Internet" } } ] } }
```

A) Correctly defined
B) Route name should be more specific
C) nextHopType should be "VirtualAppliance"
D) Incorrect addressPrefix
E) Missing tags for identification

QUESTION 16

Effective compliance management in Azure Virtual Desktop (AVD) deployments requires the use of specialized tools to monitor, assess, and enforce regulatory requirements. As the Azure specialist, you need to identify suitable tools for managing compliance in Azure. What tools are available for managing compliance in Azure? Select THREE.

A) Azure Policy for Policy Enforcement and Compliance Monitoring
B) Azure Security Center for Threat Detection and Regulatory Compliance
C) Microsoft Defender for Cloud for Security Assessments and Vulnerability Management
D) Azure Information Protection for Data Classification and Rights Management
E) Microsoft Compliance Manager for Risk Assessment and Compliance Reporting

QUESTION 17

Your organization is in the process of selecting Azure resources for its Azure Virtual Desktop (AVD) deployment and wants to ensure cost-effectiveness without compromising performance. As the Azure specialist, you need to devise strategies for selecting the right Azure resources. What strategies can you implement for selecting the right Azure resources based on cost-effectiveness in AVD deployments? Select THREE.

A) Right-Sizing Virtual Machines based on Workload Requirements
B) Utilizing Azure Spot Instances for Non-Critical Workloads
C) Implementing Azure Resource Policies for Cost Governance
D) Leveraging Azure Cost Calculator for Cost Estimation
E) Utilizing Azure Premium Storage for High-Performance Workloads

QUESTION 18

As part of optimizing an Azure Virtual Desktop (AVD) environment, you need to implement a solution for efficient user authentication and access control. Considering the importance of security and user management, what action should you take to achieve the desired outcome?
- Ensure secure and seamless user authentication
- Simplify access control and management tasks
- Centralize user identity and access policies Select TWO.

A) Azure Active Directory B2C
B) Azure Active Directory Domain Services
C) Azure Multi-Factor Authentication
D) Azure AD Conditional Access
E) Azure Identity Protection

QUESTION 19

Your organization is conducting a disaster recovery test for its Azure Virtual Desktop (AVD) infrastructure. The objective is to validate the effectiveness of failover procedures and assess the overall readiness to handle disruptions. Critical points include test planning, execution, and documentation of results. How would you ensure a comprehensive disaster recovery test for AVD environments? Select THREE.

A) Simulate failover scenarios in a non-production environment
B) Involve stakeholders from IT, operations, and compliance teams
C) Document test procedures, outcomes, and areas for improvement
D) Analyze network latency and bandwidth utilization during failover tests
E) Review historical incident reports for identifying potential failure points

QUESTION 20

Integration of AVD monitoring tools with other Azure services is critical for a comprehensive view of your environment's health. You are required to implement a solution that combines AVD telemetry with Azure Log Analytics for advanced query capabilities and integrated incident response. What is the essential step in integrating AVD monitoring with Azure Log Analytics?

A) Link AVD to Azure Log Analytics workspace
B) Create an Azure Event Hub
C) Deploy Azure API Management
D) Configure Azure Service Health alerts
E) Establish Azure Event Grid

QUESTION 21

You are configuring Azure Virtual Desktop for a company that requires enhanced security for user authentication when accessing resources remotely. You need to implement a solution that provides multi-factor authentication (MFA) for user logins. Which authentication method should you enable? Select TWO.

A) Windows Hello for Business
B) Biometric authentication
C) Azure Active Directory Conditional Access policies
D) Username and password authentication
E) Azure Multi-Factor Authentication (MFA)

QUESTION 22

Your organization is planning to migrate from traditional access control methods to role-based access control (RBAC) in existing Azure Virtual Desktop (AVD) setups. The focus is on understanding strategies for a smooth transition to RBAC without disrupting ongoing operations. What strategies should be adopted for migrating to RBAC in existing AVD setups? Select THREE.

A) Identify existing roles and permissions for mapping to RBAC roles
B) Conduct a comprehensive access review to identify security gaps
C) Pilot RBAC implementation in a test environment before full deployment
D) Communicate changes to users and provide training on new access management processes
E) Monitor RBAC implementation closely and address any issues promptly

QUESTION 23

Your organization is considering integrating third-party multi-factor authentication (MFA) solutions with Azure Virtual Desktop (AVD) to provide additional flexibility and features. The focus is on understanding the integration process and considerations for third-party MFA solutions with Azure AD. How can third-party multi-factor authentication (MFA) solutions be integrated with Azure Virtual Desktop (AVD) environments effectively? Select THREE.

A) Configure Azure AD to federate authentication requests with the third-party MFA provider
B) Install and configure the third-party MFA agent on AVD session hosts
C) Implement Azure AD Application Proxy for secure access to the third-party MFA solution
D) Enable conditional access controls to enforce MFA requirements for AVD connections
E) Establish trust relationships between Azure AD and the third-party MFA provider

QUESTION 24

In a scenario where Azure Virtual Desktop is being optimized for software development teams who frequently use resource-intensive applications, what are the key configurations you should implement? Select THREE.

A) Increase CPU and RAM allocations on session hosts.
B) Configure persistent desktops.
C) Deploy FSLogix app masking.
D) Implement auto-scaling based on usage.
E) Allocate additional storage for user profiles.

QUESTION 25

Implementing effective network segmentation is crucial for enhancing the security of AVD deployments. Analyze this ARM template snippet to ensure it correctly configures subnets for network segmentation.

```json
{
 "type": "Microsoft.Network/virtualNetworks/subnets",
 "properties": {
 "addressPrefix": "10.0.0.0/24",
 "networkSecurityGroup": {
 "id": "/subscriptions/subId/resourceGroups/AVDResources/providers/Microsoft.Network/networkSecurityGroups/AVDNSG"
 }
 }
}
```

A) Configuration is correct
B) AddressPrefix should be smaller
C) NetworkSecurityGroup ID is incorrectly formatted
D) Subnet type should be different
E) JSON structure is incorrect

QUESTION 26

Your organization is configuring advanced threat protection settings for Azure Virtual Desktop (AVD) to mitigate sophisticated cyber threats. The focus is on understanding the advanced threat protection settings available. Which advanced threat protection settings can be configured for AVD? Select THREE.

A) Cloud-delivered protection for real-time malware detection
B) Attack surface reduction rules to mitigate exploit techniques and vulnerabilities
C) Controlled folder access to protect sensitive data from ransomware attacks
D) Network protection to prevent outbound connections to malicious domains
E) Exploit protection to mitigate common exploit techniques and vulnerabilities

QUESTION 27

In an educational institution using AVD, you need to address cyberbullying through monitoring, ensure COPPA compliance, and protect student data privacy. What measures should be implemented? Select THREE.

A) Enable auditing and logging with Azure Monitor.
B) Use Microsoft Defender for Endpoint to detect cyber threats.
C) Implement data loss prevention (DLP) policies.
D) Enforce legal hold and eDiscovery capabilities.
E) Configure user behavior analytics.

QUESTION 28

Your organization is implementing Conditional Access based on network conditions in Azure Virtual Desktop (AVD) environments to enhance security and restrict access from untrusted networks. The focus is on understanding the considerations for implementing Conditional Access based on network conditions. What are the key considerations for implementing Conditional Access based on network conditions in AVD environments? Select THREE.

A) Define trusted and untrusted network locations based on IP address ranges
B) Configure conditional access policies to allow access only from trusted network locations
C) Implement Azure Firewall to enforce network-level security policies
D) Enable VPN access for users connecting from untrusted networks
E) Monitor network traffic and access patterns for anomalous behavior

QUESTION 29

Your organization is conducting periodic reviews of security configurations for Azure Virtual Desktop (AVD) session hosts to ensure ongoing compliance and protection against emerging threats. The focus is on periodic review and update of security configurations. What are key considerations for conducting periodic reviews and updates of security configurations for AVD session hosts? Select THREE.

A) Review security baselines and group policies to align with evolving compliance requirements and industry standards
B) Monitor security logs and audit trails for anomalous activities or unauthorized access attempts
C) Evaluate and update antivirus definitions and threat intelligence feeds to stay ahead of emerging threats
D) Implement just-in-time (JIT) access controls for administrative accounts to minimize exposure to potential attacks
E) Perform vulnerability assessments and penetration testing to identify and address potential security weaknesses

QUESTION 30

You are responsible for configuring security alerts to notify administrators of potential security breaches or misconfigurations in Azure Virtual Desktop. Which Azure service should you use to set up these alerts, and how should you configure it to ensure alerts are effective and provide actionable insights?
Consider the script snippet for setting up alert rules in Azure Monitor:
bash
```
az monitor alert create --name "SecurityAlert" --description "Alert for unusual login attempts" --action-group "AVDSecurityGroup" --condition "FailedLogins > 5"
```

A) Correctly configures security alerts
B) Condition should use a different metric
C) Action group needs to include email notifications
D) Alert name does not follow best practices
E) Description should be more detailed

QUESTION 31

Your organization is deploying FSLogix in an AVD environment to optimize user experience and reduce administrative overhead. You need to configure FSLogix with the following considerations:
1. Minimizing storage costs while ensuring efficient profile management.
2. Centralizing FSLogix configuration to streamline management across multiple AVD host pools.
3. Enhancing security by implementing encryption for FSLogix profiles.

A) Implement Profile Containers with deduplication enabled
B) Utilize Azure Automation DSC for FSLogix configuration
C) Configure FSLogix settings via Azure Policy

D) Enable OneDrive Known Folder Move for FSLogix profiles
E) Encrypt FSLogix profiles using Azure Disk Encryption

QUESTION 32

As an Azure Virtual Desktop administrator responsible for managing updates and patches for Office Containers, you need to ensure seamless delivery of updates while minimizing disruptions. Consider the following scenario:
- Office application updates must be deployed efficiently to all user sessions without interrupting productivity.
- Updates should be tested and validated in a staging environment before deployment to production.
- Rollback procedures must be in place to address any issues that arise during the update process.
How can updates and patches be managed for Office Containers? Select THREE.

A) Utilize Azure Update Management to automate patch deployment for Office Containers.
B) Implement a staged rollout strategy for Office application updates across user sessions.
C) Configure Office Containers to automatically download and apply updates during off-peak hours.
D) Leverage Azure Monitor to track Office application performance post-update.
E) Enable FSLogix Profile Containers to capture application state before updates.

QUESTION 33

An AVD setup in the healthcare sector must adhere to HIPAA regulations, ensure data integrity, and facilitate secure data exchange between sites. What configurations are critical? Select THREE.

A) Enable Azure Information Protection.
B) Configure inter-site connectivity with Azure ExpressRoute.
C) Implement Azure Health Data Services.
D) Use Azure Private Link for secure data transmission.
E) Set up Azure Key Vault for managing encryption keys.

QUESTION 34

Your organization is experiencing performance impacts resulting from device redirection in Azure Virtual Desktop (AVD) deployments. Consider the following scenario:
- Users frequently connect to AVD sessions from low-bandwidth networks and remote locations, leading to delays and disruptions during device redirection.
- Some users encounter latency issues while accessing redirected peripherals such as printers and scanners, affecting productivity.
- IT administrators aim to mitigate performance impacts associated with device redirection while ensuring a seamless user experience for AVD sessions.
How can you address performance impacts and optimize device redirection for the given scenario? Select TWO.

A) Implement Azure Bastion for secure RDP access to AVD instances, reducing the need for device redirection over low-bandwidth networks.
B) Configure FSLogix Profile Containers to streamline user profile management and reduce the overhead of device redirection operations.
C) Leverage Azure AD Conditional Access policies to prioritize device redirection traffic based on user roles and session priorities.
D) Utilize Azure Network Watcher to monitor network connectivity and identify bottlenecks affecting device redirection performance.
E) Deploy GPU-accelerated virtual machines (VMs) to offload device redirection processing and improve overall session performance.

QUESTION 35

Security is a priority in your AVD setup, particularly for network printing. Implement security best practices by configuring encryption for all print jobs. Analyze the Azure CLI command intended to enforce encryption:
```bash
az network vnet subnet update --name PrintSubnet --vnet-name AVDVnet --encrypt-traffic true
```

A) Properly secures print traffic
B) Encryption should be set at the printer level
C) Subnet update is unnecessary
D) Command does not target print jobs
E) Encrypt-traffic flag is incorrectly used

QUESTION 36

An e-commerce company is deploying AVD to handle peak sales periods. The requirements are to manage high traffic loads, ensure transaction security, and provide a responsive user experience. What configurations should be prioritized? Select THREE.

A) Implement Azure Front Door for global load balancing.
B) Enable Azure Application Gateway with Web Application Firewall (WAF).
C) Use Azure AutoScale to manage VM load dynamically.
D) Configure Azure AD B2C for customer identity management.
E) Set up Azure Sentinel for real-time security monitoring.

QUESTION 37

When implementing the Start VM on Connect feature in Azure Virtual Desktop (AVD), what security consideration is essential to prevent unauthorized access to resources?

A) Enabling Multi-Factor Authentication (MFA) for all AVD users
B) Restricting access to virtual machines based on user roles and permissions
C) Encrypting data transmission between client devices and AVD instances
D) Implementing network-level firewalls to control inbound traffic to AVD infrastructure
E) Configuring Azure AD Conditional Access policies to enforce access controls

QUESTION 38

Security best practices are essential when deploying applications to Azure Virtual Desktop (AVD) environments. Which deployment method offers enhanced security by encapsulating applications and preventing unauthorized access to sensitive data?

A) MSIX App Attach
B) PowerShell script execution
C) Azure Marketplace integration
D) RDP-based application deployment
E) MSI deployment

QUESTION 39

To support a hybrid work model for a tech company, Azure Virtual Desktop must offer seamless connectivity, robust security for proprietary software, and enable scalable resources during product launches. What configurations are necessary? Select THREE.

A) Set up Azure Bastion on a dedicated AzureBastionSubnet for secure access.
B) Enable Azure Scale Sets to manage resource scaling.
C) Deploy Azure Firewall for enhanced network security.
D) Configure Azure AD for seamless single sign-on (SSO) across applications.
E) Implement Azure Application Gateway for load balancing.

QUESTION 40

Implementing OneDrive in a multisession AVD environment requires setting up user profiles correctly. What is missing in the following ARM template snippet to configure OneDrive for all users?

```
"properties": { "userProfile": { "storageUri": "[concat('https://',
parameters('storageAccountName'), '.blob.core.windows.net/')] } }
```

A) Add "multisessionEnabled": true to the userProfile properties.
B) Insert "optimizePerformance": true under userProfile.
C) Include "type": "Standard_LRS" for the storage account type.
D) No changes are needed.
E) Add "useOneDrive": true to enable OneDrive.

QUESTION 41

To manage license compliance for Microsoft 365 Apps deployed on AVD, you need a PowerShell script that will report on the current activation status of apps across all session hosts. What script would provide this information?
Get-M365AppLicenseStatus -Output "detailed"

A) Script is correct as is.
B) Change -Output "detailed" to -DetailLevel "Full".
C) Use Get-AVDAppLicense -Type "M365" -Detail $true.
D) Replace with Get-M365AppStatus -ShowLicenseType $true.
E) Remove -Output "detailed" for a default summary report.

QUESTION 42

A technology startup using AVD requires a configuration that supports dynamic scaling for their development environments, ensures data isolation for security, and optimizes for cost efficiency. Which FSLogix settings are most appropriate? Select THREE.

```
A) HKLM\SOFTWARE\FSLogix\Profiles\DynamicVHDAllocation
B) HKLM\SOFTWARE\FSLogix\Profiles\Enabled
C) HKLM\SOFTWARE\FSLogix\Profiles\ProfileType
D) HKLM\SOFTWARE\FSLogix\Profiles\DiskType
E) HKLM\SOFTWARE\FSLogix\Profiles\LocalCacheSize
```

QUESTION 43

You need to identify the potential impact of network configurations on session health in an Azure Virtual Desktop (AVD) environment. Which factors should you consider to assess this impact effectively? Select CORRECT answers that apply.

A) Bandwidth limitations
B) Latency
C) Firewall rules
D) VPN connections
E) Subnet configurations

QUESTION 44

Security considerations play a crucial role in managing diagnostic data within Azure Virtual Desktop (AVD) environments. Key factors to consider include:
1. Access control and RBAC (Role-Based Access Control) for managing permissions to view and export diagnostic logs.
2. Encryption and data protection measures to safeguard sensitive information contained in diagnostic logs.
3. Monitoring and auditing mechanisms to track access and changes to diagnostic settings and logs.
Which mechanism provides granular access control and audit capabilities for managing diagnostic logs in AVD environments?

A) Azure Key Vault
B) Azure Monitor Alerts
C) Azure Security Center
D) Azure AD DS (Azure Active Directory Domain Services)
E) Azure RBAC (Role-Based Access Control)

QUESTION 45

Implement a rollback strategy for updates that cause issues. Describe a command to revert to the previous version of a VM image in an AVD host pool.

```
Set-AzVm -ResourceGroupName "AVDResourceGroup" -Name "SessionHost1" -ToLastKnownGoodState $true
```

A) Command is correct.
B) Replace Set-AzVm with Update-AzVmImage.
C) Change -ToLastKnownGoodState $true to -Redeploy $true.
D) Add -Confirm:$false to execute without confirmation.
E) Use az vm redeploy --name "SessionHost1" --resource-group "AVDResourceGroup" as the command.

QUESTION 46

Improving network performance is essential for enhancing user experience in Azure Virtual Desktop (AVD) environments. As the AVD administrator, you need to implement best practices for network configuration to optimize performance. Which best practice should you prioritize to improve network performance?

A) Implementing Quality of Service (QoS) policies
B) Configuring Azure Bastion for secure remote access
C) Optimizing Virtual Network Gateway settings
D) Enabling Webrtc for Microsoft Teams optimization
E) Implementing Azure Firewall for network security

QUESTION 47

An Azure Virtual Desktop (AVD) deployment is experiencing resource inefficiencies, leading to increased operational costs. The IT team needs to implement measures to optimize resource usage for cost-efficiency. What strategies should the IT team employ to address resource inefficiencies and reduce operational costs? Select THREE.

A) Implementing proactive monitoring and alerting
B) Using Azure Policies to enforce cost-saving measures
C) Enabling autoscaling based on user demand
D) Leveraging Azure Reserved Instances for VMs
E) Configuring network Quality of Service (QoS) policies

QUESTION 48

For a digital marketing agency that requires high graphics performance, frequent data backups, and robust security, which Windows operating systems are best suited for Azure Virtual Desktop session hosts? Select THREE.

A) Windows 10 Enterprise multi-session
B) Windows 11 Enterprise
C) Windows Server 2022
D) Windows Server 2016
E) Windows 7 Virtual Desktop

QUESTION 49

A company is seeking strategies to optimize licensing costs for its Azure Virtual Desktop (AVD) deployment while maintaining compliance. Which approaches should the company consider for effective license optimization? Select TWO.

A) Implementing user-based licensing to align costs with actual usage
B) Leveraging Azure Reservations for predictable pricing and cost savings
C) Utilizing Azure Hybrid Benefit to reduce licensing costs for on-premises workloads
D) Configuring license reassignment policies for unused or underutilized AVD instances
E) Integrating Azure Advisor recommendations for optimizing license usage and costs

QUESTION 50

A company wants to gain actionable insights from logs generated in its Azure Virtual Desktop (AVD) environment to proactively identify and address potential issues. Which tools should they use for log analysis and insight generation? Select THREE.

A) Leveraging Azure Monitor for querying and visualizing log data with customizable dashboards
B) Utilizing Azure Log Analytics for advanced log query and analysis capabilities
C) Implementing Azure Sentinel for security-focused log analysis and threat detection
D) Enabling Azure Data Explorer for real-time log analysis and visualization
E) Using Microsoft Defender for Cloud for log-based threat intelligence and incident response

PRACTICE TEST 8 - ANSWERS ONLY

QUESTION 1

Answer - C) Azure AD Connect

Option A - Incorrect. Enhances connectivity but doesn't address identity integration.
Option B - Incorrect. Connects networks but doesn't manage identities.
Option C - Correct. Synchronizes on-premises AD with Azure AD, crucial for identity management.
Option D - Incorrect. Connects Azure VNets, not on-prem to Azure.
Option E - Incorrect. Secures network traffic, not related to identity management.

EXAM FOCUS	*Always start by configuring Azure AD Connect for identity synchronization when integrating on-premises and Azure networks. This ensures seamless user authentication and minimizes disruptions to identity management in hybrid setups.*
CAUTION ALERT	*Avoid assuming that Azure ExpressRoute or VPN Gateway directly manages identity. They focus on connectivity and do not address the synchronization of identities.*

QUESTION 2

Answer - B) Optimize codec settings for audio and video compression

Option A - Incorrect. Increasing network bandwidth allocation may not fully address audio and video quality issues.
Option B - Correct. Optimizing codec settings for audio and video compression can improve quality without sacrificing performance. Option C - Incorrect. Disabling RDP Shortpath may introduce latency and is not recommended for multimedia-intensive sessions.

Option D - Incorrect. Webrtc is not directly related to optimizing audio and video quality within RDP sessions.
Option E - Incorrect. Upgrading AVD client devices may help but does not directly address codec optimization.

EXAM FOCUS	*Optimize codec settings in RDP Shortpath for multimedia tasks to ensure smooth playback for audio and video. Prioritize network settings that balance compression quality and bandwidth usage, particularly for multimedia-intensive departments like marketing.*
CAUTION ALERT	*Don't disable RDP Shortpath—it may solve one issue but introduce latency, harming overall performance. Avoid assuming that increasing bandwidth alone fixes multimedia quality—it often requires codec optimization.*

QUESTION 3

Answer - [D]

Option D - WVDUserSessions: This table contains detailed logs of user session activities, including session start and end times and application usage, making it suitable for retention purposes to meet compliance standards.
Option A - WVDUserActivityLogs: While it may seem relevant, this table does not exist, and user activity logs are typically stored in WVDUserSessions.

Option B - WVDSessionEvent: This table contains session event logs but may not provide detailed user activity information. Option C - WVDAuditLogs: This contains audit logs but may not capture detailed user activity information.
Option E - WVDServiceHealth: This provides overall service health information, not user-specific activity logs.

EXAM FOCUS	*Query WVDUserSessions for detailed user activity logs. These logs capture session start and end times, essential for compliance-related data retention. Ensure retention policies meet organizational and legal standards.*

CAUTION ALERT	Avoid selecting tables like WVDUserActivityLogs, which do not exist, or WVDAuditLogs, which focus on auditing rather than detailed user activity. Misidentifying the table could lead to non-compliance.

QUESTION 4

Answer - A) Encryption at rest and in transit; B) Role-based access control (RBAC) for data access; C) Data residency and regulatory requirements; D) Auditing and logging of data access and modifications

Option A - Correct. Encryption at rest and in transit helps protect sensitive AVD user data from unauthorized access and ensures compliance with data security standards. Option B - Correct. Implementing RBAC ensures that only authorized users have access to AVD user data, reducing the risk of data breaches and compliance violations.

Option C - Correct. Considering data residency and regulatory requirements helps ensure that AVD user data is stored in compliance with applicable laws and regulations. Option D - Correct. Auditing and logging data access and modifications provide visibility into data usage and help meet compliance requirements by tracking user activities in AVD storage.

Option E - Incorrect. While integration with Azure Active Directory is important for user authentication, it may not directly address data security and compliance considerations related to AVD storage.

EXAM FOCUS	Prioritize encryption at rest and in transit, RBAC, and data residency requirements when configuring storage for AVD user data. Compliance with these factors ensures adherence to industry regulations and robust data security.
CAUTION ALERT	Stay alert to neglecting auditing and logging—it's vital for tracking data access and meeting compliance standards. Avoid over-relying on Azure AD integration, as it doesn't address all data security aspects like encryption or RBAC.

QUESTION 5

Answer - D) Remove rootSquashType for SMB

Option A - Correct: Updating the API version can ensure compatibility with the latest features.
Option B - Incorrect: 'SMB' is correct for Azure file shares in an AVD context.
Option C - Correct: Adding an RBAC role assignment is necessary for securing access with Azure AD.
Option D - Correct: 'rootSquashType' is not applicable for SMB protocol and should be removed.
Option E - Incorrect: Changes are needed to optimize security settings.

EXAM FOCUS	Always remove rootSquashType when configuring SMB protocol for Azure file shares. Include RBAC role assignments to secure access, ensuring that access permissions align with user roles and security policies.
CAUTION ALERT	Avoid leaving unsupported properties like rootSquashType in SMB configurations. Be cautious not to confuse NFS with SMB, as protocols have different requirements and use cases.

QUESTION 6

Answer - [A, C, E]

Option A - Azure Functions: Functions can be used to trigger scaling actions based on user demand, fulfilling the requirement for dynamic scaling. Option C - Azure Automation with Azure Logic Apps: Logic Apps can automate workflows, including scaling session hosts based on demand, meeting the specified requirements.

Option E - Azure Virtual Machine Scale Sets: Scale Sets can automatically adjust the number of session hosts based on demand, ensuring availability during peak usage hours and minimizing administrative overhead. Option B - Azure Monitor Alerts: Alerts notify you of potential issues but are not specifically designed for managing resource scaling based on demand. Option D - Azure Resource Manager templates: While templates enable you to deploy and manage Azure resources, they are not specifically designed for dynamically scaling resources based on demand.

EXAM FOCUS	*Combine Azure Functions, Azure Automation with Logic Apps, and VM Scale Sets for dynamic scaling of AVD session hosts. These tools ensure automated scaling based on user demand, reducing administrative overhead and optimizing resource utilization.*
CAUTION ALERT	*Avoid using Azure Monitor Alerts as the primary scaling mechanism—it notifies issues but does not automate scaling. Avoid manual scaling methods like templates for dynamic requirements.*

QUESTION 7

Answer - A) Regulatory Requirements and Compliance Standards; B) Software Asset Management (SAM) and License Audits; D) Data Privacy and Protection Regulations

Option A - Correct. Regulatory requirements and compliance standards influence licensing agreements, ensuring adherence to industry regulations and organizational policies. Option B - Correct. Software Asset Management (SAM) and license audits help maintain compliance with licensing agreements, preventing potential penalties or legal issues.

Option D - Correct. Data privacy and protection regulations impact licensing agreements, especially concerning the storage and processing of sensitive information within AVD deployments. Option C - Incorrect. While end-user agreements and acceptable use policies are important, they are not directly related to licensing considerations for AVD deployments. Option E - Incorrect. Contractual obligations and vendor relationships may impact licensing negotiations, but they are broader aspects of procurement and vendor management, rather than specific to AVD licensing.

EXAM FOCUS	*Ensure compliance by addressing regulatory requirements, SAM and license audits, and data privacy regulations in AVD deployments. Highlight these points during discussions to secure proper licensing and maintain compliance.*
CAUTION ALERT	*Don't assume end-user agreements directly impact licensing—they focus more on user behavior. Similarly, vendor relationships matter for procurement but aren't primary licensing concerns.*

QUESTION 8

Answer - A) Application Crashes and Hangs; B) Slow Login and Profile Loading Times; D) Disk I/O Bottlenecks and Storage Latency

Option A - Correct. Application crashes and hangs can indicate compatibility issues or resource constraints within AVD sessions, requiring investigation and resolution. Option B - Correct. Slow login and profile loading times impact user experience and may result from network or storage-related issues, necessitating performance troubleshooting.

Option D - Correct. Disk I/O bottlenecks and storage latency affect application performance and session responsiveness in AVD environments, requiring optimization and potentially storage configuration adjustments. Option C - Incorrect. While high network latency and packet loss are performance issues, they are not specific case scenarios for troubleshooting within AVD deployments. Option E - Incorrect. While excessive CPU utilization and memory leaks can impact performance, they are not direct case scenarios typically encountered in AVD performance troubleshooting.

EXAM FOCUS	*Focus on application crashes, slow login times, and disk I/O bottlenecks for AVD performance troubleshooting. These are common causes of degraded performance and require targeted investigation.*
CAUTION ALERT	*Avoid spending too much time on issues like high network latency, which may not directly affect AVD performance. Excessive CPU utilization is important but not always a first-line troubleshooting scenario.*

QUESTION 9

Answer - [A, D, E]

Option A - Set up autoscale rules based on CPU and memory utilization: This allows for dynamic adjustment of resources based on performance metrics, maintaining optimal performance and cost efficiency.

Option D - Implement predictive analytics to forecast resource demands: Predictive analytics can anticipate resource needs and proactively adjust capacity, aligning with the requirement for predictive scaling. Option E - Configure alerts for abnormal resource usage patterns: Alerts can notify administrators of unusual resource usage, enabling proactive management and optimization.

Option B - Scheduling recurring scaling events during off-peak hours is a manual approach and does not align with the requirement for dynamic adjustment based on user activity. Option C - While Azure Advisor recommendations are valuable for optimizing resources, they do not directly address the requirement for dynamic scaling based on user activity.

EXAM FOCUS	*Implement autoscale rules for CPU/memory, predictive analytics, and alerts for abnormal usage to meet scaling requirements. These steps ensure resource availability during peak times and cost-efficiency during low demand.*
CAUTION ALERT	*Avoid relying solely on recurring schedules—they lack real-time adaptability. Ensure predictive analytics are well-configured to avoid under-provisioning during unexpected peaks.*

QUESTION 10

Answer - A) Change maxSessionLimit to an integer

Option A - Correct: JSON does not accept strings for integer values; thus, "25" should be without quotes.
Option B - Incorrect: The value format is incorrect for 'maxSessionLimit'.
Option C - Correct: Type and location might be needed depending on the context.
Option D - Incorrect: A deployment script isn't strictly necessary for this change.
Option E - Incorrect: There is no syntax error related to JSON formatting.

EXAM FOCUS	*Ensure JSON values like maxSessionLimit are integers, not strings. Validate all template configurations for data type consistency before deployment to avoid errors during implementation.*
CAUTION ALERT	*Don't assume all property values can be strings in JSON; always check specific requirements for each field. Avoid overlooking type errors, as they can lead to deployment failures or misconfigured host pool settings.*

QUESTION 11

Answer - A) Azure Portal or Azure CLI for VM Management; B) Sysprep Tool for Image Generalization; C) Azure Storage Account for Image Storage

Option A - Correct. The Azure Portal or Azure CLI provides interfaces for managing virtual machines, including configuring, provisioning, and managing the virtual machine used for golden image creation. Option B - Correct. The Sysprep tool is essential for generalizing the virtual machine, removing unique system identifiers and configurations to prepare it for image capture and deployment across multiple devices.

Option C - Correct. Azure Storage Account serves as the storage repository for the captured virtual machine image, providing scalability, reliability, and accessibility for image deployment within the AVD environment. Option D - Incorrect. Desired State Configuration (DSC) is used for configuration management but is not directly related to the golden image creation process, which focuses on preparing a standardized image template for deployment.

Option E - Incorrect. While the Windows Assessment and Deployment Kit (Windows ADK) offers tools for image customization and deployment, it is not specifically required for manual golden image creation in Azure Virtual Desktop.

EXAM FOCUS	*Always use Azure Portal or CLI, Sysprep, and Azure Storage for golden image creation. These tools simplify processes like VM management, image generalization, and centralized storage. Test the image in a non-production environment to ensure it works seamlessly with AVD deployments.*
CAUTION	*Avoid assuming DSC is mandatory for golden image creation—it's primarily used for managing post-*

ALERT	*deployment configurations. Similarly, don't confuse Windows ADK as a necessary tool unless advanced customizations are explicitly required for your deployment.*

QUESTION 12

Answer - [B]

Option B - Azure Site Recovery: Azure Site Recovery provides disaster recovery as a service and supports automatic failover of AVD host pools to a secondary Azure region, ensuring minimal data loss and downtime during failover operations.

Option A - Azure Traffic Manager provides DNS-based traffic routing but does not directly support failover and disaster recovery for AVD host pools. Option C - Azure Backup is primarily used for data backup and recovery and is not designed for failover and disaster recovery of AVD host pools. Option D - Azure Monitor provides monitoring and analytics capabilities but does not directly support failover and disaster recovery for AVD host pools. Option E - Azure Blob Storage is a storage service and is not directly related to failover and disaster recovery of AVD host pools.

EXAM FOCUS	*You need Azure Site Recovery for failover and continuity in AVD disaster recovery plans. It automates replication and failover to secondary regions, minimizing downtime and data loss. Test failover frequently to identify gaps and refine recovery procedures for real-world scenarios.*
CAUTION ALERT	*Stay alert about relying on Azure Traffic Manager alone—it only routes traffic and lacks host pool failover capabilities. Also, avoid assuming Azure Backup is sufficient for disaster recovery; it focuses on data recovery, not continuity of operations in AVD setups.*

QUESTION 13

Answer - A) Validating Digital Signatures of Updates; C) Scanning Images for Known Vulnerabilities

Option A - Correct. Validating digital signatures ensures the authenticity and integrity of updates, guarding against tampering and malicious alterations. Option B - Incorrect. While RBAC is important for access control, it is not specifically related to security considerations when updating OS and applications in AVD images.

Option C - Correct. Scanning images for known vulnerabilities helps identify and mitigate security risks before deployment, reducing the likelihood of exploitation. Option D - Incorrect. While encrypting image data enhances security, it is not directly related to security considerations during updates of OS and applications in AVD images. Option E - Incorrect. Enforcing MFA enhances authentication security but is not specifically focused on security considerations during updates of OS and applications in AVD images.

EXAM FOCUS	*Always validate updates with digital signatures to ensure authenticity and protect against tampering. Regularly scan AVD images for vulnerabilities to identify and mitigate potential threats before deployment. Automate these steps using tools like Azure Update Management for consistency and security.*
CAUTION ALERT	*Avoid assuming RBAC for update repositories ensures update integrity—it only manages access permissions. Encryption of image data is vital for data security but does not replace the need for validating the integrity and security of updates during deployment processes.*

QUESTION 14

Answer - A) Utilize Azure Blob Storage Cool Tier for Infrequently Accessed Images; B) Implement Azure Storage Account Reservations for Predictable Workloads; D) Implement Azure Policy for Tagging and Cost Allocation

Option A - Correct. Utilizing Azure Blob Storage Cool Tier for infrequently accessed images can reduce storage costs while maintaining accessibility for AVD deployments. Option B - Correct. Implementing Azure Storage Account Reservations allows you to pre-purchase storage capacity at a discounted rate, optimizing costs for predictable workloads in AVD deployments.

Option C - Incorrect. While Azure Hybrid Benefit can help reduce licensing costs for certain Azure services, it may not directly apply to image storage in AVD deployments. Option D - Correct. Implementing Azure Policy for tagging and cost allocation helps track and manage image storage costs by applying tags for cost attribution and resource organization.

Option E - Incorrect. While monitoring and optimizing storage consumption are essential cost management practices, this option does not specifically address strategies for image storage in AVD deployments.

EXAM FOCUS	*Optimize costs by using Azure Blob Storage Cool Tier for infrequent image access, Storage Account Reservations for predictable workloads, and Azure Policy for tagging. These strategies lower expenses, ensure accountability, and maintain storage reliability for AVD environments.*
CAUTION ALERT	*Don't confuse Azure Hybrid Benefit with storage-specific savings—it applies to licensing costs, not image storage. Avoid neglecting tagging with Azure Policy—this is crucial for tracking costs and identifying areas for optimization across multiple AVD storage resources.*

QUESTION 15

Answer - A) Correctly defined

Option A - Correct: The JSON snippet accurately sets up a default route to direct all traffic to the internet, which can be part of optimized traffic management. Option B - Incorrect: 'defaultRoute' is a valid name for a generic route setup.

Option C - Incorrect: 'nextHopType' as "Internet" is correct for directing traffic outward; 'VirtualAppliance' would be used if routing through a specific device. Option D - Incorrect: '0.0.0.0/0' is the correct address prefix for a default route.

Option E - Incorrect: Tags are useful but not required for the route table configuration.

EXAM FOCUS	*Ensure route tables have accurate addressPrefix and nextHopType values for proper traffic flow. For internet-bound traffic, set nextHopType to "Internet." Validate ARM templates using deployment tools like Azure Resource Manager to catch errors and enforce consistency across configurations.*
CAUTION ALERT	*Avoid misconfiguring nextHopType by selecting inappropriate values like "VirtualAppliance" unless specifically routing traffic through a device. While tagging isn't required for functionality, overlooking it can hinder efficient management and troubleshooting in larger setups.*

QUESTION 16

Answer - A) Azure Policy for Policy Enforcement and Compliance Monitoring; B) Azure Security Center for Threat Detection and Regulatory Compliance; E) Microsoft Compliance Manager for Risk Assessment and Compliance Reporting

Option A - Correct. Azure Policy enables policy enforcement and compliance monitoring to ensure adherence to organizational standards and regulatory requirements in AVD deployments. Option B - Correct. Azure Security Center provides threat detection and regulatory compliance capabilities, helping organizations assess and maintain compliance in AVD environments. Option C - Incorrect. While Microsoft Defender for Cloud offers security assessments, it may not be specifically tailored for compliance management in AVD deployments. Option D - Incorrect. While Azure Information Protection is important for data protection, it may not be directly related to compliance management in AVD deployments. Option E - Correct. Microsoft Compliance Manager allows for risk assessment and compliance reporting, assisting organizations in meeting regulatory requirements in AVD environments.

EXAM FOCUS	*Use Azure Policy to enforce compliance, Azure Security Center for threat detection and regulatory assessments, and Microsoft Compliance Manager for detailed compliance reporting. Regular audits with these tools ensure regulatory adherence and secure your AVD environment from potential violations.*
CAUTION ALERT	*Stay clear of assuming Microsoft Defender for Cloud is sufficient for compliance management—it mainly focuses on threat detection and security assessments. Azure Information Protection, while important, is more about data protection than comprehensive compliance management.*

QUESTION 17

Answer - A) Right-Sizing Virtual Machines based on Workload Requirements; B) Utilizing Azure Spot Instances for Non-Critical Workloads; D) Leveraging Azure Cost Calculator for Cost Estimation

Option A - Correct. Right-sizing virtual machines based on workload requirements ensures optimal performance and cost-effectiveness by matching resources to workload demands in AVD deployments. Option B - Correct. Utilizing Azure Spot Instances for non-critical workloads can provide significant cost savings by leveraging spare capacity at discounted prices in AVD deployments.

Option C - Incorrect. While Azure Resource Policies can help with cost governance, they may not directly impact resource selection based on cost-effectiveness in AVD deployments. Option D - Correct. Leveraging Azure Cost Calculator for cost estimation helps organizations evaluate the cost-effectiveness of different Azure resource configurations and make informed decisions in AVD deployments. Option E - Incorrect. While Azure Premium Storage may offer high performance, it may not always be the most cost-effective option for all workloads in AVD deployments.

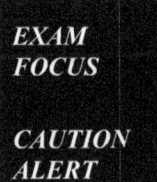

EXAM FOCUS

Right-size VMs based on workload requirements to prevent over-provisioning and save costs. Utilize Azure Spot Instances for non-critical workloads to leverage lower pricing. Always use Azure Cost Calculator to evaluate the cost-effectiveness of different configurations before deploying AVD resources.

CAUTION ALERT

Don't assume Premium Storage is always necessary—it's ideal for high-performance tasks but can inflate costs for workloads not requiring premium speeds. Avoid bypassing cost estimation; Azure Cost Calculator is a critical tool for informed resource selection decisions.

QUESTION 18

Answer - [B, D]

Option B - Azure Active Directory Domain Services: Azure Active Directory Domain Services provides managed domain services, including domain join, group policy, LDAP, and Kerberos/NTLM authentication, for Azure Virtual Desktop environments, enabling secure user authentication and access control.

Option D - Azure AD Conditional Access: Azure AD Conditional Access allows you to apply access controls and policies based on conditions such as user identity, device health, and session risk, enhancing security and simplifying access management tasks for Azure Virtual Desktop users. Option A - Azure Active Directory B2C is a customer identity and access management service and is not designed for managing user authentication and access in Azure Virtual Desktop environments.

Option C - Azure Multi-Factor Authentication provides additional security through multi-factor authentication but does not address access control and management tasks for Azure Virtual Desktop environments.
Option E - Azure Identity Protection offers risk-based identity protection capabilities but is not specific to user authentication and access control in Azure Virtual Desktop environments.

EXAM FOCUS

Implement Azure Active Directory Domain Services for managed authentication and Azure AD Conditional Access to enforce access policies based on user identity and device health. These enhance security and simplify management by centralizing user identity and enforcing access rules across AVD environments.

CAUTION ALERT

Avoid using Azure AD B2C—it's designed for external customer identities, not internal AVD users. While Multi-Factor Authentication (MFA) improves security, it alone doesn't simplify access control or manage policies like Azure AD Conditional Access does for AVD users.

QUESTION 19

Answer - A) Simulate failover scenarios in a non-production environment; B) Involve stakeholders from IT, operations, and compliance teams; C) Document test procedures, outcomes, and areas for improvement

Option A - Correct. Simulating failover scenarios in a non-production environment allows organizations to test recovery procedures without impacting live AVD deployments, ensuring minimal disruption.

Option B - Correct. Involving stakeholders from various teams ensures comprehensive test coverage and alignment with business objectives during disaster recovery tests. Option C - Correct. Documenting test procedures, outcomes, and areas for improvement provides valuable insights for refining the disaster recovery plan and enhancing AVD resilience.

Option D - Incorrect. Analyzing network latency and bandwidth utilization is important but does not directly contribute to the comprehensiveness of disaster recovery tests in AVD environments. Option E - Incorrect. While reviewing historical incident reports can provide insights, it does not substitute for comprehensive disaster recovery testing in AVD environments.

EXAM FOCUS	*Conduct failover simulations in non-production environments to test recovery procedures. Involve stakeholders from IT, operations, and compliance teams to ensure all perspectives are addressed. Document procedures, outcomes, and improvements to strengthen the disaster recovery plan and prepare for real-world scenarios.*
CAUTION ALERT	*Avoid skipping documentation—it's essential for identifying gaps and improving processes. Don't limit tests to IT teams; failure to include compliance and operations stakeholders can result in incomplete assessments and overlooked regulatory or operational considerations.*

QUESTION 20

Answer - A) Link AVD to Azure Log Analytics workspace

Option A - Correct: Linking AVD to an Azure Log Analytics workspace is essential for leveraging its data query and incident response features. Option B - Incorrect: Event Hub is used for event ingestion and distribution, not directly for AVD monitoring integration. Option C - Incorrect: API Management is unrelated to direct monitoring integration.

Option D - Incorrect: Service Health alerts are for Azure service incidents, not specific to AVD or Log Analytics integration. Option E - Incorrect: Event Grid deals with event routing, which is not required for direct AVD and Log Analytics integration.

EXAM FOCUS	*Link AVD to an Azure Log Analytics workspace to integrate telemetry data with advanced query and incident response capabilities. This enables centralized monitoring, detailed analysis, and seamless incident management across your AVD deployment, ensuring performance and operational efficiency.*
CAUTION ALERT	*Don't assume Event Hub or Event Grid are required—they focus on event distribution and routing, not log integration. Avoid relying on Service Health alerts for AVD-specific monitoring; they address broader Azure service incidents, not AVD telemetry insights.*

QUESTION 21

Answer - C,E

Option C - Azure Active Directory Conditional Access policies allow you to enforce multi-factor authentication (MFA) for user logins, enhancing security by requiring additional verification steps beyond username and password authentication. By configuring Conditional Access policies, you can enforce MFA based on specific conditions and user contexts, ensuring secure access to Azure Virtual Desktop resources.

Option E - Azure Multi-Factor Authentication (MFA) adds an additional layer of security by requiring users to provide two or more forms of authentication before accessing resources. Enabling Azure MFA ensures that user logins to Azure Virtual Desktop are protected with an additional verification step, strengthening authentication security.

EXAM FOCUS	*You should combine Conditional Access policies with Azure Multi-Factor Authentication (MFA) to enforce robust authentication. Conditional Access applies rules based on risk levels and locations, while MFA adds a secondary verification layer. This ensures only verified users access AVD securely. Test your configurations in a pilot environment before full deployment.*
CAUTION ALERT	*Avoid confusing Conditional Access with MFA itself—they complement each other but serve different purposes. Don't rely on password-only authentication as it exposes your AVD to credential theft. Stay alert*

to configure rules for trusted locations and device compliance.

QUESTION 22

Answer - A) Identify existing roles and permissions for mapping to RBAC roles; C) Pilot RBAC implementation in a test environment before full deployment; D) Communicate changes to users and provide training on new access management processes

Option A - Correct. Identifying existing roles and permissions helps in mapping them to RBAC roles, ensuring a smooth transition without disrupting user access. Option C - Correct. Piloting RBAC implementation in a test environment allows for identifying potential issues and fine-tuning the implementation before full deployment. Option D - Correct. Communicating changes to users and providing training on new access management processes helps in ensuring user awareness and adoption of RBAC.

Option B - Incorrect. While conducting a comprehensive access review is important, it is not specifically a strategy for migrating to RBAC in existing AVD setups. Option E - Incorrect. While monitoring RBAC implementation is essential, it is not specifically a strategy for migrating to RBAC in existing AVD setups.

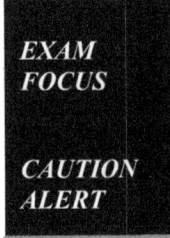

EXAM FOCUS
Make sure to map existing permissions to Azure RBAC roles carefully to avoid unnecessary disruptions. You should test RBAC implementations in a staging environment before applying them in production. Communicating changes and providing training ensures users understand new processes, reducing resistance and confusion.

CAUTION ALERT
Stay clear of assuming RBAC roles directly match existing access control lists (ACLs)—they differ in scope and structure. Avoid rushing the transition without testing, as it could lead to misconfigured permissions and accidental access disruptions.

QUESTION 23

Answer - A) Configure Azure AD to federate authentication requests with the third-party MFA provider; B) Install and configure the third-party MFA agent on AVD session hosts; E) Establish trust relationships between Azure AD and the third-party MFA provider

Option A - Correct. Configuring Azure AD to federate authentication requests with the third-party MFA provider enables seamless integration for AVD environments. Option B - Correct. Installing and configuring the third-party MFA agent on AVD session hosts ensures that MFA is enforced for user authentication.

Option C - Incorrect. While Azure AD Application Proxy provides secure remote access, it is not specifically related to integrating third-party MFA solutions with AVD environments. Option D - Incorrect. While conditional access controls are important for enforcing MFA requirements, they are not directly related to integrating third-party MFA solutions with Azure AD.

Option E - Correct. Establishing trust relationships between Azure AD and the third-party MFA provider is essential for secure authentication in AVD environments.

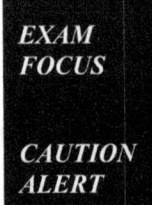

EXAM FOCUS
You need to establish trust relationships between Azure AD and third-party MFA providers to enable secure federated authentication. Installing the provider's agent on AVD session hosts ensures MFA policies are enforced during user authentication. Federation simplifies management across hybrid environments and enhances security seamlessly.

CAUTION ALERT
Don't confuse third-party MFA with Azure MFA—they integrate differently. Stay alert to configure authentication policies correctly in Azure AD to avoid gaps. Avoid overlooking compatibility requirements between third-party MFA solutions and your AVD environment.

QUESTION 24

Answer - A, D, E

A) Correct - Increasing CPU and RAM allocations is crucial for handling resource-intensive development applications.
B) Incorrect - Persistent desktops are more about user experience and data retention, not specifically enhancing performance for resource-intensive tasks.

C) Incorrect - FSLogix app masking is used for managing application visibility, not directly enhancing performance for resource-intensive usage. D) Correct - Auto-scaling ensures that resources are dynamically adjusted to meet the needs of the development team as they use intensive applications. E) Correct - Allocating additional storage for user profiles can improve performance, especially when dealing with large development projects.

EXAM FOCUS	*Always remember to increase CPU, RAM, and storage allocations for development teams using resource-intensive applications. Implement auto-scaling to dynamically adjust resources based on demand, ensuring performance and cost-efficiency. Align these optimizations with developers' needs for a seamless and productive experience.*
CAUTION ALERT	*Avoid enabling persistent desktops unless absolutely necessary—they increase management overhead and cost. Stay cautioned about over-provisioning resources without monitoring usage, as this could lead to unnecessary expenses and wasted resources.*

QUESTION 25

Answer - A) Configuration is correct

Option A - Correct: The JSON snippet correctly assigns an NSG to a subnet, which is a fundamental part of creating effective network segmentation.

Option B - Incorrect: The address prefix "10.0.0.0/24" is typical for subnetting and appropriate depending on the network design. Option C - Incorrect: The NSG ID is correctly formatted and points to a valid resource. Option D - Incorrect: The type "Microsoft.Network/virtualNetworks/subnets" is correct for defining subnets in ARM templates. Option E - Incorrect: The JSON structure is properly formatted for defining properties of a subnet within an ARM template.

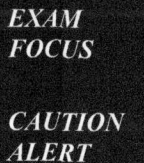

EXAM FOCUS	*Ensure network security by assigning Network Security Groups (NSGs) to subnets as demonstrated in the ARM template. Use appropriate addressPrefix values for subnet ranges based on your IP planning. NSGs provide traffic filtering at the subnet level, enforcing security best practices in AVD environments.*
CAUTION ALERT	*Don't confuse subnet address ranges (e.g., /24) with default configurations—they must be carefully planned for scalability and security. Stay clear of misformatted NSG IDs or JSON structures; validate templates before deployment to avoid deployment failures.*

QUESTION 26

Answer - A) Cloud-delivered protection for real-time malware detection; B) Attack surface reduction rules to mitigate exploit techniques and vulnerabilities; D) Network protection to prevent outbound connections to malicious domains

Option A - Correct. Cloud-delivered protection provides real-time malware detection and protection for AVD session hosts. Option B - Correct. Attack surface reduction rules help mitigate exploit techniques and vulnerabilities on AVD session hosts, enhancing security.

Option D - Correct. Network protection helps prevent AVD session hosts from making outbound connections to known malicious domains, reducing the risk of compromise. Option C - Incorrect. While controlled folder access is a valuable security feature, it is not specifically mentioned in the context of advanced threat protection settings for AVD as described in the question.

Option E - Incorrect. While exploit protection is important, it is not directly related to the advanced threat protection settings available for AVD as described in the question.

EXAM FOCUS	*You need to enable cloud-delivered protection for real-time malware detection and attack surface reduction rules to mitigate vulnerabilities. Network protection blocks outbound traffic to malicious domains, reducing exposure to threats. Use these configurations together for comprehensive advanced threat protection in AVD environments.*
CAUTION ALERT	*Stay cautioned about relying solely on one protection layer; advanced threats require a multi-faceted approach. Avoid assuming controlled folder access replaces full endpoint protection; both are needed to safeguard against diverse cyber threats in AVD environments.*

QUESTION 27

Answer - A, C, E

A) Correct - Auditing and logging enable monitoring activities which can help identify instances of cyberbullying.
B) Incorrect - Defender for Endpoint is critical for cyber threat detection but does not specifically address COPPA compliance or the broader context of cyberbullying.
C) Correct - DLP policies help protect sensitive student information, ensuring compliance with privacy laws like COPPA.
D) Incorrect - Legal hold and eDiscovery are important for compliance and legal investigations but do not directly contribute to the prevention of cyberbullying or privacy protection.
E) Correct - User behavior analytics can detect anomalous behavior potentially related to cyberbullying, thus enhancing student protection.

EXAM FOCUS	*Make sure to enable auditing and logging to monitor activities for identifying cyberbullying. Implement DLP policies to protect sensitive student data and ensure compliance with laws like COPPA. Use user behavior analytics to detect and respond to patterns indicative of harmful activities or data misuse.*
CAUTION ALERT	*Avoid neglecting comprehensive monitoring—missing activity logs can hinder detection efforts. Don't assume Defender for Endpoint alone ensures compliance with COPPA; it focuses on threat protection, not behavior monitoring or regulatory alignment.*

QUESTION 28

Answer - A) Define trusted and untrusted network locations based on IP address ranges; B) Configure conditional access policies to allow access only from trusted network locations; C) Implement Azure Firewall to enforce network-level security policies

Option A - Correct. Defining trusted and untrusted network locations based on IP address ranges provides the basis for configuring Conditional Access policies to allow or restrict access accordingly. Option B - Correct. Configuring conditional access policies to allow access only from trusted network locations enhances security by restricting access from untrusted networks.

Option C - Correct. Implementing Azure Firewall helps enforce network-level security policies, including restricting access based on network conditions, enhancing security for AVD environments. Option D - Incorrect. While enabling VPN access for users connecting from untrusted networks can enhance security, it is not directly related to implementing Conditional Access based on network conditions. Option E - Incorrect. While monitoring network traffic and access patterns is important for detecting anomalous behavior, it is not directly related to implementing Conditional Access based on network conditions.

EXAM FOCUS	*You should define trusted networks using IP ranges in Conditional Access policies. Pair this with Azure Firewall to enforce network-level security. Restricting access to trusted networks minimizes exposure to risks, enhancing the security of AVD sessions without affecting legitimate connections.*
CAUTION ALERT	*Stay clear of enabling untrusted network access without VPNs or additional controls—this undermines the intent of Conditional Access. Don't rely solely on traffic monitoring for security—it's reactive, not*

preventive, compared to proactive network access controls.

QUESTION 29

Answer - A) Review security baselines and group policies to align with evolving compliance requirements and industry standards; B) Monitor security logs and audit trails for anomalous activities or unauthorized access attempts; C) Evaluate and update antivirus definitions and threat intelligence feeds to stay ahead of emerging threats

Option A - Correct. Reviewing security baselines and group policies ensures ongoing compliance and alignment with evolving security standards and requirements. Option B - Correct. Monitoring security logs and audit trails helps detect and respond to suspicious activities or security breaches in a timely manner.

Option C - Correct. Evaluating and updating antivirus definitions and threat intelligence feeds ensures that session hosts are protected against emerging threats and malware. Option D - Incorrect. While implementing just-in-time (JIT) access controls is important, it may not be directly related to periodic reviews of security configurations for session hosts.

Option E - Incorrect. While vulnerability assessments and penetration testing are important, they may not be conducted as part of routine security configuration reviews.

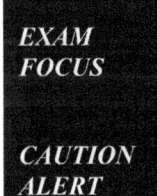

EXAM FOCUS	*Always evaluate antivirus definitions and update threat intelligence feeds regularly to counter emerging threats. Reviewing group policies and baselines ensures alignment with updated compliance standards. Monitoring logs and audit trails helps detect anomalies, enabling quick responses to security incidents in AVD environments.*
CAUTION ALERT	*Avoid assuming JIT controls replace comprehensive security reviews—they are a complementary measure. Stay alert for misconfigurations in group policies or outdated antivirus signatures—they are common entry points for attackers targeting AVD deployments.*

QUESTION 30

Answer - A) Correctly configures security alerts

Option A - Correct: The script sets an alert for an essential security metric, appropriate for monitoring failed login attempts. Option B - Incorrect: "FailedLogins > 5" is a relevant and actionable condition for security alerts.

Option C - Incorrect: While including email notifications is best practice, the scenario does not provide details on the action group's configuration. Option D - Incorrect: The alert name is descriptive and aligns with its function.

Option E - Incorrect: The description is sufficient for understanding the alert's purpose; further details can be adjusted based on specific administrative needs.

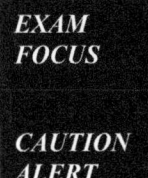

EXAM FOCUS	*Keep in mind to configure alerts for critical security metrics like failed logins to proactively detect potential breaches. Linking alerts to action groups ensures administrators are notified promptly. Use Azure Monitor's capabilities to define actionable thresholds and detailed alert descriptions for effective incident management.*
CAUTION ALERT	*Don't overlook email notifications in action groups—they are vital for immediate awareness. Stay cautioned against setting vague alert conditions, as they could lead to missed incidents or false positives, impacting the efficiency of your response processes.*

QUESTION 31

Answer - C) Configure FSLogix settings via Azure Policy

Option A - Incorrect. Deduplication may reduce storage costs but isn't directly related to FSLogix or profile management.

Option B - Incorrect. Azure Automation DSC is more suited for configuration drift management, not FSLogix configuration. Option C - Correct. Azure Policy allows centralized and consistent configuration of FSLogix settings, aligning with the requirements. Option D - Incorrect. OneDrive Known Folder Move is unrelated to FSLogix profile management.

Option E - Incorrect. Azure Disk Encryption encrypts disks, not FSLogix profiles.

EXAM FOCUS	*You should configure FSLogix settings using Azure Policy to achieve consistent and centralized management. Policies simplify deployment and maintenance across host pools. Implement encryption for FSLogix profiles to align with security standards and minimize risks to sensitive user data.*
CAUTION ALERT	*Avoid using tools like DSC unless managing configuration drift. Stay clear of assuming deduplication applies directly to FSLogix—it optimizes storage but isn't inherently part of FSLogix management. Encryption at the disk level doesn't secure FSLogix profiles alone.*

QUESTION 32

Answer - A) Utilize Azure Update Management to automate patch deployment for Office Containers, B) Implement a staged rollout strategy for Office application updates across user sessions, E) Enable FSLogix Profile Containers to capture application state before updates.

A) Utilize Azure Update Management to automate patch deployment for Office Containers - Azure Update Management automates patch deployment processes, ensuring timely and efficient updates for Office Containers while minimizing disruptions. B) Implement a staged rollout strategy for Office application updates across user sessions - Staged rollout strategies allow updates to be tested and deployed gradually, reducing the impact on productivity and enabling quick rollback if issues arise.

E) Enable FSLogix Profile Containers to capture application state before updates - FSLogix Profile Containers capture application state, allowing administrators to restore previous configurations in case of update-related issues. C) Configure Office Containers to automatically download and apply updates during off-peak hours - While automating updates may be convenient, it may not align with user productivity or testing requirements. D) Leverage Azure Monitor to track Office application performance post-update - Azure Monitor focuses on monitoring performance rather than managing updates for Office Containers.

EXAM FOCUS	*Make sure to automate updates with Azure Update Management for efficiency and reduce disruption. Implement a staged rollout to identify issues early, minimizing production risks. Use FSLogix Profile Containers to save user states, ensuring seamless rollback if updates disrupt user sessions.*
CAUTION ALERT	*Don't confuse Office Container updates with application-specific processes—they must follow distinct deployment plans. Avoid skipping staging environments as production environments demand validated updates. Stay alert for incomplete rollback setups that may fail during issues.*

QUESTION 33

Answer - B, D, E

A) Incorrect - Azure Information Protection is useful for data classification and protection but not specifically designed for healthcare data compliance or inter-site data exchange.
B) Correct - Azure ExpressRoute ensures private connectivity between sites, facilitating secure and compliant data exchange.

C) Incorrect - Azure Health Data Services provide tools for managing health data but do not directly address HIPAA compliance in the context of AVD. D) Correct - Azure Private Link provides a secure way to access Azure services privately, ensuring data transmitted between services remains off the public internet, crucial for HIPAA compliance.
E) Correct - Azure Key Vault manages encryption keys securely, crucial for maintaining data integrity and compliance with HIPAA.

EXAM FOCUS	Always implement Azure ExpressRoute for private, compliant connectivity between healthcare sites. Combine Azure Private Link and Azure Key Vault for secure, encrypted transmissions and reliable key management to meet HIPAA requirements. These configurations maintain data integrity and resilience.
CAUTION ALERT	Avoid assuming Azure Information Protection alone satisfies HIPAA—it focuses on classification, not transport security. Stay clear of using public internet routes for sensitive healthcare data. Misconfigured key vaults can expose encryption keys, undermining data security.

QUESTION 34

Answer - B) Configure FSLogix Profile Containers to streamline user profile management and reduce the overhead of device redirection operations, D) Utilize Azure Network Watcher to monitor network connectivity and identify bottlenecks affecting device redirection performance.

B) Configure FSLogix Profile Containers to streamline user profile management and reduce the overhead of device redirection operations - FSLogix Profile Containers optimize user profile management by providing a unified profile experience across sessions, reducing the impact of device redirection on performance. D) Utilize Azure Network Watcher to monitor network connectivity and identify bottlenecks affecting device redirection performance - Network Watcher helps identify and address network issues impacting device redirection, ensuring optimal performance for AVD sessions.

A) Implement Azure Bastion for secure RDP access to AVD instances, reducing the need for device redirection over low-bandwidth networks - While Azure Bastion enhances access security, it may not directly address performance impacts associated with device redirection. C) Leverage Azure AD Conditional Access policies to prioritize device redirection traffic based on user roles and session priorities - While Conditional Access policies enhance access control, they may not directly optimize device redirection performance across diverse user scenarios.

E) Deploy GPU-accelerated virtual machines (VMs) to offload device redirection processing and improve overall session performance - While GPU-accelerated VMs enhance performance for certain workloads, they may not directly address performance impacts specific to device redirection operations.

EXAM FOCUS	Consider monitoring network health with Azure Network Watcher to identify bottlenecks affecting device redirection. Use FSLogix Profile Containers to streamline user profiles and reduce redirection delays. These tools optimize performance and enhance user productivity during low-bandwidth operations.
CAUTION ALERT	Avoid enabling device redirection without validating user connectivity—it can increase latency. Stay cautioned about using GPU-accelerated VMs unless required for graphics workloads, as they may not optimize redirection performance. Don't rely solely on access policy changes.

QUESTION 35

Answer - B) Encryption should be set at the printer level

Option A - Incorrect: While encrypting network traffic is beneficial, this command does not specifically secure print jobs.

Option B - Correct: Encryption for print jobs should ideally be configured at the printer or print server level to ensure that the data remains secure from end to end. Option C - Incorrect: Updating the subnet can be part of securing the network, but it does not directly relate to securing print jobs.

Option D - Correct: This command configures general network traffic encryption, not specifically for print jobs. Option E - Incorrect: The flag is used correctly for the command, but the focus should be on printer-specific settings.

EXAM FOCUS	You should prioritize encryption at the printer server level to secure print jobs end-to-end. Configuring encryption for print jobs protects sensitive data during transmission and aligns with network security standards. Verify each printer supports encryption to maintain uniform security.
CAUTION ALERT	Stay clear of relying solely on network traffic encryption—it doesn't ensure end-to-end print job security. Avoid overlooking legacy printers that may not support modern encryption features. Misplaced

configurations at the subnet level won't directly secure print traffic.

QUESTION 36

Answer - A, B, C

A) Correct - Azure Front Door provides efficient global load balancing, essential for managing high traffic loads during peak periods. B) Correct - Azure Application Gateway with WAF secures web transactions, protecting against web vulnerabilities and attacks.

C) Correct - Azure AutoScale dynamically adjusts resources to handle varying loads, ensuring a responsive user experience during high traffic. D) Incorrect - Azure AD B2C is vital for managing customer identities but does not directly contribute to traffic management or transaction security in an AVD setup. E) Incorrect - Azure Sentinel is important for security monitoring but the priority here is managing traffic and ensuring responsiveness and transaction security.

EXAM FOCUS	*Always enable Azure Front Door for effective global load balancing and traffic management. Pair it with Azure Application Gateway and WAF to protect transactions and adjust Azure AutoScale dynamically. This ensures high availability, security, and scalability during peak periods like sales events.*
CAUTION ALERT	*Avoid relying on static configurations during peak loads—they cannot handle spikes effectively. Stay alert for misconfigured scaling rules that lead to resource underutilization or over-commitment. Overlooking web app firewall settings exposes your system to threats.*

QUESTION 37

Answer - B) Restricting access to virtual machines based on user roles and permissions

Restricting access based on user roles and permissions ensures that only authorized users can connect to VMs, preventing unauthorized access to resources.

Option A - Incorrect. While MFA enhances security, it does not directly control access to VMs.
Option C - Incorrect. Data encryption secures data transmission but does not control VM access.
Option D - Incorrect. Network-level firewalls control inbound traffic but do not enforce user access policies.
Option E - Incorrect. Conditional Access policies enforce access controls but are not specific to VM access.

EXAM FOCUS	*You need to implement role-based access control (RBAC) to restrict VM access to authorized users. RBAC prevents unauthorized access by defining granular permissions, ensuring only validated users can start VMs using the Start VM on Connect feature, enhancing overall resource security.*
CAUTION ALERT	*Don't rely solely on MFA for access—it secures authentication but doesn't restrict resource access. Stay alert for gaps in RBAC assignments where roles are overly permissive, as they may inadvertently grant unnecessary privileges.*

QUESTION 38

Answer - A) MSIX App Attach
MSIX App Attach encapsulates applications, ensuring security by preventing unauthorized access to sensitive data and offering enhanced protection compared to other deployment methods.

Option B - PowerShell script execution: PowerShell scripts lack encapsulation, making them less secure than MSIX App Attach. Option C - Azure Marketplace integration: While Azure Marketplace offers various applications, it does not provide the same level of security as MSIX App Attach.

Option D - RDP-based application deployment: RDP-based deployment methods may expose applications to security risks due to the nature of remote access. Option E - MSI deployment: MSI deployment lacks encapsulation, making it less secure than MSIX App Attach.

EXAM FOCUS	Always prioritize MSIX App Attach for secure application deployment. MSIX isolates applications, reduces dependency conflicts, and prevents unauthorized access to sensitive app data. It provides seamless updates and enhanced security compared to traditional deployment methods, especially in AVD environments.
CAUTION ALERT	Avoid using MSI installers for sensitive apps—they lack containerization and don't ensure security. Stay clear of deployment methods like RDP or unmanaged installations, as they introduce vulnerabilities and make updates harder to control or standardize.

QUESTION 39

Answer - A, B, D

A) Correct - Azure Bastion on a dedicated subnet provides secure and seamless access for remote employees.
B) Correct - Azure Scale Sets automatically adjust resources, which is crucial during high demand periods like product launches. C) Incorrect - While Azure Firewall is crucial for network security, it doesn't directly support seamless connectivity or scalability as required in the scenario.

D) Correct - Azure AD with single sign-on enhances user experience by providing seamless access across applications, supporting a hybrid work model. E) Incorrect - Azure Application Gateway focuses on load balancing web traffic, which isn't specified as a requirement for the AVD setup in this scenario.

EXAM FOCUS	Ensure seamless hybrid work by deploying Azure Bastion for secure remote access, Scale Sets for adaptive resource management, and Azure AD SSO to unify access across apps. These configurations enhance connectivity, scalability, and user productivity during hybrid work and product launch scenarios.
CAUTION ALERT	Stay alert for improperly sized scale sets—they may fail to meet scaling demands during peak times. Avoid assuming Azure Firewall addresses hybrid access—it's focused on network filtering and not remote access. Incomplete AD SSO setups can disrupt user authentication flows.

QUESTION 40

Answer - A

Option A - Correct. Enabling multisession is essential and should be specified.
Option B - Incorrect. optimizePerformance is not a valid property here.
Option C - Incorrect. Storage account type is unrelated to OneDrive settings.
Option D - Incorrect. Multisession needs to be enabled.
Option E - Incorrect. "useOneDrive": true is not a valid configuration.

EXAM FOCUS	You need to enable multisession configurations explicitly in the OneDrive setup for a seamless multiuser experience. This ensures profiles are correctly optimized for shared environments. Verify all dependencies like FSLogix and storage performance to avoid user disruptions in Azure Virtual Desktop deployments.
CAUTION ALERT	Avoid assuming OneDrive settings in single-session environments work the same for multisession. Stay clear of mismatched configurations for user profiles, as this can cause data loss or session conflicts. Incorrect storage dependencies can degrade performance or fail during heavy usage.

QUESTION 41

Answer - B

Option A - Incorrect. The parameter -Output "detailed" is not correctly formulated. Option B - Correct. The parameter -DetailLevel "Full" provides a complete report on license activation status across session hosts.

Option C - Incorrect. The cmdlet and parameters are not valid for this purpose. Option D - Incorrect. The cmdlet Get-M365AppStatus does not exist.

Option E - Incorrect. A summary report might not provide the necessary details for license compliance monitoring.

EXAM FOCUS	*You need to use PowerShell cmdlets like Get-M365AppLicenseStatus for license compliance checks. Replace vague parameters like -Output "detailed" with specific ones like -DetailLevel "Full" to retrieve detailed reports. Such precision ensures comprehensive insights for managing license compliance.*
CAUTION ALERT	*Avoid vague parameters that don't yield actionable data. Stay alert for invalid cmdlets like Get-M365AppStatus which do not exist. Ensure scripts are tested for compliance readiness to avoid inaccurate data that can compromise licensing audits.*

QUESTION 42

Answer - A, B, E

A) Correct - 'DynamicVHDAllocation' helps dynamically manage disk space, essential for cost efficiency and scalability in development environments. B) Correct - Ensuring 'Enabled' is set allows FSLogix to function and manage user profiles, crucial for operational efficiency.
C) Incorrect - 'ProfileType' dictates the type of profile but doesn't directly impact scalability or security.
D) Incorrect - 'DiskType' configures the disk usage style but is not a primary concern for the specified requirements.
E) Correct - 'LocalCacheSize' affects the amount of data stored locally, impacting performance and cost-efficiency.

EXAM FOCUS	*Always configure DynamicVHDAllocation in FSLogix for scalable disk management. Set LocalCacheSize to balance performance and cost efficiency. Enable FSLogix Profiles for proper functioning. These settings optimize development environments, particularly for startups requiring flexibility and isolation.*
CAUTION ALERT	*Don't ignore enabling FSLogix Profiles, as skipping this will disable profile management. Avoid setting rigid cache sizes without monitoring usage—over-provisioning can inflate costs while under-provisioning causes latency. Stay clear of misusing disk types for scaling purposes.*

QUESTION 43

Answer - A), B), C), D), E)

Option A - Bandwidth limitations can affect the performance and responsiveness of AVD sessions, especially for bandwidth-intensive tasks such as multimedia streaming or file transfers.

Option B - Latency refers to the delay in data transmission over a network, which can cause session lag and affect user experience in AVD deployments. Option C - Firewall rules determine the accessibility and security of network traffic, affecting the connectivity and availability of AVD sessions. Option D - VPN connections may introduce additional latency and bandwidth constraints, impacting the responsiveness of AVD sessions, particularly for remote users accessing corporate resources.

Option E - Subnet configurations define network segmentation and routing, which can influence the network paths and traffic flow for AVD sessions, potentially affecting session stability and performance.

EXAM FOCUS	*You should evaluate bandwidth, latency, and subnet configurations when troubleshooting AVD network issues. Ensure VPNs don't create bottlenecks, and firewall rules are optimized. These aspects collectively affect session stability and health, directly influencing user experience.*
CAUTION ALERT	*Stay cautioned about overlooking bandwidth as a root cause of lag, especially during peak times. Don't misconfigure subnet routing, as it can fragment traffic flow. Mismanaged firewall rules can inadvertently block essential AVD communication, degrading session performance.*

QUESTION 44

Answer - E) Azure RBAC (Role-Based Access Control)

Option E - Azure RBAC provides granular access control and audit capabilities, allowing administrators to define permissions for managing diagnostic logs in AVD environments. Option A - Azure Key Vault is used for key management and secrets storage, not for managing diagnostic logs.

Option B - Azure Monitor Alerts focus on alerting, not access control for diagnostic logs. Option C - Azure Security Center offers security posture management but does not provide granular access control for diagnostic logs. Option D - Azure AD DS is a managed domain service and not directly related to managing diagnostic logs.

EXAM FOCUS	*Make sure to use Azure RBAC for fine-grained access control over diagnostic logs. Role assignments should be scoped to avoid granting excessive permissions. Implement encryption and audit logs to ensure secure management of sensitive diagnostic data.*
CAUTION ALERT	*Avoid granting broad permissions in RBAC—it increases the risk of unauthorized access. Stay clear of assuming Azure Monitor Alerts can manage permissions; they only provide notifications. Ensure encryption settings are applied consistently to protect diagnostic data.*

QUESTION 45

Answer - E

Option A - Incorrect. The cmdlet and parameters are not valid for rolling back a VM in Azure.
Option B - Incorrect. Update-AzVmImage does not provide functionality for rollback.
Option C - Incorrect. -Redeploy $true is used for redeploying the same instance but doesn't roll back any updates.
Option D - Incorrect. -Confirm:$false is a valid parameter but irrelevant without the correct base command.
Option E - Correct. Using az vm redeploy forces the redeployment of the session host, which can help mitigate issues by moving VMs to a new node, but it does not roll back updates per se. For actual rollback, backup and restore strategies should be in place.

EXAM FOCUS	*Keep in mind that rollback for VM updates requires preconfigured backup strategies. The command az vm redeploy mitigates issues by moving VMs but doesn't revert updates. Use VM snapshots or backup solutions to restore prior states effectively, particularly in AVD environments where uptime is critical.*
CAUTION ALERT	*Don't rely on redeploy commands to roll back updates; they only reposition VM instances. Avoid skipping backup preparations, as recovery becomes impossible without prior snapshots or images. Misinterpreting rollback tools can delay resolution in high-pressure situations.*

QUESTION 46

Answer - A) Implementing Quality of Service (QoS) policies

Option A - Implementing Quality of Service (QoS) policies allows administrators to prioritize network traffic based on application requirements, ensuring optimal performance for critical workloads such as AVD. QoS policies help mitigate network congestion and prioritize bandwidth allocation, improving user experience in AVD environments.

Option B - Configuring Azure Bastion enhances remote access security but may not directly impact network performance. Option C - Optimizing Virtual Network Gateway settings is important but may not address specific network performance issues in AVD environments. Option D - Enabling Webrtc for Microsoft Teams optimization focuses on collaboration tools but may not directly impact overall network performance. Option E - Implementing Azure Firewall enhances network security but may not directly improve network performance in AVD environments.

EXAM FOCUS	*Always implement Quality of Service (QoS) policies to prioritize network traffic for critical AVD workloads. QoS ensures bandwidth allocation is optimized, improving user experience during high-demand periods. Combine this with monitoring tools to adjust configurations dynamically as usage patterns evolve.*
CAUTION ALERT	*Avoid assuming QoS works automatically without thorough configuration. Misconfigured policies can deprioritize critical workloads. Stay alert to WebRTC settings for apps like Teams—they complement, but do not replace, broader network performance strategies.*

QUESTION 47

Answer - B) Using Azure Policies to enforce cost-saving measures
C) Enabling autoscaling based on user demand
D) Leveraging Azure Reserved Instances for VMs

B) Using Azure Policies to enforce cost-saving measures - Azure Policies can enforce resource tagging, shutdown schedules, and other cost-saving measures. C) Enabling autoscaling based on user demand - Autoscaling ensures resources are dynamically adjusted to meet demand, minimizing unnecessary costs.

D) Leveraging Azure Reserved Instances for VMs - Reserved Instances offer significant discounts for VM usage, providing cost savings. A, E) While proactive monitoring and network QoS policies are important for overall AVD performance, they are not directly related to cost optimization.

EXAM FOCUS	*You need to enable autoscaling to align resource allocation with user demand. Utilize Azure Policies for shutdown schedules and cost governance. Leverage Azure Reserved Instances for predictable workloads, as they provide significant cost savings for consistent usage scenarios like AVD session hosts.*
CAUTION ALERT	*Don't overlook autoscaling rules, as static configurations can inflate costs during off-peak times. Stay clear of using Reserved Instances for highly variable workloads—they work best for predictable usage patterns. Inconsistent policy enforcement leads to inefficiencies.*

QUESTION 48

Answer - A, B, C

A) Correct - Windows 10 Enterprise multi-session can handle high graphic loads and supports multiple users.
B) Correct - Windows 11 Enterprise offers the latest security and performance optimizations for high-end graphics applications. C) Correct - Windows Server 2022 provides enhanced security features and performance improvements suitable for high-demand applications.

D) Incorrect - Windows Server 2016, while stable, lacks the modern graphical performance and security features needed. E) Incorrect - Windows 7 is unsupported and insecure for a professional digital marketing environment.

EXAM FOCUS	*Always prioritize Windows 10/11 Enterprise multi-session for AVD environments requiring high graphics performance. Combine it with Windows Server 2022 for robust security and enhanced features. These systems offer the scalability and support needed for professional and resource-intensive workloads.*
CAUTION ALERT	*Avoid using outdated OS versions like Windows 7—they are unsupported and expose environments to security risks. Stay alert for misconfigurations in multi-session environments, which can degrade performance. Incorrect licensing can invalidate deployments.*

QUESTION 49

Answer - B) Leveraging Azure Reservations for predictable pricing and cost savings
C) Utilizing Azure Hybrid Benefit to reduce licensing costs for on-premises workloads

B) Leveraging Azure Reservations for predictable pricing and cost savings - Azure Reservations offer discounted pricing for reserved instances, providing cost savings and predictability for AVD licensing. C) Utilizing Azure Hybrid Benefit to reduce licensing costs for on-premises workloads - Azure Hybrid Benefit allows organizations to apply existing Windows Server licenses to AVD deployments, reducing licensing costs. A, D, E) While user-based licensing, license reassignment policies, and Azure Advisor recommendations are important considerations for license optimization, they are not specifically focused on achieving cost savings for AVD deployments.

EXAM FOCUS	*Make use of Azure Hybrid Benefit to reduce costs by leveraging existing licenses. Pair this with Azure Reservations for predictable pricing and significant savings over extended periods. These strategies maximize cost efficiency while ensuring compliance in Azure Virtual Desktop environments.*

| CAUTION ALERT | Stay cautioned about reallocating licenses without monitoring usage, as it may violate compliance. Avoid neglecting Azure Advisor recommendations for optimization opportunities—they can provide actionable insights for additional cost savings. Mismanaged license policies increase audit risks. |

QUESTION 50

Answer - A) Leveraging Azure Monitor for querying and visualizing log data with customizable dashboards
B) Utilizing Azure Log Analytics for advanced log query and analysis capabilities
C) Implementing Azure Sentinel for security-focused log analysis and threat detection

A) Leveraging Azure Monitor for querying and visualizing log data with customizable dashboards - Azure Monitor provides robust querying and visualization capabilities for log data, enabling proactive monitoring and troubleshooting with customizable dashboards.

B) Utilizing Azure Log Analytics for advanced log query and analysis capabilities - Azure Log Analytics offers advanced log query and analysis capabilities, facilitating deep insights into AVD environment performance and health.

C) Implementing Azure Sentinel for security-focused log analysis and threat detection - Azure Sentinel specializes in security-focused log analysis and threat detection, helping organizations identify and respond to security incidents effectively.

D, E) While Azure Data Explorer and Microsoft Defender for Cloud offer valuable capabilities, they are not specifically designed for log analysis in AVD.

| EXAM FOCUS | Utilize Azure Monitor for customizable dashboards, Log Analytics for detailed analysis, and Azure Sentinel for security-specific insights. These tools together provide a comprehensive approach to identifying, analyzing, and resolving issues within Azure Virtual Desktop environments. |
| CAUTION ALERT | Don't rely solely on one tool like Azure Monitor for deep analysis—combine it with Log Analytics for granular insights. Avoid assuming security tools like Microsoft Defender suffice for all log-related tasks. Use Azure Sentinel for proactive threat detection, not just reactive responses. |

PRACTICE TEST 9 - QUESTIONS ONLY

QUESTION 1

Troubleshooting connectivity issues in AVD deployments is crucial for your role, focusing on scenarios where users experience intermittent access problems. You must:
- Analyze network traffic patterns.
- Identify potential configuration errors.
- Optimize network performance for consistent connectivity.

Which Azure CLI command would you use to monitor and diagnose these network issues?

```
A) az network watcher test-connectivity
B) az network vnet list
C) az network watcher flow-log configure
D) az network watcher troubleshooting start
E) az network watcher packet-capture create
```

QUESTION 2

You need to monitor Quality of Service (QoS) performance and RDP efficiency in your Azure Virtual Desktop (AVD) environment. The HR department recently migrated to AVD for remote work, relying on critical HR management applications. However, ensuring consistent performance and identifying potential bottlenecks pose challenges. How would you effectively monitor QoS performance and RDP efficiency to ensure a seamless experience for the HR department?

A) Utilize Azure Monitor with custom log queries for QoS metrics
B) Implement Azure Network Watcher with packet capture for RDP analysis
C) Deploy Microsoft Defender for Cloud for network performance monitoring
D) Configure Azure Application Gateway for load balancing AVD sessions
E) Monitor AVD client devices using Microsoft Endpoint Manager

QUESTION 3

- You are tasked with optimizing network performance in an Azure Virtual Desktop (AVD) environment to ensure seamless user experience.
- You need to identify and analyze network traffic patterns between client devices and session hosts.
- Your task involves selecting the appropriate Log Analytics table to monitor network traffic.

Which table should you query to access detailed logs of network traffic between client devices and session hosts, including latency and bandwidth usage?

```
A) WVDNetworkTrafficLogs
B) WVDConnections
C) WVDAuditLogs
D) WVDSessionEvent
E) WVDServiceHealth
```

QUESTION 4

Your organization needs to estimate storage needs for Azure Virtual Desktop (AVD) user data based on user and application data volumes. As the IT specialist, you must accurately assess the storage requirements to provision adequate resources for AVD deployments. What factors should you consider when estimating storage needs for AVD user data? Select CORRECT answers that apply.

A) User profile sizes and growth projections

B) Application installation and data caching requirements
C) Temporary data storage and disk caching mechanisms
D) Data deduplication and compression techniques
E) Forecasted user concurrency and session persistence

QUESTION 5

You are implementing data replication strategies for Azure file shares used in AVD. Which configuration ensures data availability and disaster recovery? Evaluate this JSON snippet.

```json
{
  "type": "Microsoft.Storage/storageAccounts",
  "sku": { "name": "Standard_GRS" },
  "properties": { "accessTier": "Hot" }
}
```

A) SKU should be Standard_LRS
B) Access tier should be Cool
C) SKU and properties are configured correctly
D) Change access tier to Archive
E) Include additional redundancy options

QUESTION 6

You are responsible for managing session hosts in an Azure Virtual Desktop (AVD) environment to optimize costs. The solution must meet the following requirements:
- Automatically start session hosts at 8:00 AM and shut them down at 6:00 PM.
- Only be in effect Monday to Friday.
- Minimize manual intervention and administrative effort.
Which Azure service should you leverage to achieve this? Select TWO.

A) Azure Monitor Alerts
B) Azure Automation with Azure Functions
C) Azure Resource Manager templates
D) Azure Automation with Azure Runbooks
E) Azure Virtual Machine Scale Sets

QUESTION 7

Your organization has unique custom scenarios that require tailored licensing needs for Azure Virtual Desktop (AVD) deployments. As the Azure architect, you need to address these specific requirements. What considerations should you take into account? Select THREE.

A) Hybrid Cloud Environments and Multi-Cloud Deployments
B) Non-Profit or Educational Institution Discounts and Special Offers
C) Industry-Specific Regulations and Compliance Requirements
D) Seasonal or Temporary Workforce Flexibility and Scalability
E) Legacy Application Support and Compatibility Challenges

QUESTION 8

Your organization is assessing the impact of different application types on performance requirements for Azure Virtual Desktop (AVD) deployments. As the Azure architect, you need to consider various factors. What factors should you evaluate? Select THREE.

A) Resource Intensiveness and Workload Patterns
B) Application Dependencies and Interactions
C) User Access Patterns and Session Characteristics
D) Compatibility with AVD Configuration and Environment
E) Security Vulnerabilities and Patching Requirements

QUESTION 9

You are implementing autoscale for host pools in an Azure Virtual Desktop (AVD) environment to optimize resource utilization. Consider the following considerations:
- Scale resources based on user demand to ensure responsiveness.
- Minimize costs by deallocating idle resources during off-peak hours.
- Ensure seamless user experience by avoiding scaling actions during active sessions.
Which actions should you take to address these considerations? Select THREE.

A) Configure autoscale rules based on CPU and memory utilization.
B) Set up recurring scaling events to deallocate resources during off-peak hours.
C) Implement logic to prevent scaling actions during active user sessions.
D) Utilize Azure Monitor to monitor user activity and trigger scaling actions.
E) Configure alerts for unexpected resource usage patterns.

QUESTION 10

During a review, you notice that session hosts are inconsistently applying compliance policies. Which Bicep script ensures all hosts apply a standard set of policies for security compliance?
bicep
resource sessionHost 'Microsoft.DesktopVirtualization/applicationGroups@2020-11-10-preview' = { name: 'ComplianceHosts' }

A) Resource type is incorrect
B) API version is outdated
C) Correct configuration
D) Name is inappropriate
E) Missing properties for policy application

QUESTION 11

Your organization is experiencing challenges with manual golden image creation for Azure Virtual Desktop (AVD), leading to delays in deployment and inconsistencies across session hosts. As the Azure administrator, you need to identify common pitfalls in manual image creation and how to avoid them. What are common pitfalls in manual image creation, and how can they be avoided? Select THREE.

A) Incomplete Application Installation and Configuration
B) Failure to Sysprep and Generalize the Image Properly
C) Lack of Version Control and Documentation
D) Overly Large Image Size and Complexity
E) Dependency on Manual Image Capture and Deployment Processes

QUESTION 12

You are planning a disaster recovery strategy for an Azure Virtual Desktop (AVD) infrastructure deployed across multiple Azure regions. Consider the following requirements:
- Ensure automatic failover of AVD host pools to a secondary region in case of a primary region outage.

- Minimize data loss and downtime during failover operations.

Which combination of Azure services should you implement to meet these requirements? Select TWO.

A) Azure Monitor
B) Azure Traffic Manager
C) Azure Site Recovery
D) Azure Load Balancer
E) Azure Backup

QUESTION 13

Your organization emphasizes testing and validation of updates before deployment to ensure system stability and user satisfaction in Azure Virtual Desktop (AVD) environments. As the Azure specialist, you need to assess strategies for testing and validation of updates. Which of the following strategies can help in testing and validation of updates before deployment in AVD environments? Select THREE.

A) Implementing Canary Deployments
B) Utilizing Blue-Green Deployment Patterns
C) Conducting A/B Testing with Pilot Users
D) Employing Pre-Production Environment Mirroring
E) Enforcing Change Management Approval Workflows

QUESTION 14

Your organization is planning to scale up its Azure Virtual Desktop (AVD) environment and ensure accessibility of images for deployment across multiple regions. As the Azure specialist, you need to consider scalability and accessibility considerations for image storage. What scalability and accessibility considerations should be taken into account for image storage in AVD deployments? Select THREE.

A) Replicate Images Across Azure Regions for Redundancy
B) Utilize Content Delivery Networks (CDNs) for Image Distribution
C) Implement Azure Availability Zones for High Availability
D) Leverage Azure ExpressRoute for Low-Latency Image Access
E) Ensure Compatibility with Azure Resiliency Services for Disaster Recovery

QUESTION 15

For enhanced security, you need to implement network security groups (NSGs) with strict rules for AVD. What is the best practice when creating NSGs using Azure CLI?

```bash
az network nsg create --resource-group MySecurityGroup --name MyNsg --location EastUS
```

A) Command is complete
B) Should specify default security rules
C) Missing parameters for rules
D) NSG location should match AVD deployment
E) Command lacks tags for management

QUESTION 16

Regular audits and compliance reports are essential for maintaining regulatory compliance and ensuring adherence to industry standards in Azure Virtual Desktop (AVD) deployments. As the Azure specialist, you need to implement effective audit and compliance reporting mechanisms. What options are available for conducting regular audits and compliance reports for AVD? Select THREE.

A) Azure Monitor for Log Analytics and Audit Logging
B) Azure Policy for Policy Enforcement and Compliance Assessment
C) Azure Security Center for Compliance Score Monitoring and Reporting
D) Microsoft 365 Compliance Center for Data Governance and Compliance Insights
E) Azure Sentinel for Security Incident Detection and Response

QUESTION 17

Your organization is looking to optimize costs in its Azure Virtual Desktop (AVD) deployment by leveraging reserved instances and spot pricing. However, you need to understand the implementation details to maximize cost savings. How can you effectively implement reserved instances and spot pricing in AVD deployments? Select TWO.

A) Purchase Reserved Instances for Fixed-Term Workloads with Predictable Usage
B) Utilize Azure Spot Instances for Temporary Workloads with Flexible Resource Requirements
C) Combine Reserved Instances with Pay-As-You-Go Pricing for Cost Flexibility
D) Implement Azure Cost Management Policies for Reserved Instance Optimization
E) Leverage Spot Instance Interruption Notices for Graceful Shutdowns

QUESTION 18

You are designing an Azure Virtual Desktop (AVD) infrastructure and need to implement a solution for centralized management and monitoring of session host performance and resource utilization. Considering this requirement, what approach should you take to achieve effective management and monitoring?
- Ensure comprehensive visibility into session host performance metrics
- Simplify management tasks for administrative efficiency
- Proactively identify and address performance bottlenecks Select TWO.

A) Azure Monitor
B) Azure Log Analytics
C) Azure Application Insights
D) Azure Advisor
E) Azure Security Center

QUESTION 19

Your organization is exploring Azure services to support disaster recovery initiatives for Azure Virtual Desktop (AVD) environments. The focus is on leveraging native Azure capabilities to enhance resilience and minimize recovery time objectives (RTO) and recovery point objectives (RPO). Which Azure services would you recommend integrating into the disaster recovery plan for AVD deployments? Select TWO.

A) Azure Blob Storage for storing backup data
B) Azure Automation for orchestrating recovery workflows
C) Azure Monitor for proactive monitoring and alerting
D) Azure ExpressRoute for private connectivity and enhanced network reliability
E) Azure Function Apps for serverless event-driven logic

QUESTION 20

Proactive maintenance and issue resolution are key to maintaining AVD service health. You plan to use Azure Automation together with Azure Monitor alerts to automate response actions for common AVD issues like service downtimes or performance degradation. Which PowerShell script would effectively set up an automated response to a specific performance alert in Azure Monitor?

A) Create an automation rule in Azure Monitor
B) Write a runbook to restart services on alert

C) Use Set-AzMetricAlertRule
D) Configure New-AzAlertRule
E) Implement Manage-AzAutomation

QUESTION 21

You are configuring Azure Virtual Desktop for a company that requires centralized management of user identities and access control. You need to implement a solution that integrates with Azure Active Directory (Azure AD) to provide identity authentication and authorization for users. Which feature should you use for this purpose? Select TWO.

A) Azure AD Domain Services
B) Azure Active Directory B2C
C) Azure Active Directory Connect
D) Azure Active Directory Identity Protection
E) Azure Active Directory Privileged Identity Management (PIM)

QUESTION 22

Your organization is concerned about auditing and compliance considerations associated with role-based access control (RBAC) in Azure Virtual Desktop (AVD) environments. The focus is on ensuring adherence to regulatory requirements and industry standards while implementing RBAC. What auditing and compliance considerations should be taken into account with RBAC in Azure Virtual Desktop (AVD) environments? Select THREE.

A) Regularly audit role assignments and permissions for compliance
B) Implement access reviews to ensure alignment with regulatory requirements
C) Enforce separation of duties to prevent conflicts of interest
D) Retain audit logs for a specified period to meet regulatory retention requirements
E) Conduct periodic security assessments to identify vulnerabilities and gaps

QUESTION 23

Your organization has implemented multi-factor authentication (MFA) for Azure Virtual Desktop (AVD) to enhance security, but users are experiencing challenges with the new authentication process. The focus is on addressing user training and support challenges associated with MFA in AVD environments effectively. How can user training and support challenges with multi-factor authentication (MFA) in Azure Virtual Desktop (AVD) environments be addressed? Select THREE.

A) Provide comprehensive training materials and resources on MFA usage and best practices
B) Offer hands-on workshops or webinars to demonstrate MFA setup and usage for AVD connections
C) Establish a dedicated helpdesk or support team to assist users with MFA-related issues
D) Implement user feedback mechanisms to gather insights and improve the MFA user experience
E) Enable self-service options for users to manage their MFA settings and preferences

QUESTION 24

For an organization relying heavily on AVD for their remote workforce, which measures should be implemented to ensure a robust disaster recovery plan? Select THREE.

A) Deploy session hosts across multiple Azure regions.
B) Regular backup of user data and applications.
C) Configure Azure Site Recovery for AVD.
D) Utilize Azure Backup for session hosts.
E) Periodically test failover to a secondary region.

QUESTION 25

To ensure proactive network monitoring in your AVD environment, you need to set up an alert rule using Azure Monitor. This PowerShell script is intended to create an alert when network traffic exceeds a specified threshold. Determine if the script meets the requirements.

```powershell
New-AzMetricAlertRuleV2 -Name "HighNetworkTraffic" -WindowSize "PT5M" -Frequency "PT1M" -Condition "TotalRequests > 1000" -TargetResourceId "/subscriptions/subId/resourceGroups/AVDResources/providers/Microsoft.Network/networkInterfaces/AVDVMNic"
```

A) Correct as is
B) WindowSize should be increased
C) Condition syntax is incorrect
D) Frequency should be less frequent
E) TargetResourceId should point to a virtual network

QUESTION 26

Your organization has implemented Windows Threat Protection features for Azure Virtual Desktop (AVD) and wants to evaluate the effectiveness of threat protection measures. The focus is on understanding how to assess the effectiveness of threat protection. How can the effectiveness of threat protection for AVD be evaluated? Select TWO.

A) Review security reports and analytics provided by Windows Defender Security Center
B) Conduct penetration testing and vulnerability assessments on AVD session hosts to identify security gaps
C) Monitor security alerts and events generated by Windows Defender Antivirus and other security features
D) Perform regular audits and compliance checks to ensure adherence to security policies and configurations
E) Collect and analyze threat intelligence data from various sources to identify emerging threats and trends

QUESTION 27

For a financial institution leveraging AVD, ensuring PCI DSS compliance, protecting against data breaches, and enabling secure remote work are priorities. Which security measures should you prioritize? Select THREE.

A) Implement network segmentation with Azure Virtual Network.
B) Deploy tokenization of sensitive data.
C) Enable Azure AD Privileged Identity Management.
D) Integrate with Microsoft Cloud App Security.
E) Establish robust endpoint protection with Microsoft Defender ATP.

QUESTION 28

Your organization is tasked with managing exceptions and policy updates for Conditional Access in Azure Virtual Desktop (AVD) environments to ensure effective access control while accommodating legitimate business needs. The focus is on understanding the process of managing exceptions and policy updates. What are the steps involved in managing exceptions and policy updates for Conditional Access in AVD environments? Select THREE.

A) Identify legitimate business scenarios requiring exceptions to Conditional Access policies
B) Review and update Conditional Access policies based on changing business requirements
C) Implement bypass mechanisms for exceptions, such as Azure AD Conditional Access exclusions
D) Test policy updates in a non-production environment before deployment to production
E) Monitor policy effectiveness and user feedback for continuous improvement

QUESTION 29

Your organization is exploring automation tools to streamline the management of security settings for Azure Virtual Desktop (AVD) session hosts. The focus is on the use of automation tools for security settings. Which automation tools can be leveraged to automate security settings management for AVD session hosts? Select THREE.

A) Azure Policy for enforcing compliance requirements and security baselines
B) Azure Security Center for continuous security monitoring and threat detection
C) Azure Automation for scheduling and executing security configuration tasks and remediation
D) Azure DevOps for version control and deployment of security configuration scripts
E) Azure Monitor for proactive alerting and notification of security incidents

QUESTION 30

To ensure that all administrative actions within Azure Virtual Desktop are logged and auditable, which Azure services should be used, and how should they be configured? Consider the following PowerShell command for enabling diagnostic settings to log all relevant activities:

```powershell
Set-AzDiagnosticSetting -ResourceId "/subscriptions/sub-id/resourceGroups/AVDGroup" -WorkspaceId "/subscriptions/sub-id/resourcegroups/AVDLogs" -Enabled $true
```

A) Correctly enables logging
B) WorkspaceId should reference a specific log analytics workspace
C) ResourceId should target specific AVD resources
D) Enabled parameter should be set to $false
E) Command lacks necessary logging categories

QUESTION 31

As part of a large-scale AVD deployment, you are tasked with avoiding common pitfalls during FSLogix installation and configuration. You aim to ensure a smooth deployment by considering the following challenges:
1. Avoiding conflicts with existing profile management solutions, such as roaming profiles.
2. Preventing profile bloat and performance degradation over time.
3. Ensuring compatibility with legacy applications and user settings during migration to FSLogix.

A) Disable Windows Search indexing within FSLogix profiles
B) Perform thorough testing in a non-production environment before full deployment
C) Set up FSLogix with VHD disk format to ensure compatibility
D) Implement a comprehensive backup strategy for FSLogix profiles
E) Use Group Policy to enforce FSLogix settings uniformly across all users

QUESTION 32

As an Azure Virtual Desktop administrator responsible for security considerations, you need to implement robust measures to protect Office Containers from potential threats. Consider the following scenario:
- Office Containers should be hardened to prevent unauthorized access and data breaches.
- Security policies must be enforced to ensure compliance with regulatory requirements.
- User authentication mechanisms should be implemented to verify user identities before accessing Office applications.
What are the security considerations for Office Containers? Select THREE.

A) Implement role-based access control (RBAC) to restrict access to Office Containers.
B) Enable Azure Active Directory (Azure AD) conditional access policies for Office application access.
C) Encrypt Office Containers to protect sensitive data from unauthorized access.
D) Utilize Azure Defender for Cloud to detect and respond to security threats in Office Containers.

E) Implement multi-factor authentication (MFA) for user access to Office applications.

QUESTION 33

To support a hybrid workforce using AVD, you need to ensure consistent user experience, secure access from various locations, and compliance with GDPR. What are the best configurations to implement? Select THREE.

A) Deploy Azure VPN Gateway for secure remote connections.
B) Configure host pools across multiple Azure regions.
C) Use Azure Policy for enforcing compliance standards.
D) Enable Multi-Factor Authentication (MFA) for additional security.
E) Implement Azure Virtual WAN for optimized connectivity.

QUESTION 34

Your organization intends to implement custom policies for device type restrictions in Azure Virtual Desktop (AVD) deployments. Consider the following scenario:
- The organization operates in a highly regulated industry with strict compliance requirements governing device usage and access.
- Users need to access AVD sessions from corporate-managed devices with specific configurations and security features enabled.
- IT administrators aim to enforce device type restrictions to ensure that only approved devices can connect to AVD sessions, maintaining compliance and security standards.
What strategies should you adopt to implement custom policies for device type restrictions in the given scenario? Select TWO.

A) Utilize Azure AD Conditional Access policies to enforce device compliance and restrict access based on device attributes and configurations.
B) Configure Azure AD Identity Protection policies to detect risky sign-in attempts from unauthorized or non-compliant devices.
C) Implement Azure AD Device Enrollment restrictions to limit AVD access to devices enrolled in a corporate device management solution.
D) Utilize Group Policy settings to enforce device configuration requirements and restrict access to AVD sessions based on device compliance status.
E) Deploy Azure Bastion as a secure remote access solution for AVD instances, restricting access to corporate-approved devices only.

QUESTION 35

Troubleshooting printing issues is part of your responsibility. Users report delays and errors when printing. You suspect network issues are to blame. To diagnose, you plan to implement logging for all print job statuses. Which PowerShell command could you use to enable detailed logging?

```powershell
Set-PrinterProperty -Name "NetworkPrinter" -PropertyName "JobLogEnabled" -Value $true
```

A) Correctly enables logging
B) JobLogEnabled is not a valid property
C) Set-PrinterProperty does not apply to network issues
D) Logging should be enabled on the server
E) Value should be set to $false

QUESTION 36

For a global news agency using AVD, ensuring fast content delivery, securing sensitive news data, and enabling efficient content management are crucial. What should you configure? Select THREE.

A) Deploy Azure Content Delivery Network (CDN).
B) Implement Azure Rights Management Services (RMS) for data security.
C) Use Azure Media Services for content management.
D) Configure Azure Bastion for secure administrative access.
E) Enable Azure Information Protection for document encryption and tracking.

QUESTION 37

You are tasked with evaluating the impact of implementing the Start VM on Connect feature in an Azure Virtual Desktop (AVD) environment. What factor should you consider when assessing the effect on resource utilization and cost management?

A) Monitoring network bandwidth usage to ensure efficient data transmission
B) Analyzing CPU and memory usage patterns during peak and off-peak hours
C) Reviewing user login times and session durations to optimize VM startup schedules
D) Implementing GPU acceleration to enhance graphics performance for AVD users
E) Enabling Azure AD Join to seamlessly integrate AVD resources with organizational identities

QUESTION 38

In Azure Virtual Desktop (AVD) environments, automating app deployments can streamline operations and improve efficiency. Which tool or technology is most suitable for automating the deployment of applications across multiple user sessions in AVD?

A) PowerShell scripts
B) Azure CLI (Command Line Interface)
C) Azure Resource Manager (ARM) Templates
D) FSLogix profile containers
E) MSIX App Attach

QUESTION 39

An educational institution requires their Azure Virtual Desktop to be optimized for online learning, ensure compliance with educational data protection standards, and provide access based on user roles. What configurations should you implement? Select THREE.

A) Configure Azure Bastion for secure VM access.
B) Use Azure Policy to enforce data protection standards.
C) Set up role-based access control (RBAC) with Azure AD.
D) Enable Azure Site Recovery for data resilience.
E) Deploy Azure Firewall to regulate e-learning traffic flows.

QUESTION 40

A challenge in multisession environments is ensuring that OneDrive syncs data efficiently without performance lag. Which PowerShell command best achieves this?
`Set-ODSyncClientPolicy -TenantId "54321" -MaxDownloadRate 50 -MaxUploadRate 50 -ThrottleRate $true`

A) Command is correct.
B) Replace -ThrottleRate $true with -BandwidthThrottling $true.

C) Change -MaxDownloadRate 50 and -MaxUploadRate 50 to -MaxDownloadBandwidth 50 -MaxUploadBandwidth 50.
D) Add -EnableSessionOptimization $true.
E) No changes are necessary.

QUESTION 41

During a security audit, you need to adjust the deployment of Microsoft 365 Apps on AVD to restrict access based on user location. Which ARM template adjustment would correctly implement this requirement?

`{ "type": "Microsoft.AVD/sessionHosts", "properties": { "restrictAccess": { "byLocation": true } } }`

A) Configuration is correct.
B) Add "allowedLocations": ["HQ", "Branch1"] to the properties.
C) Change "byLocation": true to "locationBasedRestrictions": "enabled".
D) Replace "type": "Microsoft.AVD/sessionHosts" with "type": "Microsoft.Office365/Apps".
E) Remove the restrictAccess section and manage through Azure AD policies.

QUESTION 42

An educational institution's AVD setup needs to maintain high system availability, manage large number of user profiles, and ensure quick logon times during peak hours. Which FSLogix settings should be focused on? Select THREE.

```
A) HKLM\SOFTWARE\FSLogix\Profiles\CloudCache
B) HKLM\SOFTWARE\FSLogix\Profiles\CloudCacheLocations
C) HKLM\SOFTWARE\FSLogix\Profiles\LocalCacheSize
D) HKLM\SOFTWARE\FSLogix\Profiles\DeleteLocalProfileWhenVHDShouldApply
E) HKLM\SOFTWARE\FSLogix\Profiles\PreventLoginWithFailure
```

QUESTION 43

You are tasked with automating health checks for Azure Virtual Desktop (AVD) session hosts to ensure proactive monitoring and maintenance. Which PowerShell cmdlet would you use to retrieve diagnostic information about AVD session hosts?

```
A) Get-RdsDiagnosticActivities
B) Get-RdsSessionHost
C) Get-RdsDiagnosticProperty
D) Get-RdsSessionConfiguration
E) Get-RdsSession
```

QUESTION 44

As part of performance tuning for Azure Virtual Desktop (AVD) deployments, you need to utilize diagnostic settings effectively. Considerations include:
1. Identifying performance bottlenecks and resource utilization patterns through diagnostic data analysis.
2. Implementing proactive measures based on diagnostic insights to optimize AVD infrastructure and user experience.
3. Continuously monitoring and adjusting diagnostic settings to align with evolving AVD deployment requirements.
Which diagnostic data source provides insights into performance metrics and resource utilization for AVD deployments?

A) Azure Monitor Logs
B) Azure Activity Log
C) Azure Diagnostic Logs
D) Azure Application Insights
E) Azure Network Watcher

QUESTION 45

Develop a strategy to report on update compliance and success rates within AVD. Draft an ARM template snippet to deploy diagnostic settings to track update activity.
```json
{"type": "Microsoft.Insights/diagnosticSettings", "properties": {"logs": [{"category": "UpdateLogs", "enabled": true}], "workspaceId": "/subscriptions/subId/resourceGroups/RG1/providers/Microsoft.OperationalInsights/workspaces/wsId"}}
```

A) Snippet is correct as is.
B) Add "retentionPolicy": {"days": 365, "enabled": true} to the logs section.
C) Replace "UpdateLogs" with "UpdateManagementLogs".
D) Change "workspaceId" to "logAnalyticsWorkspaceId".
E) Include "metrics": [{"category": "AllMetrics", "enabled": true}] in the properties.

QUESTION 46

Security considerations are paramount when monitoring network performance in Azure Virtual Desktop (AVD) environments. As the AVD administrator, you need to ensure that network monitoring practices adhere to security standards and compliance requirements. Which security consideration should be addressed when monitoring network performance in AVD environments?

A) Implementing Role-Based Access Control (RBAC)
B) Encrypting network traffic with Azure VPN Gateway
C) Enabling Just-In-Time (JIT) access for administrative tasks
D) Configuring Azure Security Center for threat detection
E) Enforcing Multi-Factor Authentication (MFA) for user access

QUESTION 47

A company is planning its budget for Azure Virtual Desktop (AVD) operations for the upcoming fiscal year. The IT department needs to implement best practices for budget planning and management to ensure efficient resource allocation. What steps should the IT department take to effectively plan and manage the AVD budget for the upcoming fiscal year? Select THREE.

A) Regularly reviewing Azure Cost Management reports
B) Forecasting future AVD usage and growth
C) Implementing RBAC to control spending permissions
D) Setting up alerts for budget thresholds
E) Using Azure Advisor recommendations for cost optimization

QUESTION 48

A construction company is deploying Azure Virtual Desktop to facilitate remote site management. The system must support legacy applications, provide reliable connectivity under low bandwidth conditions, and ensure data integrity. Which operating systems should you select? Select THREE.

A) Windows Server 2019
B) Windows 10 Pro
C) Windows Server 2012 R2
D) Windows 11 Enterprise
E) Windows 10 Enterprise multi-session

QUESTION 49

An organization is concerned about the legal implications of non-compliance with licensing agreements in its Azure Virtual Desktop (AVD) environment. What legal risks should the organization be aware of regarding non-compliance with AVD licensing agreements? Select TWO.

A) Potential fines and penalties for unauthorized use of software
B) Legal actions from software vendors for copyright infringement
C) Risk of data breaches and security vulnerabilities due to unlicensed software
D) Loss of reputation and trust among customers and partners
E) Impact on business continuity and productivity due to license enforcement actions

QUESTION 50

An organization is concerned about the security implications of log management in its Azure Virtual Desktop (AVD) environment and wants to implement appropriate security measures. What security considerations should they take into account for log management? Select TWO.

A) Implementing RBAC controls to restrict access to log data based on role and responsibility
B) Enabling encryption for log data at rest and in transit to protect against unauthorized access
C) Utilizing Azure Key Vault for secure storage and management of log data encryption keys
D) Implementing Azure AD Conditional Access policies to control access to log management tools and data
E) Configuring Azure Security Center for continuous monitoring and threat detection of log data

PRACTICE TEST 9 - ANSWERS ONLY

QUESTION 1

Answer - E) az network watcher packet-capture create

Option A - Incorrect. Tests connectivity, not for ongoing monitoring.
Option B - Incorrect. Lists VNets, not diagnostic.
Option C - Incorrect. Configures flow logs, not immediate troubleshooting.
Option D - Incorrect. Starts troubleshooting session, but less detailed.
Option E - Correct. Captures network packets, ideal for analyzing intermittent issues.

EXAM FOCUS	*Make sure to use az network watcher packet-capture create for deep packet-level analysis. It provides detailed insights into network traffic issues, especially intermittent access problems, helping you pinpoint root causes effectively. Always ensure Network Watcher is enabled for monitoring.*
CAUTION ALERT	*Avoid relying on commands like az network vnet list, which provide static configurations but no live traffic insights. Stay cautioned against skipping packet-level data when diagnosing intermittent issues, as this can lead to incomplete troubleshooting.*

QUESTION 2

Answer - B) Implement Azure Network Watcher with packet capture for RDP analysis

Option A - Incorrect. While Azure Monitor can provide insights, it may not offer granular QoS and RDP performance monitoring. Option B - Correct. Azure Network Watcher with packet capture allows for detailed analysis of network traffic, essential for monitoring QoS and RDP efficiency.

Option C - Incorrect. Microsoft Defender for Cloud focuses on security rather than performance monitoring. Option D - Incorrect. Azure Application Gateway is for load balancing web traffic and does not monitor AVD sessions. Option E - Incorrect. Microsoft Endpoint Manager is more focused on device management and may not provide detailed network performance analytics.

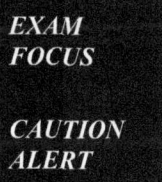

EXAM FOCUS	*You should use Azure Network Watcher for granular packet capture to monitor QoS and RDP efficiency. Focus on identifying latency spikes and bandwidth bottlenecks affecting HR-critical apps. This tool allows you to diagnose specific performance problems impacting remote sessions.*
CAUTION ALERT	*Don't confuse tools like Microsoft Defender for Cloud with performance monitoring—they focus on security. Stay alert against misusing Azure Application Gateway for load balancing AVD—it's for web traffic, not session optimization.*

QUESTION 3

Answer - [A]

Option A - WVDNetworkTrafficLogs: This table contains detailed logs of network traffic between client devices and session hosts, including latency and bandwidth usage, making it essential for monitoring network performance.
Option B - WVDConnections: While it may seem relevant, this table typically contains information about user connections rather than detailed network traffic logs.

Option C - WVDAuditLogs: This contains audit logs but may not capture detailed network traffic information.
Option D - WVDSessionEvent: This table contains session event logs but may not provide detailed network traffic information.
Option E - WVDServiceHealth: This provides overall service health information, not detailed network traffic logs.

EXAM	*Always query the WVDNetworkTrafficLogs table for network-related metrics like latency and bandwidth.*

FOCUS	This table is optimized for analyzing performance between session hosts and client devices. Focus on trends that may indicate bottlenecks in communication paths.
CAUTION ALERT	Stay cautioned against using tables like WVDConnections or WVDAuditLogs, as they don't provide traffic-level details. Avoid assuming session logs are sufficient for network analysis; detailed traffic logs are necessary for actionable insights.

QUESTION 4

Answer - A) User profile sizes and growth projections; B) Application installation and data caching requirements; C) Temporary data storage and disk caching mechanisms; E) Forecasted user concurrency and session persistence

Option A - Correct. Estimating user profile sizes and growth projections helps determine the amount of storage required to accommodate user data in AVD environments over time. Option B - Correct. Considering application installation and data caching requirements helps assess additional storage needs for application-related data and temporary files in AVD setups.

Option C - Correct. Factoring in temporary data storage and disk caching mechanisms ensures sufficient storage capacity for transient data generated during AVD sessions. Option D - Incorrect. While data deduplication and compression techniques may optimize storage utilization, they may not be directly applicable or supported in all AVD storage scenarios. Option E - Correct. Forecasting user concurrency and session persistence helps determine the level of storage performance and scalability required to support simultaneous user sessions and persistent data storage in AVD deployments.

EXAM FOCUS	Consider factors like user profiles, temporary storage, and concurrency when estimating storage needs for AVD. This ensures adequate provisioning for performance and scalability while accounting for future growth. Use storage calculators for accurate projections.
CAUTION ALERT	Don't neglect application caching or concurrency factors—they can lead to underestimated storage needs. Stay clear of solely relying on deduplication or compression to optimize storage; these techniques may not apply to all scenarios or user workloads.

QUESTION 5

Answer - C) SKU and properties are configured correctly

Option A - Incorrect: 'Standard_GRS' (Geo-redundant storage) is appropriate for disaster recovery.
Option B - Incorrect: The 'Hot' access tier is suitable for frequently accessed data.
Option C - Correct: This setup is appropriate for ensuring data availability and supporting disaster recovery.
Option D - Incorrect: 'Archive' is not suitable for frequently accessed AVD environments.
Option E - Incorrect: Geo-redundant storage already provides sufficient redundancy.

EXAM FOCUS	Keep in mind that Standard_GRS is ideal for disaster recovery due to its geo-redundancy. Pair it with the Hot tier for frequently accessed AVD data. This configuration balances availability, recovery capabilities, and performance for AVD deployments.
CAUTION ALERT	Avoid selecting the Archive tier—it's unsuitable for active workloads. Stay alert to the access tier mismatch; using Cool for frequently accessed data can degrade performance and user experience. Ensure redundancy settings align with recovery objectives.

QUESTION 6

Answer - [B, D]

Option B - Azure Automation with Azure Functions: Functions can be scheduled to start and stop session hosts at the specified times, meeting the requirements and minimizing manual intervention.

Option D - Azure Automation with Azure Runbooks: Runbooks can automate tasks such as starting and stopping session hosts based on a schedule, fulfilling the requirements efficiently. Option A - Azure Monitor Alerts: Alerts notify you of potential issues but are not specifically designed for managing session host schedules based on demand.

Option C - Azure Resource Manager templates: While templates enable you to deploy and manage Azure resources, they are not specifically designed for managing session host schedules based on demand. Option E - Azure Virtual Machine Scale Sets: While Scale Sets can help with scaling resources, they are not specifically designed for managing session host schedules based on demand.

EXAM FOCUS	*You should leverage Azure Automation with Runbooks for automating host schedules. Combine it with Azure Functions for precise timing control to reduce manual intervention. These tools are efficient for repetitive tasks like starting and stopping hosts based on work schedules.*
CAUTION ALERT	*Don't rely on Azure Monitor Alerts for automation—they are designed for notifications. Avoid assuming Scale Sets alone can meet scheduling requirements—they are more suited for load-based scaling rather than fixed time intervals.*

QUESTION 7

Answer - A) Hybrid Cloud Environments and Multi-Cloud Deployments; C) Industry-Specific Regulations and Compliance Requirements; D) Seasonal or Temporary Workforce Flexibility and Scalability

Option A - Correct. Hybrid cloud environments and multi-cloud deployments may require flexible licensing models to accommodate diverse infrastructure configurations and usage patterns. Option C - Correct. Industry-specific regulations and compliance requirements influence licensing agreements, ensuring alignment with legal and regulatory standards for data protection and privacy.

Option D - Correct. Seasonal or temporary workforce flexibility and scalability require licensing models that can adapt to fluctuating user counts and usage demands, such as Consumption-based Pricing. Option B - Incorrect. While non-profit or educational institution discounts and special offers may exist, they are not universally applicable to all custom scenarios and may not address unique licensing needs. Option E - Incorrect. While legacy application support and compatibility challenges are important, they are primarily technical considerations and may not directly impact licensing requirements for AVD deployments.

EXAM FOCUS	*Always prioritize licensing models that accommodate hybrid environments and seasonal workforce needs. Evaluate compliance requirements specific to your industry to avoid penalties. Flexible licensing, such as consumption-based plans, can reduce costs for temporary workloads.*
CAUTION ALERT	*Stay cautioned about underestimating the impact of regulations on licensing. Avoid assuming discounts for non-profits or education apply universally; these are case-specific. Misaligned licenses can lead to non-compliance and financial liabilities.*

QUESTION 8

Answer - A) Resource Intensiveness and Workload Patterns; B) Application Dependencies and Interactions; D) Compatibility with AVD Configuration and Environment

Option A - Correct. Assessing resource intensiveness and workload patterns helps determine the impact of different applications on AVD performance requirements, considering factors such as CPU, memory, and disk usage. Option B - Correct. Understanding application dependencies and interactions helps identify potential performance bottlenecks and compatibility issues within AVD deployments, ensuring optimal application performance.

Option D - Correct. Evaluating compatibility with AVD configuration and environment ensures that applications can function effectively within the virtual desktop environment, minimizing performance issues and compatibility conflicts. Option C - Incorrect. While user access patterns and session characteristics are important considerations, they are more related to user behavior and management rather than application impact on performance requirements.

Option E - Incorrect. Security vulnerabilities and patching requirements are critical but are not directly related to assessing the impact of application types on AVD performance requirements.

EXAM FOCUS — *Ensure compatibility between applications and AVD configuration to avoid performance issues. Evaluate resource intensiveness and workload patterns to provision appropriate session hosts. Understanding dependencies ensures smooth operation across user sessions and applications.*

CAUTION ALERT — *Don't overlook application dependencies—they can cause performance bottlenecks. Avoid deploying incompatible applications on AVD configurations, as this can disrupt user experience and reduce overall efficiency. Always test applications before full deployment.*

QUESTION 9

Answer - [A, B, C]

Option A - Configure autoscale rules based on CPU and memory utilization: This allows for dynamic adjustment of resources based on performance metrics, ensuring responsiveness and cost efficiency. Option B - Set up recurring scaling events to deallocate resources during off-peak hours: This helps minimize costs by deallocating idle resources when demand is low.

Option C - Implement logic to prevent scaling actions during active user sessions: This ensures that scaling actions do not disrupt user experience during active sessions. Option D - While Azure Monitor can monitor user activity, it is not specifically mentioned as a requirement to prevent scaling actions during active sessions. Option E - Configuring alerts for unexpected resource usage patterns may be useful but does not directly address the requirement to prevent scaling actions during active sessions.

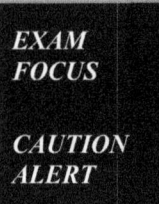

EXAM FOCUS — *Implement autoscaling rules based on resource utilization to maintain responsiveness and cost efficiency. Use logic to avoid scaling during active sessions to ensure a seamless user experience. Schedule recurring scale-down events for off-peak hours to minimize operational costs.*

CAUTION ALERT — *Avoid abrupt scaling actions during user sessions—it can disrupt active workloads. Stay cautioned about over-provisioning resources; it leads to unnecessary expenses. Mismanaged scaling rules can result in under-resourced sessions and degraded performance.*

QUESTION 10

Answer - E) Missing properties for policy application

Option A - Incorrect: Resource type is potentially correct but misaligned with the intended setting.
Option B - Correct: The API version may need updating to support new features.
Option C - Incorrect: This configuration does not ensure policy compliance on its own.
Option D - Incorrect: 'ComplianceHosts' could be a valid name.
Option E - Correct: Essential properties for enforcing policies are missing.

EXAM FOCUS — *You need to include properties in the Bicep script to enforce policy compliance. Always use the latest API versions for new features and functionality. Ensure configurations explicitly align with compliance requirements to avoid gaps in enforcement.*

CAUTION ALERT — *Don't overlook missing policy properties—they are critical for security compliance. Stay clear of using outdated API versions—they may lack features necessary for enforcing policies effectively. Misconfigured scripts can lead to inconsistent policy application across hosts.*

QUESTION 11

Answer - A) Incomplete Application Installation and Configuration; B) Failure to Sysprep and Generalize the Image Properly; D) Overly Large Image Size and Complexity

Option A - Correct. Incomplete application installation and configuration can result in missing dependencies or functionality, leading to issues during deployment and user productivity. Option B - Correct. Failure to sysprep and generalize the image properly can lead to unique system identifiers and configurations, causing conflicts and errors when deploying session hosts from the golden image.

Option D - Correct. Overly large image size and complexity can impact deployment times, storage costs, and performance of session hosts within the AVD environment, requiring additional resources and management overhead. Option C - Incorrect. While lack of version control and documentation is a concern, it is not directly related to the image creation process itself but rather to image management and governance practices. Option E - Incorrect. Dependency on manual image capture and deployment processes may introduce human errors and inconsistencies but is not a specific pitfall of manual image creation and can be mitigated through automation and standardization.

EXAM FOCUS	*Always ensure proper application installation and configuration when creating golden images. Use Sysprep to generalize images and avoid deployment errors. Simplify the image to reduce size and complexity, which minimizes storage costs and speeds up deployment. Centralized documentation aids governance.*
CAUTION ALERT	*Avoid skipping the Sysprep step; it leads to conflicts during deployment. Stay alert against creating overly complex or large images; they hinder scalability and performance. Don't ignore standardization; inconsistencies increase administrative effort.*

QUESTION 12

Answer - [B, C]

Option B - Azure Traffic Manager: Azure Traffic Manager enables DNS-based traffic routing to the closest available endpoint, facilitating automatic failover of AVD host pools to a secondary region in case of a primary region outage. Option C - Azure Site Recovery: Azure Site Recovery supports replication and failover of AVD host pools to a secondary region, minimizing data loss and downtime during failover operations.

Option A - Azure Monitor provides monitoring and analytics capabilities but does not directly support failover and disaster recovery for AVD host pools. Option D - Azure Load Balancer is a network load balancer and does not provide failover capabilities at the application level for AVD host pools. Option E - Azure Backup is primarily used for data backup and recovery and is not designed for failover and disaster recovery of AVD host pools.

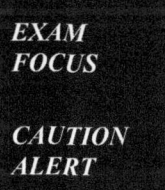

EXAM FOCUS	*You need to combine Azure Traffic Manager for DNS-based failover and Azure Site Recovery for replication and failover of AVD host pools. This combination ensures business continuity with minimal data loss and downtime during regional outages. Test failover configurations regularly.*
CAUTION ALERT	*Stay clear of assuming Azure Backup alone suffices for disaster recovery; it handles data backups, not failover. Avoid using only Load Balancers; they don't cover regional failover. Stay cautioned about failing to test disaster recovery scenarios regularly.*

QUESTION 13

Answer - A) Implementing Canary Deployments; B) Utilizing Blue-Green Deployment Patterns; C) Conducting A/B Testing with Pilot Users

Option A - Correct. Implementing canary deployments involves rolling out updates to a small subset of users or devices before wider deployment, allowing for early detection of issues. Option B - Correct. Utilizing blue-green deployment patterns involves maintaining two identical environments (blue and green) and switching between them during updates, minimizing downtime and risk.

Option C - Correct. Conducting A/B testing with pilot users allows for comparison between different versions of updates, enabling validation of changes and user feedback before full deployment. Option D - Incorrect. While mirroring pre-production environments can aid in testing, it is not specifically a strategy for testing and validation of updates before deployment in AVD environments.

Option E - Incorrect. Enforcing change management approval workflows is important for governance but does not directly facilitate testing and validation of updates before deployment in AVD environments.

EXAM FOCUS	*Always implement canary deployments and blue-green deployment patterns for risk-free updates. Test updates with pilot users in controlled environments to gather feedback and detect issues. This minimizes risks and ensures a smooth user experience in production environments.*
CAUTION ALERT	*Don't rely solely on pre-production mirrors for validation; they lack real-world user interactions. Stay alert to skipping canary or blue-green strategies, as these are critical for phased deployments. Avoid rushing updates without proper pilot user testing.*

QUESTION 14

Answer - A) Replicate Images Across Azure Regions for Redundancy; B) Utilize Content Delivery Networks (CDNs) for Image Distribution; E) Ensure Compatibility with Azure Resiliency Services for Disaster Recovery

Option A - Correct. Replicating images across Azure regions provides redundancy and ensures availability of images for deployment in different geographical locations. Option B - Correct. Utilizing CDNs for image distribution improves accessibility and reduces latency by caching images closer to end-users in AVD deployments.

Option C - Incorrect. While Azure Availability Zones enhance availability for virtual machines, they may not directly relate to image storage accessibility in AVD deployments. Option D - Incorrect. Azure ExpressRoute provides private connectivity to Azure services but may not specifically address image storage access requirements for AVD deployments. Option E - Correct. Ensuring compatibility with Azure resiliency services, such as Azure Site Recovery, helps implement disaster recovery strategies for image storage in AVD deployments, enhancing availability and resilience.

EXAM FOCUS	*Replicate images across regions for redundancy and use CDNs for efficient distribution to enhance performance and scalability. Ensure compatibility with Azure resiliency services like Site Recovery for disaster recovery. These strategies optimize accessibility and reliability for global AVD deployments.*
CAUTION ALERT	*Don't depend solely on Azure Availability Zones for image accessibility—they don't cover multi-region needs. Stay clear of ignoring CDN benefits; latency can degrade performance without caching. Avoid overlooking resiliency testing for disaster recovery strategies.*

QUESTION 15

Answer - C) Missing parameters for rules

Option A - Incorrect: While the command creates an NSG, it doesn't specify rules, which are critical for enhanced security. Option B - Incorrect: Default rules are automatically created, but custom rules need explicit definition.

Option C - Correct: The command needs additional parameters to define specific security rules tailored to AVD requirements. Option D - Correct: Ideally, NSG location should match AVD deployment for optimal performance and management. Option E - Incorrect: While tags are helpful for management, their absence doesn't affect NSG functionality.

EXAM FOCUS	*You must define custom security rules when creating NSGs to tailor them for AVD-specific requirements. Match the NSG location with the AVD deployment region to optimize management. Use tags to organize resources and simplify auditing and compliance tracking.*
CAUTION ALERT	*Avoid creating NSGs without specifying rules—they're ineffective for securing environments. Don't confuse default rules with custom configurations; defaults may not meet security needs. Stay cautioned against mismatched NSG and AVD deployment locations; it complicates troubleshooting.*

QUESTION 16

Answer - A) Azure Monitor for Log Analytics and Audit Logging; C) Azure Security Center for Compliance Score Monitoring and Reporting; D) Microsoft 365 Compliance Center for Data Governance and Compliance Insights

Option A - Correct. Azure Monitor enables log analytics and audit logging, providing visibility into user actions and system activities for compliance purposes in AVD deployments. Option B - Incorrect. While Azure Policy is valuable for policy enforcement, it may not be specifically designed for conducting audits and compliance reports in AVD environments.

Option C - Correct. Azure Security Center offers compliance score monitoring and reporting features, helping organizations track and assess compliance status in AVD deployments. Option D - Correct. The Microsoft 365 Compliance Center provides data governance and compliance insights, assisting organizations in meeting regulatory requirements and industry standards in AVD environments. Option E - Incorrect. While Azure Sentinel is useful for security incident detection and response, it may not be directly related to conducting audits and compliance reports in AVD deployments.

EXAM FOCUS	*Utilize Azure Monitor for log analytics, Azure Security Center for compliance scores, and Microsoft 365 Compliance Center for detailed insights. These tools collectively provide a robust mechanism for audit and compliance reporting in AVD deployments.*
CAUTION ALERT	*Avoid relying solely on Azure Policy; it enforces compliance but doesn't generate reports. Stay cautioned against neglecting Azure Security Center—it provides critical compliance tracking. Don't skip data governance insights in Microsoft 365 Compliance Center for enhanced reporting.*

QUESTION 17

Answer - A) Purchase Reserved Instances for Fixed-Term Workloads with Predictable Usage; B) Utilize Azure Spot Instances for Temporary Workloads with Flexible Resource Requirements

Option A - Correct. Purchasing reserved instances for fixed-term workloads with predictable usage allows organizations to commit to VM usage over a specific term, leading to significant cost savings in AVD deployments. Option B - Correct. Utilizing Azure Spot Instances for temporary workloads with flexible resource requirements enables organizations to take advantage of spare capacity at discounted prices, reducing costs in AVD deployments.

Option C - Incorrect. While combining reserved instances with pay-as-you-go pricing may provide cost flexibility, it may not be the most cost-effective approach for maximizing savings in AVD deployments. Option D - Incorrect. Azure Cost Management Policies may help with cost optimization but may not specifically address the implementation details of reserved instances and spot pricing in AVD deployments. Option E - Incorrect. While leveraging spot instance interruption notices is useful for graceful shutdowns, it may not directly impact the implementation of reserved instances and spot pricing in AVD deployments.

EXAM FOCUS	*Purchase Reserved Instances for predictable workloads and leverage Spot Instances for temporary workloads to reduce costs. Plan workloads carefully to balance resource needs and cost efficiency. Monitor usage patterns to adjust commitments or reservations effectively.*
CAUTION ALERT	*Don't combine reserved instances with pay-as-you-go without cost analysis—it may negate savings. Stay alert to interruption notices in Spot Instances; they require workload flexibility. Avoid overlooking tools like Cost Management for tracking and optimizing savings.*

QUESTION 18

Answer - [B, C]

Option B - Azure Log Analytics: Azure Log Analytics offers centralized log management and analytics for monitoring session host performance metrics, identifying trends, and diagnosing issues, ensuring effective management and proactive performance optimization.

Option C - Azure Application Insights: Azure Application Insights provides application performance monitoring (APM) capabilities, including performance counters, traces, and logs, for monitoring session host applications and workloads, complementing Azure Log Analytics for comprehensive monitoring and management.

Option A - Azure Monitor provides centralized monitoring and alerting capabilities but is more focused on infrastructure and service-level monitoring rather than detailed session host performance monitoring. Option D - Azure Advisor offers recommendations for optimizing Azure resources but does not provide detailed session host performance monitoring capabilities. Option E - Azure Security Center focuses on security posture management and threat protection rather than performance monitoring and management of session hosts.

EXAM FOCUS	*Combine Azure Log Analytics for centralized performance monitoring with Azure Application Insights for application-level insights. These tools provide a comprehensive view of session host performance and resource utilization, helping you proactively address performance bottlenecks.*
CAUTION ALERT	*Stay clear of relying solely on Azure Monitor—it focuses on service-level metrics, not session hosts. Avoid using Azure Advisor for detailed performance tracking—it provides high-level recommendations. Don't skip Application Insights for in-depth workload monitoring.*

QUESTION 19

Answer - A) Azure Blob Storage for storing backup data; B) Azure Automation for orchestrating recovery workflows

Option A - Correct. Azure Blob Storage provides scalable and durable storage for backup data, supporting efficient data retention and recovery in AVD environments. Option B - Correct. Azure Automation enables organizations to automate recovery workflows and streamline disaster recovery operations in AVD deployments.

Option C - Incorrect. While Azure Monitor offers monitoring and alerting capabilities, it is not specifically designed for disaster recovery purposes in AVD environments. Option D - Incorrect. Azure ExpressRoute enhances network connectivity but is not a primary component of disaster recovery plans for AVD deployments. Option E - Incorrect. While Azure Function Apps offer serverless event-driven logic, they are not directly related to disaster recovery initiatives in AVD environments.

EXAM FOCUS	*Use Azure Blob Storage for durable and scalable data backup in disaster recovery plans. Automate recovery workflows with Azure Automation to minimize RTO and RPO. These services complement each other to provide a robust disaster recovery strategy for AVD environments.*
CAUTION ALERT	*Avoid assuming Azure Monitor alone can address disaster recovery—it focuses on alerts and monitoring. Stay cautioned against relying on Azure ExpressRoute for disaster recovery; it enhances connectivity but doesn't cover recovery scenarios. Don't neglect testing automation workflows.*

QUESTION 20

Answer - B) Write a runbook to restart services on alert

Option A - Incorrect: Automation rules in Azure Monitor direct the workflow but do not execute specific actions.

Option B - Correct: Writing a runbook that automatically restarts services or performs other remediation actions upon receiving an alert from Azure Monitor is a proactive approach to maintaining AVD health. Option C - Incorrect: This command configures alert conditions, not actions. Option D - Incorrect: This configures new alert rules but doesn't automate responses. Option E - Incorrect: This command is not valid for automating responses in Azure; the correct context is needed.

EXAM FOCUS	*Write runbooks in Azure Automation to automate remediation actions like restarting services upon alerts. Use Azure Monitor alerts to trigger these runbooks for proactive issue resolution. This combination ensures service health and minimizes downtime in AVD environments.*
CAUTION ALERT	*Don't use generic commands like Set-AzMetricAlertRule—they only configure conditions, not responses. Stay clear of neglecting detailed action scripts in runbooks; incomplete configurations lead to failures.*

> *Avoid assuming alert rules alone can automate responses without linking them to actions.*

QUESTION 21

Answer - A,C

Option A - Azure AD Domain Services provides managed domain services that integrate with Azure AD, enabling centralized management of user identities and access control. By using Azure AD Domain Services, you can extend Azure AD capabilities to Azure Virtual Desktop environments, allowing users to authenticate and access resources securely.

Option C - Azure Active Directory Connect enables synchronization of on-premises identities with Azure AD, providing seamless integration between on-premises Active Directory environments and Azure services. By configuring Azure AD Connect, you can ensure that user identities are synchronized and managed centrally, facilitating identity authentication and authorization for Azure Virtual Desktop users.

EXAM FOCUS	*You should use Azure AD Domain Services for centralized management and Azure AD Connect for seamless identity synchronization between on-premises and Azure AD. Always ensure compatibility between your environment and Azure AD configurations for efficient authentication and access control.*
CAUTION ALERT	*Avoid using Azure AD B2C or Identity Protection; these are for specific scenarios unrelated to enterprise identity integration for AVD. Stay clear of overlooking role mappings and synchronization details—they're critical for successful implementation.*

QUESTION 22

Answer - A) Regularly audit role assignments and permissions for compliance; B) Implement access reviews to ensure alignment with regulatory requirements; D) Retain audit logs for a specified period to meet regulatory retention requirements

Option A - Correct. Regularly auditing role assignments and permissions ensures compliance with regulatory requirements and industry standards. Option B - Correct. Implementing access reviews helps ensure that access rights align with regulatory requirements and organizational policies.

Option D - Correct. Retaining audit logs for a specified period is essential to meet regulatory retention requirements and facilitate compliance audits. Option C - Incorrect. While enforcing separation of duties is important, it is not specifically related to auditing and compliance considerations with RBAC. Option E - Incorrect. While conducting periodic security assessments is important for overall security, it is not specifically related to auditing and compliance considerations with RBAC.

EXAM FOCUS	*You need to regularly audit role assignments in Azure AD to maintain compliance. Enforce access reviews to validate alignment with regulatory standards. Ensure audit logs are retained as per policy for accountability and easy access during compliance checks.*
CAUTION ALERT	*Don't neglect the retention period for audit logs—it is essential for regulatory audits. Stay alert to permissions creep; regular audits help mitigate risks. Avoid assuming that access reviews are optional—they are integral to managing RBAC compliance in AVD.*

QUESTION 23

Answer - A) Provide comprehensive training materials and resources on MFA usage and best practices; B) Offer hands-on workshops or webinars to demonstrate MFA setup and usage for AVD connections; C) Establish a dedicated helpdesk or support team to assist users with MFA-related issues

Option A - Correct. Providing comprehensive training materials and resources helps users understand MFA usage and best practices, reducing support challenges.

Option B - Correct. Offering hands-on workshops or webinars allows users to learn MFA setup and usage for AVD connections effectively. Option C - Correct. Establishing a dedicated helpdesk or support team ensures timely assistance for users encountering MFA-related issues, improving user experience.

Option D - Incorrect. While gathering user feedback is valuable, it may not directly address training and support challenges associated with MFA in AVD environments as described in the question. Option E - Incorrect. While enabling self-service options can empower users, it may not fully address the need for comprehensive training and support with MFA in AVD environments.

EXAM FOCUS	*You can reduce MFA-related challenges by offering training sessions, workshops, and detailed resources for users. Establish a helpdesk team to address issues and build confidence. Keep communication clear and focused to ease the transition. These steps ensure smooth MFA adoption in AVD environments.*
CAUTION ALERT	*Don't skip user feedback—it reveals pain points and areas for improvement. Stay alert to overcomplicating the setup process for MFA; simplicity encourages user acceptance. Avoid relying solely on self-service options; users often need guided assistance for effective adoption.*

QUESTION 24

Answer - A, C, E

A) Correct - Deploying session hosts across multiple Azure regions ensures continuity in case one region goes down.
B) Incorrect - Regular backup is important but does not directly address the immediate availability needs in disaster scenarios. C) Correct - Configuring Azure Site Recovery for AVD ensures that you can quickly recover in another region if the primary is compromised.

D) Incorrect - While Azure Backup is essential for data integrity, it does not ensure operational continuity like Azure Site Recovery. E) Correct - Periodically testing failover to a secondary region ensures the disaster recovery plan is effective and can be executed smoothly during an actual event.

EXAM FOCUS	*Always ensure that session hosts are deployed across multiple regions to provide failover options. Combine this with Azure Site Recovery for seamless replication. Periodically test failover scenarios to validate the robustness of your disaster recovery plan. These measures ensure operational continuity.*
CAUTION ALERT	*Don't overlook testing your failover strategy; untested plans often fail under real conditions. Avoid relying solely on Azure Backup for disaster recovery—it secures data but doesn't ensure operational continuity. Stay cautioned against neglecting regional redundancy for host pools.*

QUESTION 25

Answer - C) Condition syntax is incorrect

Option A - Incorrect: The script syntax needs corrections for creating an effective alert rule.
Option B - Incorrect: The window size "PT5M" is typically adequate for monitoring traffic spikes.
Option C - Correct: The condition syntax "TotalRequests > 1000" does not correctly use Azure Monitor's metric alert rule format and needs to be adjusted to match Azure's Kusto query language (KQL).

Option D - Incorrect: A frequency of "PT1M" ensures timely detection of traffic spikes, which is critical for prompt response.
Option E - Incorrect: The resource ID should indeed point to network interfaces if the goal is to monitor traffic specific to AVD session hosts.

EXAM FOCUS	*Make sure the alert condition syntax follows Azure Monitor's expected format (KQL). Use a narrow window size to capture short-lived spikes effectively. Accurate targeting of resources, like NICs, ensures actionable insights from alerts. Proper configuration minimizes false positives or incomplete monitoring.*
CAUTION	*Stay alert to syntax errors in conditions—they render alerts ineffective. Avoid broad target scopes that*

| ALERT | dilute the relevance of alerts. Don't configure overly frequent alert intervals without a clear need—it may overwhelm systems with non-critical notifications. |

QUESTION 26

Answer - A) Review security reports and analytics provided by Windows Defender Security Center; C) Monitor security alerts and events generated by Windows Defender Antivirus and other security features

Option A - Correct. Reviewing security reports and analytics provided by Windows Defender Security Center allows for assessment of threat protection effectiveness and identification of areas for improvement. Option C - Correct. Monitoring security alerts and events generated by Windows Defender Antivirus and other security features helps detect and respond to threats in real-time, enhancing overall security posture.

Option B - Incorrect. While penetration testing and vulnerability assessments are important, they are not specifically mentioned in the context of evaluating the effectiveness of threat protection for AVD as described in the question. Option D - Incorrect. While regular audits and compliance checks are valuable, they are not directly related to assessing the effectiveness of threat protection for AVD as described in the question. Option E - Incorrect. While threat intelligence data analysis is important for proactive threat detection, it is not specifically mentioned in the context of evaluating the effectiveness of threat protection for AVD as described in the question.

| EXAM FOCUS | *You need to review reports from Windows Defender Security Center and actively monitor security alerts to evaluate threat protection. These steps ensure that you can measure the effectiveness of implemented safeguards and identify potential areas for improvement in real time.* |
| CAUTION ALERT | *Avoid relying solely on audits; real-time monitoring is essential for identifying immediate threats. Stay clear of skipping periodic reviews of security analytics—they highlight trends and vulnerabilities. Don't confuse threat intelligence analysis with protection effectiveness evaluation.* |

QUESTION 27

Answer - A, B, C

A) Correct - Network segmentation helps control and limit access to cardholder data environments, essential for PCI DSS compliance. B) Correct - Tokenization reduces the risk of data breaches by replacing sensitive data elements with non-sensitive equivalents. C) Correct - Azure AD Privileged Identity Management enhances security by managing, controlling, and monitoring access to critical resources, crucial for secure remote work and compliance.

D) Incorrect - While Microsoft Cloud App Security is vital for app security, it is less directly involved in PCI DSS compliance or preventing data breaches specifically within AVD setups. E) Incorrect - Although robust endpoint protection is important, the options more directly aligned with PCI DSS and protecting sensitive financial data are A, B, and C.

| EXAM FOCUS | *Prioritize network segmentation with Azure Virtual Networks to isolate sensitive data. Implement tokenization for added security and use Privileged Identity Management for enhanced access control. These measures address PCI DSS compliance and provide robust data security in financial AVD environments.* |
| CAUTION ALERT | *Don't overlook the need for tokenization; it is a critical PCI DSS requirement. Avoid neglecting the implementation of identity management tools like PIM—they reduce risk from unauthorized access. Stay clear of considering endpoint protection alone—it's not sufficient for compliance standards.* |

QUESTION 28

Answer - A) Identify legitimate business scenarios requiring exceptions to Conditional Access policies; B) Review and update Conditional Access policies based on changing business requirements; C) Implement bypass mechanisms for exceptions, such as Azure AD Conditional Access exclusions

Option A - Correct. Identifying legitimate business scenarios requiring exceptions to Conditional Access policies ensures that access control measures do not unduly restrict legitimate business activities.

Option B - Correct. Reviewing and updating Conditional Access policies based on changing business requirements ensures that access control measures remain aligned with organizational needs and security policies. Option C - Correct. Implementing bypass mechanisms for exceptions, such as Azure AD Conditional Access exclusions, allows administrators to accommodate legitimate business needs while maintaining security controls.

Option D - Incorrect. While testing policy updates in a non-production environment is important for ensuring stability, it is not directly related to managing exceptions and policy updates for Conditional Access. Option E - Incorrect. While monitoring policy effectiveness and user feedback is important for continuous improvement, it is not directly related to managing exceptions and policy updates for Conditional Access.

EXAM FOCUS	*You need to identify valid business cases for Conditional Access exceptions and review policies regularly to align with organizational needs. Use exclusion mechanisms cautiously, ensuring they don't compromise overall security. Testing in non-production helps refine updates without risking live environments.*
CAUTION ALERT	*Avoid creating broad exclusions—they can undermine access controls. Stay alert to unverified policy updates in production; they may disrupt workflows. Don't assume user feedback is unnecessary—it often highlights unintended impacts or loopholes in Conditional Access policies.*

QUESTION 29

Answer - A) Azure Policy for enforcing compliance requirements and security baselines; C) Azure Automation for scheduling and executing security configuration tasks and remediation; D) Azure DevOps for version control and deployment of security configuration scripts

Option A - Correct. Azure Policy can be used to enforce compliance requirements and security baselines across AVD session hosts, ensuring consistent security configurations. Option B - Incorrect. While Azure Security Center provides security monitoring and threat detection capabilities, it may not directly automate security settings management for session hosts.

Option C - Correct. Azure Automation enables scheduling and execution of security configuration tasks and remediation actions, reducing manual effort and ensuring consistency. Option D - Correct. Azure DevOps facilitates version control and deployment of security configuration scripts, promoting automation and collaboration among development and operations teams. Option E - Incorrect. While Azure Monitor offers proactive alerting for security incidents, it may not directly automate security settings management for AVD session hosts.

EXAM FOCUS	*Leverage Azure Policy to enforce compliance across session hosts. Use Azure Automation for repetitive security tasks and Azure DevOps for streamlined deployment of scripts. These tools reduce manual effort and ensure consistent security configurations in AVD deployments.*
CAUTION ALERT	*Avoid using Azure Security Center as a replacement for automation; it focuses on monitoring, not direct settings management. Stay clear of neglecting version control in security scripts—Azure DevOps ensures accurate tracking. Don't skip Automation workflows; they standardize security operations.*

QUESTION 30

Answer - B) WorkspaceId should reference a specific log analytics workspace

Option A - Incorrect: The command generalizes the logging but may not capture all necessary details. Option B - Correct: WorkspaceId must reference an existing Log Analytics workspace configured for AVD logging to ensure comprehensive auditing. Option C - Incorrect: The ResourceId broadly targets the resource group, which is generally acceptable unless more granular logging is required.

Option D - Incorrect: Logging should be enabled, not disabled.

Option E - Incorrect: While adding specific logging categories could enhance the detail and relevance of logs, the basic command structure is correct for enabling logging.

EXAM FOCUS	*Ensure WorkspaceId is linked to a dedicated Log Analytics workspace for detailed logging. Use diagnostic settings to capture all relevant logs for auditing. Comprehensive logging enables effective monitoring and compliance tracking, enhancing administrative transparency in AVD environments.*
CAUTION ALERT	*Don't omit necessary logging categories—they provide granularity. Stay cautioned against pointing ResourceId at incorrect resources—it skews log data. Avoid disabling logging or setting incorrect retention policies—it undermines the auditability and compliance capabilities of the system.*

QUESTION 31

Answer - B) Perform thorough testing in a non-production environment before full deployment

Option A - Incorrect. Disabling Windows Search indexing may impact user experience but doesn't directly address profile management challenges. Option B - Correct. Thorough testing in a non-production environment helps identify and mitigate potential issues before a full deployment.

Option C - Incorrect. VHD disk format is less efficient and may not be necessary for compatibility. Option D - Incorrect. While backup is important, it's not specific to avoiding installation pitfalls. Option E - Incorrect. Group Policy enforcement doesn't replace the need for thorough testing.

EXAM FOCUS	*Make sure to conduct thorough testing in a non-production environment to identify and mitigate conflicts with legacy applications or existing profile management tools like roaming profiles. Testing ensures smooth migration and avoids pitfalls like profile bloat or performance degradation over time.*
CAUTION ALERT	*Avoid skipping pre-deployment testing; it's essential for identifying incompatibilities. Stay clear of assuming default settings are optimal for your environment. Don't confuse Group Policy enforcement with proper testing—it doesn't address environment-specific issues.*

QUESTION 32

Answer - A) Implement role-based access control (RBAC) to restrict access to Office Containers, C) Encrypt Office Containers to protect sensitive data from unauthorized access, E) Implement multi-factor authentication (MFA) for user access to Office applications.

A) Implement role-based access control (RBAC) to restrict access to Office Containers - RBAC ensures that only authorized users have access to Office Containers, reducing the risk of unauthorized access and data breaches. C) Encrypt Office Containers to protect sensitive data from unauthorized access - Encrypting Office Containers helps safeguard sensitive data stored within Containers, ensuring confidentiality and compliance with security standards.

E) Implement multi-factor authentication (MFA) for user access to Office applications - MFA adds an extra layer of security by requiring users to provide multiple forms of authentication, reducing the risk of unauthorized access even if login credentials are compromised. B) Enable Azure Active Directory (Azure AD) conditional access policies for Office application access - While conditional access policies can enhance security, they may not specifically address security considerations within Office Containers. D) Utilize Azure Defender for Cloud to detect and respond to security threats in Office Containers - Azure Defender for Cloud focuses on threat detection and response but may not directly address security measures within Office Containers.

EXAM FOCUS	*You need to enforce RBAC for restricting access, encrypt Office Containers for data security, and implement MFA to strengthen authentication. These measures collectively enhance security and ensure compliance with regulatory requirements, safeguarding sensitive data in Office applications.*
CAUTION ALERT	*Avoid relying on Azure Defender alone for protection—it focuses on detection, not proactive access control. Stay alert to gaps in encryption practices; unencrypted data can lead to breaches. Don't neglect MFA implementation—it's crucial for reducing unauthorized access risks.*

QUESTION 33

Answer - A, D, E

A) Correct - Azure VPN Gateway ensures secure and private connections for remote users, important for a hybrid workforce. B) Incorrect - Configuring host pools in multiple regions improves performance but doesn't directly ensure GDPR compliance or secure access.

C) Incorrect - Azure Policy is crucial for compliance but does not specifically address user experience or secure access requirements. D) Correct - MFA provides an additional layer of security, crucial for protecting data and complying with GDPR. E) Correct - Azure Virtual WAN optimizes network connectivity, ensuring a consistent user experience across global locations.

EXAM FOCUS	*Always implement Azure VPN Gateway for secure connections, enable MFA for added security, and deploy Azure Virtual WAN for optimized network performance. These configurations ensure a consistent and secure user experience while supporting GDPR compliance for hybrid workforce setups.*
CAUTION ALERT	*Don't rely on regional host pools alone—they improve performance but don't secure data or ensure compliance. Stay alert to improper VPN configurations—they can expose sensitive data. Avoid omitting MFA—it's a key requirement for protecting access to resources in hybrid setups.*

QUESTION 34

Answer - A) Utilize Azure AD Conditional Access policies to enforce device compliance and restrict access based on device attributes and configurations, D) Utilize Group Policy settings to enforce device configuration requirements and restrict access to AVD sessions based on device compliance status.

A) Utilize Azure AD Conditional Access policies to enforce device compliance and restrict access based on device attributes and configurations - Conditional Access policies provide granular control over device access based on compliance status, ensuring that only compliant devices can connect to AVD sessions. D) Utilize Group Policy settings to enforce device configuration requirements and restrict access to AVD sessions based on device compliance status - Group Policy settings allow administrators to enforce specific device configurations and compliance requirements, ensuring that only compliant devices can access AVD sessions.

B) Configure Azure AD Identity Protection policies to detect risky sign-in attempts from unauthorized or non-compliant devices - While Identity Protection policies enhance security, they may not directly address device type restrictions and compliance requirements for AVD sessions. C) Implement Azure AD Device Enrollment restrictions to limit AVD access to devices enrolled in a corporate device management solution - While Device Enrollment restrictions enforce device enrollment policies, they may not directly address device type restrictions for AVD sessions.

E) Deploy Azure Bastion as a secure remote access solution for AVD instances, restricting access to corporate-approved devices only - While Azure Bastion enhances access security, it may not directly enforce device type restrictions for AVD sessions.

EXAM FOCUS	*Utilize Conditional Access policies and Group Policy settings to enforce compliance and restrict device access. These strategies ensure only corporate-managed devices meet security requirements for AVD connections, maintaining industry compliance and secure access standards.*
CAUTION ALERT	*Don't confuse Azure Bastion deployment with device restrictions; it secures access but doesn't enforce compliance policies. Stay alert to misconfigured Conditional Access policies—they can inadvertently allow non-compliant devices. Avoid assuming Identity Protection addresses device restrictions.*

QUESTION 35

Answer - A) Correctly enables logging

Option A - Correct: Enabling detailed logging on the printer can help identify issues with print jobs, including delays and errors.

Option B - Incorrect: JobLogEnabled is a hypothetical valid property for enabling logging in this context. Option C - Incorrect: While the command is specific to a printer property, it is relevant as part of broader network troubleshooting.

Option D - Incorrect: While server-level logging is crucial, printer-specific logging is also necessary for comprehensive diagnostics. Option E - Incorrect: Setting the value to $true is correct to enable the feature.

EXAM FOCUS	*You can enable detailed logging with the correct PowerShell command to track job statuses, helping identify and resolve delays or errors. Use the logs to analyze network-related issues affecting printing and ensure seamless troubleshooting and performance improvements.*
CAUTION ALERT	*Avoid enabling logging only at the server level—it's crucial to capture printer-specific logs for comprehensive diagnostics. Stay clear of disabling logs after troubleshooting; they're valuable for ongoing performance monitoring. Don't assume logs are enabled by default.*

QUESTION 36

Answer - A, B, E

A) Correct - Azure CDN accelerates the delivery of high-bandwidth content, crucial for a global news agency.
B) Correct - Azure Rights Management Services secure sensitive information, protecting against unauthorized access and leaks.

C) Incorrect - While Azure Media Services is useful for managing media content, it does not directly impact the security or delivery speed of textual news content in an AVD environment. D) Incorrect - Azure Bastion provides secure access but is not directly related to content delivery or content management. E) Correct - Azure Information Protection secures and tracks sensitive documents, ensuring data security in news reporting.

EXAM FOCUS	*Deploy Azure CDN for fast content delivery, Azure Rights Management Services for protecting sensitive data, and Azure Information Protection for document tracking and encryption. These configurations ensure secure, efficient content management for a global news agency.*
CAUTION ALERT	*Don't overlook Azure CDN for content delivery—it's critical for performance. Stay alert to not encrypting sensitive documents; it risks breaches. Avoid relying on Azure Media Services for text-based content delivery; it's tailored for multimedia.*

QUESTION 37

Answer - C) Reviewing user login times and session durations to optimize VM startup schedules

Reviewing user login times and session durations allows for the optimization of VM startup schedules, which impacts resource utilization and cost management.

Option A - Incorrect. Network bandwidth usage is important but not directly tied to VM startup schedules. Option B - Incorrect. CPU and memory usage patterns are relevant but do not directly influence VM startup scheduling. Option D - Incorrect. GPU acceleration enhances graphics performance but does not specifically address VM startup schedules. Option E - Incorrect. Azure AD Join integrates identities but does not directly impact VM startup schedules.

EXAM FOCUS	*Review user login patterns and session durations to optimize Start VM on Connect schedules. These insights reduce idle VM runtime, balancing resource utilization with user demand, and contribute to effective cost management in AVD environments.*
CAUTION ALERT	*Avoid focusing only on CPU or memory usage—they don't provide actionable data for VM scheduling. Stay clear of enabling VM startup for all users indiscriminately; it leads to inefficiencies. Don't ignore session data; it's crucial for tailored cost-effective scaling.*

QUESTION 38

Answer - C) Azure Resource Manager (ARM) Templates

ARM Templates provide a declarative way to automate the deployment of resources, including applications, across multiple user sessions in AVD environments, ensuring efficiency and consistency.

Option A - PowerShell scripts: While PowerShell is versatile, ARM Templates offer a more structured approach to automation, ensuring consistency and scalability. Option B - Azure CLI (Command Line Interface): Azure CLI may be used for automation but lacks the declarative nature and consistency of ARM Templates.

Option D - FSLogix profile containers: FSLogix profiles manage user settings but do not directly automate application deployment. Option E - MSIX App Attach: MSIX App Attach facilitates application delivery but does not directly address automation of deployment tasks.

EXAM FOCUS	*Always choose ARM Templates for automating app deployments in AVD. Their declarative structure ensures consistency, scalability, and efficient resource deployment across sessions. It's a robust tool for managing complex environments with minimal manual intervention.*
CAUTION ALERT	*Avoid relying on PowerShell scripts for large-scale automation—they lack the structure of ARM Templates. Stay alert to incorrect or outdated resource definitions in templates—they can lead to deployment failures. Don't assume MSIX App Attach replaces deployment automation; it's for app delivery.*

QUESTION 39

Answer - A, B, C

A) Correct - Azure Bastion ensures secure and private access to desktop environments, important for protecting student data.

B) Correct - Azure Policy helps enforce compliance with educational data protection standards, ensuring that data handling meets regulatory requirements. C) Correct - RBAC in Azure AD allows for access control based on user roles, essential in an educational setup to differentiate between student, teacher, and admin access.

D) Incorrect - While Azure Site Recovery is important for resilience, it is not directly required for role-based access or compliance enforcement. E) Incorrect - Azure Firewall is critical for network security but does not directly support role-based access or specific compliance needs in online learning environments.

EXAM FOCUS	*Implement Azure Bastion for secure access, Azure Policy for compliance enforcement, and RBAC for role-based access control. These configurations align with educational data standards and ensure differentiated access for students, teachers, and admins in an AVD environment.*
CAUTION ALERT	*Avoid neglecting role differentiation—it's critical in educational setups. Stay clear of depending solely on Azure Firewall for access control—it regulates traffic, not roles. Don't assume Azure Site Recovery addresses access needs—it's for disaster recovery, not day-to-day management.*

QUESTION 40

Answer - C

Option A - Incorrect. The parameter names for rates are incorrect.
Option B - Incorrect. While related, BandwidthThrottling isn't the correct parameter.
Option C - Correct. The terms should be Bandwidth not Rate.
Option D - Incorrect. The proposed flag does not exist.
Option E - Incorrect. Changes are needed to the rate parameters.

EXAM FOCUS	*Use the correct parameter names (MaxDownloadBandwidth and MaxUploadBandwidth) to ensure efficient OneDrive syncing in multisession environments. Proper configurations prevent performance lags and maintain user productivity during data synchronization tasks.*

	*Avoid using incorrect parameters for bandwidth control—it can lead to inefficient sync processes. Stay alert to performance drops caused by unoptimized configurations. Don't assume throttling alone resolves issues; use session-specific optimization where possible.*

QUESTION 41

Answer - E

Option A - Incorrect. The specified configuration doesn't correctly relate to Microsoft 365 Apps.
Option B - Incorrect. While specifying allowed locations is a valid approach, it must be implemented differently.
Option C - Incorrect. The adjustment doesn't exist in this form within ARM templates.
Option D - Incorrect. The resource type for Microsoft 365 Apps is not correctly specified.
Option E - Correct. Managing access based on location should ideally be handled through Azure AD policies, not directly through session host configurations, providing more granular control and better integration with other Microsoft services.

Always remember location-based access is best managed through Azure AD Conditional Access policies for granularity and scalability. ARM templates alone cannot enforce dynamic access controls effectively. Opt for integration with identity solutions for seamless management.

Avoid assuming ARM templates directly handle app-level access restrictions. Stay clear of misconfiguring session hosts when access control must align with organizational policies. Conditional Access offers a more comprehensive approach.

QUESTION 42

Answer - A, B, C

A) Correct - 'CloudCache' enables the use of multiple storage points, essential for high availability and quick access.
B) Correct - 'CloudCacheLocations' provides redundancy, ensuring that user profiles are accessible even if one location fails.

C) Correct - 'LocalCacheSize' controls the cache size, affecting the speed of profile loading and logon times.
D) Incorrect - 'DeleteLocalProfileWhenVHDShouldApply' is useful for managing local profile cleanup but does not impact availability or logon speed directly. E) Incorrect - 'PreventLoginWithFailure' enhances security but does not directly contribute to system availability or logon speed.

Make sure to enable CloudCache and configure redundancy for high availability. LocalCacheSize ensures profiles load efficiently during peak hours. These settings are critical for large-scale, fast user logons in AVD setups, especially in dynamic environments like education.

Stay alert to not defining multiple CloudCache locations—it undermines redundancy. Avoid neglecting cache size configurations; insufficient sizing may lead to delays in profile loading. Don't confuse cleanup policies with availability optimization settings.

QUESTION 43

Answer - B) Get-RdsSessionHost

Option B - Get-RdsSessionHost cmdlet retrieves detailed information about AVD session hosts, including their status, health, and configuration. It enables administrators to perform health checks and diagnostic tasks programmatically.

Option A - Get-RdsDiagnosticActivities cmdlet is used to retrieve diagnostic activity logs for AVD, but it does not specifically target session hosts. Option C - Get-RdsDiagnosticProperty cmdlet retrieves diagnostic properties of AVD deployments, but it may not provide detailed information about individual session hosts.

Option D - Get-RdsSessionConfiguration cmdlet retrieves session configuration settings, which are not directly related to health checks for session hosts. Option E - Get-RdsSession cmdlet retrieves information about active user sessions within AVD deployments, rather than focusing on session host health.

EXAM FOCUS	You need to use Get-RdsSessionHost for proactive health checks, which provides detailed insights into host status. Incorporate it into scripts for automated monitoring to maintain optimal session host health in AVD environments.
CAUTION ALERT	Don't confuse Get-RdsSessionHost with commands targeting user sessions or general diagnostics. Stay clear of relying on manual checks alone; automation improves efficiency. Avoid overlooking this cmdlet for periodic host-level diagnostics.

QUESTION 44

Answer - A) Azure Monitor Logs

Option A - Azure Monitor Logs provide insights into performance metrics and resource utilization for AVD deployments, enabling proactive performance tuning measures.
Option B - Azure Activity Log focuses on operational events, not performance metrics for AVD deployments.
Option C - Azure Diagnostic Logs capture platform-level logs, not specific to AVD performance metrics.
Option D - Azure Application Insights is used for application performance monitoring, not for AVD infrastructure monitoring.
Option E - Azure Network Watcher focuses on network diagnostics, not AVD performance metrics.

EXAM FOCUS	Leverage Azure Monitor Logs for performance metrics and resource utilization in AVD. Always align diagnostic settings with the deployment's evolving needs, and periodically review the collected insights to address bottlenecks and improve user experiences.
CAUTION ALERT	Don't confuse platform logs with application-specific logs. Stay alert to misconfiguring diagnostic settings; irrelevant categories waste resources. Avoid assuming Azure Activity Log provides the detailed metrics required for performance tuning.

QUESTION 45

Answer - B

Option A - Incorrect. While the snippet sets up basic diagnostic settings, it does not define how long the logs should be retained. Option B - Correct. Adding a retention policy is crucial for compliance and long-term analysis, making it possible to track update activities and compliance over time.

Option C - Incorrect. "UpdateLogs" may be correct depending on the specific Azure service; the exact category name should be verified. Option D - Incorrect. "workspaceId" is the correct property name for linking to a Log Analytics workspace in ARM templates. Option E - Incorrect. Including metrics is useful but not directly related to monitoring update compliance and success rates.

EXAM FOCUS	Always include a retention policy in diagnostic settings to meet compliance requirements and ensure long-term data availability for analysis. Retaining update logs ensures a clear audit trail for monitoring compliance trends over time.
CAUTION ALERT	Avoid missing retention configurations; logs without defined retention periods may be purged prematurely. Stay clear of incorrect log categories; verify they match the intended data source. Don't assume defaults meet regulatory or operational requirements.

QUESTION 46

Answer - D) Configuring Azure Security Center for threat detection

Option D - Configuring Azure Security Center for threat detection helps identify and respond to network security threats in AVD environments, ensuring the integrity and confidentiality of network traffic. Monitoring network performance alongside threat detection enhances overall security posture and enables timely incident response.

Option A - Implementing Role-Based Access Control (RBAC) is important for access management but may not directly relate to network performance monitoring. Option B - Encrypting network traffic with Azure VPN Gateway enhances data confidentiality but may not specifically address network performance monitoring.

Option C - Enabling Just-In-Time (JIT) access enhances access control but may not directly impact network performance monitoring. Option E - Enforcing Multi-Factor Authentication (MFA) enhances authentication security but may not directly relate to network performance monitoring.

EXAM FOCUS	*You should configure Azure Security Center for network threat detection in AVD environments. Proactively identifying vulnerabilities enhances the security of monitored networks and ensures compliance with organizational policies.*
CAUTION ALERT	*Avoid assuming RBAC or VPN encryption alone is sufficient for network security. Stay alert to leaving diagnostic data unsecured; encryption and access controls are mandatory. Don't neglect Security Center alerts—they provide actionable insights for response.*

QUESTION 47

Answer - A) Regularly reviewing Azure Cost Management reports
B) Forecasting future AVD usage and growth
D) Setting up alerts for budget thresholds

A) Regularly reviewing Azure Cost Management reports - Regular reviews help identify spending trends and areas for optimization. B) Forecasting future AVD usage and growth - Accurate forecasting ensures budget allocations align with expected usage and growth.

D) Setting up alerts for budget thresholds - Alerts notify administrators when spending approaches or exceeds predefined thresholds, enabling timely action. C, E) While implementing RBAC and utilizing Azure Advisor recommendations are important, they are not specific to budget planning and management.

EXAM FOCUS	*Always review Azure Cost Management reports and forecast future AVD usage trends to align budgets with expected growth. Alerts for budget thresholds provide real-time notifications, helping prevent overspending and ensure cost efficiency.*
CAUTION ALERT	*Don't rely solely on post-spend reviews; proactive measures like alerts are critical. Stay clear of assuming RBAC alone controls costs—it doesn't address forecasting or trends. Avoid overlooking Azure Cost Management's insights when planning budgets.*

QUESTION 48

Answer - A, D, E

A) Correct - Windows Server 2019 offers good support for legacy applications and robust data management capabilities. B) Incorrect - Windows 10 Pro is suitable for general use but does not provide the session control needed for a complex remote management scenario. C) Incorrect - Windows Server 2012 R2 is outdated and may not provide the connectivity and data integrity features needed.

D) Correct - Windows 11 Enterprise provides modern features that can enhance connectivity and support for new applications. E) Correct - Windows 10 Enterprise multi-session is ideal for managing multiple remote sessions efficiently under varied network conditions.

EXAM FOCUS	*Select operating systems like Windows 10 Enterprise multi-session and Windows Server 2019 for legacy support and reliable management under low-bandwidth conditions. Modern options like Windows 11 Enterprise enhance compatibility and connectivity.*
CAUTION ALERT	*Avoid selecting outdated systems like Server 2012 R2—they lack modern features. Stay alert to the lack of multi-session support in some editions; verify compatibility. Don't assume Pro versions suffice for enterprise-scale AVD environments.*

QUESTION 49

Answer - A) Potential fines and penalties for unauthorized use of software
B) Legal actions from software vendors for copyright infringement

A) Potential fines and penalties for unauthorized use of software - Non-compliance with licensing agreements may result in financial penalties and legal consequences for the organization. B) Legal actions from software vendors for copyright infringement - Software vendors have legal recourse to protect their intellectual property rights and may pursue legal actions against non-compliant organizations.

C, D, E) While data breaches, loss of reputation, and impact on business continuity are potential consequences of non-compliance, they are not direct legal risks associated with AVD licensing agreements.

EXAM FOCUS	*Keep in mind that non-compliance with licensing can lead to fines and legal action. Regular audits and adherence to agreements mitigate risks and protect intellectual property. Licensing compliance also safeguards the organization's reputation and operational continuity.*
CAUTION ALERT	*Don't assume non-compliance is a minor issue—it can result in significant financial and legal repercussions. Stay alert to using unlicensed software; it exposes the organization to copyright infringement claims. Avoid ignoring license agreements to cut costs.*

QUESTION 50

Answer - A) Implementing RBAC controls to restrict access to log data based on role and responsibility
B) Enabling encryption for log data at rest and in transit to protect against unauthorized access
D) Implementing Azure AD Conditional Access policies to control access to log management tools and data

A) Implementing RBAC controls to restrict access to log data based on role and responsibility - RBAC controls help restrict access to log data based on users' roles and responsibilities, minimizing the risk of unauthorized access and data breaches. B) Enabling encryption for log data at rest and in transit to protect against unauthorized access - Encryption ensures that log data is protected both at rest and in transit, safeguarding it from unauthorized access and potential data breaches.

D) Implementing Azure AD Conditional Access policies to control access to log management tools and data - Conditional Access policies help control access to log management tools and data based on specified conditions, enhancing security and compliance. C, E) While utilizing Azure Key Vault and configuring Azure Security Center are important security measures, they are not directly related to log management security considerations in AVD.

EXAM FOCUS	*You need to implement RBAC and encryption for secure log management. This ensures logs remain protected from unauthorized access, both at rest and in transit. Conditional Access policies enhance control over tools and data access, bolstering compliance and security.*
CAUTION ALERT	*Avoid neglecting encryption for logs—it's critical for protecting sensitive information. Stay clear of granting broad access to logs; use RBAC for role-specific permissions. Don't overlook Conditional Access—it offers enhanced control over log access tools.*

PRACTICE TEST 10 - QUESTIONS ONLY

QUESTION 1

You are planning a scenario-based virtual network setup for AVD that requires high availability and robust recovery options. The setup must:
• Support rapid scaling and deployment of new AVD instances.
• Ensure data resiliency and backup.
• Maintain high availability across multiple Azure regions.
What is the most effective Azure configuration to implement in this scenario?

A) Azure Site Recovery
B) Azure Load Balancer
C) Azure Availability Zones
D) Azure Scale Sets
E) Azure Backup

QUESTION 2

A department within your organization is experiencing intermittent connectivity issues and degraded performance during Azure Virtual Desktop (AVD) sessions. The sales team heavily relies on AVD to access CRM tools and collaborate with clients remotely. However, identifying the root cause of the connectivity issues and implementing effective solutions pose significant challenges. How would you troubleshoot and resolve the intermittent connectivity issues to ensure seamless AVD sessions for the sales team?

A) Check for any network latency issues using Azure Network Watcher
B) Review Azure AD Connect configuration for user authentication issues
C) Analyze Azure Bastion logs for connection errors
D) Verify AVD host pool configurations for resource allocation
E) Increase Azure VM sizes for improved performance

QUESTION 3

- Your organization requires real-time monitoring of user sessions in an Azure Virtual Desktop (AVD) environment for compliance and security purposes.
- You need to identify the appropriate Log Analytics table to monitor active user sessions and detect any suspicious activities.
- Your task involves selecting the table that provides real-time session monitoring capabilities.

Which table in Log Analytics should you query to monitor active user sessions and detect suspicious activities in real-time?

A) WVDActiveUserSessions
B) WVDSessionEvent
C) WVDAuditLogs
D) WVDUserSessions
E) WVDServiceHealth

QUESTION 4

Your organization is reviewing case studies of effective storage planning for Azure Virtual Desktop (AVD) to learn from real-world implementations. As the Azure administrator, you need to analyze these case studies and extract key insights to inform future storage planning initiatives for AVD deployments. What lessons can be learned from successful case studies of AVD storage planning? Select THREE.

A) Balancing performance and cost with appropriate storage tier selections
B) Implementing data redundancy and fault tolerance for high availability
C) Leveraging caching mechanisms to optimize storage performance
D) Automating storage provisioning and management tasks
E) Integrating storage solutions with identity and access management controls

QUESTION 5

Security best practices are paramount when managing storage for AVD. Analyze this Bicep script for creating a secured storage account. What security enhancements are recommended?

```bicep
resource secureStorage 'Microsoft.Storage/storageAccounts@2021-06-01' = {
 name: 'SecuredStorage',
 location: 'westus2',
 sku: { name: 'Standard_RAGRS' },
 properties: {
 supportsHttpsTrafficOnly: true,
 networkAcls: {
 bypass: 'AzureServices',
 defaultAction: 'Deny'
 }
 }
}
```

A) Enable MFA for access control
B) Set networkAcls defaultAction to Allow
C) Disable supportsHttpsTrafficOnly
D) Configuration is already secure
E) Change location to eastus

QUESTION 6

Your organization aims to optimize costs in its Azure Virtual Desktop (AVD) environment by implementing an efficient solution for managing session host usage. The solution must meet the following requirements:
- Automatically scale session hosts based on user demand to ensure optimal resource utilization.
- Ensure that session hosts are available 24/7.
- Minimize administrative overhead.
Which Azure service or feature should you use to fulfill these requirements? Select TWO.

A) Azure Functions
B) Azure Automation with Azure Logic Apps
C) Azure Monitor Alerts
D) Azure Virtual Machine Scale Sets
E) Azure Resource Manager templates

QUESTION 7

Your organization needs to stay updated on the latest updates and changes in Azure licensing policies, particularly regarding Azure Virtual Desktop (AVD) deployments. As the Azure specialist, you are responsible for monitoring and communicating these changes. What measures should you take? Select THREE.

A) Regularly Review Microsoft Documentation and Official Announcements
B) Participate in Microsoft Partner Programs and Training Sessions
C) Engage with Microsoft Account Representatives and Licensing Experts

D) Join Online Communities and Forums for Azure Professionals
E) Conduct Internal Training and Knowledge Sharing Sessions for IT Staff

QUESTION 8

Your organization aims to maintain consistent user experience across various devices in its Azure Virtual Desktop (AVD) environment. As the Azure administrator, you are tasked with implementing techniques to achieve this goal. What techniques should you prioritize? Select THREE.

A) Profile Management and Roaming User Profiles
B) Application Virtualization and Containerization
C) Network Optimization and Quality of Service (QoS)
D) Load Balancing and Session Affinity
E) Endpoint Security and Device Management Policies

QUESTION 9

You are planning to implement autoscale for host pools in an Azure Virtual Desktop (AVD) environment to optimize resource utilization. Consider the following factors:
- Scale resources based on both user demand and performance metrics.
- Ensure seamless scaling without impacting user sessions.
- Minimize administrative effort for managing autoscale configurations.
Which of the following strategies should you prioritize to meet these requirements? Select THREE.

A) Implement autoscale rules based on CPU and memory utilization.
B) Configure a grace period to avoid scaling actions during active user sessions.
C) Utilize Azure Advisor recommendations for autoscale configuration.
D) Set up recurring scaling events during off-peak hours.
E) Implement custom scripts for autoscale management.

QUESTION 10

Troubleshooting common configuration issues in AVD involves ensuring session hosts can manage traffic effectively. Analyze this PowerShell command for setting up a new host pool with Quality of Service (QoS) configurations:

```powershell
New-AzAVDHostPool -Name "ManagedHosts" -LoadBalancerType "BreadthFirst" -CustomRdpProperty "qos:dscp=46"
```

A) Command is correctly configured
B) LoadBalancerType is inappropriate
C) CustomRdpProperty is incorrectly formatted
D) Missing network profile
E) All are incorrect

QUESTION 11

Your organization is planning to implement version control and update management for golden images used in Azure Virtual Desktop (AVD) deployments to ensure consistency and reliability. As the Azure specialist, you need to understand the recommended strategies for maintaining version control and managing updates for golden images. What are recommended strategies for version control and update management of golden images? Select CORRECT answers that apply.

A) Use Azure Image Builder for Automated Image Creation
B) Implement Tagging and Metadata for Image Versioning

C) Schedule Regular Image Maintenance and Updates
D) Leverage Azure DevOps for Image Pipeline Automation
E) Implement Rollback Procedures for Image Deployment Failures

QUESTION 12

You are tasked with configuring a disaster recovery strategy for an Azure Virtual Desktop (AVD) infrastructure to ensure business continuity. Consider the following requirements:
- Implement failover of AVD host pools to a secondary Azure region in case of a primary region failure.
- Minimize data loss and downtime during failover operations.
Which Azure service should you utilize to fulfill these requirements?

A) Azure Active Directory
B) Azure Traffic Manager
C) Azure Backup
D) Azure Monitor
E) Azure Site Recovery

QUESTION 13

Your organization aims to manage downtime and minimize user impact during updates of Azure Virtual Desktop (AVD) images to maintain productivity and user satisfaction. As the Azure specialist, you need to evaluate approaches for managing downtime and user impact. Which of the following approaches can help in managing downtime and user impact during updates of AVD images? Select THREE.

A) Implementing Rolling Updates
B) Utilizing Maintenance Windows for Scheduled Updates
C) Employing Automated Rollback Mechanisms
D) Enforcing Session Persistence Across Updates
E) Distributing Updates During Non-Business Hours

QUESTION 14

Your organization recognizes the importance of backup and disaster recovery planning for image storage in Azure Virtual Desktop (AVD) deployments to mitigate potential data loss and minimize downtime. As the Azure specialist, you need to identify backup and disaster recovery options for image storage. What backup and disaster recovery options should be considered for image storage in AVD deployments? Select THREE.

A) Implement Azure Backup for Automated Image Snapshots
B) Configure Azure Site Recovery for Image Replication and Failover
C) Utilize Azure Blob Storage Versioning for Image History Tracking
D) Implement Geo-Redundant Storage for Cross-Region Disaster Recovery
E) Establish Backup Policies with Azure Policy for Image Lifecycle Management

QUESTION 15

Monitoring network performance is critical in maintaining an efficient AVD environment. What PowerShell script would you use to retrieve network performance metrics?

```powershell
Get-AzMetric -ResourceGroupName "Network-RG" -ResourceType "Microsoft.Network/networkInterfaces" -Name "MyNic" -MetricName "NetworkInTotal"
```

A) Correctly retrieves metrics
B) Incorrect ResourceType

C) MetricName should be "TotalNetworkIn"
D) Missing TimeGrain parameter
E) Name parameter is unnecessary

QUESTION 16

Maintaining continuous compliance in Azure Virtual Desktop (AVD) deployments requires adherence to best practices and ongoing monitoring of regulatory requirements and industry standards. As the Azure specialist, you need to implement strategies for ensuring continuous compliance effectively. What are the best practices for maintaining continuous compliance in AVD deployments? Select THREE.

A) Implement Automated Compliance Checks and Remediation
B) Conduct Regular Security Awareness Training for End Users
C) Monitor Configuration Changes and Vulnerability Assessments
D) Implement Role-Based Access Controls (RBAC) and Least Privilege Principles
E) Establish Incident Response Plans and Security Incident Management Procedures

QUESTION 17

Your organization is interested in analyzing cost trends and generating reports to understand spending patterns in its Azure Virtual Desktop (AVD) deployment. As the Azure specialist, you need to employ cost analysis and reporting techniques to provide insights for cost optimization. What techniques can you utilize for cost analysis and reporting in AVD deployments? Select THREE.

A) Utilizing Azure Cost Management and Billing Reports for Cost Allocation
B) Implementing Azure Log Analytics Workbooks for Customized Cost Dashboards
C) Leveraging Power BI for Data Visualization and Cost Trend Analysis
D) Enabling Azure Monitor Alerts for Cost Anomalies and Overspending Notifications
E) Integrating Azure Budgets with Resource Tagging for Granular Cost Tracking

QUESTION 18

You are tasked with designing a disaster recovery solution for an Azure Virtual Desktop (AVD) environment to ensure business continuity in the event of a primary site failure. Considering this scenario, what solution should you recommend to achieve seamless failover and data protection?
- Minimize downtime and data loss during failover
- Ensure automatic failover and recovery processes
- Simplify management and monitoring tasks Select TWO.

A) Azure Site Recovery
B) Azure Backup
C) Azure File Sync
D) Azure Blob Storage
E) Azure Import/Export

QUESTION 19

Your organization is analyzing case studies of disaster recovery implementations in Azure Virtual Desktop (AVD) environments to learn from best practices and real-world scenarios. The focus is on understanding challenges, successful strategies, and lessons learned from previous deployments. Which aspects of these case studies would you prioritize for improving the disaster recovery plan for your AVD environment? Select THREE.

A) Analyze failover performance metrics and optimization strategies
B) Evaluate communication and coordination among stakeholders during recovery operations
C) Review post-mortem reports and identify areas for process refinement

D) Implement Azure Policy for compliance enforcement and audit trail generation
E) Utilize Azure Security Center for threat detection and response

QUESTION 20

Best practices for ongoing monitoring and reporting of AVD involve continuous assessment of user experience and resource utilization. You need to implement a strategy that not only monitors but also optimizes session host scaling based on time-of-day and user load. Which Azure service or feature should you primarily utilize to automatically scale session hosts in AVD based on predefined metrics and schedules?

A) Azure Monitor autoscale
B) Azure Logic Apps
C) Azure Automation Account
D) Azure Kubernetes Service
E) Azure Scale Sets

QUESTION 21

You are configuring Azure Virtual Desktop for a company that requires secure access to on-premises resources via Remote Desktop Gateway (RD Gateway). You need to implement a security measure that encrypts communication between the RD Gateway server and client devices. Which protocol should you configure for this purpose?

A) TLS
B) IPSec
C) SSH
D) SSL/TLS
E) SMB

QUESTION 22

Your organization is exploring the implementation of Azure role-based access control (RBAC) for Azure Virtual Desktop (AVD) environments and seeks guidance on the design aspects of an effective RBAC system. The focus is on designing a system that aligns with organizational requirements and ensures secure access management. What design considerations should be prioritized when implementing RBAC for AVD environments? Select THREE.

A) Define granular roles based on job functions and responsibilities
B) Implement role assignments using groups for scalability and ease of management
C) Utilize built-in RBAC roles whenever possible to minimize complexity
D) Establish role inheritance to streamline access management and reduce redundancy
E) Enforce least privilege principle to minimize the risk of unauthorized access

QUESTION 23

Your organization has implemented multi-factor authentication (MFA) for Azure Virtual Desktop (AVD) environments and aims to evaluate its effectiveness in enhancing security measures. The focus is on assessing the impact and effectiveness of MFA implementations in AVD environments comprehensively. What factors should be considered when evaluating the effectiveness of multi-factor authentication (MFA) implementations in Azure Virtual Desktop (AVD) environments? Select THREE.

A) Reduction in unauthorized access attempts or security incidents
B) User feedback on the MFA experience and usability
C) Compliance with regulatory requirements and industry standards
D) Comparison of MFA implementation metrics with industry benchmarks
E) Analysis of MFA-related support tickets and resolution times

QUESTION 24

You are tasked with enhancing the performance and scalability of an existing Azure Virtual Desktop deployment used by a multinational corporation. What strategies should you employ to meet these requirements efficiently? Select CORRECT answers that apply.

A) Optimize network routes with Azure Traffic Manager.
B) Implement application layer gateways.
C) Set up host pools based on user location.
D) Utilize Azure Monitor for performance metrics.
E) Scale out session hosts using Azure Automation.

QUESTION 25

After recent updates, you need to verify and adjust firewall settings to ensure only authorized traffic can access your AVD environment. This Azure CLI command is used to update a firewall rule. Check if the modification aligns with best practices for securing AVD access.

```bash
az network firewall network-rule create --name "AllowAVD" --resource-group "AVDResources" --protocols "TCP" --source-addresses "10.0.0.0/24" --destination-ports "3389" --action "Allow" --priority "100"
```

A) Command aligns with best practices
B) Source-addresses should be broader
C) Destination-ports should include more ports
D) Action should be "Deny"
E) Priority should be higher

QUESTION 26

Your organization is troubleshooting issues related to Windows Threat Protection features for Azure Virtual Desktop (AVD) and wants to identify potential causes and resolutions. The focus is on understanding how to troubleshoot threat protection feature issues. What are the steps to troubleshoot threat protection feature issues for AVD? Select TWO.

A) Verify the configuration and deployment status of Windows Defender Antivirus on AVD session hosts
B) Check for conflicts or compatibility issues with third-party security solutions or endpoint management tools
C) Review event logs and error messages generated by Windows Defender Antivirus and other security features
D) Ensure that AVD session hosts have the latest updates and security patches installed from Windows Update
E) Engage Microsoft Support for assistance with troubleshooting and resolving complex threat protection issues

QUESTION 27

An international law firm uses AVD and requires stringent measures for client data confidentiality, secure client communication, and compliance with global data protection regulations. What configurations are vital? Select THREE.

A) Enable end-to-end encryption for data in transit.
B) Implement Azure Information Protection for document classification and protection.
C) Use Azure Sentinel for continuous threat detection and response.
D) Configure geofencing with Azure AD Conditional Access.
E) Deploy Azure Front Door for global web traffic management.

QUESTION 28

Your organization is evaluating the effectiveness and security improvements achieved through the implementation of Conditional Access in Azure Virtual Desktop (AVD) environments. The focus is on understanding the impact of Conditional Access on security and user experience. What are the key effectiveness and security improvements achieved with the implementation of Conditional Access in AVD environments? Select THREE.

A) Enhanced access control based on user roles, locations, and device compliance status
B) Improved protection against unauthorized access attempts and data breaches
C) Reduced risk of malware infections and other security threats
D) Increased visibility and control over access permissions and policies
E) Streamlined user experience with seamless access to resources from trusted locations

QUESTION 29

Your organization has experienced a security breach involving Azure Virtual Desktop (AVD) session hosts, leading to unauthorized access and data exposure. The focus is on identifying the breach and implementing mitigation strategies. How can your organization identify security breaches involving AVD session hosts and implement effective mitigation strategies? Select CORRECT answers that apply.

A) Analyze security logs and audit trails to identify suspicious activities or unauthorized access attempts
B) Conduct forensic analysis of compromised session hosts to determine the extent of the breach and data exposure
C) Implement network segmentation and access controls to isolate compromised session hosts from the rest of the infrastructure
D) Disable compromised user accounts and reset passwords to prevent further unauthorized access
E) Deploy security updates and patches to address vulnerabilities exploited in the breach and strengthen defenses

QUESTION 30

Admin training and policy updates are critical to maintaining security within Azure Virtual Desktop environments. How should you implement a strategy for regular updates and training sessions to ensure all administrative staff are aware of the latest security practices and compliance requirements? Consider the integration of Microsoft Teams to facilitate ongoing training and updates.
Review the following setup for using Microsoft Teams for security training sessions:
bash
az deployment group create --template-file "training-session.json" --resource-group "AVDTraining"

A) Correct setup for training sessions
B) Template file should be more specific to security training
C) Resource group name does not reflect its purpose
D) Should integrate with Azure AD for user management
E) Deployment should be automated

QUESTION 31

Your organization has successfully deployed FSLogix in an AVD environment, and you need to validate the post-installation configuration to ensure optimal performance and user experience. You must consider the following aspects:
1. Verifying that FSLogix profiles are correctly applied to user sessions.
2. Ensuring that FSLogix settings, such as profile size limits, are enforced as intended.
3. Identifying any potential issues or misconfigurations that could impact user productivity.

A) Monitor event logs on AVD session hosts for FSLogix-related errors
B) Use PowerShell script to retrieve FSLogix profile sizes and compare with configured limits
C) Conduct user surveys to gather feedback on login times and application performance

D) Enable FSLogix diagnostic logging and analyze logs for anomalies
E) Use Azure Monitor to track FSLogix profile performance metrics

QUESTION 32

As an Azure Virtual Desktop administrator troubleshooting Office Container deployment issues, you need to identify common problems and solutions to ensure smooth operation. Consider the following scenario:
- Common deployment pitfalls and their resolutions must be identified to expedite troubleshooting efforts.
- The integrity and functionality of Office Containers post-deployment should be validated to ensure user satisfaction.
- Monitoring and alerting systems should be in place to detect and address Office Container issues proactively.
What are the troubleshooting techniques for Office Containers? Select THREE.

A) Analyze event logs for Office Container-related errors.
B) Utilize FSLogix diagnostic tools to identify performance bottlenecks.
C) Test Office Container functionality by creating and accessing user profiles.
D) Monitor storage usage and performance metrics for Office Containers.
E) Use PowerShell scripts to automate Office Container maintenance tasks.

QUESTION 33

For a media company utilizing AVD for content creators scattered globally, you need to ensure high bandwidth, low latency, and robust security for intellectual property. What actions should you take? Select THREE.

A) Enable Azure Content Delivery Network (CDN).
B) Configure Azure ExpressRoute for dedicated connectivity.
C) Implement Azure DDoS Protection Standard.
D) Use Azure Front Door for smart traffic routing.
E) Deploy Azure Application Gateway with WAF.

QUESTION 34

Your organization is encountering troubleshooting challenges related to device redirection problems in Azure Virtual Desktop (AVD) deployments. Consider the following scenario:
- Users report issues with connecting and accessing redirected devices such as printers and USB drives during AVD sessions.
- Some users experience intermittent disconnections or failures while attempting to use redirected peripherals, impacting productivity.
- IT administrators aim to diagnose and resolve device redirection problems promptly to ensure uninterrupted AVD sessions for users.
How can you troubleshoot device redirection problems effectively for the given scenario? Select THREE.

A) Utilize Azure Monitor to track device redirection events and identify patterns or anomalies indicative of underlying issues.
B) Enable verbose logging for device redirection components in AVD session hosts to capture detailed diagnostic information.
C) Implement Azure Network Watcher to analyze network traffic between client devices and AVD resources, identifying potential connectivity issues.
D) Use PowerShell scripts to reset device redirection configurations and refresh device redirection policies on AVD session hosts.
E) Leverage FSLogix diagnostic tools to analyze user profile and session data for any conflicts or inconsistencies affecting device redirection.

QUESTION 35

To enhance printing performance for remote users, you aim to reduce the data load by compressing print jobs. Evaluate the Bicep module snippet intended for configuring print job compression at deployment:

```bicep
resource printJobCompression 'Microsoft.Compute/virtualMachines@2021-04-01' = {
  name: 'EnableCompression'
  properties: {
    setting: 'Compressed'
  }
}
```

A) Compresses print jobs effectively
B) Module targets the wrong resource type
C) 'Compressed' is not a valid setting
D) Bicep module cannot configure print settings
E) Name should reflect the virtual machine's name

QUESTION 36

A university using AVD needs to ensure robust cybersecurity for research data, enable secure remote access for international researchers, and maintain compliance with educational data regulations. What configurations are essential? Select THREE.

A) Configure Azure Firewall to secure network traffic.
B) Enable Multi-Factor Authentication (MFA) for secure access.
C) Implement Azure Private Link for private connectivity.
D) Use Azure Information Protection for data classification and encryption.
E) Deploy Azure Bastion for secure, seamless access to AVD environments.

QUESTION 37

You are troubleshooting issues related to the Start VM on Connect feature in Azure Virtual Desktop (AVD). Users report delays in accessing their desktops after login. Which action can help identify common issues and improve the performance of the Start VM on Connect feature?

A) Configuring custom diagnostics in Azure Monitor to track VM startup times
B) Enabling verbose logging for the AVD service to capture detailed connection data
C) Analyzing network latency using Azure Network Watcher to identify connectivity issues
D) Reviewing Azure Activity Logs to monitor changes in VM startup configurations
E) Deploying Azure Bastion to provide secure RDP access to AVD instances

QUESTION 38

Troubleshooting app deployment issues in Azure Virtual Desktop (AVD) environments requires a comprehensive understanding of the deployment methods and associated challenges. What is the recommended approach for resolving issues related to application compatibility and performance?

A) Reviewing Azure Activity Logs for deployment errors
B) Analyzing network performance metrics to identify bottlenecks
C) Checking Azure Bastion logs for access issues
D) Monitoring Azure AD for authentication failures
E) Utilizing FSLogix profile status to verify application configurations

QUESTION 39

A healthcare provider using AVD needs to ensure PHI security, support emergency remote access during crises, and maintain high system availability. What should be configured? Select THREE.

A) Deploy Azure Bastion with AzureBastionSubnet for secure remote access.
B) Implement Azure Site Recovery across multiple regions.
C) Configure Azure AD Conditional Access based on user roles and conditions.
D) Set up Azure Monitor for system performance and availability monitoring.
E) Use Azure VPN Gateway for additional remote access routes.

QUESTION 40

To enhance collaboration through OneDrive in AVD, what script adjustment should be made to this Bicep configuration to include all necessary features for AVD users?
resource onedrive 'Microsoft.OneDrive/sites@2021-06-01' = { name: 'AVDSite' properties: { enableSharing: true } }

A) Add features: ['multiSession', 'dataSecurity'] under properties.
B) Include isAVDEnvironment: true in the properties.
C) Change enableSharing: true to allowSharing: true.
D) Add optimizePerformance: true under properties.
E) The configuration is correct as it is.

QUESTION 41

Your team is facing frequent issues with Microsoft 365 Apps update deployments on AVD. You decide to script a solution using Azure CLI to enforce update consistency. Which command correctly achieves this?
az avd m365app update -Policy "Consistent" -AllUsers $true

A) Command is correct.
B) Replace -Policy "Consistent" with -UpdateChannel "Monthly".
C) Add -ForceUpdate $true to ensure all devices receive updates.
D) Use az m365app deployment enforce -UpdateChannel "Broad" -Force $true.
E) Change az avd to az m365app.

QUESTION 42

A legal firm using AVD requires enhanced security for client data, the ability to quickly revert to previous system states, and low latency access. What FSLogix settings should be prioritized? Select THREE.

```
A) HKLM\SOFTWARE\FSLogix\Profiles\Encrypt
B) HKLM\SOFTWARE\FSLogix\Profiles\CloudCache
C) HKLM\SOFTWARE\FSLogix\Profiles\BackupInterval
D) HKLM\SOFTWARE\FSLogix\Profiles\LocalCacheSize
E) HKLM\SOFTWARE\FSLogix\Profiles\CloudCacheLocations
```

QUESTION 43

You need to implement network load balancing for Azure Virtual Desktop (AVD) to ensure optimal session performance and availability. Which Azure service would you use to distribute incoming traffic across multiple session hosts efficiently?

A) Azure Traffic Manager
B) Azure Load Balancer
C) Azure Network Watcher
D) Azure Application Gateway

E) Azure Firewall

QUESTION 44

You are tasked with exporting diagnostic logs from Azure Virtual Desktop (AVD) to Azure Storage for analysis and troubleshooting purposes. To ensure efficient log exportation, you need to select the appropriate method considering:
1. The scalability and performance requirements for exporting large volumes of diagnostic data.
2. The availability and reliability of the export mechanism to avoid data loss and interruption of analysis workflows.
3. The integration with existing Azure services and tooling for seamless log analysis and correlation.
Which method offers scalable and reliable export of diagnostic logs from AVD to Azure Storage for analysis?

A) Azure CLI (Command Line Interface)
B) Azure Monitor Agent
C) Azure PowerShell Module
D) Azure Diagnostic Settings
E) Azure Storage Explorer

QUESTION 45

Write a PowerShell script to automatically update session hosts in AVD when CPU usage is consistently below 20%, indicating low usage times.

```
Register-AzAutomationScheduledRunbook -AutomationAccountName "AutoUpdateAccount" -RunbookName "UpdateVMs" -ScheduleName "LowUsageSchedule" -ResourceGroupName "AVDResourceGroup"
```

A) Script is correct as is.
B) Add -Parameter @{ "CpuThreshold" = 20 } to specify the CPU usage condition.
C) Change Register-AzAutomationScheduledRunbook to Start-AzAutomationRunbook.
D) Include -Condition "CPU < 20%" in the script.
E) Replace -ScheduleName "LowUsageSchedule" with -ScheduleId $(Get-AzAutomationSchedule -Name "LowUsageSchedule" -ResourceGroupName "AVDResourceGroup" -AutomationAccountName "AutoUpdateAccount").Id

QUESTION 46

Reporting network status to stakeholders is essential for transparency and accountability in Azure Virtual Desktop (AVD) environments. As the AVD administrator, you need to provide regular updates on network performance and connectivity to relevant stakeholders. Which method should you use to generate comprehensive network status reports for stakeholders?

A) Azure Monitor alerts and dashboards
B) Azure Network Watcher logs
C) Azure Log Analytics queries
D) Azure Resource Graph visualizations
E) Azure Diagnostics reports

QUESTION 47

An organization needs to analyze and report on Azure Virtual Desktop (AVD) costs to ensure effective cost management and budget control. The IT team is tasked with implementing strategies to achieve this goal. What actions should the IT team take to analyze and report on AVD costs effectively? Select THREE.

A) Utilizing Azure Resource Manager (ARM) templates for cost tracking
B) Using Azure Policy initiatives for cost governance
C) Implementing role-based access control (RBAC) for cost management

D) Leveraging Azure Monitor for performance insights
E) Configuring budgets and spending limits in Azure Cost Management

QUESTION 48

A healthcare provider needs to deploy Azure Virtual Desktop to access medical applications that require regulatory compliance, high availability, and multi-region support. Which Windows operating systems should be used? Select THREE.

A) Windows Server 2022
B) Windows 10 Enterprise multi-session
C) Windows Server 2016
D) Windows 11 Enterprise
E) Windows Server 2019

QUESTION 49

An organization needs to generate reports on licensing and compliance status for its Azure Virtual Desktop (AVD) environment to ensure transparency and accountability. Which actions should the organization take to generate comprehensive reports on AVD licensing and compliance? Select TWO.

A) Utilizing Azure Cost Management for tracking AVD licensing costs and usage trends
B) Configuring Azure Policy initiatives for enforcing compliance rules and generating compliance reports
C) Leveraging Azure Resource Graph for querying AVD resource metadata and license information
D) Integrating Azure Sentinel with AVD for monitoring and alerting on compliance violations
E) Implementing Power BI dashboards for visualizing AVD licensing metrics and compliance status

QUESTION 50

A company is experiencing performance issues in its Azure Virtual Desktop (AVD) environment and wants to leverage logs for troubleshooting and performance tuning. What steps should they take to effectively utilize logs for this purpose? Select TWO.

A) Analyzing log data to identify patterns and trends indicative of performance bottlenecks
B) Using log data to correlate user activities with performance degradation events for targeted troubleshooting
C) Leveraging log data to fine-tune resource allocation and optimize AVD environment performance
D) Implementing log-based alerts to proactively notify administrators of potential performance issues
E) Integrating log data with performance monitoring tools for comprehensive performance analysis

PRACTICE TEST 10 - ANSWERS ONLY

QUESTION 1

Answer - C) Azure Availability Zones

Option A - Incorrect. Focuses on disaster recovery, not high availability.
Option B - Incorrect. Balances load but doesn't address regional availability.
Option C - Correct. Ensures high availability across multiple regions.
Option D - Incorrect. Manages scaling but not specific to high availability.
Option E - Incorrect. Provides backup solutions, not availability.

EXAM FOCUS	*Always consider Azure Availability Zones for regional high availability in AVD environments. This ensures resilient failover while maintaining performance, scalability, and rapid recovery. Combine with Scale Sets for deployment efficiency.*
CAUTION ALERT	*Avoid assuming that backup solutions or load balancers alone address high availability across regions. Stay clear of solutions that lack redundancy across Azure zones for critical workloads.*

QUESTION 2

Answer - A) Check for any network latency issues using Azure Network Watcher

Option A - Correct. Checking for network latency issues using Azure Network Watcher is essential for troubleshooting connectivity problems. Option B - Incorrect. Azure AD Connect configuration is primarily for identity synchronization and does not directly impact connectivity.

Option C - Incorrect. Azure Bastion logs are for RDP/SSH access and may not provide insights into AVD session connectivity issues. Option D - Incorrect. While host pool configurations are important, they may not be the root cause of intermittent connectivity issues. Option E - Incorrect. Increasing Azure VM sizes may improve performance but does not address underlying connectivity issues.

EXAM FOCUS	*You need to start by diagnosing latency and packet loss using Azure Network Watcher. Network troubleshooting ensures seamless AVD access, particularly for remote teams relying on real-time collaboration tools like CRM platforms.*
CAUTION ALERT	*Don't confuse authentication or host pool issues with connectivity problems. Stay cautious about increasing VM sizes—it only addresses performance bottlenecks, not network-related degradation.*

QUESTION 3

Answer - [B]

Option B - WVDSessionEvent: This table contains session event logs, allowing real-time monitoring of active user sessions and detection of suspicious activities. Option A - WVDActiveUserSessions: While it may seem relevant, this table does not exist, and real-time session monitoring is typically performed using WVDSessionEvent.

Option C - WVDAuditLogs: This contains audit logs but may not provide real-time session monitoring capabilities.
Option D - WVDUserSessions: This table contains historical logs of user session activities rather than real-time session monitoring. Option E - WVDServiceHealth: This provides overall service health information, not real-time session monitoring capabilities.

EXAM FOCUS	*Always query WVDSessionEvent for real-time monitoring of active user sessions and detecting anomalies. It is designed to support compliance and security in AVD environments, ensuring actionable insights into user activity.*

| CAUTION ALERT | *Avoid relying on tables like WVDAuditLogs for real-time monitoring—they're better suited for historical data. Stay alert to non-existent tables like WVDActiveUserSessions. Verify documentation for accurate Log Analytics sources.* |

QUESTION 4

Answer - A) Balancing performance and cost with appropriate storage tier selections; B) Implementing data redundancy and fault tolerance for high availability; C) Leveraging caching mechanisms to optimize storage performance

Option A - Correct. Successful case studies highlight the importance of balancing performance and cost by selecting appropriate storage tiers based on workload requirements and cost-effectiveness in AVD environments. Option B - Correct. Implementing data redundancy and fault tolerance ensures high availability and data integrity in AVD storage solutions, reducing the risk of data loss and downtime.

Option C - Correct. Leveraging caching mechanisms, such as Azure Disk Cache or FSLogix profile containers, can significantly improve storage performance and user experience in AVD deployments. Option D - Incorrect. While automation streamlines storage provisioning and management, it may not be a specific lesson learned from successful AVD storage planning case studies.

Option E - Incorrect. While integrating storage solutions with identity and access management controls is important for data security, it may not be a primary focus or lesson learned from AVD storage planning case studies.

| EXAM FOCUS | *Keep in mind that successful storage planning in AVD relies on balancing cost with performance. Use caching for faster data access and implement redundancy for fault tolerance, ensuring uninterrupted services during hardware or storage failures.* |
| CAUTION ALERT | *Avoid neglecting redundancy mechanisms; data loss from single points of failure is costly. Stay clear of focusing solely on automation—it complements but doesn't replace strategic planning for storage performance optimization.* |

QUESTION 5

Answer - D) Configuration is already secure

Option A - Incorrect: MFA is not directly configurable via storage account settings but should be enforced where possible.
Option B - Incorrect: The 'Deny' default action is a secure setup, only allowing specified traffic.
Option C - Incorrect: 'supportsHttpsTrafficOnly' set to true enhances security.
Option D - Correct: The current configuration aligns with security best practices.
Option E - Incorrect: The location 'westus2' is a valid choice and does not impact security.

| EXAM FOCUS | *You should validate storage security by ensuring HTTPS traffic enforcement and restrictive ACL configurations. These steps align with best practices, safeguarding AVD environments against unauthorized access while maintaining functionality.* |
| CAUTION ALERT | *Stay cautious of disabling HTTPS traffic—it compromises data security. **Avoid altering ACL settings to "Allow" without thorough review—it might expose sensitive resources unnecessarily.* |

QUESTION 6

Answer - [B, D]

Option B - Azure Automation with Azure Logic Apps: Logic Apps can be used to trigger scaling actions based on user demand, ensuring optimal resource utilization and availability, while minimizing administrative overhead.
Option D - Azure Virtual Machine Scale Sets: Scale Sets can automatically adjust the number of session hosts based on demand, ensuring availability 24/7 and minimizing administrative overhead.

Option A - Azure Functions: While Functions provide event-driven serverless compute, Azure Virtual Machine Scale Sets are more suitable for dynamically scaling resources based on demand.

Option C - Azure Monitor Alerts: Alerts notify you of potential issues but are not specifically designed for managing resource scaling based on demand.

Option E - Azure Resource Manager templates: While templates enable you to deploy and manage Azure resources, they are not specifically designed for dynamically scaling resources based on demand.

EXAM FOCUS	*Leverage Azure Automation and Scale Sets for dynamic scaling. Automation minimizes manual interventions, while Scale Sets ensure resource adjustments align with real-time demand, optimizing cost without compromising user experience.*
CAUTION ALERT	*Don't rely solely on manual templates for scaling—they are not dynamic. Stay alert to misconfiguring Scale Sets; improper setup can cause over-provisioning or user disruptions during scaling actions.*

QUESTION 7

Answer - A) Regularly Review Microsoft Documentation and Official Announcements; C) Engage with Microsoft Account Representatives and Licensing Experts; D) Join Online Communities and Forums for Azure Professionals

Option A - Correct. Regularly reviewing Microsoft documentation and official announcements ensures awareness of updates and changes in Azure licensing policies, including those related to AVD deployments. Option C - Correct. Engaging with Microsoft account representatives and licensing experts provides access to up-to-date information and guidance on licensing policies and best practices for AVD.

Option D - Correct. Joining online communities and forums for Azure professionals allows for knowledge sharing and discussions on recent developments and experiences with AVD deployments and licensing. Option B - Incorrect. While participating in Microsoft partner programs and training sessions may offer valuable insights, they may not be the most direct or timely sources of information for monitoring Azure licensing policies.

Option E - Incorrect. While internal training and knowledge sharing sessions are beneficial for building expertise, they may not provide the latest updates and changes in Azure licensing policies as effectively as direct engagement with Microsoft and online communities.

EXAM FOCUS	*Always monitor licensing policies through Microsoft documentation and community forums. Staying informed ensures compliance, avoiding potential disruptions from policy changes or unintentional license violations in AVD setups.*
CAUTION ALERT	*Avoid ignoring updates from trusted Microsoft sources. Stay clear of relying solely on internal knowledge-sharing sessions; they often lack real-time updates critical for compliance.*

QUESTION 8

Answer - A) Profile Management and Roaming User Profiles; B) Application Virtualization and Containerization; D) Load Balancing and Session Affinity

Option A - Correct. Implementing profile management and roaming user profiles ensures that user settings and configurations remain consistent across different devices and AVD sessions, enhancing user experience. Option B - Correct. Utilizing application virtualization and containerization technologies allows for centralized application management and delivery, ensuring consistent application behavior across devices and sessions.

Option D - Correct. Configuring load balancing and session affinity mechanisms helps distribute user sessions evenly across AVD hosts, preventing overloading and maintaining consistent performance and user experience. Option C - Incorrect. While network optimization and QoS are important, they primarily address network performance rather than ensuring consistent user experience across devices.

Option E - Incorrect. While endpoint security and device management policies are essential for security, they do not directly contribute to achieving consistent user experience in AVD environments.

EXAM FOCUS	Focus on consistent profiles, virtualized applications, and session load balancing for seamless user experience. This reduces variability in settings, performance, and access across different devices in AVD environments.
CAUTION ALERT	Don't overlook profile management—it directly impacts user satisfaction. Avoid relying solely on network optimization to fix inconsistencies; user profiles and application management play critical roles.

QUESTION 9

Answer - [A, B, C]

Option A - Implement autoscale rules based on CPU and memory utilization: This allows for dynamic adjustment of resources based on performance metrics, aligning with the requirement to scale resources based on both user demand and performance.

Option B - Configure a grace period to avoid scaling actions during active user sessions: This ensures that scaling actions do not disrupt user sessions, meeting the requirement for seamless scaling without impacting user sessions.

Option C - Utilize Azure Advisor recommendations for autoscale configuration: This helps minimize administrative effort by providing best practices and recommendations for autoscale configuration.

Option D - Setting up recurring scaling events during off-peak hours is a manual approach and may not align with the requirement for dynamic scaling based on user demand.

Option E - Implementing custom scripts for autoscale management may introduce complexity and additional administrative effort, which conflicts with the requirement to minimize administrative effort.

EXAM FOCUS	You can achieve dynamic scaling with autoscale rules tied to CPU/memory usage. A grace period avoids disruptions during active sessions, ensuring scaling actions don't degrade user experiences. Azure Advisor provides valuable recommendations.
CAUTION ALERT	Stay cautious of scaling during peak usage without a grace period—it disrupts active users. Avoid custom scripting unless necessary; it increases complexity and administrative overhead compared to native autoscale solutions.

QUESTION 10

Answer - C) CustomRdpProperty is incorrectly formatted

Option A - Incorrect: The command has an error in how it sets QoS.
Option B - Incorrect: 'BreadthFirst' is a valid load balancer type for distributing connections.
Option C - Correct: The format of 'CustomRdpProperty' for QoS settings is incorrect.
Option D - Incorrect: A network profile is not mandatory for this command.
Option E - Incorrect: Not all elements are incorrect.

EXAM FOCUS	Ensure correct formatting of CustomRdpProperty to enable Quality of Service (QoS) settings. Properly implemented QoS improves AVD session traffic handling and prioritization, especially under network congestion scenarios.
CAUTION ALERT	Don't misconfigure QoS parameters; incorrect formatting renders QoS ineffective. Stay alert to errors in RDP property settings—they directly impact session performance and user experience.

QUESTION 11

Answer - A) Use Azure Image Builder for Automated Image Creation; B) Implement Tagging and Metadata for Image Versioning; C) Schedule Regular Image Maintenance and Updates; D) Leverage Azure DevOps for Image Pipeline Automation

Option A - Correct. Using Azure Image Builder enables automated image creation and customization, streamlining the image management process and ensuring consistency across deployments.

Option B - Correct. Implementing tagging and metadata for image versioning provides visibility and traceability into image changes, facilitating effective version control and management. Option C - Correct. Scheduling regular image maintenance and updates ensures that golden images remain up-to-date with the latest security patches, software updates, and configuration changes, reducing vulnerabilities and enhancing stability.

Option D - Correct. Leveraging Azure DevOps for image pipeline automation enables organizations to establish continuous integration and deployment (CI/CD) pipelines for golden image management, improving efficiency and reducing manual intervention. Option E - Incorrect. While implementing rollback procedures is important for handling deployment failures, it is not specifically related to version control and update management but rather to deployment and incident management processes.

EXAM FOCUS	*You should use tools like Azure Image Builder and DevOps pipelines to automate image creation and versioning. Tagging helps maintain clarity in version control. Schedule regular maintenance to keep images updated and aligned with security and performance standards.*
CAUTION ALERT	*Avoid skipping metadata tagging; it ensures traceability in versioning. Stay cautious about manual update procedures—they are prone to errors and lack the consistency automation provides.*

QUESTION 12

Answer - [E]

Option E - Azure Site Recovery: Azure Site Recovery provides disaster recovery as a service and supports failover of AVD host pools to a secondary Azure region, minimizing data loss and downtime during failover operations.
Option A - Azure Active Directory is an identity and access management service and is not directly related to failover and disaster recovery of AVD host pools.

Option B - Azure Traffic Manager provides DNS-based traffic routing but does not directly support failover and disaster recovery for AVD host pools. Option C - Azure Backup is primarily used for data backup and recovery and is not designed for failover and disaster recovery of AVD host pools. Option D - Azure Monitor provides monitoring and analytics capabilities but does not directly support failover and disaster recovery for AVD host pools.

EXAM FOCUS	*Always prioritize Azure Site Recovery for comprehensive disaster recovery. It ensures minimal data loss, orchestrates failovers, and maintains business continuity. Use replication policies to manage recovery objectives effectively.*
CAUTION ALERT	*Don't confuse services like Azure Backup with disaster recovery tools like Site Recovery. Backup focuses on data integrity, while Site Recovery addresses operational continuity during region failures.*

QUESTION 13

Answer - A) Implementing Rolling Updates; B) Utilizing Maintenance Windows for Scheduled Updates; C) Employing Automated Rollback Mechanisms

Option A - Correct. Implementing rolling updates involves gradually updating subsets of AVD instances while others remain operational, minimizing downtime and user impact. Option B - Correct. Utilizing maintenance windows for scheduled updates allows for planned downtime during off-peak hours, reducing user disruption.

Option C - Correct. Employing automated rollback mechanisms enables automatic restoration to a previous state in case of update failures, mitigating downtime and user impact. Option D - Incorrect. Enforcing session persistence across updates may lead to resource contention and user disruption during maintenance.

Option E - Incorrect. Distributing updates during non-business hours can reduce user impact, but it does not directly address downtime management or provide mechanisms for rollback in case of issues.

EXAM FOCUS	*Implement rolling updates to keep some AVD instances operational during updates. Schedule updates during non-peak hours and use rollback mechanisms for fast recovery if issues arise. These strategies minimize user impact and downtime.*
CAUTION ALERT	*Stay alert to risks of incomplete rollback plans; they can prolong downtime. Avoid overlooking maintenance windows—failing to schedule properly could disrupt business-critical operations.*

QUESTION 14

Answer - A) Implement Azure Backup for Automated Image Snapshots; B) Configure Azure Site Recovery for Image Replication and Failover; C) Utilize Azure Blob Storage Versioning for Image History Tracking

Option A - Correct. Implementing Azure Backup allows automated snapshots of images, enabling easy restoration in case of data loss or corruption in AVD deployments. Option B - Correct. Configuring Azure Site Recovery facilitates image replication and failover, ensuring continuity of operations and minimizing downtime in disaster scenarios for AVD deployments.

Option C - Correct. Utilizing Azure Blob Storage versioning provides image history tracking, allowing you to revert to previous versions in case of accidental changes or deletions in AVD deployments. Option D - Incorrect. While geo-redundant storage enhances data resilience by replicating data across multiple regions, it may not specifically address backup and disaster recovery options for image storage in AVD deployments. Option E - Incorrect. While establishing backup policies with Azure Policy is important for image lifecycle management, it may not directly relate to backup and disaster recovery options for image storage in AVD deployments.

EXAM FOCUS	*Consider Azure Backup for image snapshots and Blob Storage versioning for historical tracking. Azure Site Recovery enhances replication for cross-region disaster recovery, ensuring operational continuity during failures.*
CAUTION ALERT	*Don't assume geo-redundant storage alone is sufficient—it complements but does not replace disaster recovery planning. Avoid neglecting snapshot versioning—it is critical for quick rollbacks in case of image corruption.*

QUESTION 15

Answer - A) Correctly retrieves metrics

Option A - Correct: The PowerShell command correctly retrieves the specified network metric, which is crucial for monitoring AVD environments.
Option B - Incorrect: 'Microsoft.Network/networkInterfaces' is a valid resource type for this context.
Option C - Incorrect: 'NetworkInTotal' is a valid Azure metric name for incoming network traffic.
Option D - Incorrect: 'TimeGrain' is optional and can be specified if needed for granularity.
Option E - Incorrect: 'Name' parameter is necessary to specify which network interface's metrics are being retrieved.

EXAM FOCUS	*Always monitor network metrics like NetworkInTotal using PowerShell to proactively identify performance bottlenecks. Granular monitoring helps detect abnormal patterns impacting AVD operations and ensures timely remediation.*
CAUTION ALERT	*Avoid neglecting optional parameters like TimeGrain; while not mandatory, they improve data granularity. Stay cautious about incorrect metric names—they result in failed monitoring and misdiagnosis.*

QUESTION 16

Answer - A) Implement Automated Compliance Checks and Remediation; C) Monitor Configuration Changes and Vulnerability Assessments; D) Implement Role-Based Access Controls (RBAC) and Least Privilege Principles

Option A - Correct. Implementing automated compliance checks and remediation processes helps ensure continuous compliance with regulatory requirements and industry standards in AVD deployments. Option B - Incorrect. While conducting regular security awareness training is important, it may not directly contribute to maintaining continuous compliance in AVD environments.

Option C - Correct. Monitoring configuration changes and performing vulnerability assessments allows organizations to identify and address compliance gaps proactively in AVD deployments. Option D - Correct. Implementing role-based access controls (RBAC) and following least privilege principles helps enforce security policies and access controls to maintain continuous compliance in AVD environments. Option E - Incorrect. While establishing incident response plans is crucial for security incident management, it may not be specifically focused on maintaining continuous compliance in AVD deployments.

EXAM FOCUS	*You need to implement automated compliance checks to enforce policies continuously. Use RBAC to enforce least privilege principles and monitor vulnerabilities regularly to align with compliance and security standards.*
CAUTION ALERT	*Don't overlook continuous monitoring—it ensures compliance even as deployments evolve. Avoid assigning broad privileges in RBAC; they violate compliance principles and expose systems to unnecessary risks.*

QUESTION 17

Answer - A) Utilizing Azure Cost Management and Billing Reports for Cost Allocation; C) Leveraging Power BI for Data Visualization and Cost Trend Analysis; E) Integrating Azure Budgets with Resource Tagging for Granular Cost Tracking

Option A - Correct. Utilizing Azure Cost Management and Billing Reports allows for detailed cost allocation and analysis, providing insights into spending patterns and cost optimization opportunities in AVD deployments. Option B - Incorrect. While Azure Log Analytics Workbooks can provide customized dashboards, they may not specifically focus on cost analysis and reporting in AVD deployments.

Option C - Correct. Leveraging Power BI for data visualization and cost trend analysis enables organizations to gain deeper insights into cost drivers and identify areas for optimization in AVD deployments. Option D - Incorrect. While Azure Monitor Alerts can help with cost anomalies and overspending notifications, they may not cover comprehensive cost analysis and reporting in AVD deployments. Option E - Correct. Integrating Azure Budgets with resource tagging allows for granular cost tracking and management, facilitating better cost optimization decisions in AVD deployments.

EXAM FOCUS	*Use Azure Cost Management for detailed cost reports, Power BI for visual trend analysis, and tagging with budgets for granular tracking. These techniques reveal cost drivers and optimize spending in AVD environments.*
CAUTION ALERT	*Avoid focusing solely on alerts—they notify but do not provide comprehensive analysis. Stay clear of ignoring resource tagging; it enables accurate allocation and cost tracking.*

QUESTION 18

Answer - [A, B]

Option A - Azure Site Recovery: Azure Site Recovery provides disaster recovery orchestration and replication capabilities for Azure Virtual Desktop environments, ensuring seamless failover and data protection with minimal downtime and data loss.

Option B - Azure Backup: Azure Backup offers data backup and recovery services for Azure Virtual Desktop environments, enabling automatic failover and recovery processes while simplifying management and monitoring tasks. Option C - Azure File Sync synchronizes files between on-premises servers and Azure file shares but does not provide disaster recovery capabilities for Azure Virtual Desktop environments. Option D - Azure Blob Storage is a scalable object storage service and does not offer disaster recovery capabilities specifically for Azure Virtual Desktop environments.

Option E - Azure Import/Export is used for importing/exporting large amounts of data to/from Azure but does not address disaster recovery requirements for Azure Virtual Desktop environments.

EXAM FOCUS	*Leverage Azure Site Recovery for automated failovers and Azure Backup for data restoration. Combining these ensures seamless disaster recovery with minimal manual intervention and downtime, critical for business continuity.*
CAUTION ALERT	*Stay cautious about relying on synchronization tools like Azure File Sync—they support data syncing but lack failover orchestration. Avoid assuming object storage alone meets DR needs; it doesn't handle failovers effectively.*

QUESTION 19

Answer - A) Analyze failover performance metrics and optimization strategies; B) Evaluate communication and coordination among stakeholders during recovery operations; C) Review post-mortem reports and identify areas for process refinement

Option A - Correct. Analyzing failover performance metrics and optimization strategies provides insights for improving the efficiency and effectiveness of disaster recovery operations in AVD environments. Option B - Correct. Evaluating communication and coordination among stakeholders during recovery operations helps identify areas for enhancing collaboration and response times in AVD deployments.

Option C - Correct. Reviewing post-mortem reports and identifying areas for process refinement enables organizations to learn from past experiences and implement continuous improvements in the disaster recovery plan for AVD environments. Option D - Incorrect. While Azure Policy can contribute to compliance enforcement, it is not directly related to improving the disaster recovery plan for AVD environments. Option E - Incorrect. While Azure Security Center offers threat detection and response capabilities, it is not specifically focused on improving disaster recovery plans for AVD deployments.

EXAM FOCUS	*Prioritize analyzing failover metrics and stakeholder coordination from case studies to refine processes. Post-mortem reviews provide actionable insights to enhance disaster recovery strategies for your AVD deployment.*
CAUTION ALERT	*Avoid overlooking communication strategies during disaster recovery—they are vital for timely execution. Don't assume threat detection like Azure Security Center directly improves disaster recovery planning—it focuses on threats.*

QUESTION 20

Answer - A) Azure Monitor autoscale

Option A - Correct: Azure Monitor's autoscale feature allows for the dynamic scaling of session hosts based on specific metrics and schedules, optimizing resource utilization and cost.

Option B - Incorrect: While Logic Apps can automate workflows, they do not directly handle scaling based on performance metrics. Option C - Incorrect: Automation accounts automate tasks but are not specifically designed for scaling based on real-time performance data. Option D - Incorrect: Kubernetes is a container orchestration service, not suited for AVD scaling. Option E - Incorrect: Scale Sets are used for scaling VM instances but need to be combined with Azure Monitor for the dynamic, metric-based scaling required here.

EXAM FOCUS	*Always utilize Azure Monitor Autoscale for dynamic, metric-based scaling. It automates resource adjustments based on time-of-day or load metrics, ensuring cost efficiency and consistent performance in AVD environments.*
CAUTION ALERT	*Stay clear of using manual scripts for scaling—they lack real-time adaptability and increase administrative burden. Avoid depending on container services like Kubernetes—they are not designed for AVD scaling scenarios.*

QUESTION 21

Answer - D

Option D - SSL/TLS (Secure Sockets Layer/Transport Layer Security) provides encryption and secure communication between the RD Gateway server and client devices, ensuring confidentiality and integrity of data transmitted over the network. Configuring Azure Virtual Desktop to use SSL/TLS for RD Gateway connections enhances security by encrypting communication channels, protecting sensitive information from unauthorized access.

Option A - TLS (Transport Layer Security) is a cryptographic protocol used for securing internet communications but is not specifically designed for RD Gateway connections. Option B - IPSec (Internet Protocol Security) is a suite of protocols used for secure internet communications but is not specific to RD Gateway connections.

Option C - SSH (Secure Shell) is a protocol used for secure remote access to systems but is not typically used for RD Gateway connections. Option E - SMB (Server Message Block) is a file sharing protocol and is not used for securing RD Gateway connections.

EXAM FOCUS	*Always configure SSL/TLS for RD Gateway to ensure encrypted communication. This protects sensitive data and secures connections between the server and client devices. Use certificates from trusted authorities for added security.*
CAUTION ALERT	*Avoid assuming TLS alone will configure SSL/TLS. SSL/TLS works together for encrypted RD Gateway communication. Stay cautious about self-signed certificates—they might not meet enterprise-level security standards.*

QUESTION 22

Answer - A) Define granular roles based on job functions and responsibilities; B) Implement role assignments using groups for scalability and ease of management; D) Establish role inheritance to streamline access management and reduce redundancy

Option A - Correct. Defining granular roles based on job functions and responsibilities allows for precise access control tailored to individual user roles. Option B - Correct. Implementing role assignments using groups enhances scalability and ease of management, especially in large organizations.

Option D - Correct. Establishing role inheritance streamlines access management by allowing users to inherit permissions from higher-level roles, reducing the need for manual role assignments. Option C - Incorrect. While utilizing built-in RBAC roles can simplify role management, it may not always align with organizational requirements, necessitating the creation of custom roles. Option E - Incorrect. Enforcing the least privilege principle is important but is not specifically a design consideration for implementing RBAC in AVD environments.

EXAM FOCUS	*You should define RBAC roles with clear job function mappings. Use groups for role assignments to enhance scalability. Role inheritance reduces redundancy, improving efficiency in access control across large AVD environments.*
CAUTION ALERT	*Don't rely solely on built-in roles—they may not meet all organizational requirements. Stay alert to over-provisioning; ensure least privilege access is enforced to mitigate unauthorized access risks.*

QUESTION 23

Answer - A) Reduction in unauthorized access attempts or security incidents; B) User feedback on the MFA experience and usability; C) Compliance with regulatory requirements and industry standards

Option A - Correct. Evaluating the reduction in unauthorized access attempts or security incidents helps assess the effectiveness of MFA implementations in enhancing security. Option B - Correct. Gathering user feedback on the MFA experience and usability provides insights into user satisfaction and potential areas for improvement.

Option C - Correct. Ensuring compliance with regulatory requirements and industry standards validates the effectiveness of MFA implementations in meeting security mandates.

Option D - Incorrect. While comparing MFA implementation metrics with industry benchmarks may provide insights, it is not specifically mentioned in the question as a factor for evaluating MFA effectiveness in AVD environments. Option E - Incorrect. While analyzing MFA-related support tickets is important for support management, it may not directly assess the effectiveness of MFA implementations in enhancing security measures as described in the question.

EXAM FOCUS	*Evaluate MFA effectiveness by analyzing reductions in unauthorized access and aligning implementations with compliance standards. Collect user feedback for usability insights and ensure the solution meets regulatory needs without affecting workflows.*
CAUTION ALERT	*Stay clear of ignoring user feedback—poor usability may discourage adoption. Avoid neglecting compliance reviews, as they ensure MFA configurations align with industry regulations and mitigate potential audit findings.*

QUESTION 24

Answer - A, C, D, E

A) Correct - Optimizing network routes with Azure Traffic Manager can significantly improve performance by directing traffic more efficiently. B) Incorrect - Application layer gateways are more about security than performance and scalability. C) Correct - Setting up host pools based on user location reduces latency and improves user experience.

D) Correct - Using Azure Monitor allows for real-time tracking of performance metrics and can help in identifying bottlenecks. E) Correct - Scaling out session hosts using Azure Automation ensures that resources are available to meet demand without manual intervention, enhancing scalability.

EXAM FOCUS	*Optimize user experience by implementing host pools per location, leveraging Azure Monitor for performance tracking, and using Automation to scale resources dynamically. Azure Traffic Manager improves routing for global performance.*
CAUTION ALERT	*Don't overuse application gateways for performance—they are primarily for security. Avoid neglecting monitoring metrics like session responsiveness; they are critical for identifying bottlenecks and enhancing scalability.*

QUESTION 25

Answer - A) Command aligns with best practices

Option A - Correct: The command sets a specific rule to allow RDP traffic from a controlled IP range, which aligns with best practices for secure remote desktop access.

Option B - Incorrect: A broader source address range could expose the network to unauthorized access. Option C - Incorrect: Limiting the destination ports to only those necessary (e.g., 3389 for RDP) enhances security. Option D - Incorrect: The action "Allow" is necessary for authorized access; "Deny" would block legitimate traffic.

Option E - Incorrect: A lower priority number has higher precedence in firewall rules, and 100 is typically adequate unless more specific rules are necessary.

EXAM FOCUS	*Ensure firewall rules are specific to required ports (e.g., 3389 for RDP) and restrict source addresses to known ranges for security. Regularly review and audit these settings to align with access and compliance policies.*
CAUTION ALERT	*Avoid using broad source ranges—they increase the risk of unauthorized access. Stay cautious about overlapping or conflicting rules; they can inadvertently allow unintended traffic through the firewall.*

QUESTION 26

Answer - A) Verify the configuration and deployment status of Windows Defender Antivirus on AVD session hosts; C) Review event logs and error messages generated by Windows Defender Antivirus and other security features

Option A - Correct. Verifying the configuration and deployment status of Windows Defender Antivirus ensures proper functioning of threat protection features on AVD session hosts. Option C - Correct. Reviewing event logs and error messages helps identify issues and troubleshoot them effectively, enabling prompt resolution of threat protection feature issues. Option B - Incorrect. While checking for conflicts or compatibility issues with third-party solutions is important, it is not specifically mentioned in the context of troubleshooting threat protection feature issues for AVD as described in the question.

Option D - Incorrect. While ensuring that AVD session hosts have the latest updates and security patches is essential, it is not directly related to troubleshooting threat protection feature issues as described in the question. Option E - Incorrect. While engaging Microsoft Support can be helpful for complex issues, it is not the first step in troubleshooting threat protection feature issues for AVD as described in the question.

EXAM FOCUS	*Check antivirus configurations on session hosts and review logs for error patterns. Regular monitoring ensures that Windows Defender and other tools operate effectively, identifying and resolving issues early.*
CAUTION ALERT	*Don't overlook logs generated by Windows Defender—they are crucial for troubleshooting. Avoid conflicts with third-party tools—they may interfere with threat protection configurations in your AVD environment.*

QUESTION 27

Answer - A, B, D

A) Correct - End-to-end encryption ensures that data transmitted is secure and confidential, meeting client confidentiality requirements. B) Correct - Azure Information Protection provides document classification and protection, essential for handling sensitive legal documents and maintaining compliance.

C) Incorrect - While Azure Sentinel is crucial for threat management, it does not directly impact client communication security or specific compliance needs in this context. D) Correct - Geofencing restricts access based on user locations, enhancing security and compliance with global data protection laws. E) Incorrect - Azure Front Door enhances web traffic management but is not specifically required for ensuring data confidentiality or compliance in a legal environment.

EXAM FOCUS	*Implement geofencing and Azure Information Protection for document security. Use end-to-end encryption for data in transit to secure client communications and ensure compliance with global legal regulations.*
CAUTION ALERT	*Avoid assuming encryption is the only solution—classification and access policies are equally critical. Stay cautious about neglecting compliance with regional data protection laws—it could lead to legal and reputational risks.*

QUESTION 28

Answer - A) Enhanced access control based on user roles, locations, and device compliance status; B) Improved protection against unauthorized access attempts and data breaches; D) Increased visibility and control over access permissions and policies

Option A - Correct. The implementation of Conditional Access enhances access control by allowing organizations to enforce policies based on user roles, locations, and device compliance status, thereby improving security. Option B - Correct. Conditional Access provides improved protection against unauthorized access attempts and data breaches by enforcing access policies and requiring additional verification when necessary.

Option C - Incorrect. While Conditional Access can help mitigate security threats, it is not specifically focused on reducing the risk of malware infections and other security threats. Option D - Correct. Conditional Access increases visibility and control over access permissions and policies, allowing administrators to monitor and manage access more effectively. Option E - Incorrect. While Conditional Access can streamline the user experience by providing seamless access to resources from trusted locations, it is not the primary focus of security improvements achieved through its implementation.

EXAM FOCUS	*Use Conditional Access to restrict access by role, location, and compliance status. Monitor access trends for visibility into potential security breaches and improve user experience by predefining trusted locations.*
CAUTION ALERT	*Don't confuse Conditional Access with endpoint protection—it enforces policies rather than directly mitigating malware. Stay clear of generic rules—they may not fully leverage Conditional Access for precise security control.*

QUESTION 29

Answer - A) Analyze security logs and audit trails to identify suspicious activities or unauthorized access attempts; B) Conduct forensic analysis of compromised session hosts to determine the extent of the breach and data exposure; C) Implement network segmentation and access controls to isolate compromised session hosts from the rest of the infrastructure; D) Disable compromised user accounts and reset passwords to prevent further unauthorized access

Option A - Correct. Analyzing security logs and audit trails helps identify indicators of compromise and unauthorized access attempts on AVD session hosts. Option B - Correct. Conducting forensic analysis of compromised session hosts allows organizations to understand the scope of the breach and assess data exposure.

Option C - Correct. Implementing network segmentation and access controls isolates compromised session hosts, limiting the impact of the breach on the overall infrastructure. Option D - Correct. Disabling compromised user accounts and resetting passwords helps prevent further unauthorized access and mitigate the risk of additional breaches.

Option E - Incorrect. While deploying security updates and patches is important, it may not directly address ongoing security breaches involving compromised session hosts.

EXAM FOCUS	*Analyze logs and segment networks to mitigate the spread of breaches. Forensic analysis helps identify vulnerabilities exploited during attacks, while disabling compromised accounts prevents further misuse.*
CAUTION ALERT	*Avoid delaying response to breaches—act promptly to isolate affected systems. Stay alert to recurring attack patterns in logs—they might indicate persistent threats needing more robust defensive measures.*

QUESTION 30

Answer - A) Correct setup for training sessions

Option A - Correct: Using Microsoft Teams through a deployment template for regular training sessions is an effective way to ensure administrative staff receive ongoing updates. Option B - Incorrect: The specificity of the template file is not detailed in the scenario, and "training-session.json" may already be adequately configured.

Option C - Incorrect: The resource group name "AVDTraining" appropriately indicates its purpose. Option D - Incorrect: Integration with Azure AD for user management is a separate consideration from setting up training sessions.

Option E - Incorrect: Automation of deployment is beneficial but not explicitly required in the scenario.

EXAM FOCUS	*Leverage Microsoft Teams for training sessions and Azure deployment templates for scalable, structured sessions. Regular updates ensure administrators stay informed of the latest security protocols and compliance changes.*
CAUTION ALERT	*Don't neglect training consistency; frequent updates ensure alignment with evolving security needs. Avoid assuming generic templates are sufficient—customize them to focus on AVD-specific security training needs.*

QUESTION 31

Answer - D) Enable FSLogix diagnostic logging and analyze logs for anomalies

Option A - Incorrect. While event logs provide some insight, they may not capture all FSLogix-related issues. Option B - Incorrect. PowerShell script can help monitor profile sizes but may not detect all configuration issues.

Option C - Incorrect. User surveys are subjective and may not provide comprehensive insights into technical issues. Option D - Correct. Enabling diagnostic logging allows detailed analysis of FSLogix logs for any anomalies or misconfigurations. Option E - Incorrect. Azure Monitor tracks performance metrics but may not provide granular FSLogix-specific insights.

EXAM FOCUS	*Always enable FSLogix diagnostic logging after deployment. Logs reveal hidden configuration issues affecting user profiles. Validate profile size limits regularly to ensure compliance with configured thresholds. Leverage these insights to optimize performance and reduce disruptions during user sessions.*
CAUTION ALERT	*Avoid relying solely on event logs for FSLogix diagnostics. They may not capture detailed issues causing user dissatisfaction, like slow login times. Stay alert to potential misconfigured settings that silently degrade performance.*

QUESTION 32

Answer - A) Analyze event logs for Office Container-related errors, C) Test Office Container functionality by creating and accessing user profiles, D) Monitor storage usage and performance metrics for Office Containers.

A) Analyze event logs for Office Container-related errors - Event logs provide valuable insights into any errors or issues encountered during Office Container operations, aiding in troubleshooting efforts. C) Test Office Container functionality by creating and accessing user profiles - Testing user profile creation and access helps verify the integrity and functionality of Office Containers post-deployment.

D) Monitor storage usage and performance metrics for Office Containers - Monitoring storage usage and performance metrics allows administrators to identify any anomalies or performance issues with Office Containers. B) Utilize FSLogix diagnostic tools to identify performance bottlenecks - While FSLogix diagnostic tools can help diagnose performance issues, they may not be specific to Office Container-related problems. E) Use PowerShell scripts to automate Office Container maintenance tasks - PowerShell scripts can automate maintenance tasks but may not directly address troubleshooting issues with Office Containers.

EXAM FOCUS	*Proactively analyze event logs and test profile functionality. Create test profiles to validate Office Container functionality. Monitoring storage usage and performance metrics regularly ensures stability. Combine FSLogix tools with storage metrics for a holistic troubleshooting approach.*
CAUTION ALERT	*Don't neglect post-deployment validation. Issues may arise unnoticed, affecting user productivity. Avoid relying on PowerShell scripts alone; they automate tasks but won't identify nuanced Office Container-specific performance bottlenecks.*

QUESTION 33

Answer - B, D, E

A) Incorrect - While Azure CDN is great for distributing static content, it is not specifically aimed at improving bandwidth or security for AVD. B) Correct - Azure ExpressRoute provides dedicated network connections, ensuring high bandwidth and low latency for global content creators.

C) Incorrect - Azure DDoS Protection is crucial for defending against DDoS attacks but doesn't directly enhance bandwidth or latency for AVD. D) Correct - Azure Front Door enables smart traffic routing, optimizing global access and reducing latency. E) Correct - Azure Application Gateway with WAF protects against web-based attacks, securing intellectual property transmitted over AVD.

EXAM FOCUS	Use Azure ExpressRoute for dedicated, high-bandwidth connections. Smart traffic routing with Azure Front Door minimizes latency for global users. Pair this with Application Gateway and WAF to secure intellectual property while ensuring seamless AVD connectivity.
CAUTION ALERT	Avoid assuming Azure CDN fits all scenarios. It supports static content distribution, not live AVD desktop performance. Stay cautious of neglecting security measures like DDoS Protection, which guard against external threats.

QUESTION 34

Answer - A) Utilize Azure Monitor to track device redirection events and identify patterns or anomalies indicative of underlying issues, B) Enable verbose logging for device redirection components in AVD session hosts to capture detailed diagnostic information, C) Implement Azure Network Watcher to analyze network traffic between client devices and AVD resources, identifying potential connectivity issues.

A) Utilize Azure Monitor to track device redirection events and identify patterns or anomalies indicative of underlying issues - Azure Monitor provides insights into device redirection events and helps identify root causes of problems, enabling timely troubleshooting and resolution. B) Enable verbose logging for device redirection components in AVD session hosts to capture detailed diagnostic information - Verbose logging captures comprehensive diagnostic data, facilitating in-depth analysis and troubleshooting of device redirection issues.

C) Implement Azure Network Watcher to analyze network traffic between client devices and AVD resources, identifying potential connectivity issues - Network Watcher helps diagnose network-related problems affecting device redirection, ensuring optimal connectivity for AVD sessions. D) Use PowerShell scripts to reset device redirection configurations and refresh device redirection policies on AVD session hosts - While PowerShell scripts can automate tasks, they may not directly address underlying issues causing device redirection problems.

E) Leverage FSLogix diagnostic tools to analyze user profile and session data for any conflicts or inconsistencies affecting device redirection - While FSLogix tools provide insights into user profiles, they may not directly diagnose device redirection issues or network connectivity problems.

EXAM FOCUS	Enable Azure Monitor to track device redirection metrics. Use verbose logging to capture detailed diagnostic data on redirection failures. Pair this with Network Watcher to identify bottlenecks between AVD and peripheral devices like printers and USBs.
CAUTION ALERT	Avoid skipping network traffic analysis for device disconnection issues. Problems often lie in overlooked network configurations. Stay alert to outdated drivers or user misconfigurations causing intermittent failures. Regular updates help.

QUESTION 35

Answer - B) Module targets the wrong resource type

Option A - Incorrect: The snippet is well-intended but incorrect for the purpose. Option B - Correct: The resource type 'Microsoft.Compute/virtualMachines' is not appropriate for configuring print job compression, which should be managed through print server settings or specific print management software.

Option C - Incorrect: Assuming 'Compressed' is a valid setting within the correct context, the problem lies in resource targeting. Option D - Incorrect: Bicep can configure various settings, but this snippet is misapplied. Option E - Incorrect: The name is arbitrary in this context but should ideally reflect its function for clarity.

EXAM FOCUS	Target print server configurations for print compression tasks. Resource types like Microsoft.Compute/virtualMachines are incorrect for print settings. Align deployment configurations with the correct resource type to achieve desired outcomes in AVD environments.
CAUTION ALERT	Avoid using Bicep snippets without validating the resource type. Misconfigured resources like Microsoft.Compute won't apply intended settings. Stay cautious of incorrect syntax or settings like

'Compressed' when applied in the wrong context.

QUESTION 36

Answer - A, B, E

A) Correct - Azure Firewall secures network traffic, protecting sensitive research data from potential cyber threats.
B) Correct - MFA enhances security by requiring additional verification, ensuring that only authorized researchers can access the system. C) Incorrect - While Azure Private Link provides private connectivity, it's more about enhancing performance than meeting specific cybersecurity or compliance needs.

D) Incorrect - Azure Information Protection is valuable for data classification and encryption but does not directly facilitate secure remote access or specific network security measures required here. E) Correct - Azure Bastion provides a secure and seamless way for international researchers to access AVD without exposing RDP and SSH to the internet, enhancing cybersecurity.

EXAM FOCUS	*Leverage Azure Firewall and MFA to create a strong security perimeter for researchers. Use Azure Bastion to ensure secure, seamless access without exposing RDP/SSH ports. This combination meets compliance, protects sensitive data, and enables secure international access.*
CAUTION ALERT	*Avoid overlooking global researcher access needs. While Azure Private Link offers private connectivity, it doesn't directly secure international AVD connections. Stay alert to network threats that can breach unmonitored firewalls.*

QUESTION 37

Answer - A) Configuring custom diagnostics in Azure Monitor to track VM startup times

Configuring custom diagnostics in Azure Monitor allows for tracking VM startup times and identifying common issues affecting the performance of the Start VM on Connect feature.

Option B - Incorrect. Verbose logging captures detailed data but may not specifically focus on VM startup times.
Option C - Incorrect. Network latency analysis is important but may not directly address VM startup delays.
Option D - Incorrect. Activity Logs monitor changes but do not specifically track VM startup times.
Option E - Incorrect. Azure Bastion provides secure RDP access but does not focus on VM startup performance.

EXAM FOCUS	*Enable custom diagnostics in Azure Monitor to track VM startup times. Use these diagnostics to identify delays caused by Start VM on Connect. This method provides actionable insights into resource readiness and improves user login experience during AVD sessions.*
CAUTION ALERT	*Don't assume verbose logging alone resolves issues. While detailed logs are useful, they don't always pinpoint the root cause of VM delays. Stay clear of misdiagnosing network latency as the sole reason for performance degradation.*

QUESTION 38

Answer - A) Reviewing Azure Activity Logs for deployment errors
Reviewing Azure Activity Logs helps identify deployment errors and issues, enabling effective troubleshooting of application compatibility and performance problems in AVD environments.

Option B - Analyzing network performance metrics: While network performance is important, it may not directly address application compatibility and performance issues. Option C - Checking Azure Bastion logs: Azure Bastion logs primarily relate to access issues and may not directly help resolve application compatibility and performance problems.

Option D - Monitoring Azure AD for authentication failures: Azure AD issues may affect authentication but may not directly impact application compatibility and performance.

Option E - Utilizing FSLogix profile status: FSLogix profiles manage user settings but do not directly address application deployment or compatibility issues.

EXAM FOCUS	*Review Azure Activity Logs to pinpoint deployment errors. These logs offer a clear timeline of issues affecting app compatibility. For unresolved challenges, cross-reference deployment methods with FSLogix and configuration guides to ensure compatibility and performance.*
CAUTION ALERT	*Avoid neglecting deployment methods in troubleshooting app issues. Compatibility often fails due to unaligned configurations. Stay cautious of unrelated logs like Bastion or network metrics, as they don't address app-specific errors.*

QUESTION 39

Answer - A, B, C

A) Correct - Azure Bastion provides a secure and controlled access point for accessing virtual desktops, crucial for maintaining PHI security. B) Correct - Azure Site Recovery ensures that services remain available across different regions, crucial during emergencies for a healthcare provider.

C) Correct - Azure AD Conditional Access allows for granular control based on user roles and conditions, ensuring that access is appropriately managed during crises. D) Incorrect - Azure Monitor is essential for monitoring but was not specified among the top requirements for PHI security or emergency access. E) Incorrect - While Azure VPN Gateway provides secure connectivity, Azure Bastion is already specified for secure access and fulfills the security requirement more directly in this context.

EXAM FOCUS	*Implement Azure Bastion, Site Recovery, and Conditional Access to secure PHI, ensure regional failover readiness, and enforce role-based access. This trio meets security, disaster recovery, and regulatory compliance needs, crucial for healthcare environments.*
CAUTION ALERT	*Don't overlook PHI compliance details. Azure Monitor is helpful for tracking system metrics but doesn't secure sensitive data. Stay alert to relying solely on VPN Gateways, as they lack the security focus provided by Bastion.*

QUESTION 40

Answer - A

Option A - Correct. Including multiSession and dataSecurity features are essential.
Option B - Incorrect. isAVDEnvironment is not a valid property.
Option C - Incorrect. The correct property is enableSharing.
Option D - Incorrect. optimizePerformance isn't applicable here.
Option E - Incorrect. Additional features are necessary.

EXAM FOCUS	*Add multiSession and dataSecurity features to OneDrive configurations for AVD users. These features optimize collaboration while ensuring session consistency and data protection. Validate settings align with OneDrive for Business best practices in multi-user environments.*
CAUTION ALERT	*Avoid using generic configurations for AVD setups. OneDrive's default settings may not support session-based needs. Stay clear of unsupported properties like isAVDEnvironment, which won't enhance functionality and can cause errors.*

QUESTION 41

Answer - D

Option A - Incorrect. The command structure and parameters are not correct for Azure CLI.

Option B - Incorrect. While changing the update channel is valid, the command syntax is incorrect.

Option C - Incorrect. The -ForceUpdate parameter does not exist. Option D - Correct. The command az m365app deployment enforce -UpdateChannel "Broad" -Force $true correctly enforces update consistency across all users in AVD. Option E - Incorrect. Simply changing the command to az m365app does not resolve the issues with parameters and functionality.

EXAM FOCUS	*Understand Azure CLI syntax for deployment. Use the correct command for enforcing Microsoft 365 App updates. Parameters like -UpdateChannel must match Azure CLI structures. Review Azure documentation for the correct parameter configurations to avoid deployment conflicts or failures.*
CAUTION ALERT	*Avoid assuming default commands work. Ensure you validate Azure CLI updates as syntax evolves. Mismatched commands like az avd instead of az m365app can mislead deployments. Stay alert to unused parameters like -ForceUpdate.*

QUESTION 42

Answer - A, B, E

A) Correct - 'Encrypt' secures data at rest, crucial for client confidentiality in legal scenarios.
B) Correct - 'CloudCache' provides a mechanism to maintain previous system states by leveraging multi-location caching, which can help in rapid recovery. C) Incorrect - 'BackupInterval' is not a recognized or relevant setting in FSLogix for managing performance or security.

D) Incorrect - While 'LocalCacheSize' affects performance, it is less impactful compared to encryption or caching strategies for security and recovery. E) Correct - 'CloudCacheLocations' ensures data is distributed across multiple locations, reducing latency by allowing access from the nearest point.

EXAM FOCUS	*Prioritize security and performance in FSLogix. Encrypt profiles for data confidentiality. Use CloudCache for fast access and recovery. Define CloudCacheLocations for multi-region access and low latency. Focus on compliance needs for sensitive client data handling in AVD.*
CAUTION ALERT	*Avoid ignoring encryption settings. Without Encrypt, client confidentiality is at risk. Don't rely only on LocalCacheSize for performance tuning, as caching strategies like CloudCache improve system state recovery significantly.*

QUESTION 43

Answer - B) Azure Load Balancer

Option B - Azure Load Balancer is a Layer 4 (TCP/UDP) load balancer that distributes incoming traffic across multiple session hosts based on configured rules and health probes. It ensures high availability and scalability for AVD deployments.

Option A - Azure Traffic Manager is a DNS-based traffic routing service for distributing user requests across global datacenters or endpoints, not suitable for load balancing session hosts. Option C - Azure Network Watcher provides network monitoring and diagnostic tools but does not offer load balancing capabilities. Option D - Azure Application Gateway is a Layer 7 (HTTP/HTTPS) load balancer for web traffic, not designed for load balancing AVD session hosts. Option E - Azure Firewall is a managed firewall service for controlling and monitoring network traffic, not for load balancing AVD sessions.

EXAM FOCUS	*Use Azure Load Balancer for efficient session distribution. Configure health probes and rules to manage session host traffic effectively. This ensures high availability and avoids overloading specific hosts, improving session reliability and performance.*
CAUTION ALERT	*Avoid choosing unsuitable tools like Traffic Manager. It's DNS-based, not designed for balancing session host traffic. Stay clear of Layer 7 services like Application Gateway that focus on HTTP/HTTPS traffic, not AVD session hosts.*

QUESTION 44

Answer - D) Azure Diagnostic Settings

Option D - Azure Diagnostic Settings provide a built-in mechanism for exporting diagnostic logs from AVD to Azure Storage, offering scalability, reliability, and seamless integration with other Azure services for analysis.

Option A - Azure CLI is a command-line tool for managing Azure resources but not specifically for log exportation.
Option B - Azure Monitor Agent focuses on telemetry collection and monitoring, not log exportation.
Option C - Azure PowerShell Module is used for scripting and automation tasks, not for log exportation.
Option E - Azure Storage Explorer is a graphical tool for managing Azure Storage but does not offer automated log export capabilities.

EXAM FOCUS	*Leverage Azure Diagnostic Settings for scalable log exports. Configure it to send logs to Azure Storage or Log Analytics. This ensures reliable exportation and integration with Azure Monitor, enabling seamless troubleshooting and performance analysis.*
CAUTION ALERT	*Avoid manual log exports via tools like CLI or Storage Explorer. These methods don't scale for large data volumes. Stay alert to monitor agent limitations, as it focuses on telemetry, not exporting diagnostic logs.*

QUESTION 45

Answer - E

Option A - Incorrect. The script registers the runbook but does not link it correctly to the schedule that checks for low CPU usage. Option B - Incorrect. The -Parameter is not used in this way for scheduling conditions.
Option C - Incorrect. Start-AzAutomationRunbook immediately triggers a runbook, not what's needed for conditional execution. Option D - Incorrect. -Condition is not a valid parameter in this context.
Option E - Correct. Using -ScheduleId with the specific lookup ensures that the script is associated correctly with a schedule that triggers based on CPU usage, essential for automating updates during low usage times as defined by the CPU threshold condition.

EXAM FOCUS	*Use ScheduleId to associate updates with specific conditions. Automate runbooks for low CPU usage times by linking schedules accurately using -ScheduleId. This ensures updates trigger only during minimal usage, maintaining session availability for users.*
CAUTION ALERT	*Avoid incomplete scheduling in automation scripts. Missing the precise -ScheduleId association can lead to unscheduled updates. Stay alert to invalid parameters like -Condition, which are unsupported in this context.*

QUESTION 46

Answer - A) Azure Monitor alerts and dashboards

Option A - Azure Monitor alerts and dashboards provide comprehensive network status reports to stakeholders, including real-time performance metrics, connectivity status, and alert notifications. Customizable dashboards allow stakeholders to visualize network performance data and make informed decisions based on current conditions.

Option B - Azure Network Watcher logs offer detailed network telemetry but may not provide user-friendly reports for stakeholders. Option C - Azure Log Analytics queries allow querying of log data but may require additional data manipulation to generate comprehensive reports for stakeholders.

Option D - Azure Resource Graph visualizations focus on resource relationships and dependencies but may not specifically address network status reporting. Option E - Azure Diagnostics reports capture diagnostic data but may not specialize in network performance reporting for AVD environments.

Page | 325

EXAM FOCUS	Azure Monitor dashboards are best for stakeholder reporting. Customize them for real-time network insights. Include performance trends and alerts to ensure timely, actionable updates. This offers transparency and supports proactive issue resolution in AVD environments.
CAUTION ALERT	Avoid overcomplicating stakeholder reporting. Logs from Network Watcher or Log Analytics may need extra processing. Stay cautious of Resource Graph, as it visualizes resource relationships, not network performance metrics.

QUESTION 47

Answer - B) Using Azure Policy initiatives for cost governance
D) Leveraging Azure Monitor for performance insights
E) Configuring budgets and spending limits in Azure Cost Management

B) Using Azure Policy initiatives for cost governance - Azure Policy can enforce cost-saving measures and ensure compliance with budgetary constraints. D) Leveraging Azure Monitor for performance insights - Azure Monitor provides detailed performance metrics, including cost-related data.

E) Configuring budgets and spending limits in Azure Cost Management - Budgets and spending limits help control costs and prevent overspending. A, C) While ARM templates and RBAC are essential for resource management, they are not directly related to cost analysis and reporting.

EXAM FOCUS	Use Azure Policy, Monitor, and Cost Management. Enforce cost-saving measures with Policy initiatives. Leverage Azure Monitor for insights into usage patterns and configure budgets in Cost Management to control spending and optimize resource utilization effectively.
CAUTION ALERT	Avoid relying solely on templates or RBAC. These don't provide detailed cost tracking or reporting. Stay cautious of neglecting budgets and spending limits, which are vital for avoiding unexpected expenses in AVD environments.

QUESTION 48

Answer - A, B, E

A) Correct - Windows Server 2022 offers the latest security features and compliance with healthcare regulations. B) Correct - Windows 10 Enterprise multi-session allows for efficient resource use and supports the high availability required in healthcare. C) Incorrect - Windows Server 2016 might not meet all modern compliance and security standards required in healthcare.

D) Incorrect - While Windows 11 Enterprise has many advanced features, it does not specifically support the multi-session environment needed. E) Correct - Windows Server 2019 is stable and supports multi-region deployments essential for healthcare providers.

EXAM FOCUS	Deploy Windows Server 2022, 2019, and Win10 Enterprise multi-session. These meet healthcare compliance, offer multi-session support, and ensure high availability across regions. Align OS choices with regulatory standards and application requirements.
CAUTION ALERT	Avoid outdated OS like Server 2016. It lacks modern compliance features critical for healthcare. Stay alert to single-session OS like Windows 11 Enterprise if multi-session support is necessary. Choose OS aligned to workload demands.

QUESTION 49

Answer - A) Utilizing Azure Cost Management for tracking AVD licensing costs and usage trends
B) Configuring Azure Policy initiatives for enforcing compliance rules and generating compliance reports

A) Utilizing Azure Cost Management for tracking AVD licensing costs and usage trends - Azure Cost Management provides insights into licensing costs and usage patterns, enabling organizations to generate comprehensive reports on AVD licensing. B) Configuring Azure Policy initiatives for enforcing compliance rules and generating compliance reports - Azure Policy initiatives can enforce compliance rules and generate reports on AVD compliance status, ensuring transparency and accountability.

C, D, E) While Azure Resource Graph, Azure Sentinel, and Power BI are valuable for querying metadata, monitoring, and visualization, they are not specifically tailored for generating reports on AVD licensing and compliance.

EXAM FOCUS	*Combine Cost Management and Azure Policy for compliance reporting. Use Cost Management for licensing trends and Azure Policy for compliance rule enforcement. This integration ensures comprehensive tracking and accountability in your AVD environment.*
CAUTION ALERT	*Avoid overlooking Policy initiatives for compliance. They enforce rules and generate reports automatically. Stay cautious of tools like Sentinel or Resource Graph, which are supplementary and not tailored for licensing compliance reporting.*

QUESTION 50

Answer - A) Analyzing log data to identify patterns and trends indicative of performance bottlenecks
B) Using log data to correlate user activities with performance degradation events for targeted troubleshooting
C) Leveraging log data to fine-tune resource allocation and optimize AVD environment performance

A) Analyzing log data to identify patterns and trends indicative of performance bottlenecks - Analyzing log data helps identify patterns and trends that may indicate underlying performance bottlenecks, enabling targeted troubleshooting and optimization. B) Using log data to correlate user activities with performance degradation events for targeted troubleshooting - Correlating user activities with performance degradation events in log data helps pinpoint the root cause of performance issues, facilitating more effective troubleshooting.

C) Leveraging log data to fine-tune resource allocation and optimize AVD environment performance - Utilizing log data to fine-tune resource allocation based on performance insights helps optimize AVD environment performance and enhance user experience. D, E) While implementing log-based alerts and integrating log data with performance monitoring tools are valuable practices, they are not specifically focused on leveraging logs for troubleshooting and performance tuning in AVD.

EXAM FOCUS	*Analyze logs to identify patterns and user correlations. Focus on trends and user activity logs to diagnose bottlenecks. Use findings to fine-tune resources and optimize AVD performance. Ensure consistent monitoring for long-term performance gains.*
CAUTION ALERT	*Avoid depending solely on alerts or integration tools. Alerts notify issues but don't provide deep insights into root causes. Stay clear of general metrics if you need specific log-based data for fine-tuning performance.*

ABOUT THE AUTHOR

Step into the world of Anand, and you're in for a journey beyond just tech and algorithms. While his accolades in the tech realm are numerous, including penning various tech-centric and personal improvement ebooks, there's so much more to this multi-faceted author.

At the heart of Anand lies an AI enthusiast and investor, always on the hunt for the next big thing in artificial intelligence. But turn the page, and you might find him engrossed in a gripping cricket match or passionately cheering for his favorite football team. His weekends? They might be spent experimenting with a new recipe in the kitchen, penning down his latest musings, or crafting a unique design that blends creativity with functionality.

While his professional journey as a Solution Architect and AI Consultant, boasting over a decade of AI/ML expertise, is impressive, it's the fusion of this expertise with his diverse hobbies that makes Anand's writings truly distinctive.

So, as you navigate through his works, expect more than just information. Prepare for stories interwoven with passion, experiences peppered with life's many spices, and wisdom that transcends beyond the tech realm. Dive in and discover Anand, the author, the enthusiast, the chef, the sports lover, and above all, the storyteller.

Made in the USA
Las Vegas, NV
07 March 2025